PROBLEMS OF THE MODERN ECONOMY

This volume is based on selections from the following volumes: .

THE BATTLE AGAINST UNEMPLOYMENT

CHANGING PATTERNS IN FOREIGN TRADE AND PAYMENTS

THE GOAL OF ECONOMIC GROWTH

INEQUALITY AND POVERTY

LABOR AND THE NATIONAL ECONOMY

MONOPOLY POWER AND ECONOMIC PERFORMANCE

PRIVATE WANTS AND PUBLIC NEEDS

THE UNITED STATES AND THE DEVELOPING ECONOMIES

Problems of the Modern Economy

Edited with introductions by

EDMUND S. PHELPS, *General Editor*
UNIVERSITY OF PENNSYLVANIA

BELA BALASSA
THE JOHNS HOPKINS UNIVERSITY

WILLIAM G. BOWEN
PRINCETON UNIVERSITY

EDWARD BUDD
PENNSYLVANIA STATE UNIVERSITY

EDWIN MANSFIELD
UNIVERSITY OF PENNSYLVANIA

ARTHUR M. OKUN
YALE UNIVERSITY
COUNCIL OF ECONOMIC ADVISERS

GUSTAV RANIS
YALE UNIVERSITY
AGENCY FOR INTERNATIONAL DEVELOPMENT

NEW YORK
W · W · NORTON & COMPANY · INC ·

Contents

Preface

THIS WORK BRINGS TOGETHER in one volume some of the highlights of the eight paperbound books, each on a major economic policy issue, which comprise the *Problems of the Modern Economy* series. There are about four or five important selections in each of the following policy areas: monopoly power, labor problems, poverty and inequality, public expenditure, fiscal and monetary policy, international trade and finance, economic growth, and foreign aid to underdeveloped countries. In addition, this volume contains four selections on the farm problem. Each section of the book is introduced by the editor in charge of that policy area. Essentially, then, we have in this volume the *Problems of the Modern Economy* series in miniature.

The need for such a volume has long been apparent to the editors of the *Problems of the Modern Economy* series. Despite the continuing success of the individual books in the series, there are many colleges in which the nature of the introductory course is such that there is not time to treat many of the major problems in the detail permitted by the individual books in the series. This is especially true of one-semester introductory courses. Nevertheless there is the desire, in these courses, to expose students to some of the basic aspects of the important problems in economic policy today.

The present volume fills that need. Moreover, it does so while retaining the essential features of the individual books in the series. Almost all the selections are by recognized authorities in economics. The selections for each policy problem were chosen by the editor of the corresponding individual book in the series, who is an expert in that area. Finally, the selections convey, as much as possible, the range of opinion that is a characteristic of the *Problems of the Modern Economy* series.

PROBLEMS OF THE MODERN ECONOMY

Prologue

Mythology vs. Economic Knowledge

JOHN F. KENNEDY

This selection is from the late President Kennedy's commencement address at Yale University on June 11, 1962. In it, he called for informed, dispassionate discussion of key economic problems and pointed to the issues discussed in this volume.

THE GREAT ENEMY of the truth is very often not the lie—deliberate, contrived and dishonest—but the myth—persistent, persuasive and unrealistic. Too often we hold fast to the clichés of our forebears. We subject all facts to a prefabricated set of interpretations. We enjoy the comfort of opinion without the discomfort of thought.

Mythology distracts us everywhere—in government as in business, in politics as in economics, in foreign affairs as in domestic policy. But I want to particularly consider the myth and reality in our national economy. In recent months many have come to feel, as I do, that the dialogue between the parties—between business and government—is clogged by illusion and platitude and fails to reflect the true realities of contemporary American society. . . .

Let us turn to the problem of our fiscal policy. Here the myths are legion and the truth hard to find. But let me take as a prime example the problem of the federal budget. We persist in measuring our federal fiscal integrity today by the conventional or administrative budget—with results which would be regarded as absurd in any business firm—in any country of Europe—or in any careful assessment of the reality of our national finances. The administrative budget has sound administrative uses. But for wider purposes it is less helpful. It omits our special trust funds; it neglects changes in assets or inventories; it cannot tell a loan from a straight expenditure; and, worst of all, it cannot distinguish between operating expenditures and long-term investments.

This budget—in relation to the great problems of federal fiscal policy—is not simply irrelevant; it can be actively misleading. And yet there is a mythology that measures all of our national soundness or unsoundness on the single simple basis of this same annual administrative budget. If our federal budget is to serve, not the debate, but the country, we must and will find ways of clarifying this area of discourse.

Still in the area of fiscal policy, let me say a word about deficits. The myth persists that federal deficits create inflation and budget surpluses prevent it. Yet sizable budget surpluses after the war did not prevent inflation, and persistent deficits for the last several years have not upset our basic price stability. Obviously deficits are sometimes dangerous—and so are surpluses. But honest assessment plainly requires a more sophisticated view than the old and automatic cliché that deficits automatically bring inflation.

There are myths also about our public debt. It is widely supposed that this debt is growing at a dangerously rapid rate. In fact, both the debt per person and the debt as a proportion of our gross national product have declined sharply since the Second World War. In absolute terms the national debt increased only 8 percent, while private debt was increasing 305 percent, and the debts of state and local governments increased 378 percent. Moreover, debts, public and private, are neither good nor bad, in and of themselves. Borrowing can lead to overextension and collapse—but it can also lead to expansion and strength. There is no single, simple slogan in this field that we can trust.

Finally, I come to the problem of confidence. Confidence is a matter of myth and also a matter of truth—and this time let me take the truth of the matter first.

It is true—and of high importance—that the prosperity of this country depends on assurance that all major elements within it will live up to their responsibilities. If business were to neglect its obligations to the public; if labor were blind to all public responsibility; above all, if government were to abandon its obvious

—and statutory—duty of watchful concern for our economic health—if any of these things should happen, then confidence might well be weakened and the danger of stagnation would increase. This is the true issue of confidence.

But there is also the false issue—and its simplest form is the assertion that any and all unfavorable turns of the speculative wheel—however temporary and however plainly speculative in character—are the result of "lack of confidence in the national administration." This I must tell you, while comforting, is not wholly true. Worse, it obscures the reality—which is also simple. The solid ground of mutual confidence is the necessary partnership of government with all of the sectors of our society in the steady quest for economic progress.

Corporate plans are not based on a political confidence in party leaders but on an economic confidence in the nation's ability to invest and produce and consume. Business had full confidence in the Administrations in power in 1929, 1954, 1958, and 1960—but this was not enough to prevent recession when business lacked full confidence in the economy. What matters is the capacity of the nation as a whole to deal with its economic problems and its opportunities.

The stereotypes I have been discussing distract our attention and divide our effort. These stereotypes do our nation a disservice, not just because they are exhausted and irrelevant, but above all because they are misleading—because they stand in the way of the solution of hard and complicated problems. It is not new that past debates should obscure present realities. But the damage of such a false dialogue is greater today than ever before simply because today the safety of all the world—the very future of freedom—depends as never before upon the sensible and clear-headed management of the domestic affairs of the United States.

The real issues of our time are rarely so dramatic as the issues of the age of Calhoun. The differences today are usually matters of degree. And we cannot understand and attack our contemporary problems in 1962 if we are bound by traditional labels and worn-out slogans of an earlier era. The unfortunate fact of the matter is that our rhetoric has not kept pace with the speed of social and economic change. Our political debates, our public discourse—on current domestic and economic issues—too often bear little or no relation to the actual problems the United States faces.

What is at stake in our economic decisions today is, not some grand warfare of rival ideologies which will sweep the country with passion, but the practical management of a modern economy. What we need is not labels and clichés but more basic discussion of the sophisticated and technical questions involved in keeping a great economic machine moving ahead.

The national interest lies in high employment and steady expansion of output, in stable prices, and a strong dollar. The declaration of such objectives is easy; their attainment in an intricate and interdependent economy and world is a little more difficult. To attain them, we require not automatic response but hard thought. Let me end by suggesting a few of the real questions on our national agenda.

How can our budget and tax policies supply adequate revenues and preserve our balance of payments position without slowing up our economic growth?

How are we to set our interest rates and regulate the flow of money in ways which will stimulate the economy at home, without weakening the dollar abroad? Given the spectrum of our domestic and international responsibilities, what should be the mix between fiscal and monetary policy?

With the necessity of maintaining our competitive position in the world, what should be the price and wage policies of our basic industries? Is there a public interest in such price and wage decisions, and, if so, how is it to be defined and organized and expressed?

How can we develop and sustain strong and stable world markets for basic commodities without unfairness to the consumer and without undue stimulus to the producer?

How can we generate the buying power which can consume what we produce on our farms and in our factories?

How can we take advantage of the miracles of automation with the great demand that it will put upon highly skilled labor and yet offer employment to the half million of unskilled school dropouts each year which enter the labor market, eight million of them in the 1960s?

How do we eradicate the barriers which separate substantial

minorities of our citizens from access to education and employment on equal terms with the rest?

How, in sum, can we make our free economy work at full capacity—that is, provide adequate profits for enterprise, adequate wages for labor, adequate utilization of plant and adequate opportunity for all?

These are the problems that we should be talking about—that the political parties and the various groups in our country should be discussing. They cannot be solved by incantations from the forgotten past. But the example of Western Europe shows that they are capable of solution—that governments, and many of them are conservative governments, prepared to face technical problems without ideological preconceptions, can coordinate the elements of a national economy to bring about growth and prosperity—a decade of it.

Some conversations I have heard in our own country sound like old records, long-playing, left over from the middle Thirties. The debate of the Thirties had its great significance and produced great results. But it took place in a different world with different needs and different tasks. It is our responsibility today to live in our own world—and to identify the needs and discharge the tasks of the 1960s.

If there is any current trend toward meeting present problems with old clichés, this is the moment to stop it—before it lands us all in a bog of sterile acrimony. . . .

PART ONE Monopoly Power and Economic Performance

ECONOMIC POWER in the United States is distributed very unevenly. Five hundred corporations control over one half of the total assets in the nonfarm economy. Within particular industries there is also considerable concentration of ownership; e.g., more than 75 percent of autos, sheet glass, light bulbs, aluminum, cigarettes, metal cans, and computers are produced by the four largest firms in each of these industries. These facts are viewed with concern by economists and lawyers like A. A. Berle, who asserts that the 500 largest firms "—each with its own little dominating pyramid within it—represent a concentration of power over economies which makes the medieval feudal system look like a Sunday School party. In sheer economic power this has gone far beyond anything we have yet seen." [1]

Economists have kept a wary eye on the large firm ever since Adam Smith's attack on monopolies.[2] Smith preached and generations of economists since have taught that a monopolist charges a price in excess of the price which would prevail if the product were produced by small competitive producers, no one large enough to affect the price. The result of the monopolization is that consumers have to contract their consumption of the product; resources which would have been used in that industry go elsewhere to produce other products which are less badly wanted by consumers; and there is less output of the monopolized product and more of other goods than would be produced under a regime of pure competition.

Why should the competitive outcome be desired over that re-

1. *Economic Power and the Free Society* (Fund for the Republic), p. 14.
2. Of course, hostility toward monopoly did not originate with Smith. For example, the Edict of Zeno in 483 prohibited all monopolies, whether created by imperial decree or by private action.

sulting from the monopoly? Under pure competition we know that the price of each product equals the cost of producing it; more precisely, the additional (marginal) cost of producing an extra unit. This is exactly what the economist wishes the price of every good to do: to signal or measure the cost—in terms of the value of other goods which must be foregone—of consuming one more unit of the good.[3] Then and only then will consumers' purchases in the market place take proper account of society's true productive possibilities. Hence, in the traditional view, concentration of economic power, by distorting the allocation of resources, impairs the performance of the economy in satisfying human wants. This is why economists have traditionally viewed the breakdown of competition in many industries as a threat to the efficient operation of the free market mechanism. It is the reason, in addition to the concern over the political and social implications of the concentration of power, why economists have traditionally urged the forceful application of antitrust laws to keep firms from becoming too big.

But this traditional view has many dissenters. The large firms have triumphed over competition because they have advantages over small firms. Are these advantages not advantages to society too? Does not the very size of the giant firm offer many benefits to the economy? Or are the advantages enjoyed by the large firm simply those of getting to be big before other firms do, and its size a burden to the economy, as the traditional view argues? In addition, there are continuing arguments over standards for antitrust policy, the social responsibility of big business, and the extent of monopoly in the United States. The questions at issue are of the utmost importance, since they concern the basic framework within which the nation's economic activity is carried out. They are the fundamental questions of public policy that are treated by economists interested in the workings of particular industrial markets.

E. M.

3. We presume here that the marginal private cost equals the marginal social cost. This need not always be the case.

The Case Against Big Business

GEORGE J. STIGLER

George J. Stigler is Walgreen Professor of American Institutions at the University of Chicago. The following paper first appeared in the May, 1952, issue of Fortune.

WHAT IS BIGNESS?

BIGNESS IN business has two primary meanings. First, bigness may be defined in terms of the company's share of the industry in which it operates: a big company is one that has a big share of the market or industry. By this test Texas Gulf Sulphur is big because it produces more than half the sulfur in America, and Macy's (whose annual sales are much larger) is small because it sells only a very small fraction of the goods sold by New York City retail stores. By this definition, many companies that are small in absolute size are nevertheless big—the only brick company in a region, for example—and many companies that are big in absolute size (Inland Steel, for example) are small. Second, bigness may mean absolute size—the measure of size being assets, sales, or employment as a rule. Then General Motors and U.S. Steel are the prototypes of bigness.

These two meanings overlap because most companies that are big in absolute size are also big in relation to their industries. There are two types of cases, however, in which the two meanings conflict. On the one hand, many companies of small absolute size are dominant in small markets or industries. I shall not discuss them here (although they require attention in a well-rounded antitrust program) for two reasons: they seldom have anywhere near so much power as the companies that are big relative to large markets and industries; and they raise few political problems of the type I shall discuss below. On the other hand, there are a few companies that are big in absolute size but small relative to their markets—I have already given Macy's as an example. These companies are not very important in the total picture, and I shall also put them aside in the following discussion.

For my purposes, then, big businesses will mean businesses that are absolutely large in size and large also relative to the industries in which they operate. They are an impressive list: U.S. Steel, Bethlehem, and Republic in steel; General Electric and Westinghouse in electrical equipment; General Motors, Ford, and Chrysler in automobiles; du Pont, Union Carbide, and Allied Chemical among others in chemicals; Reynolds, Liggett & Myers, and American Tobacco in cigarettes.

What bigness does not mean is perhaps equally important. Bigness has no reference to the size of industries. I for one am tired of the charge that the critics of the steel industry vacillate between finding the output too large and too small: at various times the industry's output has been too small; for fifty years the largest firm has been too large. Concerted action by many small companies often leads to over-capacity in an industry: it is the basic criticism of resale price maintenance, for example, that it encourages the proliferation of small units by fixing excessive retail margins. Industries dominated by one or a few firms—that is, big businesses—seldom err in this direction. Nor does bigness have any direct reference to the methods of production, and opposition to big business is usually compatible with a decent respect for the "economies of large-scale production," on which more later.

The fundamental objection to bigness stems from the fact that big companies have monopolistic power, and this fundamental objection is clearly applicable outside the realm of corporate business. In particular, big unions are open to all the criticisms (and possibly more) that can be levied against big business. I shall not discuss labor unions, but my silence should not be construed as a belief that we should have a less stringent code for unions than for business.

THE INDICTMENT OF BIGNESS

There are two fundamental criticisms to be made of big business: they act monopolistically, and they encourage and justify bigness in labor and government.

First, as to monopoly. When a small number of firms control most or all of the output of an industry, they can individually and collectively profit more by cooperation than by competition. This is fairly evident, since cooperatively they can do everything they can do individually, and other things (such as the charging of non-competitive prices) besides. These few companies, therefore, will usually cooperate.

From this conclusion many reasonable men, including several Supreme Court Justices, will dissent. Does not each brand of cigarettes spend huge sums in advertising to lure us away from some other brand? Do not the big companies—oligopolists, the economists call them—employ salesmen? Do not the big companies introduce constant innovations in their products?

COMPETITION OF A KIND

The answer is that they do compete—but not enough, and not in all the socially desirable ways. Those tobacco companies did not act competitively, but with a view to extermination, against the 10-cent brands in the 1930's, nor have they engaged in price competition in decades (*American Tobacco* vs. *United States, 328 U.S. 781*). The steel companies, with all their salesmen, abandoned cartel pricing via basing-point prices only when this price system was judged a conspiracy in restraint of trade in cement (*Federal Trade Commission* vs. *Cement Institute, 333 U.S. 683*). The plain fact is that big businesses do not engage in continuous price competition.

Nor is price the only area of agreement. Patent licensing has frequently been used to deprive the licensees of any incentive to engage in research; General Electric used such agreements also to limit other companies' output and fix the prices of incandescent lamps (*U.S. vs. General Electric, 82 F. Supp. 753*). The hearings of the Bone Committee are adorned with numerous examples of the deliberate deterioration of goods in order to maintain sales.

For example, Standard Oil Development (a subsidiary of the Jersey company) persuaded Socony-Vacuum to give up the sale of a higher-potency commodity (pour-point depressant) whose sale at the same price had been characterized as "merely price cutting."

Very well, big businesses often engage in monopolistic practices. It may still be objected that it has not been shown that all big businesses engage in monopolistic practices, or that they engage in such practices all, or even most of, the time. These things cannot be shown or even fully illustrated in a brief survey,[1] and it is also not possible to summarize the many court decisions and the many academic studies of big business. But it is fair to say that these decisions and studies show that big businesses usually possess monopolistic power, and use it. And that is enough.

For economic policy must be contrived with a view to the typical rather than the exceptional, just as all other policies are contrived. That some drivers can safely proceed at eighty miles an hour is no objection to a maximum-speed law. So it is no objection to an antitrust policy that some unexercised monopoly power is thereby abolished. (Should there be some big businesses that forgo the use of their dominant position, it is difficult to see what advantage accrues from private ownership, for the profit motive is already absent.)

Second, as to bigness in labor and government. Big companies have a large—I would say an utterly disproportionate—effect on public thinking. The great expansion of our labor unions has been due largely to favoring legislation and administration by the federal government. This policy of favoring unions rests fundamentally upon the popular belief that workers individually competing for jobs will be exploited by big-business employers—that U.S. Steel can in separate negotiation (a pretty picture!) overwhelm each of its hundreds of thousands of employees. In good part this is an absurd fear: U.S. Steel must compete with many other industries, and not merely other steel companies, for good workers. Yet the fear may not be wholly absurd: there may be times and

1. The most comprehensive survey is contained in Clair Wilcox' *Competition and Monopoly in American Industry* (Monograph No. 21 of the Temporary National Economic Committee [TNEC]). Some additional evidence is given in George W. Stocking and Myron W. Watkins' *Cartels in Action* (Twentieth Century Fund, 1946), and in C. Edwards' *Maintaining Competition* (1949).

places where big businesses have "beaten down" wages, although I believe such cases are relatively infrequent. (In any event, the reaction to the fear has been unwise: for every case where big business has held down workers there are surely many cases where big unions have held up employers.) But it cannot be denied that this public attitude underlies our national labor policy, the policy of local governments of condoning violence in labor disputes, etc.

Big business has also made substantial contributions to the growth of big government. The whole agricultural program has been justified as necessary to equalize agriculture's bargaining power with "industry," meaning big business. The federally sponsored milkshed cartels are defended as necessary to deal with the giant dairy companies.

BUSINESS ACROSS THE BOARD

Big business is thus a fundamental excuse for big unions and big government. It is true that the scope and evils of big business are usually enormously exaggerated, especially with reference to labor and agriculture, and that more often than not these evils are merely a soapbox excuse for shoddy policies elsewhere. To this large extent, there is need for extensive education of the public on how small a part of the economy is controlled by big business. But in light of the widespread monopolistic practices—our first criticism of bigness—it is impossible to tell the public that its fears of big business are groundless. We have no right to ask public opinion to veer away from big unions and big government —and toward big business.

EFFICIENCY AND BIG BUSINESS

Are we dependent upon big businesses for efficient methods of production and rapid advances in production methods? If we are, the policy of breaking up big businesses would lower our future standard of living and many people would cast about for other ways than dissolution to meet the problems of bigness.

A company may be efficient because it produces and sells a given amount of product with relatively small amounts of material, capital, and labor, or it may be efficient because it acquires the power to buy its supplies at unusually low prices and sell its products at unusually high prices. Economists refer to these as the social and the private costs of production respectively. Big businesses may be efficient in the social sense, and usually they also possess, because of their monopoly position, private advantages. But the ability of a company to employ its dominant position to coerce unusually low prices from suppliers is not of any social advantage.

It follows that even if big companies had larger profit rates or smaller costs per unit of output than other companies, this would not prove that they were more efficient in socially desirable ways. Actually, big businesses are generally no more and no less efficient than medium-sized businesses even when the gains wrung by monopoly power are included in efficiency. This is the one general finding in comparative cost studies and comparative profitability studies.[2] Indeed, if one reflects upon the persistence of small and medium-sized companies in the industries dominated by big businesses, it is apparent that there can be no great advantages to size. If size were a great advantage, the smaller companies would soon lose the unequal race and disappear.

When we recall that most big businesses have numerous complete plants at various points throughout the country, this finding is not surprising. Why should U.S. Steel be more efficient than Inland Steel, when U.S. Steel is simply a dozen or more Inland Steels strewn about the country? Why should G.M. be appreciably more efficient than say a once-again-independent Buick Motors? A few years ago Peter Drucker reported:

"The divisional manager . . . is in complete charge of production and sales. He hires, fires and promotes; and it is up to him to decide how many men he needs, with what qualifications and in what salary range—except for top executives whose employment is subject to a central-management veto. The divisional manager decides the factory layout, the technical methods and equipment used . . . . He buys his supplies independently from suppliers of his own choice. He determines the distribution of production within the several plants under his jurisdiction, decides which lines to push and decides on the methods of sale and distribution . . . . In everything pertaining to operations he is as much the real head

2. For studies that support this generalization, the reader is referred to J. L. McConnell, "Corporate Earnings by Size of Firm," *Survey of Current Business*, May, 1945; TNEC Monograph No. 13; and *Cost Behavior and Price Policy* (National Bureau of Economic Research, 1943).

as if his division were indeed an independent business." [3]

If big businesses are not more efficient as a rule, how did they get big? The answer is that most giant firms arose out of mergers of many competing firms, and were created to eliminate competition. Standard Oil, General Electric, Westinghouse, U.S. Steel, Bethlehem, the meat packers, Borden, National Dairy, American Can, etc.—the full list of merger-created big businesses is most of the list of big businesses. A few big businesses owe their position to an industrial genius like Ford, and of course future geniuses would be hampered by an effective antitrust law—but less so than by entrenched monopolies or by public regulatory commissions.

We do not know what share of improvements in technology has been contributed by big businesses. Big businesses have made some signal contributions, and so also have small businesses, universities, and private individuals. It can be said that manufacturing industries dominated by big businesses have had no large increases in output per worker on average than other manufacturing industries. This fact is sufficient to undermine the easy identification of economic progress with the laboratories of big businesses, but it does not inform us of the net effect of monopolies on economic progress.

At present, then, no definite effect of big business on economic progress can be established. I personally believe that future study will confirm the traditional belief that big businesses, for all their resources, cannot rival the infinite resource and cold scrutiny of many independent and competing companies. If the real alternative to bigness is government regulation or ownership, as I am about to argue, then the long-run consequences of big business are going to be highly adverse to economic progress.

REMEDIES FOR BIG BUSINESS

Let me restate the main points of the foregoing discussion in a less emphatic—and I think also a less accurate—manner:

1. Big businesses often possess and use monopoly power.

2. Big businesses weaken the political support for a private-enterprise system.

3. Big businesses are not appreciably more efficient or enterprising than medium-size businesses.

3. *Concept of a Corporation*, p. 56.

Few disinterested people will deny these facts—where do they lead?

A considerable section of the big-business community seems to have taken the following position. The proper way to deal with monopolistic practices is to replace the general prohibitions of the Sherman Act by a specific list of prohibited practices, so businessmen may know in advance and avoid committing monopolistic practices. The proper way to deal with the declining political support for private enterprise is to advertise the merits of private enterprise, at the same time claiming many of its achievements for big business. Much of this advertising has taken literally that form, apparently in the belief that one can sell a social system in exactly the same way and with exactly the same copywriters and media that one sells a brand of cigarettes.

GUARD THE SHERMAN ACT

The request for a list of specifically prohibited monopolistic practices will be looked upon by many persons as a surreptitious attack upon the Sherman Act. I am among these cynics: the powerful drive in 1949 to pass a low legalizing basing-point price systems is sufficient evidence that large sectors of big business are wholly unreconciled to the law against conspiracies in restraint of trade. Even when the request for a specific list of prohibitions is made in all sincerity, however, it cannot be granted: No one can write down a full list of all the forms that objectionable monopoly power has taken and may someday take. Moreover, almost all uncertainties over the legality of conduct arise out of the Robinson-Patman Act, not the Sherman Act, and I would welcome the complete repeal of the former act.[4]

We must look elsewhere for the solution of the problems raised by big business, and a satisfactory solution must deal with the facts I listed at the head of this section. Our present policy is not

4. The prohibition against price discrimination was partly designed to cope with a real evil: the use by a large company of its monopoly power to extort preferential terms from suppliers. This exercise of monopoly, however, constitutes a violation of the Sherman Act, and no additional legislation is necessary if this act can be made fully effective. The Robinson-Patman Act and certain other parts of the so-called "antitrust" amendments also have another and objectionable purpose: to supervise and regulate the routine operations of businesses in order to ensure that they will display the symptoms of competitive behavior.

a satisfactory solution. The Sherman Act is admirable in dealing with formal conspiracies of many firms, but—at least with the Supreme Court's present conception of competition and of the proper remedies for demonstrated restraint of trade in oligopolistic industries—it cannot cope effectively with the problem posed by big business. In industries dominated by a few firms there is no need for formal conspiracies, with their trappings of quotas, a price-fixing committee, and the like. The big companies know they must "live with" one another, and the phrase means much the same thing as in the relationships between man and woman. Any competitive action one big company takes will lead to retaliation by the others. An informal code of behavior gradually develops in the industry: Firm X announces the new price, and except in very unusual circumstances Y and Z can be relied upon to follow. So long as there are a few big businesses in an industry, we simply cannot expect more than the tokens of competitive behavior. Antitrust decrees that the big businesses should ignore each other's existence serve no important purpose.[5]

This conclusion, I must emphasize, is not merely that of "economic theorists," although most (academic) economists will subscribe to it. It is also the conclusion our generation is reaching, for our generation is not satisfied with the behavior of big business. More and more, big businesses are being asked to act in "the social interest," and more and more, government is interfering in their routine operation. The steel industry, for example, what with congressional review of prices and presidential coercion of wages, is drifting rapidly into a public-utility status. And the drift will not be stopped by slick advertising.

5. In the National Lead case (*67 Sup. Ct. 1634, 1947*) this company and du Pont were convicted of violating the Sherman Act. The two companies produced about 90 per cent of all titanium, but the Court refused to order divestiture of plants. The Court documented the "vigorous and effective competition between National Lead and du Pont" with the fact that "The general manager of the pigments department of du Pont characterized the competition with Zirconium and Virginia Chemical as 'tough' and that with National Lead as 'plenty tough.'" Economists will always find such testimony an inadequate demonstration of competition. Even more unfortunate was the refusal of the Court to order divestiture of foreign holdings of the Timken Roller Bearing company, which had also been convicted under the Sherman Act (*71 Sup. Ct. 971, 1951*). Here Mr. Justice Reed, the Chief Justice concurring, argues that so "harsh" a remedy as divestiture should be invoked only in extreme cases, perhaps forgetting that inadequate remedies for monopoly are "harsh" treatment of the public interest.

DISSOLUTION THE REMEDY

No such drastic and ominous remedy as the central direction of economic life is necessary to deal with the problems raised by big business. The obvious and economical solution, as I have already amply implied, is to break up the giant companies. This, I would emphasize, is the minimum program, and it is essentially a conservative program. Dissolution of big businesses is a one-for-all measure in each industry (if the recent anti-merger amendment to the Clayton Act is adequately enforced), and no continuing interference in the private operation of business is required or desired. Dissolution involves relatively few companies: one dissolves three or four big steel companies, and leaves the many smaller companies completely alone. Dissolution does not even need to be invoked in a large part of the economy: some of our biggest industries, such as textiles, shoes, and most food industries, will require no antitrust action.

A policy of "trust busting" requires no grant of arbitrary powers to any administrative agency; the policy can be administered by the Antitrust Division acting through the courts. It is sufficient, and it is desirable, that the policy be directed against companies whose possession of monopoly power is demonstrated, and that dissolution be the basic remedy for the concentration of control in an industry that prevents or limits competition. Indeed, the policy requires new legislation only to the extent of convincing the courts that an industry which does not have a competitive structure will not have competitive behavior.

The dissolution of big businesses is only a part of the program necessary to increase the support for a private, competitive enterprise economy, and reverse the drift toward government control. But it is an essential part of this program, and the place for courage and imagination. Those conservatives who cling to the status quo do not realize that the status quo is a state of change, and the changes are coming fast. If these changes were to include the dissolution of a few score of our giant companies, however, we shall have done much to preserve private enterprise and the liberal-individualistic society of which it is an integral part.

In Defense of Bigness in Business

SUMNER H. SLICHTER

Sumner H. Slichter was Lamont University Professor at Harvard University until his death in 1959. This essay appeared in the New York Times Magazine *on August 4, 1957.*

THE 1957 DECISION of the Supreme Court in the du Pont-General Motors case suggests the desirability of a review and an appraisal of American policy toward competition, monopoly, and bigness in business. The decision reveals the strong determination of the court to prevent competition from being weakened and the court's willingness to resort to controversial interpretations of the law in order to implement the public policy of preventing restraints on competition.

But the decision also reminds us that much thinking on the relation of bigness to competition is out of date and unrealistic. Hence, the adaptation of traditional American antitrust policy to the facts of modern industry requires that we take a fresh look at the role of large enterprises in American business—particularly the role of large enterprises as a source of vigorous and dynamic competition.

When one compares the economy of the United States with the economies of other advanced industrial countries, four characteristics stand out conspicuously.

1. The government of the United States endeavors through broad and drastic laws to prevent restraints on competition and to forestall the growth of monopoly. Most other advanced industrial countries either tolerate considerable restraint on competition or even encourage organizations of business men that are designed to control competition.

2. Competition in American industry is far more vigorous and pervasive than in the industries of any other advanced industrial

country. Indeed, the vigor of competition in the United States almost invariably attracted comment from the European productivity teams that visited this country in the years following the war.

3. The United States has many more huge business enterprises than any other country. Several years ago this country had more than 100 corporations (exclusive of purely financial ones) with assets of more than $250 million each. General Motors produces far more cars than the combined British, German and French automobile industries, and the United States Steel Corporation produces more steel than the entire British steel industry.

4. Production in many American industries (especially those requiring large capital investment) is highly concentrated in the hands of a few large concerns. As a general rule, the concentration of production in other industrial countries is far less than here.

These four characteristics of the American economy are not unrelated. It would be wrong to ascribe the widespread and intense competition in American industry *solely* to the strong public policy against restraint of trade, monopolization and interference with competition. Conditions in the United States—the absence of class lines, the abundance of opportunity, the weakness of tradition—have long made life here highly competitive in all its aspects, and competition in business is just one manifestation of this general competitive spirit. But America's unique and firm public policy against restraints on competition has undoubtedly helped greatly to keep industry here strongly competitive.

This strong policy, however, has paradoxically encouraged the development of giant industrial corporations and the concentration of production in many industries among a few large concerns. The growth of enterprises in Europe has been limited by the practice of forming cartels—a practice which governments have tolerated and even encouraged. The cartel or trade association divides markets among its members, limits the growth of the most efficient concerns, and assures the weak, high-cost concern a share of the market.

In the United States, where cartels are illegal, each concern is pretty completely exposed to competition from all other firms, and business goes to the firms that can get it. This means that in many industries production is gradually concentrated in the hands of a few industrial giants, and only a small part of the business is left for small firms.

The trend toward corporate bigness in industry has led many students of anti-monopoly policy to believe that the American policy of encouraging competition and discouraging monopoly is turning out to be a failure and to conclude that steps need to be taken to limit the influences of large enterprises in American industry. Of many proposals that have been made, two principal ones are of particular interest.

One proposal is that new restrictions be placed on mergers. Some have urged that no merger be permitted which cannot be justified by technological reasons. Some have proposed that mergers involving a corporation above a given size be prohibited unless found by the Federal Trade Commission to be in the public interest.

The second proposal deals with the concentration of production in various industries into a few enterprises. It is urged that the government undertake a comprehensive survey of American industry to determine whether enterprises exceed the size required by modern technology and that the government be authorized to break up firms that are unnecessarily large.

Both of these proposals are based on fallacy. They rest upon a mistaken conception of the role of large corporations in American business and particularly upon the relation of large corporations to competition. Each, if put into effect, would weaken rather than strengthen competition. In fact, in order to stimulate competition, existing restrictions on mergers should be relaxed, not tightened, and large enterprises, instead of being threatened with breakup, should be given a clear mandate to grow, provided they use fair means. Let us examine more completely each of these two proposals to restrict the growth of enterprises.

The proposal that new restrictions be placed on mergers arises from the fact that the United States in recent years has been experiencing a great wave of mergers. But recent mergers have not weakened competition. On the contrary, they have indirectly strengthened it because they have enabled managements to build more diversified and better-integrated enterprises—enterprises which are more capable of reaching all parts of the vast domestic market, of adapting themselves to market shifts and changes in technology, of riding out the ups and downs of business, and of supporting technological research and development. Many large firms and firms of moderate size have acquired small firms, but the acquisitions by the very largest firms have not been numerous.

The specific circumstances surrounding each merger are unique, but a case-by-case examination shows how mergers are helping to build stronger enterprises, better able to compete and to hold their own in competition.

Let us consider a few examples. A maker of cans bought a concern manufacturing plastic pipe in order to get a foothold in the plastic pipe business. A maker of railroad freight cars bought companies making electrical equipment, truck trailers and dairy supplies in order to shift from a declining business to expanding businesses. A food manufacturer bought a West Coast manufacturer of salad seasoning in order to give nation-wide distribution to its product. A maker of household ware bought a supplier in order to have a source of pressed wood handles for its appliances.

Unusually competent managements often buy other concerns so that they can spread good administrative methods to less efficiently operated enterprises.

The many advantages produced by mergers show that the proposal that mergers be prohibited unless they can be justified by technological reasons does not make sense. There are good reasons for mergers that have nothing to do with technology.

Moreover, it would be unwise to require government approval of all mergers involving an enterprise above a specified size. That would be substituting the decision of government officials for the decision of businessmen on matters that the businessmen are better able to understand. The public interest is amply protected by the present drastic provision of Section 7 of the Clayton Act.

Indeed, the fact that mergers often make for more vigorous competition by helping managements build stronger and more efficient business enterprises indicates the need for relaxing the present severe restrictions on mergers contained in Section 7 of the Clayton Act. This section prohibits any merger which is likely to lessen competition substantially in *any* line of commerce. The fact that the merger may increase the intensity of competition in *other* lines of commerce makes no difference. As Section 7 now reads, the *total effect* of the merger on competition is irrelevant. If it is likely to lessen competition substantially in any one line of commerce, it is illegal.

Obviously the section, as it now reads, conflicts with the national policy of encouraging competition. It should be rewritten to make the legality of mergers depend upon the *total* effect of competition, thus permitting any merger that has the net effect of increasing competition.

The second proposal—to remake the structure of American industry by breaking up the largest enterprises—rests upon the mistaken view that, where output is concentrated among a few concerns, effective competition does not occur. The error of this view is shown by the vigorous competition in various industries in which most of the output is made by a few firms—in such industries as the automobile, tire, refrigerator, soap, cigarette, paper products, television and many others.

There are two principal reasons why competition tends to be vigorous when production is concentrated among a few large concerns. One is that such enterprises keep close track of their rank in sales and fight hard to move ahead of rivals or to avoid being surpassed by rivals. The second reason, and one that is rapidly gaining in importance, is the fact that competition among large firms is being stimulated by the growth of technological research.

It is only within the last several decades that managements have generally discovered the big returns yielded by technological research. As a result, the outlays by private industry on research and development increased nearly six-fold between 1940 and 1953. In 1957, the total research and development expenditures of private industry, exclusive of the aircraft industry, which is a special case, are running about 71 per cent greater than they were in 1953. By 1960 outlays on research are expected to be 21 per cent above 1957.

No expenditures are more competitive than outlays on research, for the purpose of these expenditures is to improve products, develop new products and cut costs. More than 70 per cent of the outlays on research and development are made by firms with 5,000 or more employees because concerns with large sales can best afford this overhead expense. Hence the rapidly mounting outlays on research indicate both the growing competitiveness of American industry and the increasingly important role large enterprises are playing in making competition more intense.

Incidentally, competition among large firms is superior in quality to competition among small firms and serves consumers more effectively. This is because the greater research by the large firms gives the consumers a wider range of choice over a period of years than competition among a much larger number of small firms that can afford little or no research. In general, the wider the range of choice open to consumers, the more effectively is the welfare of consumers advanced.

In view of the growing importance of large enterprises as a source of competition and the superior quality of this competition, a move to break up large concerns would be a blunder. There is much to be said, however, in favor of incentives for enterprises to split themselves voluntarily, if the managements consider a split desirable. The resulting increase in the number of top managements with independent authority to make policies and to try experiments would be favorable to technological progress—provided the concerns are large enough to support extensive research. A good incentive for voluntary splits would be created by relieving stockholders from liability for the capital gains tax on the appreciation of their holdings from the time they purchased the stock up to the date of the split.

But enforced splitting of enterprises, except as a remedy for flagrant monopolizing of trade by unscrupulous methods, would be another matter. In fact, the present law needs to be clarified in order to encourage a few of the very largest concerns to strive harder for a bigger share of the market. The managements of a few very large and efficient concerns apparently feel that efforts to get more business by cutting prices will be held to be attempts to monopolize. There is need to make clear that efforts to win business by giving consumers the benefits of low costs will not be regarded as monopolistic.

Americans need to understand that a variety of conditions—rapidly changing technology, the growing importance of industrial research, the growing strength of trade unions—tend to increase in many industries the size of the enterprise that is able both to compete and to survive in competition. Hence, we are likely to see a spread of the tendency for production to be concentrated in a few large or fairly large firms.

But this trend, if it occurs, should not disturb us. It will simply represent an adaptation of industry to the conditions of the time.

Capitalism and the Process of Creative Destruction

JOSEPH A. SCHUMPETER

Joseph A. Schumpeter, Professor of Economics at Harvard University until his death in 1950, is one of the leading figures of twentieth-century economics. The following selection is taken from his book Capitalism, Socialism, and Democracy.

PLAUSIBLE CAPITALISM

UNLIKE THE CLASS of feudal lords, the commercial and industrial bourgeoisie rose by business success. Bourgeois society has been cast in a purely economic mold: its foundations, beams and beacons are all made of economic material. The building faces toward the economic side of life. Prizes and penalties are measured in pecuniary terms. Going up and going down means making and losing money. This, of course, nobody can deny. But I wish to add that, within its own frame, that social arrangement is, or at all events was, singularly effective. In part it appeals to, and in part it creates, a schema of motives that is unsurpassed in simplicity and force. The promises of wealth and the threats of destitution that it holds out, it redeems with ruthless promptitude. Wherever the bourgeois way of life asserts itself sufficiently to dim the beacons of other social worlds, these promises are strong enough to attract the large majority of supernormal brains and to identify success with business success. They are not proffered at random; yet there is a sufficiently enticing admixture of chance: the game is not like roulette, it is more like poker. They are addressed to ability, energy and supernormal capacity for work; but if there were a way of measuring either that ability in general or the personal achievement that goes into any particular success, the premiums actually paid out would probably not be found proportional to either. Spectacular prizes much greater than would have been necessary to call forth the particular effort are thrown to a small minority of winners, thus propelling much more efficaciously than a more equal and more "just" distribution would, the activity of that large majority of businessmen who receive in return very modest compensation or nothing or less than nothing, and yet do their utmost because they have the big prizes before their eyes and overrate their chances of doing equally well. Similarly, the threats are addressed to incompetence. But though the incompetent men and the obsolete methods are in fact eliminated, sometimes very promptly, sometimes with a lag, failure also threatens or actually overtakes many an able man, thus whipping up *everyone*, again much more efficaciously than a more equal and more "just" system of penalties would. Finally, both business success and business failure are ideally precise. Neither can be talked away.

The capitalist arrangement, as embodied in the institution of private enterprise, effectively chains the bourgeois stratum to its tasks. But it does more than that. The same apparatus which conditions for performance the individuals and families that at any given time form the bourgeois class, *ipso facto* also selects the individuals and families that are to rise into that class or to drop out of it. This combination of the conditioning and the selective function is not a matter of course. On the contrary, most methods of social selection, unlike the "methods" of biological selection, do not guarantee performance of the selected individual. In most cases the man who rises first *into* the business class and then *within* it is also an able businessman and he is likely to rise exactly as far as his ability goes—simply because in that schema rising to a position and doing well in it generally is or was one and the same thing. This fact, so often obscured by the auto-therapeutic effort of the unsuccessful to deny it, is much more important for an appraisal of capitalist society and its civilization than anything that can be gleaned from the pure theory of the capitalist machine.

But is not all that we might be tempted to infer from "maximum performance of an optimally selected group" invalidated by the further fact that that performance is not geared to social service—production, so we might say, for consumption—but to money-making, that it aims at maximizing profits instead of welfare? Outside of the bourgeois stratum, this has of course always been the popular opinion. Economists have sometimes fought and sometimes espoused it. In doing so they have contributed something that was much more valuable than were the final judgments themselves at which they arrived individually and which in most cases reflect little more than their social location, interests and sympathies or antipathies. They slowly increased our factual knowledge and analytic powers so that the answers to many questions we are able to give today are no doubt much more correct although less simple and sweeping than were those of our predecessors.

To go no further back, the so-called classical economists [1] were practically of one mind. Most of them disliked many things about the social institutions of their epoch and about the way those institutions worked. They fought the landed interest and approved of social reforms—factory legislation in particular—that were not all on the lines of *laissez faire*. But they were quite convinced that within the institutional framework of capitalism, the manufacturer's and the trader's self-interest made for maximum performance in the interest of all. Confronted with the problem we are discussing, they would have had little hesitation in attributing the observed rate of increase in total output to relatively unfettered enterprise and the profit motive—perhaps they would have mentioned "beneficial legislation" as a condition but by this they would have meant the removal of fetters, especially the removal or reduction of protective duties during the nineteenth century.

It is exceedingly difficult, at this hour of the day, to do justice to these views. They were of course the typical views of the English bourgeois class, and bourgeois blinkers are in evidence on almost every page the classical authors wrote. No less in evidence are blinkers of another kind: the classics reasoned in terms of a particular historical situation which they uncritically idealized and from which they uncritically generalized. Most of them, moreover, seem to have argued exclusively in terms of the English interests and problems of their time. This is the reason why, in other lands and at other times, people disliked their economics, frequently to the point of not even caring to understand it. But it

1. The term Classical Economists will be used to designate the leading English economists whose works appeared between 1776 and 1848. Adam Smith, Ricardo, Malthus, Senior and John Stuart Mill are the outstanding names.

will not do to dismiss their teaching on these grounds. A prejudiced man may yet be speaking the truth. Propositions developed from special cases may yet be generally valid. And the enemies and successors of the classics had and have only different but not fewer blinkers and preconceptions; they envisaged and envisage different but not less special cases.

From the standpoint of the economic analyst, the chief merit of the classics consists in their dispelling, along with many other gross errors, the naïve idea that economic activity in capitalist society, because it turns on the profit motive, must by virtue of that fact alone necessarily run counter to the interests of consumers or, to put it differently, that moneymaking necessarily deflects producing from its social goal; or, finally, that private profits, both in themselves and through the distortion of the economic process they induce, are always a net loss to all excepting those who receive them and would therefore constitute a net gain to be reaped by socialization. If we look at the logic of these and similar propositions which no trained economist ever thought of defending, the classical refutation may well seem trivial. But as soon as we look at all the theories and slogans which, consciously or subconsciously, imply them and which are once more served up today, we shall feel more respect for that achievement. Let me add at once that the classical writers also clearly perceived, though they may have exaggerated, the role of saving and accumulation and that they linked saving to the rate of "progress" they observed in a manner that was fundamentally, if only approximately, correct. Above all, there was practical wisdom about their doctrine, a responsible long-run view and a manly tone that contrast favorably with modern hysterics.

But between realizing that hunting for a maximum of profit and striving for maximum productive performance are not necessarily incompatible, to proving that the former will necessarily— or in the immense majority of cases—imply the latter, there is a gulf much wider than the classics thought. And they never succeeded in bridging it. The modern student of their doctrines never ceases to wonder how it was possible for them to be satisfied with their arguments or to mistake these arguments for proofs; in the light of later analysis their *theory* was seen to be a house of cards whatever measure of truth there may have been in their *vision*.

This later analysis we will take in two strides—as much of it, that is, as we need in order to clarify our problem. Historically, the first will carry us into the first decade of this century, the second will cover some of the postwar developments of scientific economics.

The first stride may be associated with two great names revered to this day by numberless disciples—so far at least as the latter do not think it bad form to express reverence for anything or anybody, which many of them obviously do—Alfred Marshall and Knut Wicksell. Their theoretical structure has little in common with that of the classics—though Marshall did his best to hide the fact—but it conserves the classic proposition that in the case of perfect competition the profit interest of the producer tends to maximize production. It even supplied almost satisfactory proof. Only, in the process of being more correctly stated and proved, the proposition lost much of its content—it does emerge from the operation, to be sure, but it emerges emaciated, barely alive. Still it can be shown, within the general assumptions of the Marshall-Wicksell analysis, that firms which cannot by their own individual action exert any influence upon the price of their products or of the factors of production they employ—so that there would be no point in their weeping over the fact that any increase in production tends to decrease the former and to increase the latter—will expand their output until they reach the point at which the additional cost that must be incurred in order to produce another small increment of product (marginal cost) just equals the price they can get for that increment, i.e., that they will produce as much as they can without running into loss. And this can be shown to be as much as it is in general "socially desirable" to produce. In more technical language, in that case prices are, from the standpoint of the individual firm, not variables but parameters; and where this is so, there exists a state of equilibrium in which all outputs are at their maximum and all factors fully employed. This case is usually referred to as perfect competition. Remembering what has been said about the selective process which operates on all firms and their managers, we might in fact conceive a very optimistic idea of the results to be expected from a highly selected group of people forced, within that pattern, by their profit motive to strain every nerve in order to maximize output and to minimize costs. In particular, it might seem at first sight that a system conforming to this pattern would display remarkable absence of some of the major sources of social waste. As a little reflection should show, this is really but another way of stating the content of the preceding sentence.

Let us take the second stride. The Marshall-Wicksell analysis of course did not overlook the many cases that fail to conform to that model. Nor, for that matter, had the classics overlooked them. They recognized cases of "monopoly," and Adam Smith himself carefully noticed the prevalence of devices to restrict competition and all the differences in flexibility of prices resulting therefrom. But they looked upon those cases as exceptions and, moreover, as exceptions that could and would be done away with in time. Something of that sort is true also of Marshall. Although he anticipated later analysis by calling attention to the fact that most firms have special markets of their own in which they set prices instead of merely accepting them, he as well as Wicksell framed his general conclusions on the pattern of perfect competition so as to suggest, much as the classics did, that perfect competition was the rule. Neither Marshall and Wicksell nor the classics saw that perfect competition is the exception and that even if it were the rule there would be much less reason for congratulation than one might think.

If we look more closely at the conditions—not all of them explicitly stated or even clearly seen by Marshall and Wicksell—that must be fulfilled in order to produce perfect competition, we realize immediately that outside of agricultural mass production there cannot be many instances of it. A farmer supplies his cotton or wheat in fact under those conditions: from his standpoint the ruling prices of cotton or wheat are data, though very variable ones, and not being able to influence them by his individual action he simply adapts his output; since all farmers do the same, prices and quantities will in the end be adjusted as the theory of perfect competition requires. But this is not so even with many agricultural products—with ducks, sausages, vegetables and many dairy products for instance. And as regards practically all the finished products and services of industry and trade, it is clear that every grocer, every filling station, every manufacturer of gloves or shaving cream or handsaws has a small and precarious market of his own which he tries—must try—to build up and to keep by price strategy, quality strategy—"product differentiation"—and advertising. Thus we get a completely different pattern which there seems to be no reason to expect to yield the results of perfect competition and which fits much better into the monopolistic schema. In these cases we speak of Monopolistic Competition. Their theory has been one of the major contributions to postwar economics.[2]

There remains a wide field of substantially homogeneous products—mainly industrial raw materials and semi-finished products such as steel ingots, cement, cotton gray goods and the like—in which the conditions for the emergence of monopolistic competition do not seem to prevail. This is so. But in general, similar results follow for that field inasmuch as the greater part of it is covered by largest-scale firms which, either individually or in concert, are able to manipulate prices even without differentiating products—the case of Oligopoly. Again the monopoly schema, suitably adapted, seems to fit this type of behavior much better than does the schema of perfect competition.

As soon as the prevalence of monopolistic competition or of oligopoly or of combinations of the two is recognized, many of the propositions which the Marshall-Wicksell generation of economists used to teach with the utmost confidence become either inapplicable or much more difficult to prove. This holds true, in the first place, of the propositions turning on the fundamental concept of equilibrium, i.e., a determinate state of the economic organism, toward which any given state of it is always gravitating and which displays certain simple properties. In the general case of oligopoly there is in fact no determinate equilibrium at all and the possibility presents itself that there may be an endless sequence of moves and countermoves, an indefinite state of warfare between firms. It is true that there are many special cases in which a state of equilibrium theoretically exists. In the second place, even in these cases not only is it much harder to attain than the equilibrium in perfect competition, and still harder to preserve, but the "beneficial" competition of the classic type seems likely to be replaced by "predatory" or "cutthroat" competition or simply by struggles for control in the financial sphere. These things are so many sources of social waste, and there are many others such as the costs of advertising campaigns, the suppression of new methods of production (buying up of patents in order not to use them) and

2. See, in particular, E. S. Chamberlin, *Theory of Monopolistic Competition,* and Joan Robinson, *The Economics of Imperfect Competition.*

so on. And most important of all: under the conditions envisaged, equilibrium, even if eventually attained by an extremely costly method, no longer guarantees either full employment or maximum output in the sense of the theory of perfect competition. It *may* exist without full employment; it is *bound* to exist, so it seems, at a level of output below that maximum mark, because profit-conserving strategy, impossible in conditions of perfect competition, now not only becomes possible but imposes itself.

THE PROCESS OF CREATIVE DESTRUCTION

The theories of monopolistic and oligopolistic competition and their popular variants may in two ways be made to serve the view that capitalist reality is unfavorable to maximum performance in production. One may hold that it always has been so and that all along output has been expanding in spite of the secular sabotage perpetrated by the managing bourgeoisie. Advocates of this proposition would have to produce evidence to the effect that the observed rate of increase can be accounted for by a sequence of favorable circumstances unconnected with the mechanism of private enterprise and strong enough to overcome the latter's resistance. However, those who espouse this variant at least avoid the trouble about historical fact that the advocates of the alternative proposition have to face. This avers that capitalist reality once tended to favor maximum productive performance, or at all events productive performance so considerable as to constitute a major element in any serious appraisal of the system; but that the later spread of monopolist structures, killing competition, has by now reversed that tendency.

First, this involves the creation of an entirely imaginary golden age of perfect competition that at some time somehow metamorphosed itself into the monopolistic age, whereas it is quite clear that perfect competition has at no time been more of a reality than it is at present. Secondly, it is necessary to point out that the rate of increase in output did not decrease from the nineties from which, I suppose, the prevalence of the largest-size concerns, at least in manufacturing industry, would have to be dated; that there is nothing in the behavior of the time series of total output to suggest a "break in trend"; and, most important of all, that the modern standard of life of the masses evolved during the period of relatively unfettered "big business." If we list the items that enter the modern workman's budget and from 1899 on observe the course of their prices not in terms of money but in terms of the hours of labor that will buy them—i.e., each year's money prices divided by each year's hourly wage rates—we cannot fail to be struck by the rate of the advance which, considering the spectacular improvement in qualities, seems to have been greater and not smaller than it ever was before. If we economists were given less to wishful thinking and more to the observation of facts, doubts would immediately arise as to the realistic virtues of a theory that would have led us to expect a very different result. Nor is this all. As soon as we go into details and inquire into the individual items in which progress was most conspicuous, the trail leads not to the doors of those firms that work under conditions of comparatively free competition but precisely to the doors of the large concerns—which, as in the case of agricultural machinery, also account for much of the progress in the competitive sector—and a shocking suspicion dawns upon us that big business may have had more to do with creating that standard of life than with keeping it down.

The essential point to grasp is that in dealing with capitalism we are dealing with an evolutionary process. It may seem strange that anyone can fail to see so obvious a fact which moreover was long ago emphasized by Karl Marx. Yet that fragmentary analysis which yields the bulk of our propositions about the functioning of modern capitalism persistently neglects it. Let us restate the point and see how it bears upon our problem.

Capitalism, then, is by nature a form or method of economic change and not only never is but never can be stationary. And this evolutionary character of the capitalist process is not merely due to the fact that economic life goes on in a social and natural environment which changes and by its change alters the data of economic action; this fact is important and these changes (wars, revolutions and so on) often condition industrial change, but they are not its prime movers. Nor is this evolutionary character due to a quasi-automatic increase in population and capital or to the vagaries of monetary systems of which exactly the same thing holds true. The fundamental impulse that sets and keeps the capitalist engine in motion comes from the new consumers' goods, the new methods of production or transportation, the new markets, the new forms of industrial organization that capitalist enterprise creates.

The contents of the laborer's budget, say from 1760 to 1940, did not simply grow on unchanging lines but they underwent a process of qualitative change. Similarly, the history of the productive apparatus of a typical farm, from the beginnings of the rationalization of crop rotation, plowing and fattening to the mechanized thing of today—linking up with elevators and railroads—is a history of revolutions. So is the history of the productive apparatus of the iron and steel industry from the charcoal furnace to our own type of furnace, or the history of the apparatus of power production from the overshot water wheel to the modern power plant, or the history of transportation from the mailcoach to the airplane. The opening up of new markets, foreign or domestic, and the organizational development from the craft shop and factory to such concerns as U.S. Steel illustrate the same process of industrial mutation—if I may use that biological term—that incessantly revolutionizes the economic structure *from within,* incessantly destroying the old one, incessantly creating a new one. This process of Creative Destruction is the essential fact about capitalism. It is what capitalism consists in and what every capitalist concern has got to live in. This fact bears upon our problem in two ways.

First, since we are dealing with a process whose every element takes considerable time in revealing its true features and ultimate effects, there is no point in appraising the performance of that process *ex visu* of a given point of time; we must judge its performance over time, as it unfolds through decades or centuries. A system—any system, economic or other—that at *every* given point of time fully utilizes its possibilities to the best advantage may yet in the long run be inferior to a system that does so at *no* given point of time, because the latter's failure to do so may be a condition for the level or speed of long-run performance.

Second, since we are dealing with an organic process, analysis of what happens in any particular part of it—say, in an individual concern or industry—may indeed clarify details of mechanism but is inconclusive beyond that. Every piece of business strategy acquires its true significance only against the background of that process and within the situation created by it. It must be seen in its role in the perennial gale of creative destruction; it cannot be understood irrespective of it or, in fact, on the hypothesis that there is a perennial lull.

But economists who, *ex visu* of a point of time, look for example at the behavior of an oligopolist industry—an industry which consists of a few big firms—and observe the well-known moves and countermoves within it that seem to aim at nothing but high prices and restrictions of output are making precisely that hypothesis. They accept the data of the momentary situation as if there were no past or future to it and think that they have understood what there is to understand if they interpret the behavior of those firms by means of the principle of maximizing profits with reference to those data. The usual theorist's paper and the usual government commission's report practically never try to see that behavior, on the one hand, as a result of a piece of past history and, on the other hand, as an attempt to deal with a situation that is sure to change presently—as an attempt by those firms to keep on their feet, on ground that is slipping away from under them. In other words, the problem that is usually being visualized is how capitalism administers existing structures, whereas the relevant problem is how it creates and destroys them. As long as this is not recognized, the investigator does a meaningless job. As soon as it is recognized, his outlook on capitalist practice and its social results changes considerably.

The first thing to go is the traditional conception of the *modus operandi* of competition. Economists are at long last emerging from the stage in which price competition was all they saw. As soon as quality competition and sales effort are admitted into the sacred precincts of theory, the price variable is ousted from its dominant position. However, it is still competition within a rigid pattern of invariant conditions, methods of production and forms of industrial organization in particular, that practically monopolizes attention. But in capitalist reality as distinguished from its textbook picture, it is not that kind of competition which counts but the competition from the new commodity, the new technology, the new source of supply, the new type of organization (the largest-scale unit of control for instance)—competition which commands a decisive cost or quality advantage and which strikes not at the margins of the profits and the outputs of the existing firms but at their foundations and their very lives. This kind of competition is as much more effective than the other as a bombardment is in comparison with forcing a door, and so much more important that it becomes a matter of comparative indifference whether competition in the ordinary sense functions more or less promptly; the powerful lever that in the long run expands output and brings down prices is in any case made of other stuff.

It is hardly necessary to point out that competition of the kind we now have in mind acts not only when in being but also when it is merely an ever-present threat. It disciplines before it attacks. The businessman feels himself to be in a competitive situation even if he is alone in his field or if, though not alone, he holds a position such that investigating government experts fail to see any effective competition between him and any other firms in the same or a neighboring field and in consequence conclude that his talk, under examination, about his competitive sorrows is all make-believe. In many cases, though not in all, this will in the long run enforce behavior very similar to the perfectly competitive pattern.

Many theorists take the opposite view which is best conveyed by an example. Let us assume that there is a certain number of retailers in a neighborhood who try to improve their relative position by service and "atmosphere" but avoid price competition and stick as to methods to the local tradition—a picture of stagnating routine. As others drift into the trade that quasi-equilibrium is indeed upset, but in a manner that does not benefit their customers. The economic space around each of the shops having been narrowed, their owners will no longer be able to make a living and they will try to mend the case by raising prices in tacit agreement. This will further reduce their sales and so, by successive pyramiding, a situation will evolve in which increasing potential supply will be attended by increasing instead of decreasing prices and by decreasing instead of increasing sales.

Such cases do occur, and it is right and proper to work them out. But as the practical instances usually given show, they are fringe-end cases to be found mainly in the sectors furthest removed from all that is most characteristic of capitalist activity. Moreover, they are transient by nature. In the case of retail trade the competition that matters arises not from additional shops of the same type, but from the department store, the chain store, the mail-order house and the supermarket which are bound to destroy those pyramids sooner or later. Now a theoretical construction which neglects this essential element of the case neglects all that is most typically capitalist about it; even if correct in logic as well as in fact, it is like *Hamlet* without the Danish prince.

MONOPOLISTIC PRACTICES

We have seen that, both as a fact and as a threat, the impact of new things—new technologies for instance—on the existing structure of an industry considerably reduces the long-run scope and importance of practices that aim, through restricting output, at conserving established positions and at maximizing the profits accruing from them. We must now recognize the further fact that restrictive practices of this kind, as far as they are effective, acquire a new significance in the perennial gale of creative destruction, a significance which they would not have in a stationary state or in a state of slow and balanced growth. In either of these cases restrictive strategy would produce no result other than an increase in profits at the expense of buyers except that, in the case of balanced advance, it might still prove to be the easiest and most effective way of collecting the means by which to finance additional investment. But in the process of creative destruction, restrictive practices may do much to steady the ship and to alleviate temporary difficulties.

Practically any investment entails, as a necessary complement of entrepreneurial action, certain safeguarding activities such as insuring or hedging. Long-range investing under rapidly changing conditions, especially under conditions that change or may change at any moment under the impact of new commodities and technologies, is like shooting at a target that is not only indistinct but moving—and moving jerkily at that. Hence it becomes necessary to resort to such protecting devices as patents or temporary secrecy of processes or, in some cases, long-period contracts secured in advance. But these protecting devices which most economists accept as normal elements of rational management are only special cases of a larger class comprising many others which most economists condemn although they do not differ fundamentally from the recognized ones.

If for instance a war risk is insurable, nobody objects to a firm's collecting the cost of the insurance from the buyers of its products. But that risk is no less an element in long-run costs, if there are no facilities for insuring against it, in which case a price strategy aiming at the same end will seem to involve unnecessary restriction and to be productive of excess profits. Similarly, if a patent cannot be secured or would not, if secured, effectively protect, other means may have to be used in order to justify the investment. Among them are a price policy that will make it possible to write off more quickly than would otherwise be rational, or additional investment in order to provide excess capacity to be used only for aggression or defense. Again, if long-period contracts cannot be entered into in advance, other means may have to be devised in order to tie prospective customers to the investing firm.

In analyzing such business strategy *ex visu* of a given point of time, the investigating economist or government agent sees price policies that seem to him predatory and restrictions of output that seem to him synonymous with loss of opportunities to produce. He does not see that restrictions of this type are, in the conditions of the perennial gale, incidents, often unavoidable incidents, of a long-run process of expansion which they protect rather than impede. There is no more of paradox in this than there is in saying that motorcars are traveling faster than they otherwise would *because* they are provided with brakes.

This stands out most clearly in the case of those sectors of the economy which at any time happen to embody the impact of new things and methods on the existing industrial structure. The best way of getting a vivid and realistic idea of industrial strategy is indeed to visualize the behavior of new concerns or industries that introduce new commodities or processes (such as the aluminum industry) or else reorganize a part or the whole of an industry (such as, for instance, the old Standard Oil Company).

As we have seen, such concerns are aggressors by nature and wield the really effective weapon of competition. Their intrusion can only in the rarest of cases fail to improve total output in quantity or quality, both through the new method itself—even if at no time used to full advantage—and through the pressure it exerts on the preexisting firms. But these aggressors are so circumstanced as to require, for purposes of attack and defense, also pieces of armor other than price and quality of their product which, moreover, must be strategically manipulated all along so that at any point of time they seem to be doing nothing but restricting their output and keeping prices high.

On the one hand, largest-scale plans could in many cases not materialize at all if it were not known from the outset that competition will be discouraged by heavy capital requirements or lack of experience, or that means are available to discourage or checkmate it so as to gain the time and space for further developments. Even the conquest of financial control over competing concerns in otherwise unassailable positions or the securing of advantages that run counter to the public's sense of fair play—railroad rebates—move, as far as long-run effects on total output alone are envisaged, into a different light; they *may* be methods for removing obstacles that the institution of private property puts in the path of progress. In a socialist society that time and space would be no less necessary. They would have to be secured by order of the central authority.

On the other hand, enterprise would in most cases be impossible if it were not known from the outset that exceptionally favorable situations are likely to arise which if exploited by price, quality and quantity manipulation will produce profits adequate to tide over exceptionally unfavorable situations provided these are similarly managed. Again this requires strategy that in the short run is often restrictive. In the majority of successful cases this strategy just manages to serve its purpose. In some cases, however, it is so successful as to yield profits far above what is necessary in order to induce the corresponding investment. These cases then provide the baits that lure capital on to untried trails. Their presence explains in part how it is possible for so large a section of the capitalist world to work for nothing: in the midst of the prosperous twenties just about half of the business corporations in the United States were run at a loss, at zero profits, or at profits which, if they had been foreseen, would have been inadequate to call forth the effort and expenditure involved.

Our argument however extends beyond the cases of new concerns, methods and industries. Old concerns and established industries, whether or not directly attacked, still live in the perennial gale. Situations emerge in the process of creative destruction in which many firms may have to perish that nevertheless would be able to live on vigorously and usefully if they could weather a particular storm. Short of such general crises or depressions, sectional situations arise in which the rapid change of data that is characteristic of that process so disorganizes an industry for the time being as to inflict functionless losses and to create avoidable unemployment. Finally, there is certainly no point in trying to conserve obsolescent industries indefinitely; but there is point in trying to avoid their coming down with a crash and in attempting to turn a rout, which may become a center of cumulative depressive effects, into orderly retreat. Correspondingly there is, in the case of industries that have sown their wild oats but are still gaining and not losing ground, such a thing as orderly advance.

All this is of course nothing but the tritest common sense. But it is being overlooked with a persistence so stubborn as sometimes to raise the question of sincerity. And it follows that, within the process of creative destruction, all the realities of which theorists are in the habit of relegating to books and courses on business cycles, there is another side to industrial self-organization than that which these theorists are contemplating. "Restraints of trade" of the cartel type as well as those which merely consist in tacit understandings about price competition may be effective remedies under conditions of depression. As far as they are, they may in the end produce not only steadier but also greater expansion of total output than could be secured by an entirely uncontrolled onward rush that cannot fail to be studded with catastrophes. Nor can it be argued that these catastrophes occur in any case. We know what has happened in each historical case. We have a very imperfect idea of what might have happened, considering the tremendous pace of the process, if such pegs had been entirely absent.

Even as now extended however, our argument does not cover all cases of restrictive or regulating strategy, many of which no doubt have that injurious effect on the long-run development of output which is uncritically attributed to all of them. And even in the cases our argument does cover, the net effect is a question of the circumstances and of the way in which and the degree to which industry regulates itself in each individual case. It is certainly as conceivable that an all-pervading cartel system might sabotage all progress as it is that it might realize, with smaller social and private costs, all that perfect competition is supposed to realize. This is why our argument does not amount to a case against state regulation. It does show that there is no general case for indiscriminate "trust-busting" or for the prosecution of everything that qualifies as a restraint of trade. Rational as distinguished from vindictive regulation by public authority turns out to be an extremely delicate problem which not every government agency, particularly when in full cry against big business, can be trusted to solve. But our argument, framed to refute a prevalent *theory* and the inferences drawn therefrom about the relation between modern capitalism and the development of total output, only yields another *theory*, i.e., another outlook on facts and another principle by which to interpret them. For our purpose that is enough. For the rest, the facts themselves have the floor.

THE STEEL PRICE CONTROVERSY, 1962

Attack on the Steel Price Increase

JOHN F. KENNEDY

In his news conference on April 11, 1962, the day after the U. S. Steel Corporation announced a $6 per ton increase in the price of steel, President Kennedy charged that U. S. Steel had acted in disregard of its "public responsibilities." The statement which he made relating to this action is reproduced here.

THE SIMULTANEOUS and identical actions of United States Steel and other leading steel corporations increasing steel prices by some $6 a ton constitute a wholly unjustifiable and irresponsible defiance of the public interest.

In this serious hour in our nation's history, when we are confronted with grave crises in Berlin and Southeast Asia, when we are devoting our energies to economic recovery and stability, when we are asking reservists to leave their homes and families for months on end, and servicemen to risk their lives—and four were killed in the last two days in Vietnam—and asking union members to hold down their wage requests, at a time when restraint and sacrifice are being asked of every citizen, the American people will find it hard, as I do, to accept a situation in which a tiny handful of steel executives whose pursuit of private power and profit exceeds their sense of public responsibility can show such utter contempt for the interest of 185 million Americans.

If this rise in the cost of steel is imitated by the rest of the industry, instead of rescinded, it would increase the cost of homes, autos, appliances and most other items for every American family. It would increase the cost of machinery and tools to every American businessman and farmer. It would seriously handicap our efforts to prevent an inflationary spiral from eating up the pensions of our older citizens, and our new gains in purchasing power. It would add, Secretary McNamara informed me this morning, an estimated one billion dollars to the cost of our defenses, at a time when every dollar is needed for national security and other purposes.

It will make it more difficult for American goods to compete in foreign markets, more difficult to withstand competition from foreign imports, and, thus, more difficult to improve our balance-of-payments position and stem the flow of gold. And it is necessary to stem it, for our national security, if we are going to pay for our security commitments abroad.

And it would surely handicap our efforts to induce other industries and unions to adopt responsible price and wage policies.

The facts of the matter are that there is no justification for an increase in steel prices.

The recent settlement between the industry and the union, which does not even take place until July 1, was widely acknowledged to be noninflationary, and the whole purpose and effect of this Administration's role, which both parties understood, was to achieve an agreement which would make unnecessary any increases in prices.

Steel output per man is rising so fast that labor costs per ton of steel can actually be expected to decline in the next 12 months. And, in fact, the acting Commissioner of the Bureau of Labor Statistics informed me this morning that, and I quote: "employment costs per unit of steel output in 1961 were essentially the same as they were in 1958." The cost of major raw materials—steel scrap and coal—has also been declining.

And, for an industry which has been generally operating at less than two thirds of capacity, its profit rate has been normal, and can be expected to rise sharply this year in view of the reduction in idle capacity. Their lot has been easier than that of 100,000 steelworkers thrown out of work in the last three years.

The industry's cash dividends have exceeded 600 million dollars in each of the last five years, and earnings in the first quarter of this year were estimated in the February 28 "Wall Street Journal" to be among the highest in history.

In short, at a time when they could be exploring how more efficiency and better prices could be obtained, reducing prices in this industry in recognition of lower costs, their unusually good labor contract, their foreign competition and their increase in production and profits which are coming this year, a few gigantic corporations have decided to increase prices in ruthless disregard of their public responsibilities.

The Steelworkers Union can be proud that it abided by its responsibilities in this agreement, and this Government also has responsibilities which we intend to meet. The Department of Justice and the Federal Trade Commission are examining the significance of this action in a free, competitive economy.

The Department of Defense and other agencies are reviewing its impact on their policies of procurement.

And I am informed that steps are under way by those members of the Congress who plan appropriate inquiries into how these price decisions are so quickly made and reached, and what legislative safeguards may be needed to protect the public interest.

Price and wage decisions in this country, except for very limited restriction in the case of monopolies and national-emergency strikes, are and ought to be freely and privately made. But the American people have a right to expect, in return for that freedom, a higher sense of business responsibility for the welfare of their country than has been shown in the last two days.

Some time ago I asked each American to consider what he would do for his country, and I asked the steel companies. In the last twenty-four hours we had their answer.

Defense of the Steel Price Increase

ROGER BLOUGH

On the day following President Kennedy's news conference Roger Blough, Chairman of the Board of U. S. Steel, defended the price rise. His statement is given below.

WHEN THE President of the United States speaks as he did yesterday regarding our corporation and its cost-price problems, I am sure a response is indicated and desirable.

Let me say respectfully that we have no wish to add to acrimony or to misunderstanding. We do not question the sincerity of anyone who disagrees with the action we have taken.

Neither do we believe that anyone can properly assume that we are less deeply concerned with the welfare, and the strength, and the vitality of this nation than are those who have criticized our action.

As employes and stockholders, we, along with thousands of other employes and stockholders, both union and nonunion, must discharge faithfully our responsibilities to United States Steel.

But as citizens we must also discharge fully our responsibilities to the nation. The action we have taken is designed to meet both those responsibilities.

One of the nation's most valuable and indispensable physical assets is its productive machinery and equipment, because its strength depends upon that. I, among others, share the responsibility of keeping a portion of that plant machinery and equipment in good working order. To do that our company, like every other employer, must be profitable. The profit which any company has left over after paying its employes, its other expenses, the tax collector and its stockholders for the use of their resources, are the main source of the plants and equipment that provide the work that thousands of workers have now.

Had it not been for those profits in the past, the millions with jobs in many varieties of business would not have those jobs.

But the machinery and equipment must be kept up to date, or no sales will be made, no work provided, no taxes available, and our international competitive position, our balance of payments, our gold reserves, and our national growth will seriously suffer.

None of us is unaware of the serious national problem and no one is unsympathetic with those in the Executive Branch of Government attempting to conduct the affairs of the nation, nationally and internationally.

But certainly, more rapid equipment modernization is one of the nation's basic problems as outlined by Secretary of the Treasury Douglas Dillon.

Speaking before the American Bankers Association last October, he said:

"More rapid equipment modernization by industry is vital to the success of our efforts to remain competitive in world markets, and to achieve the rate of growth needed to assure us prosperity and reasonably full employment."

"I think it highly significant," says Mr. Dillon, "that all the industrial countries of Western Europe, except Belgium and the United Kingdom, are now devoting twice as much of their gross national product to purchases of industrial equipment as are we in the United States."

"And Belgium and the United Kingdom," continues Mr. Dillon, "the two European countries whose economic growth has lagged in comparison with the rest of Western Europe, are devoting half again as much of their G.N.P. to the purchase of equipment as we are."

Now what this all means is that as a nation, we keep ahead in the race among nations through machinery and equipment through good productive facilities, through jobs that are vitally linked to the industrial strength. Surely our workmen are as good as any in the world, but they must have the tools with which to compete.

In other words, we compete as a company, as an industry and as a nation with better costs and better ways of production. Proper pricing is certainly part of that picture. And that is what is involved here, however it may be portrayed. For each individual company in our competitive society has a responsibility to the public, as well as to its employes and to its stockholders, to do the things that are necessary price-wise, however unpopular that may be at times to keep in the competitive race. And that is all we have attempted to do.

Now may I say several things with respect to any misunderstandings that have been talked about.

First, the President said when questioned regarding any arrangement not to increase prices, and I quote, "We did not ask either side to give us any assurance because there is a very proper limitation to the power of the Government in this free economy." So the effect of this statement is quite right. No assurances were asked and none were given regarding price action so far as I am concerned or any other individual connected with our corporation.

Furthermore, at least in my opinion, it would not have been proper for us under those circumstances to have had any understanding with anyone regarding price.

Second, I have said a number of times over the past months that the cost-price relationship in our company needed to be remedied.

As recently as Feb. 16, while the labor negotiations were going on, I referred in an interview made public to the steadily rising costs which we have experienced.

And I said, and I quote: "And you're asking me how long that can continue to increase, and how long it can be borne without any kind of a remedy? I would give you the answer that it is not reasonable to think of it as continuing. In other words, even now there should be a remedy. If any additional cost occurs, the necessity for the remedy becomes even greater."

And that was said in February.

This very real problem has been discussed in recent months with a number of individuals in Washington, and I am at a loss to know why anyone concerned with the situation would be unaware of the serious deterioration in the cost-price relationship.

In this connection President Kennedy in his letter of last Sept. 6 addressed to the executives of the steel companies said:

"Now I recognize too that the steel industry by absorbing increases in employment cost since 1958 has demonstrated a will to halt the price-wage spiral in steel."

I am sure that anyone reading the reply made on Sept. 13 to

that letter could not infer any commitment of any kind to do other than to act in the light of all competitive factors. So it is useful to repeat here that hourly employment costs have increased since 1958 by a total of about 12 per cent and that other costs have risen too. The net cost situation, taking into account employment and other costs, has risen about 6 per cent since 1958.

All this is without regard to the new labor contract. When costs keep moving upward, and prices remain substantially unchanged for four years, the need for some improvement in the cost-price relationship should be apparent.

Fourth, the thought that it costs no more to make steel today than it did in 1958 is quite difficult to accept, in view of the cost increases since that time. For U. S. Steel costs since 1958 have gone up far more than the announced price increase of yesterday.

Fifth, higher costs at the same selling prices obviously mean lower profit. Our own profits of 5.7 per cent on sales in 1961 were the lowest since 1952.

Sixth, the increase of three-tenths of a cent per pound in the price of steel adds almost negligibly to the cost of the steel which goes into the familiar everyday products that we use. Here for example is the amount by which this price change would increase the cost of steel for the following items:

A refrigerator, 65 cents; a domestic gas range, 70 cents; a wringer-type washing machine, 35 cents; a toaster, 3 cents; a compact-size car, $6.83; an intermediate-size car, $8.33; and a standard-size car, $10.64.

Seventh, it must be remembered that the process by which the human needs of people are met, and the process by which jobs are created, involves, importantly, the role of the investor.

Only when people save and invest their money in tools of production can a new productive job be brought into existence.

So our nation cannot afford to forget its obligations to these investors. Nor can we in United States Steel, who are responsible to more than 325,000 stockholders, forget the many Americans who have a stake in our enterprise, directly or indirectly.

Over half of our shares are held by individuals in all walks of life. And no one of these individuals owns as much as two-tenths of 1 per cent of the total stock. Most of the rest is held by pension funds, insurance companies, charitable and educational institutions, investment companies and trustees representing the direct or indirect ownership of large numbers of people in America. These are the owners of United States Steel.

Now, I have touched upon a few matters here in the hope that those who are so seriously interested with these matters, and the public at large, will recognize that there was nothing irresponsible about the action we have taken.

My hope is that this discussion of our responsibilities, as we see them, will lead to a greater understanding, and a more thoughtful appraisal of the reasons for that action.

On April 13, 1962, two days after President Kennedy's attack on the steel price increase, U. S. Steel rescinded its announced increase. Shortly after, the five companies that had followed its lead in raising their prices took the same action. But one year later, in April, 1963, smaller across-the-board increases in steel prices were announced by the corporations. The government voiced no objections.

The Effectiveness of the Antitrust Laws

THURMAN ARNOLD, ARTHUR R. BURNS,

EDWARD H. LEVI, EDWARD S. MASON, AND

GEORGE W. STOCKING

The following selections are from a symposium which appeared in the June, 1949, issue of the American Economic Review. *Thurman Arnold was Assistant Attorney General of the United States in charge of antitrust enforcement during 1938–1943. Arthur R. Burns is Professor of Economics at Columbia University. Edward H. Levi is Provost of the University of Chicago. Edward S. Mason is Professor of Economics at Harvard University. George W. Stocking is Professor of Economics at Vanderbilt University.*

THURMAN ARNOLD

THE ANTITRUST laws have not been effective in the real world. Therefore, the temptation of an academician is to substitute an administration which looks well on paper and compare it with the antitrust laws as they operate. This seems to me very naïve political thinking. My belief is that the only instrument which has a chance to preserve competition in America is antitrust enforcement through the courts. Traditionally we accept the courts as an institution which cannot be criticized or badgered as we badger an administrative bureau. A grand jury investigation can be conducted without public protest in a way that is impossible for an administrative tribunal to function. That is because there is a judge in a robe sitting over it. An administrative tribunal taking drastic action against a powerful political group cannot survive. We have watched the Labor Board swing too far under union pressure and then we see Congress destroying its public prestige and power. Under our tradition and habits you cannot do that to courts.

Theoretically, of course, there are many other ways to preserve a competitive system. You could arrange a tax system to regulate the amount of business which large concerns may profitably do. For instance, Fred Raymond has worked it all out along these lines in a book, which John Chamberlain endorses, entitled "The Limitist." However, my political guess is that we will not depart from the traditional ways of enforcing antitrust laws.

Unfortunately, all antitrust law enforcement under any plan depends on the public attitude. It does not make much difference what your instrument for carrying out antitrust policy is, it will not be effective unless there is a strong demand. There was such a demand when I was in office. Today, in an economy entirely dependent on government spending we are sufficiently prosperous that there is little demand. However, I expect the demand to grow as the consequences of the present centralization of economic power make themselves felt in the business world.

ARTHUR R. BURNS

ALTHOUGH FEDERAL antitrust legislation has been on the books since 1890, there is very little doubt that we have failed to achieve a competitive system at all closely resembling that which was in the minds of the economists of the last century and which provided the background for the legislation. The reasons for this failure lie partly in the forces within the economic system operating in a contrary direction to the legislation and partly to difficulties of achieving competition by law.

The primary pressure away from an organization of industry likely to operate competitively is the industrial technique of production. This technique often requires plants of considerable size for most economical operations. Where considerations affecting the most economical location of industry involve the scattering of plants throughout the country, local monopolies tend to develop from this cause alone. Even in other industries relatively few plants sometimes emerge as a result of efforts toward the most economical scale of operation.

The fact that a considerable part of the costs of industrial production are fixed (the proportion varying widely, however, from industry to industry) permits price-cutting of the short-run type to drive prices down sometimes to the point at which they cover only marginal costs well below average costs. The fact that the industrial technique also involves investments with a considerable physical life means that prices can stay at these levels for considerable periods. However desirable this situation may be in broad economic terms, businessmen, pursuing the profit motive, seek to avoid it. Where they are relatively few, they can pursue their interest by coming to agreements or by price leadership. Alternatively, firms may bring under common control plants at a number of different production points. Thus, the firm may be considerably larger than the plant of the most economical size.

In other circumstances, and particularly in the sale of consumer goods, there is a tendency to turn to the differentiation of products and the use of promotion expenditures, particularly on advertising. Consequently, considerations as to the size of the most economical distributive and promotional organization begin to affect the size of firms and again firms may be larger than the smallest plant capacity capable of production at minimum cost. Thus, there are various forces making for large firms and larger firms mean fewer firms. Tariffs tend to reduce further the number of sellers in industries which are effectively protected from foreign competition.

There has also been a number of forces operating to increase the size of firms by increasing the variety of their activities as well as the scale of their operations in any one activity. The resulting patterns of integration are varied. Vertical integration seems to occur sometimes as a solution to otherwise insoluble problems resulting when at some stage of production there are not only few sellers but also few buyers. During the last twenty-five years the organization of retailing in this country has been passing through a revolution, as a result of which numbers of small retailers have been replaced by large organizations which, in order to be large, are also territorially integrated. But the price competition which resulted at the retail level has brought forth efforts on the part of manufacturers to protect themselves from the direct or indirect pressure of price competition at the retail stage. In some industries such as oil, manufacturers have become integrated through to the retail level. In others, manufacturers have sought (in their own interest, or under pressure from that section of retailers which fears that it is about to be superseded) indirect methods of integration, more particularly through resale price maintenance contracts.

From the point of view of social control, the major question is why a law aiming at the suppression of restraint of trade and monopolies has failed to place an effective barrier in the way of many of the foregoing tendencies generated by the industrial process of production.

The most fundamental reason for the considerable measure of failure of efforts to erect such a barrier lies in the inadequacy of the economic theory underlying the legislation. Theoretically, perfect competition results in the ideal allocation of resources among uses; in a general tendency for costs to cover only the costs of the most efficient firm in the long run, and for full capacity to be utilized except when the resulting prices fail to cover marginal costs of production. But the theory is internally contradictory in some circumstances. The lowest cost may be achieved only by firms so large that they are too few to behave competitively. A choice must then be made between (1) firms of the most efficient size but operating under conditions where there is inadequate pressure to compel the firms to continue to be efficient and pass on to the consumer the benefits of efficiency and (2) a system in which the firms are numerous enough to be competitive but too small to be efficient. The courts faced with this choice have been either unwilling or unable to decide between the two horns of the dilemma. The dictum in the United States Steel Corporation case that "mere size is no offense" seems to rest upon a choice of efficiency with whatever size it may involve. Irrespective of the facts in the case regarding the most efficient size for the corporation, the court was unwilling to obstruct businessmen in the pursuit of efficiency, whatever the result as to the competitiveness of the market.

Furthermore, had the courts been willing to choose the other horn of the dilemma, namely the maintenance of enough firms to insure competition, they would have faced further difficulties in the solution of which they would not have found economists very helpful. More particularly, the number of firms necessary for the maintenance of competition is a problem that has never been satisfactorily solved, and a firm operating under a ceiling as to size cannot be expected to be fully competitive.

Facing these difficulties, the courts have been unwilling to interfere where they could find plausible reasons for keeping out of complicated difficulties. They have often made their choice as to whether or not to interfere on the basis of a judgment of the motives of businessmen. The reason for this attitude lies largely in the belief that if the market tactics or merger policies under review seem to them to be aimed at the elimination of rivals as a means to attaining a monopoly, or where there is direct evidence of such motive, interference is unlikely to impede efforts to attain efficiency. The fact that some of the prosecutions have been under the criminal clauses of the law tends, for reasons of legal tradition, to place emphasis on the motives of those under indictment. While this policy is not in itself unreasonable, it has two fundamental defects impeding the attainment of competition. First, the determination of motive is extremely difficult and, in actual market situations, may be almost impossible. Second, motive itself is, from the economic point of view, secondary. Those who desire to see the antitrust laws enforced aim ultimately at the maintenance of a competitive structure whether it is threatened by people whose motives are good or bad.

Where oligopoly already exists, economic conditions have not by their nature compelled competitive behavior. The effort to maintain competitive behavior under these conditions seems to be doomed to failure. If businessmen choose price leadership as a means of avoiding price competition, no legal device has yet been discovered by which leadership can be prevented, except perhaps where it is based on collusion. There is no form of decree that can be addressed to a leader by which he can be prevented from being accepted as a leader. It would be more appropriate to address such a decree to the price followers. But a decree preventing them from charging the same price as the biggest firm in the industry would not be feasible, and might also be rejected as unconstitutional. The same difficulties attend efforts to eliminate basing point systems. The firms in an industry may be ordered to cease and desist from the use of such a system, and possibly the non-base producer may be compelled to adopt a base price of his own. But it is not feasible to determine the height of his base price which, in fact, determines how nearly he remains a non-base producer. The requirement that producers sell to all buyers at a production point at a uniform mill price may eliminate competition by interpenetration of market territories but it remains to be seen whether competition in mill prices will be intensified, whether such prices will be lower than under a basing point system and the extent to which the delivered price of the product may be higher when demand in the vicinity of a producing point exceeds the capacity there. Economists have not been able to suggest any generally acceptable territorial pattern of prices.

Similar difficulties attend efforts to attack another important policy that has emerged from oligopoly, namely the price set and maintained at a stable level for considerable periods of time. Decrees to compel firms to change their prices from time to time are hardly feasible, because of the necessity for prescribing the frequency, and presumably also the amount of change that will comply with the requirements of the court. Here again the economist has been unable to establish criteria which would give the courts confidence in making such decrees.

If the courts do not accept monopoly or oligopoly, they are then faced with the necessity for determining the number of firms to be maintained in order to remove these conditions. In the past, they have from time to time broken up the almost single-firm monopoly but largely because they were persuaded that these monopolies had been achieved, not as the result of a quest for efficiency, but rather in the effort to achieve control of the market. Even so, they have never done more than replace almost unitary monopoly with oligopoly. If they did seek to eliminate oligopoly, they would encounter the difficulties already mentioned concerning the criteria as to the number of firms necessary for competition.

The courts have also been somewhat confused by repeated, and generally truthful, statements by business that it faces considerable competition. The difficulty here lies in the fact that competition or rivalry can take a great variety of forms ranging from the physical destruction of a rival's plant or products to pure price competition. Each of the available types of competition has its own peculiar consequences, some of them varying according to the nature of the industry. Only pure price competition can produce the results which most people have in mind when they defend what they call in general terms "the competitive system." Non-price competition by way of product differentiation and sales promotion operates to increase costs rather than reduce prices. But consumers may benefit to some extent from increased expenditures, particularly on product differentiation or quality competition. Consequently, judgment of these types of competition is extremely difficult. Here again the economist is unable to be very helpful to the court because typically where an oligopoly engages in product differentiation and service competition, the buyer has no choice as between various combinations of price, quality, service, and the like.

The foregoing does not mean that the antitrust laws have had no effect. It is customary to say that they must have had some preventive effect. The probabilities are that this statement is true, although by its nature it is unprovable. Consequently, no measure of the preventive effect can be available.

The recent modifications of the antitrust laws give considerable general support to the court in its extremely cautious attitude regarding the disturbance of existing business structures and market behavior. The legalization of resale price maintenance provides an opportunity for businessmen to prevent price competition at retail. The court is justified, therefore, in believing that Congress is not determined to maintain price competition wherever it may occur and in this case in the market for consumers goods. State legislation imposing discriminatory taxes on chain stores can be interpreted by the courts as an indication that at least the state legislators are not in all circumstances ready to permit reorganizations of business producing greater efficiency as measured by costs. The Robinson-Patman Act regarding price discrimination rests in the main upon criteria of price discrimination drawn from much economic writing. Here again the courts must realize that this legislation is a part of the struggle between the older and newer organizations in distribution in which the older group sought protection from the state presumably because it was not prepared to rely on the outcome of competition. It is stated, however, that in these circumstances competition is not likely to produce the most desirable results because the very large buyer obtains advantages accruing not only from his cost-reducing opportunities but also from his market-control opportunities. While there may be truth in this statement, it has never been very satisfactorily documented and in practice it is almost impossible to draw a line between the two sources of possible price reduction.

EDWARD H. LEVI

I THINK there are three principal reasons for the relative ineffectiveness of the antitrust laws:

1. The courts are not sufficiently aware of the monopoly problem. As an aspect of this, the courts have not sufficiently considered size rather than the abuse of monopoly position to be the violation of the law. And as another aspect of this, they have tended to think that a finding of violation and an injunction against further monopolistic actions constitute sufficient relief. I believe that this point is the result of points (2) and (3).

2. The Department of Justice has never had a sufficiently sustained and energetic policy of enforcement. Enforcement is sporadic; vigorous enforcement is branded as witch hunting and is followed by a "period of reasonableness." One result of this is that the courts are not forced to face the problems of size in monopoly. Because there are so few monopoly cases, the courts are relatively uninformed as to economic conditions in key industries and the law itself does not develop as rapidly as it would if more cases were brought. Enormous gaps in the law are permitted to remain and this makes it much easier to have an ineffective enforcement policy.

3. Economists in general, I think, must bear a great share of the blame. The general impression of the public is that monopoly is inevitable and since it is inevitable, it is silly to try to prevent it. A variation of this is the popular opinion that it is childish to be against monopoly (perhaps because it is inevitable) and that, therefore, a monopoly cannot be said to be "bad" or a violation. In other words, I think economists have failed to distinguish between descriptions of our present economy and analyses of what can or ought to be done. Thus, even critical essays on the present state of the economy become a basis for a weak enforcement policy and for a lack of understanding on the part of the courts.

EDWARD S. MASON

THE GREAT difficulty in answering the question [raised here] lies in the interpretation one is to put on the phrase "broadly competitive economic system." There are at least two sources of confusion: (1) Is competition to be understood strictly in the market sense of the term or does it also embrace considerations having to do with the structure of the *political* economy, *i.e.*, concentration of economic control? (2) In so far as attention is concentrated on competition in the market sense, how does one measure departures from competition, *i.e.*, the degree of monopoly.

1. When people speak of a decline of competition, they frequently are thinking of such phenomena as the rise of the large corporation and the relative decline in the importance of sectors of the economy associated with small scale enterprise, *e.g.*, agriculture, which may or may not have anything to do with competition in the market sense of the term. One way of characterizing the phenomena they have in mind is "concentration of economic control."

There are various ways concentration may be measured, each of which has its own significance. Among them is a number of employees per business unit. It is, of course, obvious that the ratio between the number of business units and number of employees is continually declining as a result of the continued shift from agricultural to industrial employment, the relatively rapid growth of sectors of industry characterized by large-scale enterprise, and the increase in the size of the optimum unit in almost all branches of industry.

There is, furthermore, little doubt that this changing ratio of number of firms to number of employees has great significance for the functioning of the *political* economy. It affects the location of political power, the character and size of pressure groups, employer-employee relationships, etc. It is certainly true that it is changing the character of American democracy and it may be true that it threatens the continued existence of democratic institutions.

But it has no necessary or even obvious connection with competition in the market sense of the term. No one has been able to show as yet that monopoly is more important in the economy than it was fifty or one hundred years ago or that competition has declined. Partly this has to do with ambiguities in the interpretation of competition and in difficulties connected with the measurement of departures from competition in whatever sense the term is used.

2. The most precise notion of competition is pure or atomistic

competition but this is (a) a limiting concept in (b) a purely static analysis. Although it is possible to measure *conceptually* departures from pure competition in various ways such as ratio of price to marginal cost, ratio of actual to competitive profits, ratio of actual to competitive output, etc., each of these conceptual measures is firstly only a partial measure even on its own terms and assuming static conditions, and secondly, is not susceptible to statistical application.

Moreover, this whole conception of competition and monopoly is purely static. In the American economy new products, new techniques, new locations, changing consumer tastes, etc., are continually breaking the existing patterns of market relationships and forming new ones which in turn emerge only to be broken. How is this process to be fitted into conceptions of monopoly and competition? No one has as yet provided any satisfactory answer.

In default of answers running in terms of the degree or extent of departure from pure competition people have recently sought an answer to the question whether various industries are or are not "workably competitive." Presumably this notion fastens attention on the *results* of a particular market structure. Is the existing set-up accompanied by a progressive technology, the passing on to consumers of the results of this progressiveness in the form of lower prices, larger output, improved products, etc.? Although there is a certain attractiveness to this conception, it must be admitted that no one as yet has given it any precision. Whether a given industry is judged to be workably competitive will depend to a very substantial extent on the "ideology" of the judges. And who is to say in these terms whether the American economy is or is not more "broadly competitive" now than it was in 1890?

Whatever answer is given to this question, I believe myself that the American economy is in fact substantially more "workably competitive" than it would have been without the existence of the antitrust acts. This is due, I believe, not so much to the contribution that particular judgments have made to the restoring of competition as it is to the fact that the consideration of whether a particular course of business action may or may not be in violation of the antitrust acts is a persistent factor affecting business judgment, at least in large firms.

It is frequently stated that the greatest defects of antitrust policy are in handling the monopolistic or monopsonistic bargaining power of the large firm and the problem of mutual inter-dependence which may exist when a few large firms are pre-dominant in a market. This judgment, however, usually will be found to emanate from those who have a static approach to the problem of monopoly and competition. Until it is clearer to me than it is now (a) that the large firm in the presence of manifestly dynamic influences exerts an adverse monopolistic influence on the functioning of the economy and (b) that any possible action under existing (or a modified) antitrust policy would remedy the situation, I have my fingers crossed.

GEORGE W. STOCKING

I BELIEVE the chief reason the antitrust laws have not been more successful is that no politically powerful economic group wants them to be generally enforced. This is partly due to ignorance and partly to vested interests. But regardless of the reasons neither big business, nor labor, nor the farmers believe in a free-enter-prise system. A paraphrase of Pope expresses the trend in public attitudes:

> Monopoly is a monster of such frightful mien
> That to be hated needs but to be seen (Sherman Law 1890)
> But seen too oft, familiar with her face
> We first endure (Rule of Reason 1911; *U.S.* v. *U.S. Steel Corpora-tion,* 1920), then pity (Federal Trade Commission trade practice conferences and codes; trade association activities, etc.), then embrace (NRA).

Big Business has failed to distinguish between free enterprise and private enterprise and apparently is unwilling to admit that the former is essential to the preservation of the latter. Whether this is due to ignorance or hypocrisy does not affect business' stubborn insistence that it must be left alone. The most recent illustration is the National Association of Manufacturers' charac-terization of the Federal Trade Commission's recommendation for amending Section 7 and 11 of the Clayton Act as a witch hunt.

Labor professes to oppose business monopolies, but shouts to high heaven against any proposal to curb its own monopoly power.

Farmers have become so used to subsidies for output restric-tion and destruction that they regard them as constitutional rights.

Under these circumstances not the failure of antitrust but the basic vigor of competition is amazing. Between 1911 and 1930 the oil industry's monopoly had been transformed into competition so ruinous that the states stepped in to forbid it. Between 1897 when the Supreme Court came to the rescue of the sugar trust (E. C. Knight case) and the late 'twenties sugar refining had become highly competitive—American control having declined from 97 per cent to about 40 per cent—and the industry was "demoralized" by "ruinous" competition.

Bear in mind that the technique of competitive readjustment is ruin and bankruptcy, but among modern social groups nobody wants to be the sacrificial lamb even for the good of the tribe.

If we really wanted a competitive economy it would be necessary to:

1. Revise our patent laws so as to give venture capital easier access to modern technology.

2. Prohibit mergers so as to make business firms as small and numerous as is consistent with the economies of mass production.

3. Require federal incorporation for firms the assets of which exceed a specified minimum and which do business in interstate commerce, and limit the use of the holding corporation.

4. Supply more adequate funds for the enforcement of antitrust. Eternal vigilance is the price of liberty.

5. Curb labor monopolies. Specifically, prohibit industry-wide bargaining. The ideal unit of bargaining would probably be the firm and the size of the firm would be limited in accordance with the principle set forth under (2) above.

6. Lower tariffs.

7. Through monetary and fiscal policies, stabilize the general price structure; but leave individual prices to seek competitive levels and perform their proper function of allocating resources and distributing income.

8. Curb monopolies of prestige created by advertising where the main effect is to increase costs by diverting customers from one product to a substantially similar product. This might involve limiting or taxing advertising expenditures, government grading to prevent misleading advertising, or service by a Bureau of Standards like that of Consumers' Research.

In brief, it would be necessary to create an environment conducive to the operation of a free economy. If we could solve the problem of industrial stability, *i.e.*, insure an expanding economy, the readjustments in use of resources which competition would require would be relatively painless.

This obviously is a big order and while the broad goal is generally attractive—a maximization of economic freedom, a high level of employment and income, and economical use of productive agents—its specific objectives encounter serious obstacles on every hand.

PART TWO Labor and the National Economy

MORE AND MORE, we are a nation of employees. Compensation of employees now accounts for over 70 percent of national income, and the labor markets in which compensation and working conditions are set constitute an ever more important component of our over-all economic system.

In the last twenty years, laymen, public officials, and professional economists have become increasingly aware of the extent to which the success of our economic system depends on the workings of labor markets. Policymaking groups, such as the President's Council of Economic Advisers, have found themselves devoting considerably more attention to such things as the outcome of wage negotiations in basic industries, the implications of dramatic shifts in the composition of the labor force (white-collar workers, roughly 18 percent of the labor force in 1900, now comprise close to 50 percent), and the effects of minimum-wage laws, overtime provisions, and other labor legislation on the health of the economy. "Labor monopoly," "cost inflation," and "structural unemployment"—these are some of the phrases that are used to describe key policy issues, and no one who reads a daily newspaper needs to be told that they describe an exciting, controversial, and often murky area.

The essays presented here discuss the problems confronting contemporary American unions, the major trends in the labor market in this century, the effects of unionization and other characteristics of contemporary labor markets on the efficiency with which the economy allocates its resources and on the distribution of income, and the inter-related macroeconomic problems of inflation, unemployment, and hours of work.

W. G. B.

The Squeeze on the Unions

A. H. RASKIN

A. H. Raskin covered major labor-management developments for
The New York Times *for thirty years, and is now a member of
the editorial board. In this article from* The Atlantic Monthly *he
surveys the problems confronting unions in the 1960s.*

A DISQUIETING FEELING of impotence besets many who sit behind
lordly desks in the glass and marble headquarters of giant unions.
True, they still command huge treasuries; they have a controlling
voice in the investment of billions of dollars in pension and welfare funds; their strike calls can plunge vital industries into long
periods of idleness; their political machinery can influence the
democratic process by persuading hundreds of thousands of
workers and their families to register and vote. Yet each day
brings compelling reminders that labor's strength is on the down-
grade and that, like the colonial powers of Europe, its leaders
may soon be presiding over the dismantling of their own empires
unless they can find imaginative new approaches to the challenges
thrust on them by automation, intensified foreign competition,
and a dramatic shift in the composition of the work force.

What may be the wave of the future for all labor already has
swept over John L. Lewis' United Mine Workers, the union that
set the pattern for unionizing the mass-production industries and
for modern collective bargaining and strike technique.

The miners are rich in memories and in money, poor in members. They have $100 million in their treasury and $100 million
more in pension and welfare reserves. But the industry in which
they operate has become an industry of machines, not of men.
Employment in the soft-coal field has gone down from 700,000
to fewer than 200,000 in the four decades since World War I.
In hard coal the drop has been even more precipitate, from

180,000 to 13,000.

The union's quadrennial convention in Cincinnati last October was like an assembly of the Grand Army of the Republic, its proceedings full of nostalgic hymns to faded greatness. Lewis, still majestic at eighty, was bathed in veneration even more awesome than that which enveloped him when he led the epic battles against the mine operators, the courts, and the White House.

There was much atavistic fist-shaking at the greedy "interests." The few delegates intrepid enough to suggest that the rank and file ought to have a more assertive voice in the organization's affairs were bluntly informed that what they called democracy was just another name for "labor union inefficiency," a luxury the miners could not afford unless they wanted their implacable enemies in management to restore them to serfdom.

Similar echoes of a bygone militancy reverberated through the ratification of a constitutional ban on membership in the National Association of Manufacturers and the United States Chamber of Commerce. The two employer groups were cast into outer darkness, in league with the Communist party, the Nazi Bund, the Ku Klux Klan, and the IWW; joining any of these was made the basis for expulsion from the miners' union.

All this in an industry in which there has been no strike for ten years and in which the employers cheer the union as the chief instrument of stabilization. Lewis, once the embodiment of class warfare, now sits with the operators as a director of corporations set up to keep King Coal from being pushed off his throne by competitive fuels. He and his successor, Thomas Kennedy, promote the consolidation of coal companies into ever-larger aggregations of capital, foster the maximum use of labor-saving machinery to dig and load coal, and cooperate in the squeezing out of marginal mines as a further contribution to cutting production costs.

THE PRICE OF SURVIVAL

The result of the union's shift from guerilla warfare to hospitality toward all measures that heighten efficiency through improved technology has been to keep the mine price of coal steady through the inflationary surges of the postwar years. In the process, coal's market has been protected against the inroads of oil and natural gas, and the unionists still needed in the mines have achieved the highest wages and broadest welfare benefits of all major industries.

But the human cost of this progress is starkly visible in West Virginia, Pennsylvania, Kentucky, and other coal states, where tens of thousands of miners have been tossed on the slag heap to rot in an idleness that has turned their communities into ghost towns and their families into public charges. These human discards stalk the coal-rich mountainsides, scratching out a meager existence at bootleg mines and snatching up their shotguns to fight off the union they once fought to build.

Against this backdrop of misery, the miners' union could do little but implore the government to move aggressively to revive the stricken areas and ease the hardships suffered by its stranded ex-members. It tightened the eligibility rules governing its own retirement and welfare fund to prevent the mountainous load of poverty from bankrupting it. Husbanding the union's financial resources and swelling them through strategic investments in common stock have become as much a concern for the miners as for corporate treasurers.

The union is now the chief stockholder in Washington's second largest bank and has a big chunk of its own money in a bulging portfolio of securities in big coal companies, utilities, coal-carrying railroads, and other industrial enterprises. An accounting by John Owens, the miners' secretary-treasurer, on how much the union had profited from its dabblings in big business was greeted by the delegates with the same warm approval they used to accord news that the union had emerged triumphant from a make-or-break conflict with the mine operators.

No one mistakes the union's involvement in its moneybags for a sign that it has lost either its heart or its muscle. The unfilled needs of jobless mine families so far exceed the capacities of any private group that it would be foolhardy to seek to set up an emergency relief program under direct union auspices. As for the strikes that once kept the miners popping in and out of the pits, they have been abandoned, not from an inability on the union's part to cut off production but from a knowledge on both sides that a reversion to the old warlike pattern would mean the loss of coal's principal customers, the electric power companies. They are equipped to convert almost instantaneously from coal to oil or natural gas, and they have made it plain that any irregularity in coal deliveries will cause a permanent shift to these rival sources of energy. Confronted with a choice between cooperation and suicide, the industry and the union scrapped their arsenals.

THE MARCH OF TECHNOLOGY

Indications are plentiful that automation is drying up the fields of historic union strength; the organizing slogans of the thirties hold no appeal for the new workers pouring into the labor force; surplus plant capacity makes many managements welcome strikes as a handy valve for draining inventory out of clogged warehouses; most menacing of all, increased employer toughness, the mounting pressure of low-wage imports, and public hostility toward wage increases accompanied by price increases have lowered the ceiling on the contract gains most big unions can hope to deliver.

The march of technology is like a pincer movement in its impact on unions. It eliminates large numbers of blue-collar jobs in manufacturing and transportation, thus chipping away the bedrock of union enrollment. To the extent that new jobs are created, they involve hard-to-organize engineers, technicians, and white-collar workers. That is one side of the nutcracker.

The other is the degree to which automation makes businesses invulnerable to strike harassment. When push buttons and electronic control devices regulate every operation from the receipt of raw materials to the loading of finished goods, a handful of nonunion supervisors and clerks will be able to keep acres of machines producing in the face of a total walkout by unionized factory crews. The Bell telephone system and most major electric utilities already have reached this point of immunity to large-scale disruption of service resulting from strikes. In a few years many other big companies will be so far advanced along the road to mechanized production that they, too, can cease to worry about union strike calls.

Even with existing production methods, our ability to make goods is so much greater than our ability to market them that most major industries can satisfy all the consumer demand of a prosperous year by operating their plants eight or nine months. A work stoppage of three or four months saves the employer the necessity of ordering a forced layoff or a short-work schedule to prevent his products from drowning the market.

The 116-day steel strike of 1959, which took a half million unionists from their jobs, made plain how little financial punishment labor is able to inflict on employers through the exercise of its ultimate weapon. Despite the longest union shutdown in the industry's history, the combined net profit of the leading steel producers, as computed by the First National City Bank of New York, came to $816 million for the year, a rise of 5 percent over their 1958 earnings.

To add to the union's frustrations, the excess of capacity over demand proved so great that the mills found it necessary to black out half their furnaces and furlough tens of thousands of workers within six months after a presidential order under the Taft-Hartley Act had compelled the union members to return to their jobs in the national interest. By the end of 1960 the slackness of market demand had caused a loss of tonnage almost equal to that engendered by the long strike. The industry, which is now able to show a profit when it is operating at as little as one third of capacity, decided to ease its embarrassment over the gulf between what it could make and what it could sell by abolishing the production index that advertised its lag to an unsympathetic world.

THE WORKER'S BEST FRIEND

A complex of new factors has further blunted the effectiveness of strikes. Employers are turning more and more to strike-insurance programs to cushion their strike losses: income-tax carryback provisions operate as another shield against red ink; so do unemployment insurance merit-rating taxes, which make it cheaper for a business to have workers idle because of a strike than because of a cutback ordered by the company.

Add to this a widespread feeling in management ranks that it is time to "stop letting unions push us around." This translates into a far more rigid employer stance in collective bargaining— a determination to get concessions in increased efficiency for every new union gain. Companies that once fought a rearguard

action against union demands now make all the key decisions
on how much they will give and how much they will take in
exchange.

Many unions have found themselves powerless to buck this
"take it or leave it" approach because of the vastly increased
sophistication with which employers are conducting most aspects
of employee relations. All the techniques of motivational research
are poured into multimillion-dollar programs to convince the
workers that management is their best friend. The blood-and-
guts antagonism to unions of the Tom Girdlers and Ernest T.
Weirs in the Little Steel strikes of two decades ago has been
replaced by a year-round flow of "Papa knows best" communications, the net effect of which is that unions are perfectly all
right if the workers want them, but there is nothing beneficial
they can do that management won't do at least as well without
their prodding.

By all odds, the most skillful practitioner in this field is General Electric, the nation's biggest electrical manufacturer. The
extent of its dominance in collective bargaining was forcefully
indicated by the rout of the International Union of Electrical
Workers in the three-week strike it conducted last October
[1960] in a vain effort to improve a G.E. contract offer.

The union's biggest local, representing workers at the G.E.
headquarters plant in Schenectady, quit the walkout in mid-
course. Other plants were able to restore varying measures of
production. Indeed, it was plain that the union's official order
to go back without any modification of the prestrike package
was issued just soon enough to prevent a general collapse that
would have left the union leaders without any rank and file.
The only flaw for the company was the issuance by Mayor
Richardson Dilworth of Philadelphia of a public charge that
General Electric had been guilty of "political and industrial
blackmail" in hinting that it would move to a more congenial
environment if the police of the City of Brotherly Love did not
act more vigorously to get nonstrikers through the union picket
lines. The company insisted that its sole concern was with the
maintenance of law and order.

It was not until four months after the union had limped back
on the company's terms that the first real crack developed in
the image of corporate rectitude in which General Electric had

wrapped itself. The company was fined $437,000 and three of its high officials went to jail for participation in an industry-wide price-rigging scheme that cheated government agencies and private utilities in the sale of billions of dollars in heavy electrical equipment.

The paradoxical upshot of all this weakening of labor's mastodons in the mass-production industries is that little unions are calling much more damaging strikes these days than their big brothers. Despite the unabated clamor of the Goldwaters and the Mundts for laws to prevent industry-wide strikes, a strategically placed small union often exercises far more economic leverage than one a hundred times its size. This was illustrated with particular force last January [1961] when a walkout of 664 crewmen on railroad ferries and tugs in New York Harbor generated a picket blockade that cut off service for 100,000 commuters, forced an embargo on export freight, and halted virtually all main-line service on the sprawling New York Central and New Haven rail systems.

At the very time that a covey of top federal, state, and city officials were pooling their energies in a panicky rush to relieve the disruption touched off by this tiny walkout, the Labor Department was releasing a study designed to show that there was no cause for public anxiety over the frequent national work stoppages by 500,000 steelworkers. The irritation that stems from this imbalance between union size and the capacity to hurt an army of innocent bystanders is one that damages labor's popularity.

THE END OF THE WAGE-PRICE SPIRAL

The unions have several other big headaches. One of the worst is the heightened cost-consciousness engendered in industry by the recession, by public and political anxiety over higher prices, and by the prospect of increasingly stiff competition from foreign and domestic rivals. So pressing have all these considerations become that there is solid basis for believing that we are nearing—if we have not already reached—the end of the wage-price spiral in such pivotal industries as steel, automobiles, and electrical manufacturing. The decisive battle on this front was fought, in the opinion of many observers, even before the steelworkers went out on their long strike in 1959.

No industry has been more criticized for the development of a leapfrog relationship between higher wages and higher prices than steel. Until 1959 the regular practice of the major steel producers was to give a bigger-than-average pay hike each year and follow it with an even bigger price hike. The result was that steel prices went up four times as fast as the general price level in the post-war period. The union complained that the companies took three dollars in price increases for every dollar in higher labor costs, but it never allowed its objections on this score to moderate its own pressure for bigger and better contracts.

By the time the steel companies and the union arrived at the bargaining table in 1959, it was clear to both sides that they had reached the end of the road on a wage agreement that would provide the excuse for an automatic jump in prices. President Eisenhower emphasized his determination to crack down on any inflationary settlement. The Senate Anti-Monopoly Committee, under the chairmanship of Estes Kefauver, made it equally plain that it felt steel prices were already too high.

Interestingly enough, the union's own membership manifested almost as much coldness to the idea of a wage increase based on a price increase as did consumers, who would have to pay one without the offsetting effect of the other. "It makes no sense to have the boss put a nickel in wages in your pocket with one hand and take out a dime in prices with the other" was a common sentiment in the steel towns as the contract deadline approached.

It was only when the industry demanded a freer hand in junking established work rules that the union unleashed its old militancy. It resisted so fiercely that the companies were obliged to surrender on the rules issue in the peace pact negotiated with the help of Vice President Nixon, but the cash provisions of the accord gave the union only half a loaf by the bread-and-butter measure of earlier years.

President Kennedy set forth during the campaign his resolve to oppose labor-management settlements made at the expense of the consumer. His economic messages to Congress put even heavier stress on the need for wage-price stability. The realities of foreign competition are as compelling a goad to holding down prices as the political unpopularity of inflation. The greater the disparity between costs here and abroad, the more exposed our markets will be to invasion by a fast-industrializing world and the more temptation there will be for American manufacturers to set up overseas affiliates instead of expanding or modernizing their facilities in this country.

This presents the government, industry, and labor with a joint stake in arresting a situation that threatens more import of goods and more export of jobs to the detriment of the American economy and our influence in the free world. With more than thirteen million additional job seekers expected to enter our already overcrowded labor market in the next ten years and with automation snuffing out work opportunities in many sections of industry, the horizons for dramatic improvements in wages or working conditions are murky.

The administered price system, in which union-enforced wage increases became a handy justification for pushing up prices in bad times as well as good, is breaking down under these new competitive factors. In steel, the industry's abstention from raising prices in the last two years has been based not solely on the fear of White House or congressional reprisals but also on a recognition that aluminum, plastics, prestressed concrete, fiberglass, and other domestic materials have joined foreign steel products in a bid for the markets traditionally ruled by an oligopoly of giant steel companies. With the incentive for price hikes gone, the industry is sure to use its vast reserves of unused capacity as a wall against further union advances of pre-1959 magnitude.

This does not forebode a freezing of wages at present levels. But it does create a strong probability that unions will have to be content with increases geared more or less mathematically to productivity. This means producing more to earn more under contracts that will be fairly predictable before the negotiators get to the bargaining chamber. Such a slide-rule system, with total increases of eight to ten cents an hour each year, will make it more and more difficult to explain to the average worker what economic service he obtains in return for his union dues.

THE DROP IN UNION MEMBERSHIP

Unions already are finding that the slogans which attracted millions of workers in the early years of Franklin D. Roosevelt's New Deal are ill adapted to mass organizing drives on the "new frontier." When the American Federation of Labor and the Congress of Industrial Organizations ended their twenty-year war in 1955, the architects of merger spoke optimistically about doubling union membership in the first ten years. With the decade half gone, the federation is fighting a losing battle to hold the share of the work force with which it started. Only about one worker out of every three in the nonfarm field holds a union card, and the ratio is going down.

Part of the holdback stems from the limitations put on traditional recruiting methods by the Taft-Hartley Act and the newer Landrum-Griffin Act. Part reflects the readiness of workers who reached adulthood after the Great Depression, the sit-down strikes, and the outlawing of private industrial armies to take for granted the higher economic standards and civilized grievance machinery for which earlier unionists gave their blood. The long-standing coldness of white-collar, civil service, and professional employees toward unionization has been heightened by the reaction to labor that came out of the McClellan Committee's three years of concentration on the scabrous side of union-management affairs. The firmness with which the AFL-CIO moved to kick out the Jimmy Hoffas and the Johnny Dios has been obscured by the inability of the sanctions applied by labor or the government to force any real cleanup in the freewheeling Teamsters Union, biggest and strongest of all labor organizations.

Difficulties of such dimensions clearly require a thoroughgoing evaluation by labor of the adequacy of its policies, its leadership, and its functions in the total society. Many large corporations have set up special divisions of forward planning to look into the future and decide what the company ought to do to keep growing. Such planning agencies are almost unknown in organized labor. Walter P. Reuther, the dynamic president of the United Automobile Workers, has done more in this direction than his more earthbound associates in labor's top echelon.

TRAINING ORGANIZERS

However, there is beginning to be a stirring even in the most standpat unions. George Meany, the AFL-CIO president, whose crusading for high ethical standards was principally responsible for the Teamsters' exile, is exploring ways to revive the dormant organizing drive and put new brightness in labor's public image. The federation is contemplating a school for organizers as a means of ensuring a cadre of highly qualified replacements for labor's aging general staff.

Twelve of the twenty-eight members of the federation's ruling executive council are past the social security retirement age of sixty-five, and four others are less than five years from that milestone. It is on these men that the primary responsibility falls for evolving a new sense of mission for the labor movement. Unhappily, a good deal of the enterprise they should be devoting to the task is drained off in endless jurisdictional wars. Unions with a hundred thousand workers unorganized in their industries battle over who should control a dozen already in union ranks. Personal animosities are so virulent that the merged federation has been repeatedly dragged to the edge of collapse by the inability of its aging rulers to live at peace.

Yet in many ways labor's elder statesmen have shown more receptivity to fresh ideas and to concepts of social responsibility than their rank and file. Despite the threat automation has posed to the size of their unions and the security of their treasuries, they have recognized from the start that they could not halt scientific improvement. The arguments have been less over whether to automate than over how to share the fruits of automation most equitably and provide maximum safeguards against too high a toll in layoffs.

In many industries union chiefs have been so diligent in suppressing wildcat strikes and fostering increased efficiency that their members have accused them of becoming too company-minded. On the political front, they have been careful to avoid any scramble for patronage as the price of their election support, and the bulk of their legislative program is aimed at achieving faster economic growth for the welfare of all.

THE UNIONS' LIFE EXPECTANCY

The big question is whether the rather amorphous social goals for which labor is now striving are sufficiently appealing to hold together a movement that has always prided itself on its non-ideological character and its identification with "bringing home the bacon" in the most literal market-basket sense. If democratic values are to survive in this country, a healthy union movement will have to play its important role in giving them meaning. To let it sink into a supine subservience to management, with no real grip on the loyalty or idealism of American workers, would throttle at the source much of our productive energy and reduce our chances of overcoming the challenge of Soviet industrial progress.

A labor movement excessively dependent on government would be equally empty of democratic vitality. No group in our complex society has a monopoly on wisdom. If labor defaults in its role as a balance wheel against too much concentration of power in industry or the state, we shall all be the poorer.

Obviously, the life expectancy of unions will be short if all they can promise their members is a modest dose of more of the same in each new wage contract, plus eternal worry about how long their members' jobs will last. Thus far, most of the answers to automation that have come out of collective bargaining consist of little more than termination-pay allowances and arrangements for retraining the displaced workers if there are any jobs to train them for. Developing more satisfactory answers is too big a task for labor alone. It requires a pooling of the best thinking in all parts of our economy—employers, unions, and government on an across-the-board, as well as an industry-by-industry, basis.

President Eisenhower's Secretary of Labor, James P. Mitchell, made some significant headway toward meeting this need. An even more ambitious effort was undertaken by his successor in the Kennedy cabinet, Arthur J. Goldberg. The extent to which these two men—one a Republican with a background of executive service in management, and the other a Democrat with two decades as a labor lawyer and policy maker—have pursued parallel aims is perhaps the best portent of hope that a fruitful partnership can be established on the production front, the battlefield on which Premier Khrushchev has vowed he will eventually bury us.

PROGRESS WITHOUT STRIKES

Labor's trail blazers in the sixties will not be the leaders who plan the most audacious strikes but those who are most successful in devising formulas for social justice and industrial progress without strikes. The two most powerful men in the AFL-CIO, Meany and Reuther, have long recognized that labor must go forward with the community, not by picking the community's pocket for its own benefit.

Reuther began immediately after V-J Day to enunciate the principle that labor should fight against company moves to make every wage increase an excuse for an even bigger price increase. Meany, when the McClellan Committee began demonstrating how flagrantly some union leaders were violating labor's ethical practices code, was at pains to remind his flock that Gompers was not thinking only of dollars and cents when he made his classic statement that what labor wanted was "more." This was Gompers' testament, as Meany chose to recall it: "I do not value the labor movement only for its ability to give better wages, better clothes, and better homes. Its ultimate goal is to be found in the progressively evolving life possibilities in the life of each man and woman. My inspiration comes in opening opportunities that all alike may be free to live life to the fullest."

It is easy to point to departure from this idyllic credo. Too many unions continue to be arrogant or hypocritical in their attitudes toward industry, the consumer, and their own members. But each year brings indications of an awareness that steady jobs and stable prices are more important than the kind of wage increases that erase both jobs and buying power by pricing goods out of the market. Union-built housing projects are replacing slums in many cities; union hospitals and health centers are supplementing community health facilities; hundreds of youngsters are going to college on union scholarships; labor has become a mainstay in Community Chest fund-raising drives; unions are contributing men and money to the building of free labor organizations in Asia and Africa as a defense against Communist penetration. All these are signs of hope as labor gropes for new footholds in a fast-changing society.

Wage Behavior and the Cost-inflation Problem

WILLIAM G. BOWEN

This essay, written expressly for this volume, is based on a lecture given in the basic economics course at Princeton University and on several of the author's publications dealing with wages and inflation, especially The Wage Price Issue *and* Wage Behavior in the Postwar Period.

THE ROLE OF WAGE behavior in the inflationary process has been one of the most hotly debated issues of the postwar years, both in this country and abroad. This is a new development. Prior to the end of World War II most discussions of inflation paid little, if any, attention to wage determination. Inflation was analyzed mainly in terms of changes in the stock of money and in aggregate spending relative to the supply of goods and services. Needless to say, it has long been recognized that increased demand for goods and services leads to increased demand for labor, and that inflationary pressures originating on the demand side have effects on money wages, which in turn affect prices. Recognition of these relationships has led to the adoption of anti-inflationary labor-market policies, especially in wartime, when many governments have instituted wage (and price) controls. In most situations in which wage controls have been employed, however, policymakers have tended to see an excess of demand over supply as the root problem, and to assume that labor markets play a rather passive, transmission-belt role in the inflationary process.

When World War II ended, the inflationary pressures which accompanied it did not end, although they abated considerably. Economists in many Western European countries and in the

United States began to speak of a "new" type of inflation, commonly referred to as "cost inflation." While there are almost as many versions of cost inflation as there are economists who write on the subject, all versions refer, often loosely, to situations in which prices are pushed up from the cost side (cost-push) rather than pulled up from the demand side (demand-pull), and all assign to wage behavior a much more active role than it plays in demand-inflation models.

A SIMPLE COST-INFLATION MODEL

Let us consider the sequence of events in one very simple model of the cost-inflation process. The first component of the model is a wage-determination assertion which states that, in the absence of excess demand for labor, the collective-bargaining process generates wage increases which are greater than increases in productivity. As a result, unit labor costs rise.[1] Next comes a price-determination assertion which states that businessmen price on some kind of cost-plus basis, and that therefore they will respond to increases in unit labor costs by raising product prices. The third, and last, assertion is the monetary–fiscal policy assertion: those responsible for monetary-fiscal policies will take whatever expansionary steps are necessary to enable consumers to continue to buy roughly the same quantity of goods at the higher prices now being charged.

1. At this juncture it may be helpful to some readers if we illustrate the arithmetic of the wage-productivity–unit-labor-cost relationship, since it occupies such an important place both in the model of the cost-inflation process and in the policy debate concerning the famous "guidelines" formulated by the Council of Economic Advisers. To begin with a definition, "unit labor cost" (ULC) is just what its name implies: the dollar cost of the labor needed to produce one unit of output. It can be expressed as $ULC = \frac{W}{P}$, where W is the wage rate per hour and P is "productivity" (output per man hour). Thus, if the wage rate were $1.00 and if one man could produce 5 units of output in one hour, unit labor cost would be $\frac{\$1.00}{5} = \$.20$. It follows from this definitional relationship that if both wages per hour and productivity increase at the same percentage rate, unit labor cost will be unchanged. Suppose, for instance, that both W and P go up 40 percent; then, $ULC = \frac{\$1.40}{7} = \$.20$. The basic point is that increases in wage payments per hour lead to increases in unit labor costs only if productivity increases at a slower rate than wages per hour.

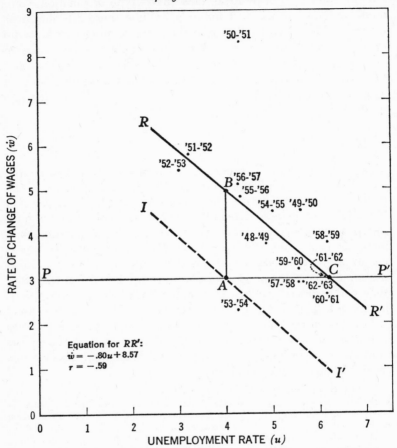

FIG. 1. *The Rate of Change of Money Wages Related to the Level of Unemployment, 1948–1963*

The "rate of change of wages" (w) is, more accurately, the percentage rate of change in gross average hourly earnings in manufacturing from one year to the next. "Unemployment" (u) is the average percentage of the civilian labor force unemployed over each two-year span. Thus, $w_{55\text{-}56} = \dfrac{w_{56} - w_{55}}{w_{55}}$ and $u_{55\text{-}56} = \dfrac{u_{55} + u_{56}}{2}$. The reasons for aligning the wage and and unemployment series in this manner are explained at length in W. G. Bowen and R. A. Berry, "Unemployment Conditions and Movements of the Money Wage Level," *Review of Economics and Statistics*, May 1963, pp. 171–172. The data are from the Economic Report of the President, 1964, pp. 230, 242.

If the figures for the Korean war ('50–'51) are omitted, the coefficient of correlation r goes up to $-.69$ and the regression equation becomes $w = -.72u + 7.51$.

This simple model has the virtue of calling attention to the interaction between the cost-push and demand-pull aspects of almost any inflationary process. That is, while in the case being considered here it is a large wage increase which initiates the process (conceptually, it could just as easily be an autonomous increase in profit margins or in the prices of imported raw materials), "appropriate" monetary- or fiscal-policy responses are necessary to prevent the process from being choked off for lack of sufficient demand. Suppose, for instance, that monetary and fiscal policymakers adopted the policy of not allowing total money spending to rise, no matter what happened. In this situation, a given increase in the price level would require an offsetting reduction in the quantity of goods sold, a derived decrease in the demand for labor, and an increase in unemployment. If wages continued to rise more rapidly than productivity, the cycle would repeat itself and unemployment would increase still more. At what point (if ever) the growing volume of unemployment would dampen wage increases sufficiently to halt the upward pressure on the price level is an empirical question, to which we shall turn shortly.

In the real world, it is of course unlikely that monetary and fiscal policymakers would be willing to tolerate increasing unemployment. Probably they would ease credit and allow money incomes and money spending to increase sufficiently to permit the same quantity of goods to be purchased as before, thus validating the increase in the price level and setting the stage for another round.

For our present purposes, the important point to note about this cost-inflation model is that it forces monetary and fiscal policymakers to wrestle with a dilemma: restrictive policies mean unemployment, but expansionary policies facilitate further rounds of inflation. For this reason, this has been called the "dilemma model" of the inflationary process.

Could things really happen this way? The answer is clearly "yes," this kind of cost-inflation model, when carefully stated, is internally consistent. The more difficult—and more interesting— questions, however, are: What kinds of evidence can be used to determine whether in fact we have experienced a significant degree of cost inflation? What does the relevant evidence show? What are the policy implications?

THE EVIDENCE

How can we identify cost inflation when we see it? This is not an easy question, and the interaction between cost and demand elements even in the simple model of the cost-inflation process described above makes empirical identification very difficult.

Our main concern here is the wage-behavior aspect of the cost-inflation problem. From this perspective the best measurement approach consists of looking at the relation between unemployment and the rate of change of money wages. This relationship as it has existed in the United States, from 1948 to 1963, is depicted in Figure 1.

The first thing to note about this scatter of points is that relatively *low* levels of unemployment have tended to be associated with relatively *large* increases in average hourly earnings. We can obtain a more precise notion of the character of the relationship by fitting a straight line to the scatter of points (RR'). The negative slope of RR' comes as no surprise, since in periods of low unemployment (and tight labor markets), competition by employers for labor leads to larger wage increases than in periods of high unemployment and relatively abundant labor. The bargaining position of a union is of course stronger when unemployment is low and the demand for the employer's product brisk than when the converse conditions hold. Collective bargaining does not operate independently of economic conditions. This simple scatter diagram indicates that it is wrong to suppose that in our economy wages are completely unresponsive to the level of unemployment.

This is certainly not to say, however, that institutional considerations, such as the extent of union organization, employer organization and the basic characteristics of our labor markets, have no influence on wage behavior. In Figure 1, these institutional characteristics can be thought of as influencing the *position* of the RR' curve. If unions were nonexistent, if employers always paid the lowest wage consistent with short-run profit maximization, and if labor were perfectly mobile, then wages would rise less rapidly (and fall more readily) at given levels of unemployment, and the entire RR' schedule might shift down to, say, II'.

We must also emphasize that, as the dispersion of observations for the individual years around the fitted line testifies, wage behavior is certainly not such a simple phenomenon that all variations in rates of increase can be explained in terms of movements along a stable RR' curve associated with variations in the level of unemployment. Other factors—such as the direction in which unemployment is changing, the level of profits, the movement of the consumer price index, overtime provisions, and the timing of key negotiations—also exert influence. Furthermore, as the effect of the outbreak of the Korean war on price and wage increases between 1950 and 1951 illustrates, sudden changes in expectations can have a pronounced short-run effect.

We could speculate further on the significance of this scatter of points for wage determination in the U.S. economy, but it is more important to return to the basic question posed at the beginning of this section: the relevance of wage behavior for the cost-inflation controversy. As noted earlier, cost inflation poses a serious policy problem because it implies that we may experience inflation even during periods of significant unemployment. From the standpoint of the contribution of wage behavior to this problem, we saw earlier that unit labor costs increase only when wages go up more rapidly than productivity. Therefore, to measure the contribution of wage-setting mechanisms to cost inflation, it is necessary to examine the movements of money wages relative to productivity at various levels of unemployment.

To translate this proposition into graphic terms, let us assume, for the sake of simplicity, that productivity increases at the rate of 3 percent per year regardless of the level of unemployment. The horizontal line PP' on Figure 1 reflects this assumption. The vertical distance between RR' and PP' indicates the approximate amount by which unit labor costs have risen at various levels of unemployment. At 4 percent unemployment, for instance, where average hourly earnings have tended to increase at the rate of about 5 percent per year, assuming a 3-percent increase in productivity, there is about a 2 percent increase in unit labor costs, measured roughly by line AB. (Strictly speaking, if our wage index increases from 100 to 105 and our productivity index increases from 100 to 103, unit labor costs increase not by 2 percent but by $\frac{105}{103} = 1.94$ percent.) Figure 1 also suggests that,

on the average, it has taken an unemployment rate of slightly
more than 6 percent to prevent labor costs from rising at all.
So, unless we are prepared to regard 6-percent unemployment
as "full employment," we must conclude that, from the wage-
setting side, our economy has been subject to "cost inflation,"
in the sense that unit labor costs have tended to rise before full
employment has been reached.

How much of a downward shift in the RR' curve would be
required to eliminate the policy dilemma altogether depends on
how one defines "full employment." If we accept the conservative
goal of 4-percent unemployment, then RR' would need to pass
through point A (as II' does), and the extent to which our present situation departs from this "ideal" can be measured in terms
of the (average) distance between II' and RR'. A simpler index
can be obtained by calculating the area of triangle ABC. This
can be done in terms of objective data (we don't need to make
assumptions about the exact slope of II'). The area of this triangle is intuitively meaningful, in that it is the sum of the
increases in unit labor costs associated with all levels of unemployment above the "full"-employment level.

Thinking about cost inflation in these terms also provides us
with a way of comparing our postwar experience with earlier
experiences. In principle, we could fit a line like RR' to the
observations for earlier years and then compare these results
(and the area of the triangle analogous to ABC) with the postwar results. Unfortunately, however, the economic history of
the United States during much of the first half of the twentieth
century was so replete with "unusual" events that many observations have to be discarded. The experience of the 1930s for
instance, is strictly *sui generis*, as is the experience with wage
controls during World War II. The figures for the first two
decades of the 1900s (excluding the World War I years) are
less subject to extreme abnormalities, and a comparison of this
period with the postwar years does yield several interesting
findings. First of all, even in the early 1900s, before the advent
of large industrial unions, average hourly earnings tended to
increase faster than productivity when the unemployment rate
was below 6 percent. So, the limited evidence that is available
indicates that cost inflation, viewed from the wage side, is by
no means a distinctly new phenomenon. The data also suggest,

however, that at comparable rates of unemployment average hourly earnings in manufacturing tended to rise more rapidly in the postwar years than in the period prior to 1930. Postwar wage behavior does seem to be somewhat less conducive to the simultaneous achievement of price stability and high-level employment than wage behavior in the early part of the century.

POLICY IMPLICATIONS

In this country, main reliance has been placed on aggregate demand measures (monetary and fiscal policies) in our efforts to achieve a reasonable degree of price stability and relatively high employment. In terms of Figure 1, these tools can be thought of as moving us along a given wage-unemployment-reaction curve (approximated by RR') to whatever point seems most desirable from the standpoint of society's preferences for low unemployment vs. price stability.[2]

The menu of choices given by the position of the RR' curve is such that, over a considerable range, the makers of monetary and fiscal policies must expect to face both an unemployment problem and some upward pressure from the cost side on the price level. Furthermore, the slope of RR' implies that by taking steps to ease one problem, they will aggravate the other problem. In short, the policy dilemma suggested by the simple cost-inflation model is real enough.[3]

2. Actually, the specific mix of monetary and fiscal policies used in a given situation will also have some influence on the shape and position of RR'. For instance, if we were to increase aggregate demand by means of a substantial increase in public expenditures for space exploration, we would be much more likely to encounter bottlenecks at relatively high levels of over-all unemployment than if the same increase in aggregate demand were brought about by a widely diffused tax cut. Thus, if the increased space-expenditure route were taken, the increase in aggregate demand would probably lead to a somewhat larger increase in wages (because of the shortage of space workers) and a somewhat smaller increase in employment than if the tax-cut route had been taken. In terms of Figure 1, RR' would be farther to the right and somewhat steeper in the space-expenditure case than in the tax-cut case.

3. To be more precise, the evidence presented here indicates that the dilemma is a real one provided that the upward pressure on prices exerted by increases in production-worker labor costs in manufacturing is not offset by decreases in other labor costs, in nonlabor costs, in profit margins, or in the prices of imported goods. Conceptually, these other elements could, of course, worsen as well as improve the menu of policy choices.

It would be wrong to infer that monetary and fiscal policies cannot be used to halt "cost inflation." A sufficient reduction in aggregate demand would presumably move us down the RR' line to point C, where unit labor costs are stable. But the important point is that by taking such action, we would allow substantial unemployment to develop at the same time. Many people have commented on the relative stability of labor costs and prices in the U.S. over the last few years, but they sometimes fail to note that relative stability has been accompanied by considerable unemployment.

This policy dilemma cannot be solved by wishing it away, or by saying that to admit that there can be a conflict of goals is to display a "lack of faith in America." Given the present nature of our labor and product markets, the makers of monetary and fiscal policies must face up to the need for making hard-headed choices. How bad is a 1-percent increase in the price level vis-à-vis an additional 1 to 1½ percent of the labor force unemployed? [4]

In addition to trying to find the optimal point on the present RR' line, policymakers may also try to shift the entire line to a more advantageous position. Proposals to reduce the market power of unions and corporations and to return to a more atomistic type of economy may have this as one objective. It is well to remember, however, that the link between union size and union power may be weak and, moreover, that the relationship between union power and the size of wage settlements may be more complex than it at first appears to be. In fact, some scholars have suggested that we move in the other direction, that we emulate some foreign countries by encouraging more centralization of bargaining so that the national interest will loom larger in the thinking of the negotiators. In evaluating proposals for institutional reform, it is very important to remember that participation in wage-setting is only one of the functions of unions (probably not the most important), and that a proposal designed to weaken a union's bargaining power in the

4. In arriving at one's own answer to this question, it is necessary to consider not only the relative costs of inflation and unemployment but also the accuracy of our measures of these phenomena. As Albert Rees indicates in his paper in this volume (pp. 95–105), there are reasons for thinking that the price indices exaggerate the true increases in prices because of their inability to allow fully for quality improvements.

wage arena may also weaken its ability to protect its members from arbitrary treatment.

Union-busting and trust-busting are certainly not the only possible ways of seeking to shift *RR'* down to a lower level. Wage controls can also be used, and have been in wartime, though they raise serious problems of administration, allocation, and equity. The exhortations of public officials and the publication of "guideposts" for wage- and price-setting constitute a less extreme, though nonetheless controversial, approach to the problem, as other articles in this volume indicate. As noted earlier, shortages of workers in particular areas or with particular skills can also put upward pressure on labor costs (by creating "bottlenecks"), and in this connection mention should be made of the increasing efforts in this country to retrain workers and promote mobility.

The purpose of this essay has not been to advocate one policy or another but to clarify the issues and present some relevant evidence as to the trade-offs which exist at the present time. In conclusion, however, I do wish to express the following personal judgments. (1) The cost-inflation problem, while real, has been exaggerated, and it is not serious enough to justify radical institutional surgery. (2) Efforts to increase the adaptability of the labor force are all to the good and will help somewhat to make high employment and price stability more compatible. (3) Carefully directed exhortations of public officials are not likely to do much harm and may even do some good. (4) Finally, what is most important at the present time is an attitude of realism and a willingness to accept somewhat greater risks of inflation than we accepted in the 1957–1963 period in order to reduce what I regard as an intolerably high level of unemployment.

Guideposts for Noninflationary Wage and Price Behavior

COUNCIL OF ECONOMIC ADVISERS

The Council of Economic Advisers was established to advise the President by the Employment Act of 1946. Of all the words published since then by various Councils, none has been so widely quoted and discussed as this statement from the January 1962 Economic Report of the President.

THERE ARE IMPORTANT segments of the economy where firms are large or employees well-organized, or both. In these sectors, private parties may exercise considerable discretion over the terms of wage bargains and price decisions. Thus, at least in the short run, there is considerable room for the exercise of private power and a parallel need for the assumption of private responsibility.

Individual wage and price decisions assume national importance when they involve large numbers of workers and large amounts of output directly, or when they are regarded by large segments of the economy as setting a pattern. Because such decisions affect the progress of the whole economy, there is legitimate reason for public interest in their content and consequences. An informed public, aware of the significance of major wage bargains and price decisions, and equipped to judge for itself their compatibility with the national interest, can help to create an atmosphere in which the parties to such decisions will exercise their powers responsibly.

How is the public to judge whether a particular wage-price decision is in the national interest? No simple test exists, and it is not possible to set out systematically all of the many considerations which bear on such a judgment. However, since the question is of prime importance to the strength and progress of the American economy, it deserves widespread public discussion and clarification of the issues. What follows is intended as a contribution to such a discussion.

Mandatory controls in peacetime over the outcomes of wage negotiations and over individual price decisions are neither desirable in the American tradition nor practical in a diffuse and decentralized continental economy. Free collective bargaining is the vehicle for the achievement of contractual agreements on wages, fringes, and working conditions, as well as on the "web of rules" by which a large segment of industry governs the performance of work and the distribution of rewards. Similarly, final price decisions lie—and should continue to lie—in the hands of individual firms. It is, however, both desirable and practical that discretionary decisions on wages and prices recognize the national interest in the results. The guideposts suggested here as aids to public understanding are not concerned primarily with the relation of employers and employees to each other, but rather with their joint relation to the rest of the economy.

WAGES, PRICES, AND PRODUCTIVITY

If all prices remain stable, all hourly labor costs may increase as fast as economy-wide productivity without, for that reason alone, changing the relative share of labor and nonlabor incomes in total output. At the same time, each kind of income increases steadily in absolute amount. If hourly labor costs increase at a slower rate than productivity, the share of nonlabor incomes will grow or prices will fall, or both. Conversely, if hourly labor costs increase more rapidly than productivity, the share of labor incomes in the total product will increase or prices will rise, or both. It is this relationship among long-run economy-wide productivity, wages, and prices which makes the rate of productivity change an important benchmark for noninflationary wage and price behavior.

Productivity is a *guide* rather than a *rule* for appraising wage and price behavior for several reasons. First, there are a number of problems involved in measuring productivity change, and a number of alternative measures are available. Second, there is nothing immutable in fact or in justice about the distribution of the total product between labor and nonlabor incomes. Third, the pattern of wages and prices among industries is and should be responsive to forces other than changes in productivity.

Industry series	Average annual percentage change [a]			
	1909 to 1960	1947 to 1960	1947 to 1954	1954 to 1960
Total private economy	2.4	3.0	3.5	2.6
Nonagriculture	2.1	2.4	2.7	2.2
Nonmanufacturing	[b]	2.2	2.6	1.9
Manufacturing	[b]	2.8	2.9	2.9
Manufacturing corrected for varying rates of capacity utilization	[b]	2.8	2.8	3.1

[a] Computed from least squares trend of the logarithms of the output per man-hour indexes.

[b] Not available.

SOURCES: Department of Labor and Council of Economic Advisers.

ALTERNATIVE MEASURES OF PRODUCTIVITY

If the rate of growth of productivity over time is to serve as a useful benchmark for wage and price behavior, there must be some meeting of minds about the appropriate methods of measuring the trend rate of increase in productivity, both for industry as a whole and for individual industries. This is a large and complex subject and there is much still to be learned. The most that can be done at present is to give some indication of orders of magnitude, and of the range within which most plausible measures are likely to fall (see table above).

There are a number of conceptual problems in connection with productivity measurement which can give rise to differences in estimates of its rate of growth. Three important conceptual problems are the following:

1. Over what time interval should productivity trends be measured? Very short intervals may give excessive weight to business-cycle movements in productivity, which are not the relevant standards for wage behavior. Very long intervals may hide significant breaks in trends; indeed in the United States— and in other countries as well—productivity appears to have risen more rapidly since the end of the Second World War than before. It would be wholly inappropriate for wage behavior in the 1960s to be governed by events long in the past. On the other hand, productivity in the total private economy appears to have advanced less rapidly in the second half of the postwar

period than in the first.

2. Even for periods of intermediate length, it is desirable to segregate the trend movements in productivity from those that reflect business-cycle forces. Where the basic statistical materials are available, this problem can be handled by an analytical separation of trend effects and the effects of changes in the rate of capacity utilization.

3. Even apart from such difficulties, there often exist alternative statistical measures of output and labor input. The alternatives may differ conceptually or may simply be derived from different statistical sources. A difficult problem of choice may emerge, unless the alternative measures happen to give similar results.

Selected measures of the rate of growth of productivity in different sectors of the economy for different time periods are shown in the table. Several measures are given because none of the single figures is clearly superior for all purposes.

THE SHARE OF LABOR INCOME

The proportions in which labor and nonlabor incomes share the product of industry have not been immutable throughout American history, nor can they be expected to stand forever where they are today. It is desirable that labor and management should bargain explicitly about the distribution of the income of particular firms or industries. It is, however, undesirable that they should bargain implicitly about the general price level. Excessive wage settlements which are paid for through price increases in major industries put direct pressure on the general price level and produce spillover and imitative effects throughout the economy. Such settlements may fail to redistribute income within the industry involved; rather they redistribute income between that industry and other segments of the economy through the mechanism of inflation.

PRICES AND WAGES IN INDIVIDUAL INDUSTRIES

What are the guideposts which may be used in judging whether a particular price or wage decision may be inflationary? The desired objective is a stable price level, within which particular prices rise, fall, or remain stable in response to economic pressures. Hence, price stability within any particular industry is not necessarily a correct guide to price and wage decisions in that industry. It is possible, however, to describe in broad outline a set of guides which, if followed, would preserve over-all price stability while still allowing sufficient flexibility to accommodate objectives of efficiency and equity. These are not arbitrary guides. They describe—briefly and no doubt incompletely—how prices and wage rates would behave in a smoothly functioning competitive economy operating near full employment. Nor do they constitute a mechanical formula for determining whether a particular price or wage decision is inflationary. They will serve their purpose if they suggest to the interested public a useful way of approaching the appraisal of such a decision.

If, as a point of departure, we assume no change in the relative shares of labor and nonlabor incomes in a particular industry, then a general guide may be advanced for noninflationary wage behavior, and another for noninflationary price behavior. Both guides, as will be seen, are only first approximations.

The general guide for noninflationary wage behavior is that the rate of increase in wage rates (including fringe benefits) in each industry be equal to the trend rate of over-all productivity increase. General acceptance of this guide would maintain stability of labor cost per unit of output for the economy as a whole —though not of course for individual industries.

The general guide for noninflationary price behavior calls for price reduction if the industry's rate of productivity increase exceeds the overall rate—for this would mean declining unit labor costs; it calls for an appropriate increase in price if the opposite relationship prevails; and it calls for stable prices if the two rates of productivity increase are equal.

These are advanced as general guideposts. To reconcile them with objectives of equity and efficiency, specific modifications must be made to adapt them to the circumstances of particular industries. If all of these modifications are made, each in the specific circumstances to which it applies, they are consistent with stability of the general price level. Public judgments about the effects on the price level of particular wage or price decisions should take into account the modifications as well as the general guides. The most important modifications are the following:

1. Wage rate increases would exceed the general guide rate in an industry which would otherwise be unable to attract sufficient labor; or in which wage rates are exceptionally low compared with the range of wages earned elsewhere by similar labor, because the bargaining position of workers has been weak in particular local labor markets.

2. Wage rate increases would fall short of the general guide rate in an industry which could not provide jobs for its entire labor force even in times of generally full employment; or in which wage rates are exceptionally high compared with the range of wages earned elsewhere by similar labor, because the bargaining position of workers has been especially strong.

3. Prices would rise more rapidly, or fall more slowly, than indicated by the general guide rate in an industry in which the level of profits was insufficient to attract the capital required to finance a needed expansion in capacity; or in which costs other than labor costs had risen.

4. Prices would rise more slowly, or fall more rapidly, than indicated by the general guide in an industry in which the relation of productive capacity to full employment demand shows the desirability of an outflow of capital from the industry; or in which costs other than labor costs have fallen; or in which excessive market power has resulted in rates of profit substantially higher than those earned elsewhere on investments of comparable risk.

It is a measure of the difficulty of the problem that even these complex guideposts leave out of account several important considerations. Although output per man-hour rises mainly in response to improvements in the quantity and quality of capital goods with which employees are equipped, employees are often able to improve their performance by means within their own control. It is obviously in the public interest that incentives be preserved which would reward employees for such efforts.

Also, in connection with the use of measures of over-all productivity gain as benchmarks for wage increases, it must be borne in mind that average hourly labor costs often change through the process of up- or down-grading, shifts between wage and salaried employment, and other forces. Such changes may either add to or subtract from the increment which is available for wage increases under the over-all productivity guide.

Finally, it must be reiterated that collective bargaining within an industry over the division of the proceeds between labor and nonlabor income is not necessarily disruptive of over-all price stability. The relative shares can change within the bounds of noninflationary price behavior. But when a disagreement between management and labor is resolved by passing the bill to the rest of the economy, the bill is paid in depreciated currency to the ultimate advantage of no one.

It is no accident that productivity is the central guidepost for wage settlements. Ultimately, it is rising output per man hour which must yield the ingredients of a rising standard of living. Growth in productivity makes it possible for real wages and real profits to rise side by side.

Rising productivity is the foundation of the country's leadership of the free world, enabling it to earn in world competition the means to discharge its commitments overseas. Rapid advance of productivity is the key to stability of the price level as money incomes rise, to fundamental improvement in the balance of international payments, and to growth in the nation's capacity to meet the challenges of the 1960s at home and abroad. That is why policy to accelerate economic growth stresses investments in science and technology, plant and equipment, education and training—the basic sources of future gains in productivity.

Restraint and National Wage Policy

ALBERT REES

Albert Rees is professor of economics at the University of Chicago. This paper, which is critical of the Council of Economic Advisers' "guideposts" policy, was first presented at a University of Pennsylvania Industrial Relations Conference in late 1960.

THERE IS WIDE agreement among economists that the United States needs a national policy to guide the movement of wages in an economy committed to reasonably full employment and to the right to collective bargaining. In the absence of such a policy, it is feared that strong unions will contribute to cost-push inflation. There is even surprising unanimity on the content of this national wage policy: the average rate of increase in hourly earnings and fringe benefits (in current dollars) should not exceed the rate of growth of man-hour productivity in the economy as a whole. Such a policy is consistent with the preservation of a stable price level and of the initial distribution of income between wage-earners and others. The policy is to be implemented by the voluntary restraint of the parties to collective bargaining and of those employers who are in a position to set wages unilaterally. In the background lurks the threat that if voluntary restraint is not forthcoming, some sort of government pressures or controls to enforce the policy will be needed. . . .

My most basic objection to the proposed policy is that it is one of extreme conservatism, not in the good sense of upholding principles that have proved their value, but in the empty, negative sense of opposing change simply because it is change. The conservative aspect of the position is, of course, that it views the existing distribution of income as fair and just, a proposition from which most unions and many employers would dissent, for different reasons. What is worse, it assumes that this distribution will continue to be fair and workable under the changed economic conditions of the future.

It is interesting to note how often economic policies designed to insure "fair shares" take the form of freezing historical income or price relationships and attempting to maintain them in changed circumstances. This concept of equity underlies many arbitration decisions that restore or continue historical wage differentials between groups of workers. In an extreme form, it underlies the position that the purchasing power of a bushel of wheat should forever remain as high as it was in the years 1910–1914, though the amount of resources needed to grow a bushel of wheat has fallen dramatically and we are accumulating surpluses faster than we can give them away. It is possible for a wheat farmer or a locomotive fireman, each in his own way, to be as reactionary as any member of the Union League Club when change threatens traditional economic privileges. A wage policy that would link wage changes to the growth of productivity and thus preserve indefinitely the initial distribution of income differs in degree from a parity price policy for farm products, but not in basic spirit.

It might be thought that the parties to collective bargaining have already accepted this kind of a wage policy in many basic industries. Have they not agreed to long-term contracts providing for periodic increases in real wages according to an "annual improvement factor" or some similar formula under another name? A moment's reflection on the history of collective bargaining in these industries will suggest that they have not. When these agreements have been renegotiated, they have provided additional wage increases for particular groups of workers and valuable and expensive improvements in fringe benefits. Real compensation has been tied to a formula only for periods of two, three, or at most five years.

If we remove from the proposed national wage formula the implication that distributive shares are to be frozen, the whole scheme is endangered. Once labor's share of national income is allowed to increase, a rate of wage increase in excess of productivity gains is consistent with price stability, while if the property share of national income is allowed to increase, the "warranted" rate of wage increase becomes too large to prevent inflation. I have no particular reason for holding that at this time labor's share is either too small or too large, but this is very different from saying that the present shares should be permanently enshrined and preserved.

Two arguments have often been advanced in support of the

proposed national wage policy: first, that labor's share has in fact been stable historically, and second, that it is already so large that it cannot get appreciably larger. Neither argument seems convincing. The stability of labor's share if it existed would be more of a statistical and historical accident than the outcome of any permanent economic principle or law. Recent statistical research, especially that of Professor Irving Kravis of the University of Pennsylvania, creates serious doubt that there ever was such stability.[1] Professor Kravis's estimates show a rise in labor's share of national income between the years 1900–1909 and the years 1949–1957 of from 3 to 10 percentage points, depending on the method of estimation that is used. On all methods, much of this rise took place before 1934, or before unions were of appreciable importance in the economy as a whole. Along with the rise in labor's share, Kravis shows a steady fall in the return to capital relative to the price of labor. I see no particular reason to believe that these trends have run their full course and can go no further. However, the position that the shares should not be frozen by policy does not depend on the prediction of a continued rise in labor's share in the absence of such a policy. It would be equally valid if the natural future tendencies of the economy would lead to a rise in the property share.

As we accumulate capital and as incomes rise, as people choose to spend more of their lives in education, in vacations, and in retirement rather than in work, as the taste for being a manager or a scientist rises and that for being a laborer or a housemaid declines, new relationships will have to develop among wages, salaries, and returns to property. Such relationships will seem strange by the standards of today, just as it would be incredible to a man of 1890 to find that a coal miner now earns more than a clerk. But such adjustments are needed to prevent gluts or shortages of capital and labor in various forms, and they cannot always be relied on to take place within a rigid framework of fixed shares. When it is first recognized that these adjustments are taking place, no doubt those who lose by them have always regarded them as unfair. In time, however, new concepts of equity develop around the new income relationships and these in their turn are defended against

1. Irving B. Kravis, "Relative Income Shares in Fact and Theory," *American Economic Review*, XLIX (December 1959), 917–949.

further change.

To be sure, we could formulate a national wage policy that set a "warranted" rate of growth of wages somewhat higher than the rate of growth of productivity, or somewhat lower, and thus implied shifting relative shares. However, any such formula implies some arbitrary projection of past trends into the future, and some arbitrary and centralized judgment about equitable distribution.

All of these difficulties could be put aside if there were some compelling reason for having a national wage policy. In my opinion, there is not. The policy is put forth primarily as a defense against peacetime inflation. This fear of inflation seems to me to be much exaggerated. In the seven years since the end of the Korean War, wholesale prices have advanced about 9 percent and the Consumers Price Index has risen about 11 percent. These would not be intolerably high rates of increase even if they could be taken at face value. After devoting a good deal of time to studying the methods by which our price indexes are constructed, I am convinced that these peacetime increases cannot be taken at face value; except during wars the indexes have important and systematic upward biases that could account for large portions of the measured price rise. Unemployment and the failure to make full use of our resources strike me as more pressing peacetime problems than creeping inflation.

If it is difficult to support the proposed national wage policy in principle, it is even more difficult to see how it would work in practice. No one proposes that wages in each occupation, industry, or locality should rise at exactly the same rate. It is possible to fail to notice that the formula most often proposed would freeze labor's share, but almost everyone has noticed that the uniform application of it would freeze relative wages and that this would have serious effects on the allocation of labor. The remedy proposed is that industries, occupations, and areas that are short of labor or growing rapidly should raise their wages by more than the average rate of increase in pro-ductivity, while industries with chronic labor surpluses should raise their wages less than the average or not at all. The basic formula thus provides a rule that is both completely general and completely empty; every actual wage determination can be viewed as an exception to the basic rule in the light of local circumstances. A unified national system of wage controls might eventually be expected to develop criteria for taking all these local circumstances into account, but this would involve a degree of interference with labor markets and collective bargaining that no one has seriously contemplated. As for putting such a policy into effect through voluntary restraint one need only imagine a Secretary of Labor attempting to persuade John L. Lewis in his prime that the United Mine Workers should not demand a wage increase because coal mining had a higher than average rate of unemployment. One can hardly doubt that the reply would have been terse, pungent, and most emphatically negative.

There can be no such thing as a wholly scientific discussion of policy; policy issues inevitably involve the tastes and values of the discussants as well as their reasoning and knowledge. My own tastes incline me strongly against any long-run reliance on voluntary restraint in our kind of political and economic system. We can and must call on individuals and organizations to make certain sacrifices for the general good in time of war, or in the settlement of a few critical emergency strikes. On the other hand, we cannot and should not rely on self-restraint as a permanent factor in the making of most important wage decisions. Our economic system is premised on the belief that if each of us pursues his individual goals in open competition, the general welfare will also be advanced. Similarly, our political system is based on the open competition of parties and interest groups with selfish but incompatible interests, no one of which is able to dominate the whole. These are basically eighteenth century ideas, but they look more rather than less attractive in comparison with the twentieth century ideologies that call on the individual continuously to sacrifice his own goals for the goals of the state.

The application of this to collective bargaining is the view that the main business of a union is to advance the interests of its members and the main business of a company is to earn a return for its stockholders. Of course, this does not mean that these goals can be pursued by fair means or foul, that the parties to bargaining should be free to engage in unethical practices simply because they are not illegal, or that it is wrong for companies or unions to make charitable contributions or to give the time of their leaders to civic causes. Nevertheless, negotiators at a bargaining table are agents, not principals, and if they can reach an agreement consistent with the interests of their principals, it is usually unwise as well as unavailing to ask them to put it aside to conform to the supposed interest of the public.

An analogy from baseball might illuminate this point. Suppose that in a ball park with a very short right-field fence, left-handed pull hitters are reaping a rich harvest of home runs. It would hardly improve the game for the umpire to urge each left-handed batter to bunt in the interests of sportsmanship. It would be far better to move back the fence and let everyone do his best. The policy of restraint seems exactly analogous to asking union leaders to bunt. If the rules of collective bargaining as they are now established result in union wages that are too high or rise too rapidly, then surely the only fair and effective solution is to change the rules. Insofar as we need a national wage policy, it should deal with the methods of setting wages and not with the substance of the determinations. It may occasionally be necessary for government to participate in setting the terms of a wage settlement in the event of an emergency strike, but such occasions should be very rare, probably rarer than they have been in the past. In any event, government participation in the settlement of emergency wage disputes is unlikely to assist a policy of wage restraint. In such situations the overriding interest of the government is in getting the strikers back to work, even if this means putting pressure on employers to make additional concessions.

All experiences with policies of wage restraint during rapid peacetime inflation suggest that they are unworkable. Where unions have exercised restraint, as in Scandinavia, there has nevertheless been a substantial increase in earnings over and above the increase in union rates as a result of the upgrading of labor, the loosening of wage incentive systems, and similar forces. This so-called wage drift is now too widely known and too well documented to require further discussion. In the United States, the experience of the Wage Stabilization Board during the Korean conflict shows that the parties to collective bargaining cannot be induced to use restraint even when the nation is engaged in active if limited warfare. It can be argued that the government did not put enough teeth in its Korean stabilization policies; my own feeling, however, is that more compulsion would have harmed rather than furthered the national interest.

Even the strict wage controls of World War II had such serious drawbacks as to suggest the need for a different approach under similar circumstances, in the unlikely event that similar circumstances can recur in the age of the hydrogen bomb. In World War II we never learned to control the general level of wages without interfering seriously with the kind of wage structure needed to attract and hold labor in areas of critical shortages. For example, essential procurement programs were crippled for lack of foundry parts because of the failure to admit that hot, dirty work in foundries commands a higher wage premium in a period of accute manpower shortages than in the depressed prewar period on which official standards of equity were based.

However, this discussion of wage restraint under demand inflation is not relevant to most of the period since 1953, when concern about national wage policy has been growing. The recent problem is that of "creeping inflation," often identified as cost-push or wage-push inflation as distinguished from demand inflation. Most of the analysis of price rises in this period has involved the role of collective bargaining as a central issue.

To the extent that there have been real, as opposed to measured, increases in the general level of prices during a period of adequate and often redundant labor supply, it is tempting to explain them as a result of wage pressures. Yet it is hard to see how collective bargaining alone could raise the general level of prices more than temporarily. This is not to deny that a convincing theoretical model of a wage-price spiral can be created; indeed, many have been. Rather, it is to say that these models do not fit the institutions and circumstances of the United States during the postwar period.

The salient point to be kept in mind is that collective bargaining covers only one-third of nonagricultural wage and salary workers, and that even within this third there are many workers whose unions do not have any substantial power over wages. When labor markets are tight, the wage patterns set by strong unions are quickly copied by weaker unions and by nonunion employers. This copying probably influences the form and timing of the wage increases more than the amount, since demand forces would justify wage increases in the nonunion sector in any case. However, the spread of union wage patterns to the nonunion sector will be severely limited in periods of loose labor markets, and probably will not extend beyond the immediate vicinity of the original bargain. In more remote parts of the nonunion sector, the effect of union wage increases at such times may be quite the opposite. By limiting the growth of employment in the union sector, the increases can reduce any pressures on nonunion employers to raise wages.

The importance of the nonunion sector of the American economy forces us to reconsider the usual model of the wage-price spiral. This model implies that strong unions will cause either inflation or persistent unemployment, if they raise wages faster than the rate of growth of productivity. Inflation will result if the government is committed to supply the aggregate demand needed to support the higher level of wages and prices. General unemployment will result if the government is committed to price-level stability and fails to provide the needed aggregate demand, or if it mops up any independent increase in aggregate demand created by or simultaneously with the wage increase. (I am considering the Federal Reserve System as part of the government in this discussion.) The unions are thus convicted of causing either inflation or depression, and government is powerless to do more than choose the crime to be committed. This model has been named the "dilemma model" by William Bowen in his book *The Wage Price Issue.*

In the past I have accepted the basic logic of the dilemma model. However, in the last year I have come to believe that it is not an appropriate model for the United States. Its most important shortcoming, as I have hinted earlier, is its failure to give enough weight to effects on the nonunion sector, and particularly the failure to take into account the autonomous rise in wages in the nonunion sector resulting from the rise in productivity there.

Suppose that we have an economy in which, without unions or with ineffective ones, prices are stable and money wages are rising at an average annual rate of say 3 percent. Suppose further that strong unions are organized in half of this economy, selected so that its preunion rate of wage increase does not differ from the average, and that the effect of these unions is to raise the rate of increase of wages in their sector to 4 percent annually. Very probably the ultimate outcome of unionization would be to reduce the rate of growth of wages in the nonunion sector to 2 percent but to leave the average annual increase unaltered for the economy as a whole. If this is correct, the whole effect would be consistent with the national wage policy usually prescribed and would not call for either government intervention or union restraint to avoid inflation.

To be sure, the situation just envisaged raises prices in the union sector, and if there is downward price rigidity in the nonunion sector, it could, at least temporarily, raise some broad price indexes. However, the nonunion sectors of the economy are not those usually characterized by substantial price rigidity, so that the effect is likely to be almost entirely on the structure of relative prices and not on the absolute level of prices. In this formulation we do not need to consider downward wage rigidity in the nonunion sector, since the effect of the unions is not to put downward pressure on wages in this sector but only to reduce the rate at which these wages rise. This result relies on our assumption that when labor markets are not tight, most nonunion employers see no need to emulate union wage increases fully in order to hold their workers. I also assume that nonunion employers are under no immediate threat of organization by an aggressively expanding union movement.

The dynamic model just discussed need not involve any unemployment as a result of union wage pressures provided that employment is initially growing in both sectors. The higher relative prices of the products of the union sector will cause some decrease in the amounts of them demanded, and rising relative wages in the union sector will lead to faster substitution of capital for labor in this sector. Unless these effects are large, however, they will merely slow the growth of employment in the sector and not cause it to decline absolutely. Even if there is an absolute decline in employment in the union sector, the workers displaced could be absorbed in the nonunion sector, whose rate of growth will have increased. The unemployment created even in this case is frictional or structural rather than the kind resulting from a deficiency of aggregate demand. Indeed, it is precisely this increased supply of labor to the nonunion sector that enables it to slacken its rate of wage increase.

The situation created by different rates of growth of wages in the two sectors as a result solely of union pressures is not entirely a happy one. It would undoubtedly contribute to under-employment in the nonunion sector—to having too many people trapped in low-productivity activities like domestic service and marginal agriculture who should be absorbed into more productive activities. It is not impossible to imagine a national wage policy designed to cope with this kind of malallocation. But such a policy would be of a totally different kind than the policy generally proposed. It would have to address itself directly to the problem of relative wages, and not to the general level of wages.

My conclusion is that we do not need a national wage policy designed to govern the general level of wages. If unions need to exercise restraint in their wage bargaining, it is not so much to prevent inflation as to preserve employment for their members. The incentives for this kind of restraint are provided by employer resistance to union demands and by short hours or layoffs and not by admonitions from public officials to act in the national interest.

Let me make it as clear as I can that my opposition to a national wage policy is not based on opposition to any sort of macroeconomic policy for the federal government. The government, including the Federal Reserve System, has the very important and difficult obligation of maintaining a reasonably stable value of money and of assuring reasonably full employment. To develop policies that will assure a proper balance between these objectives in a changing economy subject to cyclical fluctuations is a continuing challenge. But if we can control aggregate demand so that there is neither a strong pressure of excess demand nor a large nor persistent unemployment of labor and other resources, there is no need for an additional and independent policy on the rate of increase of wages. Within the restraints provided by monetary and fiscal policy, the general level of wages can be left to the determination of employers and unions. The only further purpose to be served by a wage policy would be to decide the division of income between workers and others, and this in my view the government should not do.

Perhaps we need to pay less attention to the formulation of over-all national wage policies of the kind that cannot be implemented, and ask how the actual present labor policies of the federal government affect the wage determination process. The over-all policies set forth in the Economic Reports of the President call for wage restraint, but the actual impact of policy as it works in collective-bargaining situations is more likely to be on the side of wage increases. For example, we can ask whether the main pressure of fact-finding boards in emergency disputes has not been usually on employers to give larger increases to get a settlement rather than on unions to moderate their demands. Perhaps there are changes in the procedures of handling emergency disputes or in the criteria used by fact-finders that would help to eliminate any tendency for intervention to work toward higher pay for industries that are not short of labor and already have high wages. We can ask, too, whether it makes for better wage settlements to permit strikers to collect unemployment insurance while they are on strike (as is now possible in New York state and on the railroads), or for that matter, whether we should permit employers to carry strike-loss insurance or to enter into loss-sharing contracts. We can also ask whether the Walsh-Healy Act, on the rather infrequent occasions when it is effective, is not used to support high union wages by denying government contracts to nonunion employers, even though their employees may have chosen to remain nonunion in an election conducted under the terms of other federal legislation. I do not mean to prejudge any of these issues; each might merit a long discussion in its own right, with much to be said on both sides. My only concern is to point out that the real national wage policy is made up of what the government does and not of what it says, and that the two are often at variance.

Perhaps the question of wage policy also suggests a lesson for economists. We often learn a great deal from the construction of formal theoretical models of the economy, and those whose talents lie in this direction should certainly be encouraged to expand and refine these models. It is dangerous in the extreme, however, to use these models as a guide to policy formation unless great care has been taken to assure that the assumptions of the models, both explicit and implicit, are consistent with the conditions of the problem for which policy is being made. In my judgment, the implications of formal models for wage changes are not yet sufficiently well worked out to form the basis of a national wage policy. For the time being at least I think that the process of wage determination as it has evolved in our political economy will come closer to taking account of all the relevant conditions and requirements than any formal scheme developed by economic science.

PART THREE

The Farm Problem

MANY PROBLEMS beset United States agriculture. There is the instability of farm prices; there are conservation problems. There is the technological backwardness and uneconomic scale of the typical "marginal" farmer. And many more could be mentioned.

But the essence of "the" farm problem is that there are too many resources in agriculture, especially labor. If the federal government were to cease taking measures to prop up agricultural prices, prices and the incomes of farmers would fall enormously. Large numbers of farmers would earn incomes far below median city incomes in a free market, proving to almost everyone's satisfaction that the nation is faced with a malallocation of labor between farm and city, between agriculture and industry. To alleviate poverty in agriculture, the federal government has intervened with price supports, acreage allotments and so on, measures which work through supply and demand to keep farm prices high. But these measures tend to maintain the excess of labor on the nation's farms.

The reasons for the development of the farm problem, the reasons why agriculture should (or should not) receive special public treatment, the choice of farm policies that are available and the directions which government farm policy should take are the subjects of the essays that follow.

E. S. P.

Government and Agriculture:
Is Agriculture a Special Case?

D. GALE JOHNSON

D. Gale Johnson is Dean, Division of Social Sciences, University of Chicago. The article first appeared in The Journal of Law and Economics *in October 1958.*

WHILE AGRICULTURE has received some type of special attention from government since the establishment of the federal government, programs of the present scale date from 1929 with the establishment of the Federal Farm Board and from 1933 with the emergence of a large number of New Deal agencies and programs. The land grant system of agricultural and mechanical colleges (1862), research grants (1887), extension service (1914), federal land banks (1916), and the federal intermediate credit banks (1923), all antedate the Federal Farm Board. Federal costs for these programs and other long time activities of the U.S. Department of Agriculture, such as crop and livestock estimates, inspection, disease and pest control, and certain general administrative costs amounted to a little more than 6 per cent of the total costs of agricultural programs in fiscal 1955. The rest of the costs were for programs started since 1929 and were largely the consequence of price support operations and the disposal of agricultural products accumulated through price support programs.

The purpose of this paper is not to appraise the present farm programs or those of the recent past. Instead, I wish to determine whether there are grounds for the special and extensive attention which the federal government is now lavishing upon agriculture. In other words, are there one or more aspects of agriculture that differentiate it from other types of economic activity and thus may warrant governmental intervention? With the present degree of government interference in many phases of economic activity, this is not an easy question to answer. Even if we ignore the tariff, there are many techniques now in use as a means of influencing the development of various sectors of the economy. Some are found in the federal corporate income tax structure— accelerated amortization, depletion allowances of mineral industries. Shipbuilding and ocean shipping are subsidized by various means. A limited amount of housing is subsidized. In recent years the stockpiling of certain minerals and raw materials has acted to maintain market price and encourage production.

The growth of governmental intervention in agriculture is not a unique American phenomenon. Almost all of the major industrial nations have adopted programs, especially since World War I, designed to aid agriculture in one manner or another. Perhaps the extreme case is that of the United Kingdom where in recent years the net governmental expenditures on agricultural and food subsidies have approximately equalled the net income of farm operators. For the United States to reach the same relative position would imply an increase in net governmental costs to about four times the level of the 1955 fiscal year.

In this essay I shall restrict my comments to the particular position of the United States and its agriculture. Seven major lines of argument have been used to justify various types of governmental aid to agriculture. The seven will be considered in turn. They are:

1. Depressions are farm-led and farm-fed.
2. Industry and labor are organized; agriculture needs governmental aid to offset their monopoly powers.
3. Almost all farms are small; there are certain activities that these farms cannot carry on efficiently.
4. Farm people are confronted with a great deal of economic instability.
5. Agriculture is and will continue to be a declining industry, as measured by the level of labor employment.
6. Farm incomes are too low.
7. A large and productive agriculture is required for military and strategic reasons.

Depressions Are Caused by Agriculture • A former Secretary of Agriculture, Mr. Charles Brannan, declared:

Most depressions have been farm-led and farm-fed. Farm prices traditionally go down before, faster, and farther than other prices. On the down swing of the business cycle, farm people are the major early victims of a squeeze. As their income and, therefore, purchasing power is cut by low prices or production failure, industrial producers find a contracting market for their production. This throws workers out of jobs. They in turn spend less for farm products, which in turn forces down farm prices, and farm purchasing power is further cut.

I don't mean to say that declines in farm prices are the sole cause of depressions, but they certainly contribute greatly and would do so more now than in the past because agriculture has become a bigger customer of industry.

The view that the rest of the nation cannot be prosperous unless agriculture is prosperous goes back to the beginnings of our nation and has been and still is widely held. Many presidents have accepted this view. Businessmen and financial advisers have similarly accepted it. Bernard M. Baruch said in 1921:

Agriculture is the greatest and fundamentally the most important of our American industries. The cities are but the branches of the tree of national life, the roots of which go deeply into the land. We all flourish or decline with the farmer.

The most extreme form of the argument that national prosperity depends upon agriculture is perhaps the following:

Unless Congress recognizes the simple fact that each $1 of gross farm income generates $7 of national income, theory and legislation resulting from theories can easily legislate the United States into bankruptcy and chaos. On the other hand, if Congress will use it as a yardstick, there is no reason why the United States should ever have a depression.

The latter statement rests upon the fact that for a fairly long period of time (from about 1929 to 1950) national income was approximately seven times as much as gross farm income, with only moderate departures from this ratio from year to year. Thus a statistical relationship was transformed into a cause and effect relationship, with the cause being farm income and the effect being national income. The exact converse could be deduced, namely that for each $7 change in national income, gross farm income changed by $1. It could also be pointed out that certain other sectors of our economy have exhibited a similar close correspondence between the income of that sector and national incomes. One such sector happens to be the fishing industry. If the same line of reasoning could be applied it obviously would be much easier to maintain national prosperity by subsidizing the fishing industry since its gross income constitutes less than 1 per cent of the national income.

One could present many statistics that would, at least for some, throw doubt on the view that changes in agricultural prices and incomes are responsible for changes in national income. For example, there has been a fairly steady decline in the percentage of gross farm income of national income from about 23 per cent in 1910 to almost half that today, yet national income, in real terms, has trebled. But the argument cannot be proved or disproved by simple statistical comparisons. This is true because we live in an economy with strong interrelationships among the various parts of that economy. Thus a decline in national income will almost certainly be accompanied by a decline in farm income and in the income from the production of steel, automobiles, movies, and confetti. In some cases, the relative declines will be more than in the national income; in others, less, and in some, almost the same. But, depending upon the particular characteristics of the commodity, there will be a fairly consistent pattern of changes relative to national income. By the criterion used above in the $1 to $7 analogy, many sectors of the economy could be found to be strategic factors in causing depression or prosperity. This is why simple comparisons of statistical series will not provide us with much insight concerning the role of agriculture in national economic stability.

Let us try to trace through the effects of important changes in agricultural incomes upon the rest of the economy. These changes can occur in a relatively short period of two or three years either because of changes in production or changes in demand. Compared to most other parts of the economy, farm production in the aggregate is remarkably stable. In the last 45 years, the largest change in the volume of farm marketings and home consumption from one year to the next was 12.5 per cent; only two other changes exceeded 10 per cent. Over 90 per cent of the year-to-year changes have been less than 5 per cent, and these are small year-to-year changes compared with steel, automobiles, or other durable goods. In the United States changes in farm production are too small to have any significant effect on general business activity.

Farm prices, responding mainly to changes in demand, do change a great deal from year to year. Most of the changes in gross farm income are due to changes in prices since the quantity sold changes little from year to year. It is at this point that a crucial difference between agriculture and many other parts of the economy becomes apparent in terms of effects of declines in income upon the level of incomes in the rest of the economy. When farm prices decline, as they did by about 55 per cent between 1929 and 1932, output changes little if at all. Thus the economy as a whole has as large a volume of farm products available for use after prices have dropped as before. The major change is that consumers pay less for the same amount of food and farmers receive less. The loss to farmers is approximately equal to the gain to consumers. Thus it is correct to say that no income is lost in the process. Farmers have less to spend; the rest of the population has more to spend after purchasing the same amount of food.

It should also be noted that a decline in farm income will have disadvantageous effects upon those producers in the economy who receive much of their income from selling to farmers, such as farm machinery manufacturers and machinery dealers. To a large extent, however, these losses are offset by gains of firms that produce for or sell to the nonfarm population which has more income to spend upon nonfarm products.

There is little or no basis for government aids to agriculture on the ground that depressions originate in agriculture. The reasoning underlying such a position is surely faulty. However, this conclusion does not imply that there is no basis for some special measures for agriculture as a part of a general program of anti-depression measures. While major reliance should be placed upon general monetary and fiscal measures to prevent depressions and inflation, if a depression should occur and governmental expenditures are used as a means of increasing the over-all level of demand, there is as much basis for channeling some of the expenditures directly to farm people as there is for paying unemployment compensation or engaging upon a public works program. But nothing said here should imply that there is any basis for a program designed to prevent any and every decline in farm income, and especially to prevent those declines that represent adjustments to changes in demand or in relative costs of producing agricultural products during periods of full employment.

Industry and Labor Are Organized; Agriculture Needs Government Aid to Offset Their Monopoly Powers · This is a persuasive argument, at least to many people. The farmer is pictured as selling in a market dominated by the large meat packing firms, canneries, flour mills, and other firms presumed to possess monopoly powers, while buying in a market dominated by large farm machinery firms, fertilizer companies, and General Motors. The farmer has no control over the prices at which he sells, while elsewhere in the economy producers set their prices at the level they desire. Many farmers are also convinced that labor legislation has allowed organized labor to obtain more or less any wage desired, resulting in higher costs of processing agricultural products and thus lower prices for farm products and in higher costs and prices for the products bought by farm people. The answer seems to be that since farmers cannot organize themselves to obtain similar monopoly powers, the government should provide the necessary assistance to permit the farmers to create that power. Price supports, acreage limitations, and marketing quotas may be viewed as devices to give farmers a degree of monopoly power; so can marketing agreements in many fluid milk markets which are supervised and enforced by the federal government.

One counter argument to this view is that the appropriate way to fight monopoly in one part of the economy is not to create another monopoly, but to destroy the monopoly which exists. To use an analogy, nothing is gained by creating an additional monopoly since the farmers may find that, though they may be getting a larger piece of the total national income pie, the pie has so shrunk in size that the actual piece of pie is no larger than before. This analogy, like most analogies, has its defects. The larger share of the smaller pie may, in fact, be greater than the smaller piece of the larger pie. The analogy also implies that it is possible to break up monopolies elsewhere in the economy; farmers may well remain skeptics on this point.

There are two other lines of argument that are more appropriate, though I am not sure that they are any more convincing. The first is that the degree of monopoly which exists in the rest of the economy is greatly exaggerated. The second is that there is no evidence that farmers can gain economic benefits over a period of time from the measures adopted to offset the presumed monopoly powers elsewhere in the economy.

1. First, the power of labor unions to raise wages cannot be demonstrated by a comparison of wages in the unionized and the nonunion sectors, except perhaps for unions that involve no more than four million workers. Second, since the relative wages of union workers have not increased relative to nonunion, the second major goal of unions—the maintenance of full employment—is clearly inconsistent with labor receiving a larger share of the total national income than would be true in the absence of the unions. Third, most of the markets in which farmers sell their products, with the exception of fluid milk markets and perhaps tobacco, are quite competitive with a large number of buyers, including buyers representing markets from all over the world. The agricultural processing industries have not been singularly profitable in the past decade. Over the past several decades the so-called "Big Four" of the meat packers have suffered a substantial reduction in their share of total livestock slaughter and two of these firms have paid no dividends on their common stock for several years.

2. The second point, namely that farmers have not been able to gain from efforts to give them monopoly power, is the most weighty one. The nature of agricultural production is such that efforts to create a cartel under guidance and subsidy from Washington will almost certainly lead to disappointing results. There is no way to restrict entry into agriculture. Thus if a program were to result in higher returns for agriculture through price supports and acreage restrictions, potential producers will attempt to enter the field. One way that this can be done is to buy land which has attached to it the right to produce the particular commodity. After a fairly short time land prices will be bid up and new producers will find that it is no more profitable to produce this particular crop than a number of others. This is not a hypothetical case, but is essentially what has happened in tobacco, where acreage controls, marketing quotas, and price supports have been maintained for two decades.

It should be remembered by those who want greater emphasis upon price supports and production limitations that these measures were used during the recent years of declining farm income. While these measures may have stemmed the fall of farm incomes somewhat, they certainly have not provided the panacea that was hoped for.

Farms Are Small; Government Must Undertake Activities That Small Firms Cannot Maintain • American farms are small, have been small in the past, and if present trends continue will remain small in the future. Small is, of course, a relative term. Large scale farms have been defined as farms with over $25,000 in sales and in 1950 there were 103,000 such farms; these constituted less than 3 per cent of all commercial farms. The average total payment for hired labor for the year 1949 was about $9,000 for these 103,000 farms. In April of 1950 less than 16,000 farms had ten or more hired workers; the majority of the commercial farms had no hired workers.

The small size of farms justifies governmental support of research on farm production techniques, information activities about marketing conditions, and the maintenance of an extension service to bring available knowledge to the attention of farmers and help them to utilize that knowledge effectively. Measured by willingness to adopt new methods of production, American agriculture has been extremely progressive. Its record compares favorably with that of manufacturing. Much of the credit for the rapid advances achieved must be given to the experimental stations and agricultural colleges supported by the state and federal governments to undertake research and train individuals in the sciences especially important to agriculture. The extension service has also played a significant role in making the information available to farmers. The individual farm is too small to organize research on most problems that are important to it. The research has to be done by an agency larger than the farm, and the particular techniques adopted in the United States have paid very large returns for the relatively small expenditures involved. These expenditures have meant more and cheaper farm products; as consumers, we have all gained.

Farm People Are Confronted with Much Economic Instability • The income of an individual farm family varies a great deal from year to year. This is due to two things. First, farm prices fluctuate over a much wider range than do wage rates or the prices of most other products, except some mineral raw materials like copper. Second, the output of a given year is subject to many influences beyond the control of the farmer—the weather, diseases, insects, and pests. Sometimes the gods of chance smile on him and a large production coincides with favorable prices; other times the opposite occurs. The higher degree of instability makes planning of farm operations and family consumption difficult.

I am not certain how much farm people dislike the risk which confronts them. We do know that federal crop insurance, which is designed to remove part of the risk from natural hazards affecting yields, has not been widely accepted by farmers even though the premiums have never covered the actuarial risks involved. On the other hand, many farmers do insure against certain specific risks, such as hail damage.

Available evidence supports the view that when the price risks are reduced by a government price support program farmers do produce more than they would for the same average price in a free market. This stems from the fact that with the reduction of price risks greater quantities of some production items, such as fertilizer, are used and investments are made in machinery that would not be made if the chances of loss were greater. Several years ago I outlined a method of reducing and transferring the price risks of farming, calling the method forward prices. The basic idea was that the government would estimate the price of product prior to the time the most important production decisions were made and then guarantee to the farmers a large fraction of that estimated price when the product was actually sold several months hence. There are economic difficulties with this scheme, especially arising out of errors in the estimates of future prices. Nonetheless, I felt then and I feel now that such a scheme could result in more efficient agricultural production.

One basic objection to the proposal is political; the pressure to estimate prices at levels that are too high would be ever present. Whether any methods can be devised for protecting the administrators of such a program from these pressures is uncertain. If prices are set too high, the gains from reducing the price risks would soon be offset by inducing too much production of agricultural products, which is the situation to which price supports have now brought us.

The instability of farm incomes provides grounds for some kind of governmental intervention in agricultural markets. But the gains to the economy are not so large that they cannot soon be dissipated by misguided efforts to "try to help the farmer" through overdoing a good thing and setting prices at levels above those

that would equate supply and demand. I should point out that I
do not see any substantial political support for the views expressed
in the previous paragraphs.

Agriculture Is a Declining Industry · Since about 1915 farm employment has been declining more or less continuously, and while
employment has declined by more than 40 per cent, output has increased by about 80 per cent. Thus decline in employment has
not meant stagnation, but it has meant that the migration from
farms to cities has had to continue at a rapid pace throughout the
past 40 years. Since 1910 the net migration from farm to nonfarm
areas has been about double the present farm population of 20
million. The high rate of migration has been required more by
the relatively high fertility of the farm population than by the
decline in the number of profitable job opportunities in agriculture. But the two factors taken together have meant, and will
continue to mean, that if farm earnings are to come into balance
with nonfarm earnings for people of comparable skills and
capacities net migration rates of perhaps 5 per cent per annum
will be required for some time to come.

An industry in which employment is continuously declining is
always confronted with difficult adjustments. Many people must
change to very different types of work. If a declining industry is
located in a diversified urban area, the adjustment problem is
simplified by not hiring new workers and thus employment decreases with retirements and quits. But agriculture, organized as
it is around family farms, has a more or less built-in training
system that trains almost every male youth in the farm families as
a farmer. Thus the rather impersonal process of not hiring new
workers does not function, and farm youth must make a positive
decision not to be a farmer. Furthermore, when a farm person
decides to change occupations, he usually must change location
and move away from familiar surroundings which may increase
his reluctance to move to more remunerative employment.

The necessity for a continual movement of workers trained for
farming to other occupations means that the returns to workers
in agriculture must remain somewhat below the level in occupations requiring comparable workers. Because of the inherent difficulties of measuring and comparing farm incomes with nonfarm
incomes, we do not know how large a differential is required to

induce a million people a year to move away from farms.

I would argue that the government might well play a valid role in minimizing the difference in earnings required to achieve a given rate of migration. Perhaps the most appropriate role that the government could perform would be that of supplying adequate and reliable information. Under present circumstances, information about job opportunities in the nonfarm economy is extremely difficult for a farm youth to obtain; the most common source is from relatives or friends who have moved to a certain area. The state employment services, as now organized, are essentially designed to meet the needs of urban people. Undoubtedly, their efforts could be expanded to meet more fully the needs of farm people. However, this would require close liaison between services of several states since much interstate movement is involved. Whether additional information alone would be adequate to reduce the difference between farm and nonfarm earnings to an acceptable level is uncertain. Finding jobs before a person leaves the home community and loans or grants to finance the movement for families might also have merit.

Professor T. W. Schultz has dramatized the need for some measures to speed up the flow out of farming by suggesting that the government establish homesteads in reverse by making a substantial payment to a farm family now actively farming which moves to a nonfarm area and takes a nonfarm job. The homestead idea was used to settle a large part of the United States. Perhaps it might also be used to "unsettle" agriculture. In any case, it seems clear that it would be much more economical to approach the farm problem by this route than by the present expensive, but almost wholly ineffectual, methods.

Farm Incomes Are too Low · Probably the most frequent reason given for special governmental programs for agriculture, especially the price support and allied measures, is the low income level of farm population compared to nonfarm population. Since World War II, farm per capita income has ranged from 45 to 63 per cent of nonfarm per capita income. The lower figure was for 1956 and the higher for 1948. In 1957 the corresponding figure was 49 per cent. What does such a comparison mean? It means very little as an indication of whether farm incomes are high or low. An obvious, but incorrect, implication of such a comparison is that the per capita incomes should be the same if farm people were to be as well off as nonfarm people. Such a statement has about as much meaning as the statement that families whose head member is aged sixty-five or more ought to have the same income as families whose head is aged forty to fifty years, or that manual laborers in manufacturing should have the same incomes as craftsmen and foremen in manufacturing.

Any comparisons of the incomes of two or more groups always implies certain assumptions about the degree of comparability of the groups and the incomes that they receive. Certain questions must be answered before any legitimate comparisons can be made.

1. Will each of the dollars of income that are being compared actually purchase the same amount of goods and services? In other words, does the income which is earned by the farm population have more purchasing power per dollar than does a dollar earned in a city? Farm income, as presently calculated, includes an estimate of the value of home-produced and consumer food. This food is priced at the price which the farmer would receive if he sold it. At the present time, the farmer receives less than 40 per cent as much for his products as the city consumer pays at retail. Thus if the farmer purchased these same foods at retail, he would have to pay approximately two and one half times as much for them as the value placed on them in estimating his income. A careful study made by Nathan Koffsky, based on data collected in 1941, indicated that a dollar of income of the farm population had a purchasing power of about 25 per cent more than a dollar earned in an urban setting.[1] While this result is probably not exactly applicable to the present, it would seem to be a reasonable approximation.

2. Are the groups comparable with respect to age and sex and composition, the percentage of the population actually working, and education? We know that persons in the age group of thirty-five to fifty-five earn more than do persons older or younger. Likewise, on the average, men earn substantially more than women, and earnings increase with the level of education. Thus, if the two groups being compared are substantially different in these respects, the differences in incomes may be due to the

---

1. Nathan Koffsky, "Farm and Urban Purchasing Power," in *Studies in Income and Wealth*, No. 11, National Bureau of Economic Research (1949), pp. 151, 156–72.

differences in these and related characteristics. The farm population has a larger fraction of its working population in the age groups under twenty and over sixty-five than does the nonfarm population. It also has a substantially smaller percentage of its total population in the labor force, 33.5 per cent compared to 41 per cent. The farm group has, for each age group, about two or three years less schooling. Considering only persons in the labor force, differences in age, sex, and education would indicate that the average member of the nonfarm labor force would earn about 15 per cent more than the average member of the farm labor force.

3. Are the payments of direct taxes, principally income taxes, approximately equal for individuals of the same income level in the two groups? The federal income tax, which is the most important direct tax paid, taxes only money income. Thus the non-money income of the farm population in 1955 equalled 18 per cent of the total net income of the farm population and 27 per cent of the net income of the farm population received from agriculture. Other groups in the population, principally home owners, also receive nonmoney income that is not subject to tax, but such income is much more important to the farm population. For 1953, personal income taxes were 11.3 per cent of the nonfarm personal income and 6.9 per cent of the net income of farm families.

4. Is the relative importance of labor income in total income approximately the same? Contrary to general opinion, more capital is used per worker in agriculture than in the rest of the economy. In agriculture about 40 per cent of total income is return on capital, while in the economy as a whole, after payment of corporate income taxes about 20 per cent of total income is return on capital. Thus a larger share of the income of the farm population is required as compensation for capital used than is true of the rest of the economy.

Taking all of these factors into account, if the per capita income of the farm population was roughly 65 per cent of that of the nonfarm population, the returns to workers of similar age, education, and sex would be approximately comparable. While 65 is substantially above the 48 per cent that prevailed in 1957, the discrepancy is substantially less than when one naively assumes that the two incomes must be equal.

Even if one believes that average returns to farm people are now lower than for comparable resources in the rest of the economy, as I do, this belief cannot be used to support just any measure designed to increase farm income. There is a great deal of diversity in farm income from area to area in the United States, a much greater degree of diversity than exists in urban incomes. In 1949 there were perhaps a million farm families with able-bodied male heads with net money incomes of less than $1,500. Most of these families are concentrated in the South and live on small farm units, deriving much of their income from cotton, tobacco, or subsistence farming. Their market sales are small and changes in the level of prices have rather small absolute effects upon their incomes. There is no question that the low incomes of these million families represents an important economic and social problem. But there is also no question that their low incomes should not be included in an average which is then used as evidence for the need of a program whose benefits go primarily to farmers who have substantially higher incomes.

In 1949 the 40 per cent of the farms making 88 per cent of the total farm sales, and which would receive at least that large a share of the net gains from a price support program, had average incomes somewhat higher than the average incomes of nonfarm families. Since that time the average income of these families has increased by about 10 per cent, while the incomes of nonfarm families have risen by 30 per cent. But if one takes into consideration the differences in the purchasing power of income, the income spread is now not very large.

While the concentration of low incomes in certain rural areas may well justify governmental programs to meet the problems of the farm people in those areas, the existence of these low incomes is not an adequate basis for the present expensive farm programs which are not designed to solve their problems. The incomes of the farm families that receive most of the income gains from price supports and the soil bank are not so low that they can be said to constitute an important social or economic problem.

A Large and Productive Agriculture Is Required for Military and Strategic Reasons • There can be little question that many nations in the world have subsidized their agriculture as a means of insuring a supply of food in case war disrupts the normal channels of trade. The very solicitous treatment that the English farmer has received from his government since World War II is probably in large part based on the precarious position in which Britain might find itself in another war with respect to its food supply if it still relied as heavily upon food imports as during the first third of this century. Almost all of Europe, including the Soviet Union, has related its actions in agriculture to its actual or presumed military needs.

The position of the United States is such that there seems little or no grounds for special agricultural measures to increase total agricultural production for military or strategic reasons. With or without a system of price supports and related aids to agriculture, our farm output is going to continue to expand. The use of more fertilizer, advances in animal nutrition, supplemental irrigation in the relatively nonhumid areas, improvements in plant varieties, more effective methods of controlling plant and animal diseases and other changes not now known will contribute to an expanding output. As we have discovered in the past, a decline in the farm labor force is consistent with increasing output as farmers substitute power and machinery for labor.

The United States is a major exporter of a number of food and fiber products—wheat, rice, cotton, tobacco, and a wide variety of other products. We are a major importer of sugar and a considerable number of subtropical and tropical products such as coffee, bananas, and spices. We are also a large importer of wool and jute. The variety and over-all excellence of our diet, especially the heavy emphasis upon livestock products, means that the population could be relatively well-fed even if aggregate agricultural output fell sharply as a result of war. Synthetic fibers provide reasonably satisfactory substitutes for almost any natural fiber now in use.

In adopting measures designed to increase agricultural output for military or strategic reasons, we must always recognize production somewhere else is reduced. The farm worker who is induced to continue producing cotton could and probably otherwise would contribute to the production of airplanes, guided missiles, or related items. Thus before concluding that more farm output is a good thing, we must consider the cost in terms of the alternative products that are lost in order to get more farm products. When this comparison is made, my conclusion is that there is no justification for producing more agricultural products than would be provided in the ordinary course of events through equating the demand of consumers and the amount farmers would be willing to supply.

There may be some basis for maintaining stockpiles of certain agricultural products as a safety measure. But it seems unlikely that the size of these stockpiles would be as large as the quantities of certain farm products now held by the government. Government-owned or -controlled stocks equal one and one-half years of domestic food and seed use of wheat, a third of a year's corn production, and about seven months' domestic mill use of cotton. And it should also be remembered that when we add to our stockpiles of these products, we are sacrificing the output of other products that may have equal or greater value for military and strategic reasons.

It is worth noting that our present and past policies which have led to the accumulation of large stocks of many agricultural products and a continuing excess of production relative to market demand at the supported prices are a negative strategic factor at the present time and are likely to continue to be so. These programs prevent normal economic and trade relations with many nations, particularly the underdeveloped nations that we would like to attract to our political position in the present contest between communism and the free world. This is true for two reasons. First, our price supports and accumulated stocks have led us to engage in large-scale export dumping of wheat and cotton and the use of foreign aid funds to dispose of significant quantities of these and other agricultural products. These actions have limited the access of many nations to markets that might otherwise have been theirs. Examples are Canada for wheat, Egypt, Mexico, and Brazil for cotton, Burma and Thailand for rice, and Greece and Italy for dried fruits.

Second, these policies have meant that we cannot, for economic and political reasons, provide a market for the agricultural products of many underdeveloped nations. It is quite possible that even if there were no price supports on rice, for example, the United States would still be a net exporter of rice. But there is no question that without the price support our production of rice would be less and the world market price somewhat higher.

The Soviet Union's economic and political position has been strengthened as a consequence of our domestic agricultural policies. This is probably a higher price than we want to pay for the continuance of these programs.

Summary • In this paper I have tried to analyze a number of reasons that are frequently given as arguments for particular forms of governmental aid for agriculture. The seven reasons given include all of those that might in any meaningful way distinguish agriculture from the other sectors of the economy and thus might serve as a basis for a different relation between government and agriculture than prevails elsewhere. No one or all of these considerations convince me that the present large-scale program of price supports and other subsidies are any more warranted in agriculture than in almost any other part of the economy.

Some of the characteristics of agriculture do imply a reasonable basis for some types of government aid to agriculture or the performance of a special set of functions by the government. The small size of farm firms has meant that government expenditures upon research and education have been for a function that farmers could not have satisfactorily performed. The high degree of instability confronting farmers may serve as a basis for actions designed to reduce that instability and thus permit greater efficiency in agricultural production. The difficulty exists, however, that most of the means to reduce instability are vulnerable to misuse in the American political scene.

Finally, the fact that farm employment is declining and the continued existence of large areas where most farm families have low incomes implies that the government could, with gain to the people who remain in agriculture and to the economy as a whole, institute programs that would reduce the cost of the labor transfer from farming into nonfarm occupations.

An Adaptive Program for Agriculture

COMMITTEE FOR ECONOMIC DEVELOPMENT

This selection contains the heart of the program for agriculture proposed by the Committee for Economic Development in its 1962 publication, An Adaptive Program for Agriculture. *The C. E. D. is a private research organization concerned with major economic policy problems in the United States.*

THE AGRICULTURAL policies of the past should not be continued. Recognition of this has been growing and is now widespread. The proliferation of suggestions for new programs is evidence of this. While the suggestions are endlessly varied and complex, we believe that real alternatives to the course we have been following fall into two general categories.

One alternative is a stringent, leakproof control of production, so that farmers will get higher prices for a smaller volume of sales. Whether this could be effective without policing measures that would be intolerable in America is uncertain. Such a program would change the form of the burden on the nonfarm community from high taxes to high prices. It would change the evidence of waste from mounting stocks of surplus products to idle land, labor and capital, withheld from farm use and not channeled to other uses. All other consequences of the program would be essentially the same as those of the past policy.

The other—adaptive—alternative is a program to permit and induce a large, rapid movement of resources, notably labor, out of agriculture. This is the program we recommend. In our opinion, it is the only approach that offers a solution from the standpoint either of the agricultural community or of the non-agricultural community.

We describe such a program in this statement. There are, however, two points of great importance that should be made here.

First, if we choose the adaptive course recommended here, we must pursue it in a large scale, vigorous, thorough-going way.

Small steps will not do. We are dealing with a big and difficult problem. We are proposing an alternative to programs that now cost $6 billion a year and involve massive government interference in the free economy. The alternative we offer will cost very much less after a short period. It will change government's role from supplanting the market to improving the market. But it will not be cheap and easy; if it were, it would not be effective.

We are recommending many governmental activities here that we would usually regard as inappropriate. The circumstances, however, are unusual. Agricultural policy has brought into being a vast field of governmental activity. These activities cannot simply be dropped; it is necessary for agricultural policy to work its way out of them. The relatively few, and in part temporary, governmental activities recommended here will, we confidently believe, enable national farm policy to work its way out of a large number of otherwise permanent governmental operations in the economy.

Second, we must be prepared to moderate the temporary but sharp decline in farmers' incomes that would otherwise occur in the shift from the protective approach to the adaptive approach. The program we suggest contemplates that a major part of the required adjustment in agriculture would take place over a five-year period. We recommend steps to supplement, on a diminishing scale, the incomes that farmers would earn in free markets during that period. This does not mean that no further movement of people out of agriculture will be required after the five-year transition period. As long as the rise of productivity in agriculture equals or exceeds the rise in the rest of the economy, some movement from agriculture is likely to be necessary. But after the transition period the required movement would be on a scale that would not strain normal processes of private adjustment or require special measures of assistance. There would be a continuing, gradually emerging excess of resources in agriculture, resulting from the gradual growth of productivity and population increase, but this excess would be continuously moved out of agriculture. It would not, therefore, depress farm incomes substantially below the incomes of comparable nonfarm resources.

The transition we visualize will not bring itself about in a five-year period. Action will be required to bring it about. We believe that the transition can be effected in a five-year period if the program recommended here is pursued with vigor. A relatively short transition period depends considerably upon high employment in the nonfarm economy. But we cannot be certain that our estimate is correct. Unforeseeable developments, for example, in foreign markets or in productivity, may cause difficulties. In other words, there are uncertainties in the course we recommend. The rest of the community should be prepared to share the costs of these uncertainties, and not leave them to the farmer alone. We must watch the progress of the program and be willing, if necessary, to adjust it in ways consistent with its basic philosophy. We are confident that the direction we point out is the correct one, and while there are uncertainties about rates and amounts these uncertainties are preferable to the certain wastes and frustrations of the alternatives.

It will be seen that we describe the agricultural problem in general and propose a general program for its solution. We do not have a program for hard winter wheat and a different program for long-staple cotton. Analysis and experience show that a list of programs addressed to the specific problems of specific parts of agriculture does not solve the basic problem of agriculture. At best it redistributes the problem among the parts of agriculture. There are differences within agriculture, some of which are recognized in our program and others that would have to be considered in its application. But with respect to the basic problem, the excess of resources, agriculture is a unit. Enough of the land, labor, and capital in agriculture can be shifted, and is shifted from one agricultural product to another, and the products move sufficiently between one use and another to require this total approach. An excess of resources in one part of agriculture depresses incomes throughout agriculture and withdrawal of any excess resources will improve agricultural incomes generally.

Before presenting our program for agricultural adjustment we would like to make clear our recognition that United States agriculture has been adjusting vigorously on its own, for many years, to market pressures. Our program suggests governmental action to facilitate the adjustments the American farming industry has been making privately. One of our principal reasons for thinking such a program will succeed is the evidence that American farming has exhibited a large-scale readiness to adapt to change; an adaptiveness that marks our farm industry as a vigorous participant in the free enterprise system.

We have noted that agriculture's chief need is a reduction of the number of people in agriculture. Farmers have been moving out of agriculture, on a grand scale, for at least 40 years. It is equally evident that the farmer in the United States has devoted a great part of his earnings and energies to the purchase of machinery and the use of advanced techniques, thereby contributing markedly through high farm productivity to the nation's potential overall economic efficiency. The program we are proposing is aimed at realization—for the farmer's benefit and the nation's—of the full potential of United States agricultural efficiency.

A PROGRAM FOR AGRICULTURAL ADJUSTMENT

First and fundamentally, we propose a set of measures designed to bring about a condition in which:

1. A much smaller total quantity of resources will be used in agricultural production;

2. This smaller total of resources at use in farm production will be composed of a much smaller amount of labor, and, possibly, somewhat less capital;

3. Production per unit of resources used in agriculture will be higher;

4. Earnings per unit of resources used in agriculture will be higher, on the average, and these earnings will be obtained through sale of farm products without government subsidy or support.

Adjustment of farming to this condition is basic to solution of the farm problem.

Second, we propose a set of temporary, transitional measures designed to:

1. Prevent a sharp decline in farm incomes, and

2. Avoid further additions to stocks of farm goods,

while the basic adjustment to the condition sketched above is being brought about.

It is an essential characteristic of these transitional programs that they should cushion the adjustment, but should do so in ways that do not prevent or retard the adjustment.

ATTRACTING EXCESS RESOURCES FROM USE IN FARM PRODUCTION

This is the heart of the matter in agricultural adjustment. Excess resources in use in the production of farm goods *is* the farm problem. Everything else suggested here is for the purpose of facilitating the fundamental transaction—withdrawal of excess resources from agricultural production—or serves to hold things steady while the basic transition is taking place.

Some of the measures we are suggesting here are broader than the program traditionally associated with agricultural policy, or lie outside what has been the usual farm policy scope. The fact is that the well-being of agriculture cannot be assured by programs having to do only with the production and marketing of farm goods: healthy agriculture requires a healthy economy as a whole and healthy relations between the farm and nonfarm sectors. It is obvious, therefore, that the Department of Agriculture would not be called upon to administer all the programs suggested here, but that, regardless of the fact that they are suggested in connection with solving the farm problem, they should be administered by agencies best able to do so.

1. High Employment. The maintenance of employment opportunities in non-agricultural industry and services is an essential condition for the most satisfactory agricultural adjustment. In our diagnosis, the problem of getting excess resources out of agriculture is a nonfarm employment problem: resources, particularly labor, are engaged in farming when they could produce more, and earn more, outside agriculture. This implies that opportunities for their employment exist or can be created outside of agriculture. If this were not true, the problem of agriculture would be basically different.

We believe, of course, that high and growing employment can be maintained in the nonfarm economy. We have discussed the steps necessary to achieve this result in a recent statement that emphasized: (a) The potential contribution of monetary and fiscal policy to a steady rate of growth in total expenditures for goods and services, and (b) Moderation of the rate of increase of wages and other labor costs, so that the rise of total expenditures is not absorbed by higher prices, but takes effect in raising production and employment.

The importance of high employment for a resolution of the farm problem must be emphasized. The movement of labor from agriculture has shown itself to be responsive to the state of the non-agricultural labor market. A sustained period of high employment would itself make a major contribution to agricultural adjustment, and would contribute to the success of any other measures that may be undertaken.

While emphasizing the importance of high employment in the non-agricultural economy for the speed with which agricultural adjustment can be effected, we do not mean to suggest that the other parts of the program recommended here must await the achievement of high employment or should be suspended in the event of future departures from high employment. There has been significant movement of people from agriculture even in recent years when unemployment was unsatisfactorily high, and even in such circumstances measures to facilitate the outmovement will have constructive results.

2. Education. Forty-four per cent of the farm population is presently below the age of 20. Here, in our opinion, is a main key to agricultural adjustment: we have an opportunity to secure long-lasting relief from the overburden of people pressing upon farm income by getting a large number of people out of agriculture before they are committed to it as a career.

It is obvious that the extent to which we may be successful in using this key will depend upon the impression the farm youth gets when he looks at the nonfarm economy with an eye to uprooting himself permanently from farming. If employment prospects off the farm are high and growing, the attraction to farm youth of training for nonfarm careers will be strong; if the current prospects for employment off the farm are not attractive, young people deciding whether to commit themselves to a career on the farm or in the nonfarm economy can be expected to decide in large numbers that the long term prospects are best in farming. This tends to perpetuate the farm problem.

TABLE 1. *Per cent of Males Enrolled in School*

Place of Residence
October, 1960

Age Groups	TOTAL	URBAN	RURAL NONFARM	FARM	Usual School Grade
5 years	64.1	74.1	58.0	33.7	Kindergarten
6 years	97.8	98.8	98.0	92.7	First
7 to 9 years	99.6	99.6	99.7	99.7	2-3-4
10 to 13 years	99.4	99.5	99.5	98.6	5-6-7-8
14 & 15 years	97.9	98.0	98.3	96.3	Fr & S, H.S.
16 & 17 years	84.5	85.1	85.4	79.7	Jr & Sr, H.S.
18 & 19 years	47.8	51.4	46.8	33.5	Fr & S, Col.
20 & 21 years	27.1	31.1	20.8	18.8	Jr & Sr, Col.

SOURCE: Bureau of the Census, Current Population Reports (school grades supplied).

Recent studies have brought out that fewer farm youths than others (*a*) graduate from high school, (*b*) enter college, and (*c*) graduate from college.

Attendance of boys at school falls off sharply in countryside school districts, by comparison with the nation as a whole and with urban schools, beginning with the 16-17-year-old age brackets (final years of high school) as shown in Table 1.

Another facet of education as it relates to farming is that the United States as a whole derives 4.3 per cent of its personal income from farming, and no state derives more than 26.1 per cent; yet the nation devotes 44.5 per cent of its vocational education funds, exclusive of funds for home economics training, to training for agriculture. In the 20 states getting the highest percentage of personal income from farming (North Dakota, 26.1 per cent to Texas, 6.5 per cent), all but two—Arizona and Vermont—spend over half of their vocational education funds, excepting home economics, for training in the skills of farming.

This means that in many states where farming is strongest vocational education tends to perpetuate the farm problem of too many people in agriculture by holding out extraordinary opportunities to train for farming as a vocation.

America's Resources of Specialized Talent,[1] a study published in 1954, gave the following summary of the relationship between the father's occupation and higher education (see Table 2).

The tendency for farm youths to have fewer years of school-

1. Report of the Commission on Human Resources and Advanced Training (Harper and Brothers, New York), Dael Wolfle, Director.

TABLE 2.

Father's Occupation	Percentage of High School Graduates Entering College	Percentage of High School Graduates Graduating from College
Professional and semiprofessional	67%	40%
Managerial	50	28
White collar (clerical, sales, service)	48	27
Factory, craftsman, unskilled, etc.	26	15
Farmer	24	11

SOURCE: Report of the Commission on Human Resources and Advanced Training (Harper & Brothers, New York), Dael Wolfle, Director.

ing, and the emphasis on vocational education for farming, together with the above figures showing the relatively low proportion of farm youths in colleges, indicate that it is necessary to give attention to the amount and the kind of education farm youths get below the college level.

We have three recommendations on this vital aspect of the farm problem:

(a) *This Committee has recommended a program for Federal aid to public education below the college level in the low income states.*[2] If this program were put into effect, its preponderant effects in the improvement of educational attainments would be felt in lower income farm states. *We once again urge adoption of this program, and rejection of proposals for aid to all states.*

(b) *Vocational education should be revamped to place its emphasis upon training in skills needed by expanding industries.* This means that vocational education in farming areas should be mainly for industrial, not agricultural, skills. There is need, as this Committee has pointed out elsewhere, for an expanded Federal effort to provide research and information to help guide state education departments and local school boards in what skills are in demand or coming into demand.[3]

2. *Paying for Better Public Schools.* A Statement on National Policy by the Research and Policy Committee, Committee for Economic Development. December 1959.

3. *Distressed Areas in a Growing Economy.* A Statement on National Policy by the Research and Policy Committee, Committee for Economic Development. June 1961.

(c) *Public and private policy should take dual account of the national needs (i) to reduce the number of people committed for their livelihood to farming, and (ii) to raise the national educational attainment, by measures to bring the participation of farm youths in higher education up to the national standard.* Our recommendation (a) above tends in this direction, by increasing opportunities for youths in lower income farm states to qualify for college. There should also be a general increase in the availability on the basis of need and merit of loans and scholarship grants for college education. State and private funds for this purpose have been increasing and should continue to do so. Federal loan and scholarship funds for needy farm youths qualified for college study should be provided during the transition period in which a rapid migration from agriculture is needed. Here also, as in (a) above, major effects would be felt in lower income farm states.

It should be recognized by all agencies, public and private, that on the average the farm youth, more often than the nonfarm youth, will have to live away from home while he is at college, and that a college education therefore tends to be more "expensive" for farm youths than for others. This should be taken into account in judging need for financial help.

3. Mobility. Early in 1962, a Federal Manpower Development and Training Act was enacted. The objectives of the Act are to "appraise the manpower requirements and resources of the nation, and to develop and apply the information and methods needed to deal with the problems of unemployment resulting from automation and technological changes and other types of persistent unemployment."

In farming, the counterpart of unemployment resulting from automation and technological changes is underemployment, or, as we have discussed it here, excess use of resources.

We are glad to see the problem of the excess use of resources *in farming,* particularly excess commitment of people, integrated with the *general* problem of the nation's manpower requirements, and the national, general need for policies to help the nation adapt to the ever changing skill requirements of the economy.

This coincides with our view, basic to the adaptive approach we are recommending for solution of the farm problem, that the farm problem is not unique, but is, rather, the leading case of a large class of problems where an industry is using too many resources, and, that solution of the farm problem lies in policies tending to improve, generally and overall, the efficient use of our resources, rather than in protectionist, specialized "farm policy."

The provisions of the new Manpower Act can be an important step in guiding and easing the movement out of farming of a large number of people in a short time, if the Act's purposes are interpreted as applying fully and specifically to the farm problem, and if they are vigorously pursued in that light. This includes:

JOB INFORMATION. The Act requires the Secretary of Labor to promote, encourage or directly engage in programs of information and communication concerning manpower requirements and improvement in the mobility of workers. We recommend additionally that:

The Federal-State Employment Service be expanded to rural areas, and its coverage made national and regional, rather than local only, and that:

The present farm labor service should expand its responsibility to include placement in off-farm work, instead of limiting its referrals to farm employment.

Careful attention should be given to the impact of the foreign worker program upon the wages of domestic migrant farm workers.

RETRAINING AND MOVEMENT. The new Act establishes procedures for selecting and training workers for occupations requiring new skills. It specifies that workers in farm families with annual net income under $1,200 are eligible for retraining assistance under the Act. The Act provides allowances for training, subsistence and transportation, and for Federal assistance for state and private occupational training schools.

The adjustments required in agriculture will call for the movement of many people who would not be eligible for retraining under the provisions of the Act. It confines retraining allowances and other assistance to workers in farm families with net annual income below $1,200. Basically our objective should be to provide assistance for retraining where the individual will not get it without assistance and where the retraining will substantially increase his ability to produce and earn income. Some arbitrary definition of eligibility may be necessary for administration of the Act, but *we believe that the present definition is too restrictive so far as agriculture is concerned.*

The retraining of farm workers leaving farming should be considered one of the principal objectives of the new Act. Those responsible for the administration of the Act should have it clearly in mind that farming is the leading case of misuse of resources in the American economy, that over-commitment of people to farming for their livelihood is the special form of the use of excess resources in agriculture, and that the Manpower and Training Act should consequently be applied with all vigor to solution of the farm problem.

The provisions in the Act limiting and qualifying direct help programs to avoid abuse should be fully and carefully observed.

We recommend that retrained farm workers leaving farming should be assisted in moving to nonfarm work sites, by a program of loans to cover the cost of moving themselves and their families. Such assistance should be given once only for the purpose of leaving farming. It should be given only for movement from areas where there is excess labor supply and only for movements in excess of, say, 50 miles.

It should be emphasized that all such direct help programs should apply to farm tenants, hired hands and domestic migrant workers, as well as to farm proprietors and their families.

We regard direct help to farm people in finding better opportunities in the nonfarm labor force as necessary and desirable, because we believe that a small fraction of the funds now spent on agricultural subsidies would, if spent in ways that tended positively to induce the needed movement of human resources out of farming, result in higher national income and lower national outlays on subsidies.

ADJUSTMENT OF AGRICULTURAL PRICES. The basic adjustment required to solve the farm problem, adjustment of the resources used to produce farm goods, cannot be expected to take place unless the price system is permitted to signal to farmers how much is wanted, of what.[4] *Therefore, it is recommended that a Price Adjustment Program be instituted.*

In order that the prices of our major farm products should give the correct signals for investment and production, *the prices of cotton, wheat, rice and feed grains and related products now supported should be allowed to reflect the estimated long run "adjustment price" of these products.*

The adjustment price would simultaneously satisfy two conditions. *First,* it is a price at which the total output of the commodity can be sold to domestic consumers or in commercial export markets without government subsidy. *Second,* it is a price at which resources efficiently employed in agriculture, after a period of maximum freedom to move out, could earn incomes equivalent to those earned in the nonfarm economy.

For most of these commodities the adjustment price is below the present support price and is likely to remain so even after a period of stimulated out-movement. This means that at prices below the present support prices sufficient resources would prefer to remain in agriculture, rather than move out under favorable conditions, to produce as large a volume of these commodities as would be bought by consumers, at home and abroad, at these lower prices. The willingness of labor to remain in agriculture after a period of maximum opportunity to move out, with the incomes they can earn at these lower prices, will be objective evidence that these incomes are "satisfactory." It will be possible for labor to earn satisfactory incomes at lower commodity prices because output per worker will be increased by two developments: a) the number of workers will be substantially reduced, which will increase the capital each worker has to work with, and b) restrictions on output per worker will be removed.

While the adjustment price for most of the major commodi-

4. The importance of the correct price signals for farm products was highlighted by recent developments in the dairy industry. During 1960, production and consumption of dairy products were about in balance and the government had to purchase only small amounts of surpluses. Then, in late 1960 and early 1961, the support price for dairy products was increased. This higher support price, together with lower feed grain prices, induced a sharp increase in the production of dairy products at a time when the demand for dairy products was not expanding. The result has been more resources in dairying, more output, and sharply increased expenditures for acquisition of surpluses to support prices of dairy products.

ties is below the present support level, it is above the price that would result if the total output that the resources now in agriculture would produce were sold in an unsupported market. Such a purely free market price would be lower than the adjustment price we have in mind because it would result from marketing crops without previous adjustment of the resources used in their production. We propose below two measures, an expanded Soil Bank and a Cropland Adjustment Program, to keep production from exceeding demand at the adjustment prices during the transition period while the basic out-movement of resources is taking place.

The purpose of setting the adjustment price is to give farmers the best possible indication of the prices they may expect to receive during and at the end of the transition period, so that those farmers who do not think they can earn incomes they regard as satisfactory at those prices can take advantage of the transition period to move out. It is not proposed that the government should support prices at the adjustment price levels after the transition period. Neither should it be expected that market prices will remain permanently at the adjustment price levels after the transition period. The long-run course of agricultural prices will depend mainly upon the rate of growth of agricultural productivity and the rate of movement of resources into and out of agriculture.

We do not favor a gradual lowering of farm prices to the adjustment level, although we took a position in our statement on farm policy in 1956 favoring gradualism. Gradual price reductions in recent years have not affected the resources used in farming fast enough and have not allowed total production to flow into use. Therefore, *it is recommended that the price supports for wheat, cotton, rice, feed grains and related crops now under price supports be reduced immediately to the prices that could be expected to balance output and use, after the transition period, without new additions to government stocks.* The undesirable effects on farm incomes during the transition period should be handled separately and simultaneously, as suggested later.

The importance of such price adjustments should not be underestimated. The lower price levels would discourage further commitment of new productive resources to those crops unless it appeared profitable at the lower prices. Also, the lower prices would induce some increased sales of these products both at home and abroad. Some of these crops are heavily dependent upon export markets. Finally, these price adjustments would put the United States into position to begin disentangling itself from export subsidies, import quotas, and other inconsistent policies which now surround our foreign trade in these farm products.

Specific adjustment prices to satisfy these principles will have to be estimated when the program is initiated, in terms of the facts and outlook at that time. It appears that at the present time (mid-1962) the adjustment price would be, for cotton about 22 cents a pound, for rice about $3 a hundredweight, for wheat about $1.35 a bushel, and for feed grains the equivalent of about $1 a bushel for corn.[5]

These prices for wheat, rice and cotton are believed to approximate the prices at which these crops would be sold in the market without further accumulation of surpluses. The suggested price for feed grains is about the level that had been maintained for feed grains for two years prior to 1961.

To keep feed grain production from outrunning usage at the suggested adjustment price, we recommend below a Temporary Soil Bank, designed to hold output of feed grains below 155 million tons a year.

Consequently, although government supports of the crops designated above would continue at the adjustment price levels during the five year adjustment period, *it is not expected that the government would acquire surpluses except under exceptional and temporary circumstances.*

5. These price levels were estimated by specialists in the field and are based upon their judgment as well as a number of unpublished and published statistical studies regarding the levels at which the domestic and international markets for these products would clear under the assumptions of the proposed program. Among the published studies giving estimates of market prices under different conditions are: *Report from the United States Department of Agriculture and a Statement from the Land Grant Colleges IRMI Advisory Committee on Farm Price and Income Projections 1960–65*, Senate Document 77, 86th Congress, Second Session, January 20, 1960; *Economic Policies for Agriculture in the 1960's*, Materials Prepared for the Joint Economic Committee, 86th Congress, 2nd Session, 1960; W. A. Cromarty, "Free Market Price Projections Based on a Formal Econometric Model" and Arnold Paulsen and Don Kaldor, "Methods, Assumptions and Results of Free Market Projections for the Livestock and Feed Economy," both in the *Journal of Farm Economics*, May 1961.

The effects of the adjustment prices would reach beyond our borders. The adjustment price suggested for cotton would permit our domestic cotton mills to compete on a more even basis with foreign mills, in our markets and in foreign markets. At present, foreign mills can buy United States cotton more cheaply than can our domestic cotton producers. The same would be true of our domestic flour millers and rice exporters.

An estimate of the market adjustment price for farm products will be partly a matter of judgment as long as markets are not free and earnings in farming are too low. However, this judgment must be made, and the preferable direction of error, if any, is clear in our present situation.

For several reasons it is important that price supports be moved to levels that, if wrong, will be low rather than high.

First, price supports on the low side will test the market demand for farm products. If this demand turns out to be higher than output at the support level we can meet the needs from our huge stocks.

Second, new resources (especially people) should be discouraged from entering agriculture, at least during the adjustment period, and the rate of entry in the longer run should not be excessive. Price supports set too high will tend to continue the errors of recent years.

Therefore, the costs of errors of setting supports too low initially are virtually zero as long as the income of farm people does not suffer as a result, whereas the errors of too high a level can only be corrected at considerable expense either to farmers or the public, or both. If it is demonstrated over a period of time that the adjustment prices originally determined are too high or too low, the adjustment price should be corrected accordingly.

Where support prices are reduced to an adjustment level, production restrictions should be abolished.

In explanation: Given two cushioning programs discussed later —a Cropland Adjustment Program and a Temporary Soil Bank— the output of the products for which we are suggesting reduction of supports to an adjustment price should be approximately in balance with domestic and export use at the recommended prices. Where it is exceptionally advantageous to produce these crops, producers would find it profitable to expand output at the adjustment price. Such would be the case for cotton in California and wheat in certain areas of the Plains.

On the other hand, in other areas farmers would find alternatives more attractive than continued production of the crops for which supports had been lowered. In some cases the alternative would be nonfarm employment. In other cases, the alternative would be the production of farm goods for which demand is rising fast (meat, for instance, as contrasted with wheat).

CUSHIONING THE PROCESS OF ADJUSTING THE RESOURCES USED IN FARM PRODUCTION

A Cropland Adjustment Program · What we are recommending with respect to land use is a program designed to turn land being misused in agriculture to better agricultural use. It is not a program to take land out of farming where there is no nonagricultural alternative use, since that would be wasteful. Our suggestions concern mainly the Western Plains and Mountain area. They are designed to convert land being used for the production of crops back to grassland. It is anticipated that if wheat is priced lower, farmers in this area will have better income raising livestock on this land, once it is returned to grass, than they have as arid country wheat farmers. The object of the program we are suggesting is to assist them in converting their farms from plowland to livestock grasslands.

It is recommended that a Cropland Adjustment Program be instituted, to induce the reconversion of at least 20 million acres of Western Plains and Mountain Region land from crop use to grass, as rapidly as possible.

To induce a farmer to convert from wheat production to grassland, the government would:

1. Pay an amount equal to the expected income from producing a crop, so that these conversion payments, together with the income protection payments mentioned later, would provide, over the adjustment period, an income equivalent to what the farmer would get if he produced a crop.

2. Make available technical assistance and planning in the conversion of cropland to grass, and share the costs of conservation practices, where applicable.

3. Require agreements on the part of the owner that, once

converted, the land would not be returned to the production of wheat for some specified period.

This program is an extension and enlargement of the Great Plains Conservation Program started in 1956 and continued until the present time. What is proposed is an expansion and extension of its scope to induce greater participation.

The extraordinary demands of World War II and the immediate postwar period brought favorable wheat prices. These prices induced a substantial expansion in wheat acreage in the United States, from a low of 57 million acres in the early war period to over 77 million acres in the late 1940's. The increase in production was intensified by good weather. This expansion included a marked increase in the total acreage in the low rainfall areas of the Western Great Plains.

When wheat surpluses appeared, acreage allotments were inaugurated and land was forced out of wheat. However, in this western region grain sorghums have been developed that are an alternative dry country crop to wheat—*as long as wheat and feed grain prices are maintained high enough to keep sorghum prices high.* In the Plains and Mountain region harvested wheat acreage declined by 9 million acres from 1952-53 (the last years before allotments) to 1957-58. Feed grain acreage meanwhile increased by over 12 million acres. This additional 12 million acres in feed grains can produce just about the amount of *surplus* feed grain produced annually in recent years before 1961. Moreover, total wheat production in this region still substantially exceeds prewar production despite the acreage allotments.

These basic facts point directly at what should be done:

1. Acreage converted to cropland in the dry areas must be returned to grass.

2. Wheat and feed grain prices should be allowed to tell farmers how much of each is wanted. That is, the price signals should be allowed to work.

As long as five years may be required to return this plowed land to grass. During this period farm operators would have to forego all or a major portion of their cash income and at the same time incur some out-of-pocket expenses. Even though the long run income prospects in the dry area would be higher from a grassland-livestock program than from wheat, if wheat were priced correctly, few farmers can afford to forego current income to make the change.

This is why we recommend a Cropland Adjustment Program. Payments under the plan should reflect the length of time required to establish grass. This will differ in various areas. Payments should end at the end of that time.

Payments under the Cropland Adjustment Program would be on a declining schedule, to mesh with the growth of new income from different use of the land.

A Temporary Income Protection Program · If price supports for wheat, rice, and cotton were reduced immediately to the level at which adjustment of resources would begin to take place, the income of the producers of these crops would decline sharply in the absence of any compensatory public policy. While such a quick and sharp decline in income might conceivably increase the rate at which needed adjustments took place, it would exact a high cost in terms of suffering of the farm people displaced. Therefore, we suggest that a *Temporary Income Protection Program be inaugurated,* to prevent the major impact of the required price adjustment from bearing excessively upon the farm community.

We recommend Temporary Income Protection payments only for wheat, rice and cotton because the price drop in other crops would be much less than for these three.

The Temporary Income Protection Program would have five controlling features:

1. Payments should be made only to farmers who now have acreage allotments for wheat, rice and cotton. The adjustment payments should be based upon a quantity of the product determined by the present acreage allotment and the normal yield of the farm for the previous two years prior to the beginning of the program.[6]

2. The program would continue only five years.

3. Payments would be a declining percentage of the excess of the 1960 support prices over the adjustment price.

4. Payments would be independent of further production of these crops.

---

6. Under the present production controls, each farm producing one of these crops has an acreage allotment permitting the farm to produce so many acres of the crop, without penalty. If more than the allotted acres of the crop are planted, penalties are assessed.

5. Payments would decline to zero within five years.

To illustrate the workings of the program in the case of wheat farming:

The farmer has a base period quantity of wheat, computed as above in Point 1. Let us assume that this quantity, for a particular farmer, is 1,000 bushels. The support price for wheat in 1960 was $1.78 a bushel. If the adjustment price, as described earlier, is $1.35 a bushel, this leaves a difference of 43 cents a bushel. In the first year of the program, the farmer would receive 1,000 times 43 cents, or $430. In the second year he would get 80 per cent of that amount, or $344. In the third year he would get 60 per cent of $430, or $258, and so on. In the sixth and succeeding years, there would be no income protection payments.

The farmer would get the income protection payments, based upon his former marketing quota, no matter how much wheat he grew, and even if he grew no wheat or grew something else. This provision is essential. The farmer should decide how much wheat to produce, if any, on the basis of what is profitable for him to do at $1.35 a bushel. It is essential that receipt of the supplemental payment should not be dependent upon the production of wheat. Otherwise the supplemental payment would simply be an additional price for wheat and an additional inducement to produce wheat, beyond what would be induced by the adjustment price.

The foregoing example has assumed that the adjustment price is constant during the five year period, but, as noted earlier, the adjustment price might be changed if circumstances indicated that it was too high or too low.

To put the above into the form of rules for the program, the income protection payments should:

1. be based upon (a) the acreage allotment held by the farmer and a marketing quota, converted to an income protection base derived from it, and (b) the difference between supports in 1960, and the new adjustment price;

2. decline to zero by the end of five years;

3. be made whether or not a crop was produced.[7]

7. Plans have long been proposed for the protection of farmer incomes during a period of transition to lower farm prices. While the Committee was at work on this Statement a plan very similar to the one suggested here was independently proposed by Hendrik S. Houthakker, Harvard University, in an article, "Toward Solution of the Farm Problem," in *Review of Economics and Statistics* (February 1961).

A Temporary Soil Bank · The third measure for cushioning adjustment should be a Temporary Soil Bank, to prevent feed grain production from exceeding demand in the next few years.

It is recommended that a Temporary Soil Bank should be established, to last not more than five years, and to hold feed grain output, during that time, to not over 150-155 million tons a year. The Temporary Soil Bank would extend, under conditions set forth below, the existing Soil Bank.[8]

If feed utilization per animal continued at the rate of recent years, it appears that by 1965 the domestic demand for livestock products will require the use of about 165 million tons of feed grains annually, at about 1960-61 prices. This would mean that feed grain and livestock prices should stabilize at about 1960-61 levels without the accumulation of feed grain stocks. Until such time as this balance is achieved, a Soil Bank program should be utilized in order to prevent low livestock prices or continued accumulation of feed grains.

The Temporary Soil Bank should be on a whole farm basis.

First, the retirement of whole farms is less expensive in terms of the inducement needed to obtain the necessary land. *Second,* the whole farm retirement also retires both labor and capital from farming, thereby shrinking the total resource base in agriculture.

There has been much objection to the whole farm Soil Bank Program from the nonfarm people in rural communities. They have objected to the loss of sales and to the competition from farm people in the local labor market. However, the impact of the Soil Bank on adjacent communities will depend very much on the state of economic activity in the economy generally. Moreover, the program should be operated so that its impact will be minimized on individual communities or areas.

OTHER REQUIREMENTS OF AGRICULTURAL POLICY

The Export Market · The fact that the United States is a low cost producer of foods and natural fibers should give us more advantage in foreign trade than we are realizing.

8. This is the program in effect, with various changes, since 1956 under which the government makes payments to farmers to hold cropland out of production. It is officially Title I of the Agricultural Act of 1956.

In an efficient organization of the world economy, the United States would make much larger exports of farm commodities to Europe than we do. This is so even though Europe in 1960 took a third of the grains and grain preparations we exported, and in 1959 took close to a half.

Our past price-support programs have interfered with United States efforts to achieve reduction of European barriers to imports of farm products. Our sales of farm commodities in world markets below our domestic prices, and our application of import quotas to protect our domestic prices, have been used by importing countries as justification for their own restrictions on trade. In fact, the United States has been careful not to "dump" farm products on commercial markets, and we do not believe, therefore, that our domestic farm programs justify the obstacles placed in the way of our exports. Nevertheless, so long as our domestic prices are above world prices, it has been difficult to avoid the suspension or claim of dumping. The program we recommend here would eliminate the differential between domestic and world prices. This should strengthen the effectiveness of U. S. efforts to achieve a liberalization of world agricultural trade.

Liberalization of agricultural trade, now blocked chiefly by the use of restrictive quotas in Europe, should be a cardinal point of United States trade policy. There is a danger that the agriculture policy of the European Economic Community (the Common Market) will be such as to promote agricultural self-sufficiency in Europe. This would be a mistake from the point of view of the efficiency of the entire free world. Europe should accept, as a fundamental decision in the course of its current economic integration, the idea that there is an advantage to Europe in the increased use of American farm goods, and the decreased use of high cost European farm products.

Limiting Seasonal Price Swings · Under the program recommended here farm price supports would be terminated at the end of five years and the trend of farm prices would be governed by free market forces. It would, however, be desirable to take certain limited government actions tending to moderate seasonal fluctuations of prices after the five year transition period.

Farm products come into the market in large quantities at

particular seasons, but they flow into consumption rather steadily throughout the year. Prices received by farmers are lower when the supply comes into the market than at other times of the year, because the supply is suddenly increased greatly. Unless there is an adequate supply of credit to carry the product through the year the seasonal swing of prices is very large. Farmers who must sell at the low point suffer. In some parts of the country the privately available credit supply is inadequate.

The stability of farm life and the efficiency of agricultural production would be improved if the government were prepared to moderate the effects of this problem by making non-recourse loans based on some large fraction, say 80 per cent, of the expected average prices for the year.

Two aspects of such provision for shielding farmers from the consequences of seasonal price instability should be emphasized: (1) Loans should not be large enough to result in carryover of stocks in the hands of the government from one year to the next, and (2) farmers would be responsible for storage of crops under loan.

Agricultural Research · We have stressed that the solution of the farm problem lies in eliminating the excess resources now being applied to the production of farm goods.

We want to lay equally strong stress upon our view that while we bring agricultural supply and demand into balance by reducing the resources employed in producing farm products, *we should not slack off the search for ways to produce more farm goods with fewer resources;* that is, the drive for agricultural efficiency should not be halted or even impeded by the need to eliminate the excess resources at use in farming. On the other hand, decisions to incur the costs of research for agriculture, as for other industries, should be guided by the criterion of the relation between prospective benefits and costs.

The Use of Surpluses in Economic Development · We should continue to use our existing surplus stocks of farm products to assist the economic growth of underdeveloped countries, but we should not create more surpluses simply because they can be disposed of abroad.

In using farm surpluses for development aid, certain conditions not met in the past should become standard.

1. Foreign sales of surplus farm products should not disguise the cost of the present farm programs and thereby encourage their continuation. The present practice is chiefly to "sell" surpluses at world market prices for inconvertible local currencies of which only a small fraction will ever be turned to U. S. use. The "proceeds" from such "sales" are then treated as a deduction from the costs of farm price support programs. This has minimized the apparent costs of the farm program and caused complacency about its continuation. Moreover, the foreign disposal of $9 billion of farm products abroad since 1954 at uncertain prices has disguised the extent of surplus production. This, again, has cushioned public reaction and encouraged continuation of a program that is bad for agriculture and bad for the national economy as a whole. The burden of supporting wasteful agricultural production limits our ability to give underdeveloped countries assistance of the kind they most need.

2. Costs should not be incurred to dispose of surpluses unless these costs yield a benefit sufficient to make them worthwhile. For example, it is sometimes proposed that surplus feed be converted into chickens, which would then be given to underdeveloped countries. The soundness of such a move depends upon whether the chickens are worth the cost to the recipient country of converting the feed to chickens, in the sense that it would be willing to pay that cost or would prefer the chickens to the dollar amount of the cost of conversion.

3. Disposal programs should not affect the agriculture of recipient countries in a way that retards their overall development.

4. Disposal programs should not lead to the accumulation in U. S. hands of excessive amounts of foreign inconvertible currencies that conceal the facts of the transactions and cause irritation in U. S. relations with the recipient countries.

Farming and the Low-Income Areas · There is a structural link between the problems of the low income area and the farm problem already noted in our recommendation on education of farm youths: low production farms predominate in the low income areas. Solution of the farm problem is part of the solution of the low income area problem, and solution of the low income area problem contributes to the solution of the farm problem.

The proposals we have made for improving the mobility of labor from farm to nonfarm employment would do much to relieve the excess labor problems of the low income areas, where so much of the excess labor is excess farm labor.

The programs we are suggesting would result in fewer workers in agriculture, working a smaller number of farms of greater average size and receiving substantially higher income per worker.

As to costs, in money and other terms:

1. We do not think that the effects of these recommendations on farm land values would be widespread, or large. The proposed Price Adjustment Program may create some decline in farm land values where acreage allotments have been capitalized into land values. This appears to be primarily a problem that would affect the western edge of the wheat areas. The proposed Cropland Adjustment Program and Income Protection Program would assist land owners in that area.

2. Assuming that the income protection payments for the first year were 100 per cent of the difference between 1960 support price levels and the proposed price adjustment levels, and assuming a base output of 1.1 billion bushels of wheat, 14 million bales of cotton, and 50 million hundredweight of rice, the cost of the income payments for wheat would be $473 million, for cotton $324 million, and for rice $71 million. Thus, the income adjustment payments would amount to about $900 million for the first year and less in subsequent years.

3. There are two ways to reduce government agricultural outlays without great losses to farmers. One is to tighten controls of production and marketing enough to reduce farm output to the point where all output will sell at the higher prices. This will make consumers pay more for farm products, and let the government pay less.

The other way is to attract and assist enough farmers out of farming so that farm income *per farmer* will be sustained without rising farm prices despite a decline in government spending on agriculture.

The first method reduces government costs by shifting them to consumers, forcing some resources out of productive use in agriculture without at the same time channeling them toward better alternative use. The second method results in a true net reduction of costs to the country as a whole. Government costs go down. Farmers' per-family incomes are sustained. Many people now in farming shift to work more profitable to them and to the nation. Consumers—including farmers—are not made to pay higher food and fiber prices. It is this second method we recommend.

Our program would not result in immediate reduction of government costs. Government costs could only be immediately and substantially lowered by transferring them either to consumers or to farmers. However, *the program presented here would, over a period of time, reduce government agricultural expenditures, which have been running around $6 billion a year, by roughly $3 billion a year.*

The remaining costs (of approximately $3 billion) relate to items not dealt with in this statement, including farm housing, research, rural electrification, certain commodities, such as wool, and the cost of aid to underdeveloped countries equivalent to that now provided in the form of surplus farm goods.

4. As we emphasized in the early portions of this statement, it is the very heart of the farm problem that a massive adjustment needs to be made in the human resources now committed to agricultural production. Small adjustments in the farm labor force will not suffice.

What we have in mind in our program is a reduction of the farm labor force on the order of one third in a period of not more than five years.

This, we think, would be large enough and fast enough to offset the effects on farm output of new technology and investment. It would thereby contribute to the basic goal of a net reduction of the resources—human and other—now employed in farming.

This is a high, but not an impractical, goal.

The Farm Problem and the Policy Choices

JOHN KENNETH GALBRAITH

J. Kenneth Galbraith is Professor of Economics at Harvard University, formerly U. S. Ambassador to India. This selection is taken from an address he gave before the National Farm Institute in Des Moines, Iowa, February, 1958.

IN THE LAST twenty years we have achieved something. We have come close to agreement on at least two of the underlying causes of the farm problem. We agree, first of all, that a remarkable technological and capital advance has remarkably increased output from given land and labor. A great many changes—improved machinery and tillage, more and better power, hybrids, plant foods, improved nutrition, and disease control—have all contributed to this result.

Secondly, there is agreement that this great increase in the efficiency of farm production and the resulting increase in output has occurred in a country which has a relatively low absorptive capacity. In the economist's language, both the price elasticity and the income elasticity are low. Farm products do not move readily and easily into use when there is a modest reduction in prices. For the generality of farm products only a large reduction in price will much expand consumption. Some are unresponsive to almost any likely movement. Needless to say, this makes price cutting a painful way of getting expanded consumption.

Such is the meaning of low price elasticity. Low income elasticity means that as the incomes of people rise—urban incomes in particular—they spend more on clothing, on transportation, on recreation, and on other things but not a great deal more on food. The meaning of this will be evident to everyone. While expanding prosperity and increasing purchasing power would be a cure for overproduction in other industries, they are not similarly the salvation for agriculture.

I now come to another and, in some respects, more vital cause of our farm difficulties. This is also one which is much less clearly perceived. And much of what I have to say later on depends on a clear perception of this point.

THE ORGANIZATION OF AGRICULTURE

Unlike most industry and unlike most parts of the labor market, agriculture is peculiarly incapable of dealing with the problems of expanding output and comparatively inelastic demand. This incapability is inherent in the organization of the industry. Agriculture is an industry of many small units. No individual producer can exercise an appreciable influence on price or on the amount that is sold. As a result, it is not within the power of any individual producer—and since there is no effective organization to this end, it is not within the power of the agricultural industry as a whole—to keep expanding farm output from bringing down prices and incomes. And given the inelasticity of these markets, a large increase in supply can obviously be the cause of great hardship and even demoralization.

All this, you will say (or some will say), is inevitable. It is the way things should be. This is the free market. This is competition. Perhaps so. But it is a behavior that is more or less peculiar to agriculture. In the last thirty or forty years there have been important technological improvements in the manufacture of automobiles, trucks, and tractors. The moving assembly line, special-purpose machine tools of high speed and efficiency, and automation have all worked a revolution in these industries. Did it lead to a glut on the market and a demoralization of prices? Of course it did not. It did not because the individual companies, very fortunately for them and perhaps also for the economy, were able to control their prices and regulate their output. This is a built-in power; it goes automatically with the fact that there are comparatively few firms in these industries. The steel industry is currently running at some sixty percent of capacity because it cannot sell a larger output at a price which it considers satisfactory. This it accomplishes easily without the slightest fuss or feathers. If farmers had the same market power they could, if necessary, cut hog production back by forty percent in order to defend, say, a $20 price.

The power to protect its market that is enjoyed by the corporation is also enjoyed in considerable measure by the modern union. Early in this century American workers worried, and not without reason, lest the large influx of European migrants would break down their wage scales. They were in somewhat the same position as the farmer watching the effect of a large increase in supply on his prices. But now the unionized worker is reasonably well protected against such competition. Even though the supply of labor may exceed the demand, he doesn't have to worry about his wages being slashed. He, too, has won a considerable measure of security in the market.

Thus it has come about that the farmer belongs to about the only group—certainly his is by far the most important—which is still exposed to the full rigors of the competitive market. Or this would be so in the absence of Government programs. Government price protection, viewed in this light is, or at least could be, only the equivalent of the price security that the modern corporation and the modern trade union have as a matter of course. There is this important peculiarity of the farmer's position. Because of the comparatively small scale of his operations, his large numbers, and the fact that agricultural production is by its nature scattered widely over the face of the country, he can achieve a measure of control over supply and price only with the aid of the Government. If one wishes to press the point, the market power of the modern corporation—deriving as it does from the State-issued charter—and the market power of the modern union both owe much to the State. But their debt is rather more subtle and better disguised than that of the farmer to the Agricultural Marketing Service and the CCC. So it is overlooked or perhaps conveniently ignored.

The meaning of this argument is also clear. It means that those who talk about returning the farmer to a free market are prescribing a very different fate for him than when they talk about free enterprise for General Motors or free collective bargaining for labor. In the free market the corporation and the union retain their power over prices and output. The farmer does not. What is sauce for the corporation is sourdough for the farmer. In its report, *Toward a Realistic Farm Program,* the Committee for Economic Development said that farm programs must have the basic objective of bettering the condition of the commercial farmer by means consistent with free markets and the national well-being. This means inevitably the particular kind of free market which farmers have. To prescribe the same kind of market for GM, one would have to recommend splitting the company up into a hundred or a thousand automobile-producing units. None of these would then have more influence than the average corn farmer on price; an improvement in technology would mean expanded output and lowered prices, and a glut of autos for all. And this recommendation applied to the labor market would mean the dissolution of unions. The CED is a highly responsible body. It would never think of making such silly recommendations for industry or labor. Yet this is what, in effect, it prescribes for the farmer when it asks that he be enabled to free himself from Government subsidy and control.

The special rigor with which the free market treats the farmer has always seemed to me self-evident. I have been struck by the general unwillingness to acknowledge it. While it is not usually fruitful or even wise to reflect on the reasons for the unwisdom of others, I do think some economists have resisted the idea for reasons essentially of nostalgia. Economic theory anciently assumed a market structure similar to that of agriculture. There were many producers selling in a market which none could influence or control. This was the classical case of free competition. There has been a natural hesitation to accept the conclusion that what was once (supposedly at least) the rule for all is now the rule only or chiefly for the farmer.

Also once we agree that the market operates with particular severity for the farmer we are likely to ask what should be done about it. The door is immediately opened to talk of Government programs. And that talk is not of temporary expedients but of permanent measures. Those who find such ideas abhorrent realize, perhaps instinctively, that to talk of free markets is the best defense.

I should also add that no one ever gets into trouble praising the virtues of the free market.

Finally, in recent times, the beneficence of unregulated markets has acquired some of the overtones of a religious faith. It is hinted, even though it is not quite said, that divinity is on the side of the free market. Support prices, although they may not be precisely the work of the devil, are utterly lacking in heavenly sanction. I must say I regard this whole trend of discussion not only as unfortunate but even as objectionable. I am not an expert in theology, but I doubt that providence is much concerned with the American farm program. Certainly it seems to me a trifle presumptuous for any mortal, however great or pious, to claim or imply that God is on his side. I would suggest that, following an old American tradition, we keep religion out of what had best be purely secular discussion.

THE CHOICE CONFRONTING US

It will be plain from the foregoing that expanding output, in the presence of inelastic demand, and in the absence of any internal capacity to temper the effect, can bring exceedingly painful and perhaps even disastrous movements in farm prices and incomes. And not only can it do so but on any reading of recent experience is almost certain to do so. And there is the further possibility that these effects may be sharpened by shrinking demand induced by depression. What should we do?

Within recent times, so it seems to me at least, we have come to understand more clearly the choice that confronts us. This choice rests on an increasingly evident fact of our agriculture. It is the very great difference in the ability of different classes of farmers to survive satisfactorily under the market conditions I have described. As I say, this is something of which we are only gradually becoming aware. Let me explain it in some detail.

For purposes of this explanation we may think of three classes of farmers in the United States. The first group are the subcommercial or subsistence farmers. These are the people who sell very little. Their situation is characteristic in the southern Appalachians, the Piedmont Plateau, northern New England hill towns, the cutover regions of the Lake States, and the Ozarks. Their income is inadequate less because prices are low than because they have so little to bring to market. It is plain that if these families are to have a decent income one of two things must happen. They must be assisted in reorganizing their farm enterprises so that their output is appreciably increased or they must find a better livelihood outside of agriculture. For the family grossing less than $1,000 or $1,500 from agriculture, of which there are still a great many in the United States, one or another of these remedies is inevitable. I doubt the wisdom of those who seek to make political capital out of statements of public officials which recognize this choice.

But it seems clear that we must now recognize two separate groups within the category that we are accustomed to call commercial farmers. We must distinguish the case of the very large commercial farm which, there is increasing evidence to show, has been able to return its operators a satisfactory income in recent years from that of the more conventional family enterprise which is in serious trouble. In the nature of things the dividing line here is not very sharp and it undoubtedly varies from one type of farming to another. But the growing income advantage of the large farm—the very large farm—is strongly indicated. It is shown by the trend toward farm consolidation. It is strongly suggested by farm management budgeting and programming studies. And it is borne out by the statistics. Speaking of commercial farms, Koffsky and Grove, of the United States Department of Agriculture, conclude in their recent testimony on agricultural policy for the Joint Economic Committee that between 1949 and 1954-55, although the evidence is not entirely conclusive, "net income on farms with an annual value of sales of $25,000 or more was fairly well maintained, while incomes of smaller operations, although still in the high-production category, showed substantial declines. That the large farms would even come close to maintaining their income in this period was highly significant.

We can conclude, I believe, that in many areas at least, modern technology has come to favor the large farm enterprise. Agriculture has become an industry where there are substantial economies of scale. The most successful units may, indeed, be very large by any past standards—in some areas the investment will be from half or three-quarters of a million dollars upward. This is an important point, for there is still more than a slight reluctance to admit of the size of these units and to explore the full extent of the change that is involved. We hear scholars, Professor T. W. Schultz among them, speak of the need for a further large-scale withdrawal of the human factor from commercial agriculture. But we hear less of the massive reorganization of the farm units which this withdrawal implies. The huge scale of the resulting units is not recognized—or this part of the conclusion is soft pedalled. Yet, if many fewer people run our farm plant it can only mean that each person is operating a far larger firm.

For let there be no mistake, an agriculture where the average unit has a capitalization of a half million dollars or upward will be very different, both in its social and economic structure, from the agriculture to which we are accustomed. Not many can expect to start with a small or modest stake and control a half million or million dollars of capital during their lifetime. If these are the capital requirements of the successful farm, we shall have to accept as commonplace the separation of management from ownership. Owner-operation will be confined, with rare exceptions, to those who were shrewd enough to select well-to-do parents. We shall develop in our agriculture what amounts to an aristocratic tradition. There will no doubt also be closer integration with industrial operations with capital borrowed from industry and with closer control by industry. Modern broiler feeding is a sign.

Perhaps this development will not be so bad. But we should face up to its full implications. Those who now talk about adjustments and reorganization of commercial agriculture are talking about means without facing up to results. Those who praise the free market and the family in one breath are fooling either themselves or their audience. As I have noted, it is the very large farm, not the traditional family enterprise, which from the evidence has much the greater capacity to survive.

We should also recognize that the adjustment to high capitalization agriculture will not be painless. It will continue to be very painful. And we should spare a thought for the trail of uprooted families and spoiled and unhappy lives which such adjustment involves. I would especially warn colleges, now interesting themselves in these problems, against using the word "adjustment" as though it described a neutral and painless process.

FOR THE SMALL COMMERCIAL FARM

Suppose we do not wish an agriculture of large, highly capitalized units. What is the alternative? The alternative is to have a farm policy in which the smaller commercial farm—what we have long thought of as the ordinary family enterprise—can survive. Given the technological dynamic of agriculture, the nature of its demand and the nature of the market structure, we cannot expect this from the market. It will come only as the result of Government programs that are designed to enable the family enterprise to survive. It has to be a Government program. Self-organization by farmers, of which some people are now talking, to regulate supply and protect their incomes is a pipe dream. Those who advocate it only advertize their innocence of history, economics, and human nature and their refusal to learn from past failure. I also confess my skepticism of individual commodity programs now so much in fashion. I very much fear that they will prove to be only a way of magnifying the tendency of farmers to disagree with each other—a tendency that is exceedingly well-developed—and thus to insure no action of any kind. I also deplore the belief that is currently so popular that if everyone just thinks hard enough someone, someday, will come up with a brilliant new idea for solving the farm problem and insuring everyone an adequate income. That is not going to happen either. Farmers are reputed to be hardheaded people. But a surprising number still have a sneaking faith in magic. The soil bank should stand as a warning. The good ideas have already occurred to people. So, of course, have the bad ones.

Or, to be more precise, the choices in farm policy are not very great. Any policy must provide a floor under prices or under income. As I have said on other occasions, a farm policy that doesn't deal with these matters is like a trade union which doesn't bother about wages. There must be production or marketing controls and these must be strong enough to keep the program from being unreasonably expensive. They will also inevitably interfere somewhat with the freedom of the farmer to do as he pleases. Nothing is controlled if a man can market all that he pleases. But we should also bear in mind that life involves a choice between different kinds of restraints. Inadequate income also imposes some very comprehensive restraints on the farm family.

I have long felt that there is a right way and a wrong way to support farm prices and income and that since World War II we have shown an unerring instinct for the wrong course. Production payments, either generally or specially financed, would be far more satisfactory. And since payments can be denied to over-quota production, they fit in far better with a system of production control. But this is another story.

The choice today is not the survival of American agriculture, or even its efficiency. The great and growing productivity shows that these are not in jeopardy. What is at stake is the traditional organization of this industry. We are in process of deciding between the traditional family enterprise of modest capitalization and widely dispersed ownership and an agriculture composed of much larger scale, much more impersonal, and much more highly capitalized firms. This is not an absolute choice. We shall have both types of farm enterprises for a long time to come. But a strong farm program will protect the traditional structure. The present trend to the free market will put a substantial premium on the greater survival power of the large enterprise.

My own preference would be to temper efficiency with compassion and to have a farm program that protects the smaller farm. But my purpose tonight is not to persuade you but to suggest the choice.

The Farm Problem Is *Not* Hopeless

Hendrik Houthakker is Professor of Economics at Harvard University. This selection appeared originally in the June 1962 issue of Challenge: The Magazine of Economic Affairs.

AFTER MORE THAN 30 years of active government intervention in agriculture, a durable solution to the farm problem has yet to be found. The two most influential sources of ideas on farm policy—the U.S. Department of Agriculture and the American Farm Bureau Federation—agree on one thing: that the government should take more dramatic steps to cut back production. They only disagree on methods of curtailment.

But reduction of agricultural output by government intervention can hardly be called an answer to the farm problem. If such a policy is to work at all, the cutbacks would have to be increasingly severe because farm technology is constantly improving. More seriously, it is clearly inconsistent for the government to curtail activity in this important sector while pursuing the universally accepted goal of general economic expansion elsewhere. To say that a more rational approach is politically impossible does not say much for the American system of government.

The persistence of this stalemate clearly suggests that some fundamental rethinking is needed. The deadlock is not merely a standoff between conflicting pressure groups; it is also due to a failure of analysis. To reconcile opposing interests, after all, is the daily work of politicians. But before this can be done, the nature of these interests has to be clearly recognized. In agriculture, however, a number of widely held but fallacious convictions becloud the main issues and complicate the search for a lasting solution. Before we can consider a solution, then, we must refute seven basic fallacies about farm problems and policies.

SEVEN FALLACIES ABOUT FARM PROBLEMS

First of all, there is the *farm income fallacy*—the belief that the aggregate income derived from farming should rise at least proportionately to nonfarm income, and any falling behind of farm income is an inequity which the government should correct. But the fact is that in a growing economy the shares earned by different sectors inevitably vary over time. Since farm products are mostly "necessities," consumers do *not* increase their purchases from farmers proportionately as their incomes rise. Thus, a rise in agricultural productivity will not benefit farmers as long as they fail to adjust their production plans. For, if this increased farm output is to be sold, prices will have to fall, and this offsets the gain in volume.

By improving their techniques, then, farmers work themselves (or other farmers) out of a job. The less efficient farmers must find more useful work—which, of course, enables those who do stay on farms to keep their income on a par with the rest of the economy. The resulting gradual reduction of the farm labor force has now gone on for hundreds of years, and it will no doubt continue in the future. If there is anything unfair about it, the blame must be laid on Engel's law, which says that people spend proportionately (but not absolutely) less on food as their incomes rise. This is perhaps the best-established proposition of economics.

Any attempt to obscure the necessity of reducing the farm labor force by establishing high price supports merely perpetuates the problem and creates a spiral of ever-higher surpluses and ever-higher expenditures. The recent history of farm policy amply demonstrates this process. This does not mean that the government should be indifferent to the income of farmers (or the income of any other group); it does mean that farm supports have to be administered in such a way as to facilitate rather than counteract the needed adjustments in the labor force. To keep up farm income by keeping up farm prices is impossibly expensive in the long run. As we shall see, there is a better way.

Second, there is the *family farm fallacy*. Many people feel that the government should preserve the family type of farm production—even though it has lost its economic viability—because of its alleged noneconomic benefits. Whatever moral virtue there is in independent country living, however, will be eroded if it can be achieved only by government handouts, no matter how disguised. Rural politicians are fond of arguing that agriculture is the nation's backbone, but this is hardly a reason for government intervention. Of what use is a backbone that needs to be supported?

Moreover, a large share of the benefits of programs purporting to help the family farm now go to large-scale operators (often corporations). According to the 1954 *Census of Agriculture* (still the most recent source available), three per cent of the country's cotton farms were receiving, at that time at least, 30 per cent of the support benefits. (This pattern is even more pronounced in wheat.) Several cotton-growing corporations receive more than $1 million a year each from the Commodity Credit Corporation.

It should not be thought that the benefits could be spread more evenly by limiting the "loans" that any farm can receive: as long as prices are kept high, it makes little or no difference whether a large grower sells his crop in the open market or receives a "loan" on it from the government. Even if there are reasons for favoring the family farm, price supports are too blunt a tool for the purpose.

A third misconception is the *acreage fallacy*—the belief that production can be controlled by restricting acreage. Although there can be no doubt that farmers will abandon the least productive acreage, the Agriculture Department still chooses to ignore this fact in such schemes as the Emergency Feed Grain Plan.

In fact, this scheme, which allows farmers to wait until crops are grown before deciding which acreage to abandon, puts a positive premium on harvesting only the most productive acres. To take an extreme case, a field that yielded no crop at all because of flooding can still serve to meet the farmer's commitment to reduce acreage in return for an incentive payment. It is not surprising, therefore, that the very costly Emergency Feed Grain Plan of 1961 had only a very slight effect on feed grain output.

Fourth, we must consider the *research fallacy*. This amounts to a belief that agricultural research will improve the relative position of farmers in the economy. As was argued above, improved productivity (the principal result of research) will not help farmers as long as all of them stay on farms. Such research may, of course, benefit the economy as a whole, but it only intensifies the need for adjustments in the farm sector. The government should promote research only if it is prepared for its economic consequences. This principle also applies to other productivity-raising government programs such as irrigation and conservation.

The fifth mistaken conviction about farm problems—the *free market fallacy*—is that farmers are too numerous and too weak to bargain effectively and, thus, in a free market they will always come out on the bottom. But bargaining between various sectors of the economy has little influence on the distribution of national income. Far more important is the willingness of producers to supply even at low prices. Farmers are willing to do this because their purchased inputs are small in relation to their output, largely because most of the land and labor they use is their own.

Because the supply elasticity of farm products is low (at least in the short run), farm prices in a free market are likely to fluctuate considerably. From the farmers' point of view, this is a more serious defect of the free market than the alleged bargaining weakness. The fluctuations can be mitigated by greater foresight (including more use of the futures market by farmers) and, if necessary, losses can be compensated for by social security and welfare devices.

Sixth, we have the *middleman fallacy*, which is related to the free market fallacy. Because the farmer's share of the consumer's dollar is steadily declining, many feel that there must be a conspiracy on the part of middlemen. But the simple truth is that farm products are reaching the consumer in ever more highly processed form. Not only does the proportion of income spent on food decline as income goes up, but production on the farm accounts for a diminishing share of the proportion that continues to be devoted to food, while the share of processing, distribution and transportation increases. It is not a conspiracy, therefore, that causes the farmer to receive less and less of the total value of food sold in a growing economy. This is equally true in the clothing sector.

Indeed, if the "middlemen" were powerful enough to deprive the farmer of his just reward, they would be making a much bigger profit than they do. But meat packing, cotton textiles, transportation and food retailing are all low-return industries. The plight of the cotton textiles industry is probably due primarily to the high support price of raw cotton and not to imports, as the industry prefers to think.

Finally, the *idea that agriculture can be isolated from the rest of the economy is perhaps the most dangerous fallacy of all.* I refer to the belief that the purpose of agriculture is to provide an income to farmers rather than to supply the world with food and fibers. The corollary is that only the farmers themselves should decide what farm output and farm prices should be. "Supply management," which refers to the centralized control of output under government-sponsored cartels, is unlikely to improve the farmers' bargaining position. Such a system would force the more efficient farmers to operate far below capacity and therefore discourage their cooperation. Supply management is on a level with the medieval guilds in terms of economic sophistication: it protects the inefficient at the expense of the efficient. Supply management would make it legal, even compulsory, for farmers to adopt the same practices for which the executives of General Electric and Westinghouse were sent to jail. "Supply management," in fact, is merely a euphemism for "monopoly." Farm policy is judged by odd standards.

Ideas of this sort are wholly out of place in a democratic society devoted to the freedom and welfare of *all* its members. The frequency with which they appear is all the more alarming. Congressional committees on agriculture listen every year to literally hundreds of witnesses representing farm interests, but rarely, if ever, to a single witness with any claim to speak for the consumer. This one-sided approach is hardly likely to lead to balanced legislation—nor, as recent experience indicates, to any permanent legislation at all.

SEPARATING PRICES FROM INCOMES

So much for the basic fallacies underlying past, present and proposed agricultural policies. The alternative I have in mind avoids all of these pitfalls. It is, I believe, a rational policy which recognizes the needs of farmers without putting unnecessary burdens on the rest of the economy. Essentially, I believe an attempt should be made to restore agriculture to a healthy and useful condition by separating the issue of farm *income* from the issue of farm *prices*. Farm prices should be allowed to return to levels at which supply and demand would reach equilibrium without an accompanying build-up in surpluses or the necessity of ever-tighter controls.

Obviously, sudden changes in farm income are undesirable. Thus, to cushion the initial shock of a return to market prices, acreage payments should be made, over a limited number of years, to the present holders of acreage allotments for basic commodities. The acreage payment should be set at a level equal to the value per acre of current price supports at current levels of output. Thus, if the price of cotton were to drop by 10 cents per pound upon the restoration of free markets, and the average yield per acre is 400 pounds, then the acreage payment would start at $40 per acre and taper off gradually in subsequent years. Each farmer would be free to produce more or less than he does now, or to abandon production.

Unlike other schemes, this plan does not require farmers to continue production in order to receive the benefits—a requirement which would hinder the needed adjustments in output. On the other hand, the acreage payment is not a reward for not producing, as is the case under the Soil Bank and Emergency Feed Grain Plans; the incentive for output reduction (where needed) is provided by lower prices. New entrants to farming would not receive acreage payments, but otherwise they would not meet any restrictions. There would consequently be no problems of enforcement.

Another advantage of the acreage payment scheme is that the distribution of its benefits would correspond more closely to need than is the case under the present program, which gives large farms an inordinate share. This is so because, on the average, large farms have higher yields per acre and thus get more under bushel supports than they would under acreage payments.

The cost of acreage payments for cotton, corn and wheat, using Department of Agriculture estimates of free market prices, would be somewhat less than $3 billion in the first year (about a billion each for corn and wheat, and $750 million for cotton). In contrast, the current agriculture budget amounts to $7 billion; in fact, the Emergency Feed Grain Plan alone, ineffective as it is, last year cost the taxpayers about $800 million—and this leaves out the cost to consumers. In addition, lower U.S. farm prices would eliminate the need for export subsidies and the "equalization" tariff on cotton textiles.

From the point of view of implementation, the advantage of the plan is its flexibility. It could be put into effect, to begin with, on only one commodity. (Cotton is the logical candidate, but the problems in corn are perhaps even more pressing.) *If necessary,* the plan could be combined with some form of price stabilization —but with support prices set at much lower levels than they are at present. And if Congress should be unwilling to see the acreage payments taper off, there would be no problem as far as resource allocation is concerned, since the program, even at the beginning, would be far less expensive than the agricultural program currently in effect.

The most important advantage of the acreage payment plan is that it would restore agriculture to its proper role in the economy. When supply and demand are in equilibrium, farm produce will no longer be a burden on the economy but will contribute significantly to its steady and orderly growth.

The farm problem is not as hopeless as it seems.

PART FOUR Inequality and Poverty

IF ONE WERE to ask Americans to list those economic problems they consider to be most important, income distribution might not appear high on the list. Certainly the issue has not made its share of headlines, at least until just recently, when public attention has come to be focussed on the problem of poverty. But it is clear that in reactions to other issues of public concern—tax policy, the farm question, collective bargaining, social security, price and rent controls, even tariffs—questions of income distribution—between farmers and the nonfarm population, labor and management, landlords and tenants—are barely hidden below the surface.

Although the contrast between rich and poor characterizes all ages and countries, a few figures indicating the extent of inequality in the United States may prove useful. In 1962, the last year for which data are available, the poorest fifth of income recipients (families and unattached individuals) received less than five percent of total personal income, and the richest fifth, nearly half (45%) of the total, the average income of those in the latter group being close to ten times that in the former. The share of the top five percent of income recipients was nearly 20 percent of income, implying an average income 17 times as great as that received in the lowest fifth. Translated into dollars, the average income of the bottom fifth was less than $1,700; the top fifth, about $16,500; and the top five percent, $28,500. These figures are averages, of course, not the incomes making one eligible for membership in the class. Anyone with an income below about $3,000 in 1962 would have found himself placed in the lowest group; on the other hand, it would have taken an income of just under $10,000 to have placed him in the top quintile, and of over $17,000 to have put him in the top five percent. (The range between $3,000 and $10,000 included the remaining three fifths of the income recipients.)[1]

Contrary to the conclusions reached by some early investigators, the distribution of income, including that for the United States, does not remain constant over time. Indeed, since 1929 (the earliest year for which the data are even close to being adequate), there has been a rather significant reduction in inequality. For example, the share of the top quintile fell from 54 percent in that year to 45 percent in 1962, or by a sixth; that of the top five percent, from 30 percent to 20 percent, or by a third; that of the top one percent of income recipients, from 16 percent to under 8 percent, or by more than a half. On the other hand, the share of the two bottom quintiles together (the lowest 40 percent of recipients) rose from 13 to 16 percent, or by about 25 percent.[2] These figures imply in turn that in 1929 the average income of the top quintile was nine times as great as the average in the two bottom quintiles, and in 1962 only six times as great. For the top five percent of income recipients compared with the two bottom quintiles, the ratios were close to twenty times in 1929 and ten times in 1962.

The change has been so striking that some writers have referred to it as an "income revolution." If a revolution it was, then its time span was considerably less than that involved in the above comparisons, which cover a third of a century; the revolution was completed before the end of World War II. Since the end of that war the degree of inequality has shown relatively little change; if anything, the poorest fifth as well as the top five percent may have lost a little ground relative to the

1. The figures given, those of the U. S. Department of Commerce for the distribution of personal income, are not necessarily the only, or even the most ideal, for measuring inequality. Results would differ somewhat, depending on the definition of the income recipient (e.g., family unit, "spending unit," the individual), the definition of income itself, and the time period used for measuring income. For example, the above estimates are based on income before taxes. After-tax income shares would not, however, be materially different, if allowance were made not only for personal income taxes, but all other taxes as well, although the average income figures in dollars would, of course, be reduced. As another example, the data given are for annual incomes received in 1962, even though some individuals' incomes may have been temporarily high or low in that year. Considerations such as these, while important for certain problems, would not serve to alter materially the overall picture of inequality.

2. Reliable data on the share of the lowest fifth of income recipients are not available for 1929.

third and fourth quintiles.

This is not to say that changes in the postwar period have been absent; rather, the changes there have more or less offset each other in their effects on distribution. For example, fewer farmers and self-employed businessmen are currently found in the ranks of the top five percent; their places have been taken largely by professional people and managerial personnel. Only brief mention can be made of some of the factors behind the prewar trend to less inequality: a somewhat larger share of income going to wages and salaries, which are more equally distributed than are self-employment and property incomes; a reduction in the share of dividends, most of which go to the very top income groups; and a narrowing of the dispersion in wage and salary incomes.

Such is the factual background on income distribution in this country. Whether one believes there is "too much" or "too little" equality, or that any movement toward more equality has been "too fast" or "too slow" clearly depends on one's ethical judgments. Some of these ethical issues are raised in the selections by R. H. Tawney and Henry Wallich. But more than ethical issues are involved. In an economy such as ours, the distribution of income is to a large extent a market-determined phenomenon, the outcome not only of the pattern of ownership of productive resources, but of a price system, which places relatively high values on resources in scarce supply relative to the demand for them, and lower values on relatively more abundant resources. Tawney, for example, would modify inequality in the ownership of property through inheritance taxation and would in effect narrow wage and salary differentials by increasing the value of labor services sold by those in lower income groups through appropriate investment in their health and education.

The distribution of income as initially determined by market forces can, of course, be subsequently modified by taxes and transfer payments; indeed, since governments must collect taxes, their fiscal policies must effect some redistribution, whether desired or not. But taxes and transfers themselves are likely to affect the efficiency with which the price system is able to perform some of its other tasks. The selection from Wallich examines conflicts which may arise in implementing such goals as more equality, improved economic efficiency, and a more rapid rate of economic growth.

The recent upsurge of interest in the problem of poverty has focussed attention on the bottom of the distribution—roughly, on the lowest fifth of recipients whose incomes are under $3,000. The creation of a consensus on the need for undertaking policies to raise the incomes of the poor was undoubtedly assisted by Michael Harrington's book, *The Other America*. A selection from the first chapter, "The Invisible Land," is included below; in it Harrington argues that the misery of the poor has become increasingly hidden from public view. The selection from President Johnson's message on poverty couples a summary of the Administration's program in its war against poverty with a strong plea for action. The final two selections review the causes and extent of poverty and discuss alternative measures for dealing with it: Robert J. Lampman discusses a range of preventive, remedial, and alleviative policies; Harry G. Johnson emphasizes the role of income transfers. Both economists thus underline the contrast just drawn between those policies, such as public assistance programs and a negative income tax, which attempt to handle the problem of transfer payments, and those which are designed to raise the earning power of the poor themselves.

E. C. B.

Equality

R. H. TAWNEY

Professor R. H. Tawney, the distinguished British economic historian, presents a powerful argument against economic inequality in his book, Equality, *from which the following selection is taken. Delivered as the Halley Stewart Lectures for 1929 and first published in 1931, the book has become a classic.*

[THERE ARE] THOSE who have thought that a society was most likely to enjoy happiness and good will, and to turn both its human and material resources to the best account, if it cultivated as far as possible an equalitarian temper, and sought by its institutions to increase equality. It is obvious that, as things are today, no redistribution of wealth would bring general affluence, and that statisticians are within their rights in making merry with the idea that the equalization of incomes would make everyone rich. But, though riches are a good, they are not, nevertheless, the only good; and because greater production, which is concerned with the commodities to be consumed, is clearly important, it does not follow that greater equality, which is concerned with the relations between the human beings who consume them, is not important also. It is obvious that the word "Equality" possesses more than one meaning, and that the controversies surrounding it arise partly, at least, because the same term is employed with different connotations. Thus it may either purport to state a fact, or convey the expression of an ethical judgment. On the one hand, it may affirm that men are, on the whole, very similar in their natural endowments of character and intelligence. On the other hand, it may assert that, while they differ profoundly as individuals in capacity and character, they are equally entitled as human beings to consideration and respect, and that the well-being of a society is likely to be increased if it so plans its organization that whether their powers are great or small, all its members may be equally enabled to make the best of such powers as they possess.

If made in the first sense, the assertion of human equality is untenable. It is a piece of mythology against which irresistible evidence has been accumulated by biologists and psychologists. In the light of the data presented, the fact that, quite apart from differences of environment and opportunity, individuals differ widely in their natural endowments, and in their capacity to develop them by education, is not open to question.

The acceptance of that conclusion, nevertheless, makes a smaller breach in equalitarian doctrines than is sometimes supposed, for such doctrines have rarely been based on a denial of it. It is true, of course, that the psychological and political theory of the age between 1750 and 1850—the theory, for example, of thinkers so different as Helvétius and Adam Smith at the beginning of the period, and John Stuart Mill and Pierre Proudhon at the end of it—greatly underestimated the significance of inherited qualities, and greatly overestimated the plasticity of human nature. It may be doubted, however, whether it was quite that order of ideas which inspired the historical affirmations of human equality, even in the age when such ideas were still in fashion.

It is difficult for even the most sanguine of assemblies to retain for more than one meeting the belief that Providence has bestowed an equal measure of intelligence upon all its members. When the Americans declared it to be a self-evident truth that all men are created equal, they were thinking less of the admirable racial qualities of the inhabitants of the New World than of their political and economic relations with the Old, and would have remained unconvinced that those relations should continue even in the face of proofs of biological inferiority. When the French, who a century and a half ago preached the equalitarian idea with the same fervent conviction as is shown today by the rulers of Russia in denouncing it, set that idea side by side with liberty and fraternity as the motto of a new world, they did not mean that all men are equally intelligent or equally virtuous, any more than that they are equally tall or equally fat, but that the unity of their national life should no longer be torn to pieces by obsolete property rights and meaningless juristic distinctions.

Few men have been more acutely sensitive than Mill to the importance of encouraging the widest possible diversities of mind and taste. In arguing that "the best state for human nature is that in which, while no one is poor, no one desires to be richer," and urging that social policy should be directed to increasing equality, he did not intend to convey that it should suppress varieties of individual genius and character, but that it was only in a society marked by a large measure of economic equality that such varieties were likely to find their full expression and due meed of appreciation. Theologians have not, as a rule, been disposed to ignore the fact that there are diversities of gifts and degree above degree. When they tell us that all men are equal in the eyes of God, what they mean, it is to be presumed, is the truth expressed in the parable of the prodigal son—the truth that it is absurd and degrading for men to make much of their intellectual and moral superiority to each other, and still more of their superiority in the arts which bring wealth and power, because, judged by their place in any universal scheme, they are all infinitely great or infinitely small. And, when observers from the Dominions, or from foreign countries, are struck by inequality as one of the special and outstanding characteristics of English social life, they do not mean that in other countries differences of personal quality are less important than in England. They mean, on the contrary, that they are more important, and that in England they tend to be obscured or obliterated behind differences of property and income, and the whole elaborate facade of a society that, compared with their own, seems stratified and hierarchical.

The equality which all these thinkers emphasize as desirable is not equality of capacity or attainment, but of circumstances, institutions, and manner of life. The inequality which they deplore is not inequality of personal gifts, but of the social and economic environment. They are concerned, not with a biological phenomenon, but with a spiritual relation and the conduct to be based on it. Their view, in short, is that, because men are men, social institutions—property rights, and the organization of industry, and the system of public health and education—should be planned, as far as is possible, to emphasize and strengthen, not the class differences which divide, but the common humanity which unites, them.

Such a view of the life which is proper to human beings may, of course, be criticized, as it often has been. But to suppose that it can be criticized effectively by pointing to the width of the intellectual and moral differences which distinguish individuals from each other is a solecism, an *ignoratio elenchi*. It is true, of course, that such differences are important, and that the advance of psychology has enabled them to be measured with a new precision, with results which are valuable in making possible both a closer adaptation of educational methods to individual needs and a more intelligent selection of varying aptitudes for different tasks. But to recognize a specific difference is one thing; to pass a general judgment of superiority or inferiority, still more to favour the first and neglect the second, is quite another. The nightingale, it has been remarked, was placed in the fourth class at the fowl show. Which of a number of varying individuals is to be judged superior to the rest depends upon the criterion which is applied, and the criterion is a matter of ethical judgment. That judgment will, if it is prudent, be tentative and provisional, since men's estimates of the relative desirability of initiative, decision, common sense, imagination, humility and sympathy appear, unfortunately, to differ, and the failures and fools—the Socrates and St. Francis—of one age are the sages and saints of another.

It is true, again, that human beings have, except as regards certain elementary, though still sadly neglected, matters of health and development, different requirements, and that these different requirements can be met satisfactorily only by varying forms of provision. But quality of provision is not identity of provision. It is to be achieved, not by treating different needs in the same way, but by devoting equal care to ensuring that they are met in the different ways most appropriate to them, as is done by a doctor who prescribes different regimens for different constitutions, or a teacher who develops different types of intelligence by different curricula. The more anxiously, indeed, a society endeavours to secure equality of consideration for all its members, the greater will be the differentiation of treatment which, when once their common human needs have been met, it accords to the special needs of different groups and individuals among them.

It is true, finally, that some men are inferior to others in respect of their intellectual endowments, and it is possible that the same is true of certain classes. It does not, however, follow from this fact that such individuals or classes should receive less consideration than others, or should be treated as inferior in respect of such matters as legal status, or health, or economic arrangements, which are within the control of the community.

It may, of course, be deemed expedient so to treat them. It may be thought advisable, as is sometimes urged today, to spend less liberally on the education of the slow than on that of the intelligent, or, in accordance with the practice of all ages, to show less respect for the poor than for the rich. But, in order to establish an inference, a major premise is necessary as well as a minor; and, if such discrimination on the part of society is desirable, its desirability must be shown by some other argument than the fact of inequality of intelligence and character. To convert a phenomenon, however interesting, into a principle, however respectable, is an error of logic. It is the confusion of a judgment of fact with a judgment of value—a confusion like that which was satirized by Montesquieu when he wrote, in his ironical defence of slavery: "The creatures in question are black from head to foot, and their noses are so flat that it is almost impossible to pity them. It is not to be supposed that God, an all-wise Being, can have lodged a soul—still less a good soul—in a body completely black."

Everyone recognizes the absurdity of such an argument when it is applied to matters within his personal knowledge and professional competence. Everyone realizes that, in order to justify inequalities of circumstances or opportunity by reference to differences of personal quality, it is necessary to show that the differences in question are relevant to the inequalities. Everyone now sees, for example, that it is not a valid argument against women's suffrage to urge, as used to be urged not so long ago, that women are physically weaker than men, since physical strength is not relevant to the question of the ability to exercise the franchise, or a valid argument in favour of slavery that some men are less intelligent than others, since it is not certain that slavery is the most suitable penalty for lack of intelligence.

Not everyone, however, is so quick to detect the fallacy when it is expressed in general terms. It is still possible, for example, for one eminent statesman to ridicule the demand for a diminution of economic inequalities on the ground that every mother knows that her children are not equal, without reflecting whether it is the habit of mothers to lavish care on the strong and neglect the delicate; and for another to dismiss the suggestion that greater economic equality is desirable, for the reason, apparently, that men are naturally unequal. It is probable, however, that the first does not think that the fact that some children are born with good digestions, and others with bad, is a reason for supplying good food to the former and bad food to the latter, rather than for giving to both food which is equal in quality but different in kind, and that the second does not suppose that the natural inequality of men makes legal equality a contemptible principle. On the contrary, when ministers of the Crown responsible for the administration of justice to the nation, they both took for granted the desirability and existence, at any rate on paper, of legal equality. Yet in the eighteenth century statesmen of equal eminence in France and Germany, and in the nineteenth century influential thinkers in Russia and the United States, and, indeed, the ruling classes of Europe almost everywhere at a not very distant period, all were disposed to think that, since men are naturally unequal, the admission of a general equality of legal status would be the end of civilization.

Our modern statesmen do not agree with that view, for, thanks to the struggles of the past, they have inherited a tradition of legal equality, and, fortified by that tradition, they see that the fact that men are naturally unequal is not relevant to the question whether they should or should not be treated as equal before the law. But they have not inherited a tradition of economic equality, for that tradition has still to be created. Hence they do not see that the existence of differences of personal capacity and attainment is as irrelevant to the question whether it is desirable that the social environment and economic organization should be made more conducive to equality as it is to the question of equality before the law, which itself, as we have said, seemed just as monstrous a doctrine to conservative thinkers in the past as the suggestion of greater economic equality seems to them today.

Perhaps, therefore, the remote Victorian thinkers, like Matthew Arnold and Mill, who commended equality to their fellow-countrymen as one source of peace and happiness, were not speaking so unadvisedly as at first sight might appear. They did not deny that men have unequal gifts, or suggest that all of them are capable of earning £10,000 a year, or of making a brilliant show when their natural endowments are rigorously sifted and appraised with exactitude. What they were concerned to emphasize is something more elementary and commonplace. It is the fact that, in spite of their varying characters and capacities, men possess in their common humanity a quality which is worth cultivating, and that a community is most likely to make the most of that quality if it takes it into account in planning its economic organization and social institutions—if it stresses lightly differences of wealth and birth and social position, and establishes on firm foundations institutions which meet common needs, and are a source of common enlightenment and common enjoyment. The individual differences of which so much is made, they would have said, will always survive, and they are to be welcomed, not regretted. But their existence is no reason for not seeking to establish the largest possible measure of equality of environment, and circumstance, and opportunity. On the contrary, it is a reason for redoubling our efforts to establish it, in order to ensure that these diversities of gifts may come to fruition.

It may well be the case that capricious inequalities are in some measure inevitable, in the sense that, like crime and disease, they are a malady which the most rigorous precautions cannot wholly overcome. But, when crime is known as crime, and disease as disease, the ravages of both are circumscribed by the mere fact that they are recognized for what they are, and described by their proper names, not by flattering euphemisms. And a society which is convinced that inequality is an evil need not be alarmed because the evil is one which cannot wholly be subdued. In recognizing the poison it will have armed itself with an antidote. It will have deprived inequality of its sting by stripping it of its esteem.

Humanism is the antithesis of materialism. Its essence is simple. It is the attitude which judges the externals of life by their effect in assisting or hindering the life of the spirit. It is the belief that the machinery of existence—property and material wealth and industrial organization, and the whole fabric and mechanism of social institutions—is to be regarded as means to an end, and that this end is the growth towards perfection of individual human beings. Its aim is to liberate and cultivate the powers which make for energy and refinement; and it is critical, therefore, of all forms of organization which sacrifice spontaneity to mechanism, or which seek, whether in the name of economic efficiency or of social equality, to reduce the variety of individual character and genius to a drab and monotonous uniformity. But it desires to cultivate these powers in all men, not only in a few. Resting, as it does, on the faith that the differences between men are less important and fundamental than their common humanity, it is the enemy of arbitrary and capricious divisions between different members of the human family, which are based, not upon what men, given suitable conditions, are capable of becoming, but on external distinctions between them, such as those created by birth or wealth.

Sharp contrasts of opportunity and circumstances, which deprive some classes of the means of development deemed essential for others, are sometimes defended on the ground that the result of abolishing them must be to produce, in the conventional phrase, a dead-level of mediocrity. Mediocrity, whether found in the valleys of society or, as not infrequently happens, among the peaks and eminences, is always to be deprecated. But whether a level is regrettable or not depends, after all, upon what is levelled.

Those who dread a dead-level of income or wealth do not dread, it seems, a dead-level of law and order, and of security for life and property. They do not complain that persons endowed by nature with unusual qualities of strength, audacity or cunning are artificially prevented from breaking into houses, or terrorizing their neighbours, or forging cheques. On the contrary, they maintain a system of police in order to ensure that powers of this kind are, as far as may be, reduced to impotence. They insist on establishing a dead-level in these matters, because they know that, by preventing the strong from using their strength to oppress the weak, and the unscrupulous from profiting by their cleverness to cheat the simple, they are not crippling the development of personality, but assisting it. They do not ignore the importance of maintaining a high standard of effort and achievement. On the contrary, they deprive certain kinds of achievement of their fruits, in order to encourage the pursuit of others more compatible with the improvement of individual character, and more conducive to the good of society.

Violence and cunning are not the only forces, however, which hamper the individual in the exercise of his powers, or which cause false standards of achievement to be substituted for true. There are also, in most societies, the special advantages conferred by wealth and property, and by the social institutions which favour them. If men are to respect each other for what they are, they must cease to respect each other for what they own. They must abolish, in short, the reverence for riches. And, human nature being what it is, in order to abolish the reverence for riches, they must make impossible the existence of a class which is important merely because it is rich.

The existence of opportunities to move from point to point on an economic scale, and to mount from humble origins to success and affluence, is a condition both of social well-being and of individual happiness, and impediments which deny them to some, while lavishing them on others, are injurious to both. But opportunities to "rise" are not a substitute for a large measure of practical equality, nor do they make immaterial the existence of sharp disparities of income and social condition. On the contrary, it is only the presence of a high degree of practical equality which can diffuse and generalize opportunities to rise. The existence of such opportunities in fact, and not merely in form, depends, not only upon an open road, but upon an equal start. It is precisely, of course, when capacity is aided by a high level of general well-being in the *milieu* surrounding it, that its ascent is most likely to be regular and rapid, rather than fitful and intermittent.

If a high degree of practical equality is necessary to social well-being, because without it ability cannot find its way to its true vocation, it is necessary also for another and more fundamental reason. It is necessary because a community requires unity as well as diversity, and because, important as it is to discriminate between different powers, it is even more important to provide for common needs. Clever people, who possess exceptional gifts themselves, are naturally impressed by exceptional gifts in others, and desire, when they consider the matter at all, that society should be organized to offer a career to exceptional talent, though they rarely understand the full scope and implications of the revolution they are preaching. But, in the conditions characteristic of large-scale economic organization, in which ninety per cent of the population are wage-earners, and not more than ten per cent employers, farmers, independent workers or engaged in professions, it is obviously, whatever the level of individual intelligence and the degree of social fluidity, a statistical impossibility for more than a small fraction of the former to enter the ranks of the latter; and a community cannot be built upon exceptional talent alone, though it would be a poor thing without it. Social well-being does not only depend upon intelligent leadership; it also depends upon cohesion and solidarity. It implies the existence, not merely of opportunities to ascend, but of a high level of general culture, and a strong sense of common interests, and the diffusion throughout society of a conviction that civilization is not the business of an élite alone, but a common enterprise which is the concern of all. And individual happiness does not only require that men should be free to rise to new positions of comfort and distinction; it also requires that they should be able to lead a life of dignity and culture, whether they rise or not, and that, whatever their position on the economic scale may be, it shall be such as is fit to be occupied by men.

· · · · · ·

If every individual were reared in conditions as favourable to health as science can make them, received an equally thorough and stimulating education up to sixteen, and knew on reaching manhood that, given a reasonable measure of hard work and good fortune, he and his family could face the risks of life without being crushed by them, the most shocking of existing inequalities would be on the way to disappear. Sharp contrasts of pecuniary income might indeed remain, as long as society were too imperfectly civilized to put an end to them. But the range of life corrupted by their influence would be narrower than today. It would cease to be the rule for the rich to be rewarded, not only with riches, but with a preferential share of health and life, and for the penalty of the poor to be not merely poverty, but ignorance, sickness and premature death.

In reality, however, even inequalities of income would not continue in such conditions to be, either in magnitude or kind, what they are at present. They would be diminished both directly and indirectly—as a result of the diminution of large incomes by means of taxation, and through the removal of special advantages and adventitious disabilities arising from the unequal pressure of the social environment. Inherited wealth, in particular, would lose most of the importance which it has today. At present, when—after the payment of death duties—more than £400 millions pass by way of inheritance, its influence as a cause of social stratification remains overwhelming. It results, not merely in capricious disparities of fortune between individuals, but in the "hereditary inequality of economic status" between different classes. If the estate duties were increased, part of them required to be paid in land or securities, and a supplementary duty imposed, increasing with the number of times that a property passed at death, the social poison of inheritance would largely be neutralized. As the privileges conferred by it became a thing of the past, and the surplus elements in incomes were increasingly devoted to public purposes, while the means of health and education were equally diffused throughout the whole community, "the career open to talent," which today is a sham, would become a reality. The element of monopoly, which necessarily exists when certain groups have easier access than others to highly paid occupations, would be weakened, and the horizontal stratification, which is so characteristic a feature of English society, would be undermined. While diversities of income, corresponding to varieties of function and capacity, would survive, they would neither be heightened by capricious inequalities of circumstances and opportunity, nor perpetuated from generation to generation by the institution of inheritance. Differences of remuneration between different individuals might remain; contrasts between the civilization of different classes would vanish.

The Meaning of Economic Inequality

HENRY C. WALLICH

An alternative view on the problem of inequality is presented by Henry C. Wallich, Professor of Economics at Yale University and a member of the Council of Economic Advisers from 1959 to 1961, in his book, The Costs of Freedom, *first published in 1960.*

IN THE United States of America, in the year of prosperity 1957, some 5 per cent of the consumer units collected 20 per cent of total personal income. At the other end of the scale, 20 per cent had to make do with 5 per cent. Per consumer unit, the prosperous 5 per cent at the top had sixteen times more than their less successful countrymen at the bottom. These hard facts call for some hard thinking.

We have made great strides in our country toward political equality, and we have made a good advance also toward a classless society. Practically nobody in the United States thinks of himself as belonging to "the proletariat." It takes a sociologist with a research grant to discover an American aristocrat. How, then, do we reconcile economic inequality with our belief in political equality? If one man rates one soul and one vote, why should he be worth widely varying amounts of dollars?

For a partial answer, we can truthfully say that the real differences are not so big as they look in the *Statistical Abstract of the United States.* Figures don't lie, but they may distort. It can be pointed out, for instance, that the gap in living standards is much smaller than the gap in incomes. It is smaller, too, than the rich-poor gap in most other countries. And the living standards of even the lowest group in the United States are still well above the average standard of most of the people on the globe. The width of the rich-poor gap, moreover, has been shrinking during most of the industrial period, despite what many people seem to believe.

Yet the fact remains that the logic of our economic system demands some degree of economic inequality, even in the face of the egalitarianism of our political system. Economic incentives, if they work, mean that some men will earn more than others. We must now face up to the consequences of those recommendations. What have we let ourselves in for?

THE MORALS OF INEQUALITY

There is probably less to economic inequality than meets the eye. Nevertheless, there is still enough to make one uneasy and to compel one to search for either remedy or justification.

This reaction, which seems to come naturally in an egalitarian country, would not have come at all times and places. History knows many civilizations that were built on an unquestioning acceptance of inequality, political as well as economic. The glory of Greece and the grandeur of Rome were built on slavery. Plato's philosophy of government rejected equality in favor of a rigid hierarchy of classes. The teachings of the Church during the Middle Ages and its contemporary feudal society took inequality on earth as given by God and pleasing to Him. Our sensitivity to the problems of inequality is of surprisingly recent date.

This sensitivity to the injustice of unequal incomes varies not only in time, but also in space. Some European countries today seem to be more "sicklied o'er with the pale cast of thought" than the United States. But wherever the question arises, one observes two extremes between which the great majority find their places: Those who see nothing wrong with the existing distribution of incomes, or one even more unequal, and those who take for granted that the only fair shares are equal shares. Each side has its arguments to demonstrate that its position is "naturally just."

Those who approve of inequality usually point to the obvious facts of life. Human beings are biologically unequal. The equality that the Constitution speaks of is one of rights, not of condition —before God and the law, not in the market place. The basic truth of these propositions is undeniable, even though the readiness of their proponents to bear other people's poverty with fortitude is sometimes a little irritating. Yet perhaps not much is proved by truths such as these. If man is the master of his fate, why should he not correct the consequences of biological inequality if he finds them unattractive? We have gone some way in evening up what nature made uneven—why not go the whole way?

The supporters of inequality are fond also of saying that, after all, anybody can get rich if he tries hard enough. That is true enough in any particular case—leaving aside the question of whether the "case" has the ability to work his way to the top. It is conspicuously fallacious for the people as a whole. Even if the population of the United States consisted exclusively of men with the ability and determination of Rockefeller, Ford and Carnegie, they could not all be presidents of corporations. Circumstances—luck, connections and whatever—must inevitably lead a few to the top and keep the vast majority in the lower echelons. We cannot all get ahead of one another.

Finally, one often hears it said in support of income inequality that, after all, a man has a right to the fruits of his labor. If he is smart enough to make a million, why should he not be entitled to it? This principle carried conviction in the days when craftsmen and farmers really "made" what they lived by. Today it does not speak to us quite so clearly. When a man "makes" a million in business today, what is it he really makes, and how much of it is his own contribution? How much is contributed by his collaborators, his predecessors, by society at large? How much of it depends on the state of competition, the state of business and a host of other factors not demonstrably under his control? Economists believe that, under favorable conditions, they can calculate the contribution that an individual makes to the flow of production with the help of the marginal productivity doctrine. But they rarely have the courage to extract a moral claim from such calculations.

If those who regard economic inequality as "natural" fail to make a convincing case, those who go for equality as "the only just solution" perform no better. Righteous indignation and vicarious anguish at the sight of poverty do not add up to a logical demonstration. Equality of income as a principle of justice runs straight into the fact that men are unequal not only as producers but also as consumers. Some of us want an expensive education, some want to travel, some want great variety in clothes, living habits and entertainment—others may find all of this tiresome. Temperaments, moreover, may vary as well as tastes—we were created equal, but not equally cheerful. To endow everybody with equal income will certainly make for very unequal enjoyment and satisfaction. Perhaps some sort of allowance could be made for this. But in practice it would scarcely be feasible to determine for purposes of compensation how many drinks above or below par each individual happened to be born.

The plea for equality also offends the elementary feeling that there should be some relation between performance and reward. We cannot say, to be sure, that a man has a right to whatever he makes, because today there are few things of which we can say who really "made" them. Yet to say positively that a man has no right to what he makes seems to imply that someone else has a better right, which makes little sense. The right of any member of society to an equal share, moreover, would presumably depend on his having put forth a normal amount of effort. To hand a full share to those who not only do not succeed, but do not even try, will strike most people as perverse. Justice seems to escape the egalitarians as it has evaded those who believe in "natural" differences.

WHAT SORT OF INEQUALITY?

Part of this debate amounts to no more than a conflict between self-interest and sentimentality. But it has an honest core, and the wide differences that it reveals among men of good will point to a conflict deeper than pocketbook interest. This conflict can be pursued all the way up into the family history of our term "equality." Among the three sister virtues "liberty, equality, fraternity" which the French Revolution held before the world, "fraternity" originally possessed much of the emotional content today carried by equality. Equality, in turn, was closer to liberty —freedom from oppression and equal treatment under the law. But fraternity—probably too good for this world—early withdrew from public life. Equality, though a little dowdy and somewhat lacking in generosity, in part took her place. In her new and expanded guise she promptly fell out with her former ally, liberty: The compulsion to conform to uniform standards was discovered to be at odds with the right to be different.

The conflict between freedom and equality has become deeper

as equality increasingly has come to mean economic equality. By the same token, however, equality has lost a good part of its halo and much of the ready support that it formerly commanded. For looked at cold-bloodedly, what sort of an ideal is this economic equality? What claims to a fair-minded man's allegiance does it have, what sense does it make as a goal?

Equality of rights before the law is intuitively appealing as a social goal. Particular individuals might of course want for themselves greater powers and privileges than equality of rights would allow. But it is clear that their desires could be granted only at the expense of someone else. The sum total of rights and powers in a community remains fixed—it adds up to 100 per cent. In such a situation, equal sharing of rights and powers offers the obvious solution.

This obvious solution does not translate smoothly into economics. Here the obvious goal seems to be, not equal welfare, but maximum welfare. A man can have more than others and yet not take anything from them, if he creates his own surplus. Economic equality as such seems to bestow no particular blessings. A community where some were rich and the rest well provided for presumably would be considered better off than one in which all were equally poor. Economic equality, unlike its political counterpart, plainly is not an end in itself. It is only a means, designed to reduce poverty; perhaps it is not the most effective means.

That economic equality does not rank with political equality as a moral ideal is plain on several grounds. To demand that none have privileges I do not enjoy seems fair. To insist that none be richer is merely spiteful. People's behavior, moreover, makes clear that economic equality is rarely their true goal. What they strive for is betterment. Insofar as they compare themselves with others, it seems that emulation, the creation of invidious distinctions, as Thorstein Veblen has so well observed, turns out to be a stronger motive than desire for equality. Equality appears in the main as a steppingstone for the underdog on his way to becoming top dog. Once he is past the halfway mark, his interest in equality usually tends to abate. The successful self-made man characteristically seems to be far less concerned about the injustice of inequality than the man whose inheritance weighs heavily on his conscience. In matters of money, there are few who are prepared to say, as Walt Whitman did about democracy, "I will accept nothing that all cannot have on even terms."

I may have labored unnecessarily the simple conclusion that economic equality or inequality is not primarily a matter of justice. To speak against any form of equality, in our day and age, is uphill work. Yet it seems clear that the debate over justice in distribution largely misses its point. The real issue is not which division, equal or unequal, is the more just. The issue is which of the two leads to higher welfare for all. The functional, rather than the moral, aspects of distribution are what matter, and it is these we will look at now.

INEQUALITY AND PROGRESS

The Welfare Case for Equality · The case for greater equality can be established very simply. A dollar means less to a richer man than to a poorer. Therefore, if we take a dollar from the rich man and give it to the poor man, we hurt the rich man less than we help the poor. The sum total of their happiness rises by virtue of the operation. Happiness can be further increased by additional transfers and will reach its peak when everybody's income is up or down to the average and complete economic equality is achieved.

Scientific economics sees a fly in the egalitarian ointment. All we really know is that the millionth dollar means less than the thousandth *to the same man*. We cannot be sure that the millionth dollar means less to one man than the thousandth means to another. True enough, one of these men is rich, the other is poor. But perhaps the pauper is completely satisfied with what he has, while the millionaire is pressed for cash. Or perhaps the pauper is an insensitive clod, incapable of finer feelings, while the millionaire is a delicate aesthete who can exist only in complete luxury. More realistically, the millionaire is probably accustomed to his standard of living and the pauper to his. Even if they are fairly similar individuals, it may hurt the one more to cut his standard than it will cheer the other to increase his.

Rigorous economic theory, therefore, will not subscribe unqualifiedly to the egalitarians' doctrine that redistribution from rich to poor must increase total satisfaction. Nevertheless, for practical purposes, the case is pretty strong, the objections not very convincing. Individuals differ, but people in the mass fall into fairly stable patterns. I would hate to have to argue that the members of the upper income brackets are on average more sensitive and capable of greater enjoyment than the rest. And the unquestionable hardships that would result from a reduction of the upper living standards could be softened by spreading the process over a generation or two.

Thus put, the case for equality is impressive, simply on functional grounds and aside from questions of justice. It can hardly fail to predispose us in favor of greater rather than lesser equality, whenever this does not interfere with growth, or boomerang in other respects. In fact, however, it is apt to defeat itself in these respects more often than not. That will be the next step of the argument.

Growth vs. Redistribution · Once growth comes to be seen as an alternative to redistribution, its potential superiority in providing welfare becomes quickly apparent. Even those who are at the low end of the income scale stand to gain more, in the not-very-long run, from speedier progress than from redistribution. Redistribution is a one-shot operation. What it can do for the lower income groups amounts to less than its enthusiasts claim. Soaking the rich yields political dividends, but not much consumable revenue. And once it is done, the toll of a lower rate of progress is exacted continually thereafter. If the rate of income growth in an egalitarian economy is 2 per cent per year, and 4 per cent in one allowing itself a higher degree of inequality, it will not be many years before the middle class of the egalitarian economy is outdistanced by the "poor" of the other.

The proposition that rapid progress is worth more than redistribution even to the poor has been challenged occasionally. The critics argue that the standard of poverty rises with the standard of living. Accordingly, if we succeeded in doubling or quadrupling the average standard of living, those who fell below it would feel just as poor as they do today. To redistribute, to raise the poor closer to the average, would thus be a surer road to happiness.

Even on their own gloomy premises, these critics overlook one obvious flaw in their reasoning: What happens to the man above the average? If the poor man feels poor simply because he is below average no matter how well off he really is, the rich man presumably feels rich because he is above average. If some future New Deal averages the poor up, it must average the rich down. The first gain, but the others lose.

What really demands our attention here, however, is the gloomy premise itself, which says that apparently we can never get ahead of our needs. This economic relativity theory is profoundly pessimistic—in fact it seems to put an end to all meaningful economic endeavor. No matter how rich we get, the doctrine says, no matter how equally we split our wealth, as a community we shall never feel any better off.

There is probably more than a grain of truth in this doctrine. Man's capacity for enjoyment is limited, luxuries quickly become necessities, and money, as has been observed on occasion, is no guarantee of happiness. Material progress is just one part of the story. If man is constitutionally unable, as these critics seem to think, to achieve happiness, he can at least do something to reduce the positive ills of this vale of tears. Schopenhauer argued that while pleasure is an illusion, pain is real. With all our high standard of living, we still have enough sources of pain—illness, unprotected old age and, above all, lack of real leisure. So long as these are with us, there is little point in even wondering whether or not we would be made happier by more and more progress.

Those who take the gloomy view of man's capacity for happiness must bear in mind, besides, that one answer to their problem can be found precisely in the rapid progress which they want to sacrifice for the joys of equality. It is true that the satisfactions of having and being pall in time. But getting and becoming are always fresh sensations. Insofar as material welfare and creature comforts can do anything for men at all, it is their increase, more than their level, that brings satisfaction. Here lies such justification as one may find for singing the perhaps debatable praises of progress.

Creative Inequality · Let us put aside now the question of whether economic inequality is inequitable. Instead, let us look more searchingly at its constructive role in the economy.

One important explanation of, and reason for, inequality follows from the need to get the right people into the right jobs. It is wasteful if engineers do work that mechanics can handle, or if executives perform chores that could be done by their secretaries. A market economy avoids this by compelling business to compete for talent and to pay each man what he is worth in the job he can do best. The process admittedly works far from perfectly. Many of our income differentials arise from monopoly power rather than from greater productivity. This is true of some wage rates and salaries higher up the line, as well as of some of the profits of venture capital. The benefits of inequality of this sort—except to the recipients—are questionable. But even in more perfect markets, large differentials would arise.

These differentials could be taxed away, of course, as in part they are today. The effectiveness of the selection process, how-ever, suffers correspondingly. A high salary that one cannot keep is no great attraction. If the selection process results in large bonuses, efficiency demands that, in good part, they be left where they land.

Another instance of creative inequality presents itself when we turn to incentives. Here again, the logic of our system pro-duces inequalities that cannot be removed without slowing down the system itself. If we want good performance, we must hold out rewards. To be effective, rewards must raise one man above the other. Not their absolute level, but their differentiation, is what counts. Inequality once more proves to be the price of progress and efficiency.

It might be possible, of course, to shift the needed inequalities from the economic sphere to that of status, prestige and power. In part—to the extent that economic differentials are taxed away —that shift is likely to come automatically, even though unof-ficially. We should then be moving into the world of George Orwell's *Animal Farm*, where everybody is equal, but some are more equal than others. I see no reason to think that power and prestige differentials are any more "just" than economic ones. Certainly they could be a great deal more unpleasant.

If a thoroughgoing economic egalitarianism were to take hold, its chief victim probably would be the incentive to take risks. Successful risk-taking has built most of the big fortunes. It is here that the egalitarians would find their most inviting targets. It is here, also, that the conjunction between equality and stagnation might make itself felt most strongly.

The incentive to invest, to be sure, is not exclusively wedded to the profit motive. It is related to other motivations—competition, sheer expansionism, prestige. But remove profit and enough of the motive force probably will be gone to slow down the rest.

The ability to save is another important consequence of high incomes that has often been stressed. The rich, as has been correctly observed, can afford to save a good part of their incomes. The poor, unfortunately, save little or nothing. Leveling of incomes, it has therefore been thought, would perforce reduce the rate of saving. This argument was especially popular during the Great Depression, when saving tended to outrun investment opportunities. A cut in saving and a corresponding rise in consumption would then have aided recovery. Redistribution of income would have killed two birds with one tax hike.

To the credit of those who developed this doctrine and derived from it a pleasure perhaps more than intellectual, it must be said that they were also the first to discover that the doctrine may not fit the statistical evidence. What they discovered from income distribution data and personal budget studies was rather surprising. A man with $10,000 a year net may save $1,000 and a man with $4,000 may save nothing. But out of any dollar added to their respective incomes, both may save sums that are not so very different. In other words, it is true that the upper brackets save more of their *total* income; it is somewhat doubtful that they save much more than the poor also out of an *increase* in income. A change in income—up or down—seems to lead to a fairly similar change in saving for upper and lower brackets alike.

If this is so, a redistribution of income from rich to poor would cause the poor to begin saving possibly as much as the rich would cease to save. Redistribution, on these premises, would not greatly change the volume of saving out of current income. It would not help to cure a depression brought on by oversaving. By the same token, it would not greatly cut into the savings needed by a fast-growing, high-employment economy. The statistical facts which deprived the liberals of a favorite argument for redistribution have robbed conservatives of an old war horse in the struggle against the egalitarians.

The statistical findings, however, are not entirely clear cut.

It is not only the quantity but also the quality of savings that counts. Industry needs venture capital, and that is not usually supplied by insurance companies buying bonds nor even by pension funds buying blue chip stocks. Venture capital typically comes from wealthy individuals. To dry up their savings would still create an important gap in our financial structure, even though dollarwise they could be replaced from other sources. This much can fairly be argued by those who see a threat in equalization.

On the firing line against egalitarianism, we find also a belief, sometimes a little camouflaged, in the need for an elite—cultural, intellectual, political, economic. Stated in terms of a need for a privileged aristocracy, the view sounds offensive to American ears. The belief in the virtues of a leisure class, in particular, has taken a bad drubbing at the hands of Thorstein Veblen—in the one country where a leisure class proper has scarcely existed. But when the idea is reformulated in terms of "leadership," many people will probably be inclined to agree that something of this sort, based on merit, is needed. Most of the great achievements that history remembers or contemporaries admire are very clearly connected with the existence of a leadership group.

In a minor key, the need for leadership in consumption is readily arguable. Our own experience shows the advantages, for instance, of consumer pioneering. We are all ready to keep up with the Joneses, provided there are Joneses to keep up with. Anyone will buy something that is a necessity, but someone first has to smooth its transition from luxury to the more humdrum status. Conspicuous consumption, in a country constantly offering new kinds of goods, is creative consumption. An egalitarian society promises to be virtuous, frugal and dull.

These ideas do not lend themselves to quantification. It is impossible to say how concentrated wealth should be to stimulate the creation of luxuries, and how well spread to speed up their conversion to mass necessities. To push the need for consumer pioneering very hard smacks unpleasantly of snobbism. But to reject the notion altogether would be evidence of the very egalitarian conformism against which it protests.

One further point deserves to be made. Economic inequality is not purely an economic affair. It touches also upon political stability and social cohesion. In an extreme case, inequality may lead to revolution. So may overzealous efforts to reduce it. A distribution of income that is widely resented may, even though it is economically efficient, do more political harm than economic good. Slower progress would have to be written off as the cost of political and social betterment.

Added to its probable price in terms of growth, action to alter the distribution of income determined by the market is likely to impose a non-economic cost. Typically, this cost takes the form of lengthening the reach of government. Something, somebody, has to be registered, regulated, controlled. A little freedom always goes by the board. Some economic resources, too, that could perhaps be more productively employed must be shifted to this function. If anyone thinks that this is altogether a negligible matter, let him note the lack of enthusiasm with which taxpayers vote the means for even the most pressing functions of government.

How Much Inequality? · We may safely conclude that progress will come faster if some degree of inequality is tolerated. The right man must be put into the right job and given the right incentives. Savings must be kept flowing, and the taste for risk-taking kept alive. There must be scope for consumer pioneering. In addition, we can save ourselves some added regimentation if we are willing to push less hard for equality. All this supports the case for accepting a certain measure of inequality.

A certain measure—but how much? The range is wide, from literal and absolute equality to the equally implausible state of an Eastern potentate of the old days surrounded by a subsistence population. Neither condition commends itself as a base for progress.

Unfortunately, most of the considerations that argue against complete equality desert us when we want to know about the right degree of inequality. Only the market criterion has an answer. It says, in effect, "Put each man in the job which he does best, and pay him what he is worth in it." If we expand this idea to cover also the employment of peoples' savings—pay each type of capital, venturesome or timid or in between, what it produces in its proper use—we end up with a distribution of income according to the market's valuation.

But the market criterion is only one among several. If we judge the desirable degree of inequality according to the incentives that are needed, we may find that the market criterion over-shoots the goal. A man may feel himself driven to do his best in response to a reward that would underpay him according to his market value. Why not tax away the difference?

The savings criterion, too, is tantalizingly unspecific. Would a strong concentration of income, if it tends toward higher saving, mean faster progress? It probably would, if that income is con-centrated in the hands of an authoritarian government which channels into investment every cent above a low level of con-sumption. It would not lead to much progress, however, if the recipient were an old style potentate surrounded by a popula-tion without purchasing power, without wants—in short, without a market.

The consumer-pioneering criterion of inequality, finally, is likewise more emphatic than specific in its advice. What sort of inequality does it imply? The sort that enabled the Medicis to subsidize Renaissance art and literature? Or the kind that allows the Joneses to have a new portable grill ahead of the rest of us? In the absence of specific answers to such questions, the optimum inequality remains very much a matter of opinion.

The Other America

MICHAEL HARRINGTON

Michael Harrington, a free-lance writer, was perhaps the first to focus nationwide attention on the poverty issue in his book, The Other America, *first published in 1962. The following selection is from chapter one, "The Invisible Land."*

THERE IS a familiar America. It is celebrated in speeches and advertised on television and in the magazines. It has the highest mass standard of living the world has ever known.

In the 1950's this America worried about itself, yet even its anxieties were products of abundance. The title of a brilliant book was widely misinterpreted, and the familiar America began to call itself "the affluent society." There was introspection about Madison Avenue and tail fins; there was discussion of the emotional suffering taking place in the suburbs. In all this, there was an implicit assumption that the basic grinding economic problems had been solved in the United States.

While this discussion was carried on, there existed another America. In it dwelt somewhere between 40,000,000 and 50,000,000 citizens of this land. They were poor. They still are. Tens of millions of Americans are, at this very moment, maimed in body and spirit, existing at levels beneath those necessary for human decency. If these people are not starving, they are hungry, and sometimes fat with hunger, for that is what cheap foods do. They are without adequate housing and education and medical care.

The Government has documented what this means to the bodies of the poor. But even more basic, this poverty twists and deforms the spirit. The American poor are pessimistic and defeated, and they are victimized by mental suffering to a degree unknown in Suburbia.

The millions who are poor in the United States tend to become increasingly invisible. Here is a great mass of people, yet it takes an effort of the intellect and will even to see them. The other America, the America of poverty, is hidden today in a way that it never was before. Its millions are socially invisible to the rest of us. No wonder that so many misinterpreted John Kenneth Galbraith's title and assumed that "the affluent society" meant that everyone had a decent standard of life. The misinterpretation was true as far as the actual day-to-day lives of two-thirds of the nation were concerned. Thus, one must begin a description of the other America by understanding why we do not see it.

There are perennial reasons that make the other America an invisible land.

Poverty is often off the beaten track. It always has been. The ordinary tourist never left the main highway, and today he rides interstate turnpikes. He does not go into the valleys of Pennsylvania where the towns look like movie sets of Wales in the thirties. He does not see the company houses in rows, the rutted roads (the poor always have bad roads whether they live in the city, in towns, or on farms), and everything is black and dirty. And even if he were to pass through such a place by accident, the tourist would not meet the unemployed men in the bar or the women coming home from a runaway sweatshop.

Then, too, beauty and myths are perennial masks of poverty. The traveler comes to the Appalachians in the lovely season. He sees the hills, the streams, the foliage—but not the poor. Or perhaps he looks at a run-down mountain house and, remembering Rousseau rather than seeing with his eyes, decides that "those people" are truly fortunate to be living the way they are and that they are lucky to be exempt from the strains and tensions of the middle class. The only problem is that "those people," the quaint inhabitants of those hills, are undereducated, underprivileged, lack medical care, and are in the process of being forced from the land into a life in the cities, where they are misfits.

These are normal and obvious cases of the invisibility of the poor. They operated a generation ago; they will be functioning a generation hence. It is more important to understand that the very development of American society is creating a new kind of blindness about poverty. The poor are increasingly slipping out of the very experience and consciousness of the nation.

If the middle class never did like ugliness and poverty, it was at least aware of them. "Across the tracks" was not a very long way to go. There were forays into the slums at Christmas time; there were charitable organizations that brought contact with the poor. Occasionally, almost everyone passed through the Negro ghetto or the blocks of tenements, if only to get downtown to work or to entertainment.

Now the American city has been transformed. The poor still inhabit the miserable housing in the central area, but they are increasingly isolated from contact with, or sight of, anybody else. Middle-class women coming in from Suburbia on a rare trip may catch the merest glimpse of the other America on the way to an evening at the theater, but their children are segregated in suburban schools. The business or professional man may drive along the fringes of slums in a car or bus, but it is not an important experience to him. The failures, the unskilled, the disabled, the aged, and the minorities are right there, across the tracks, where they have always been. But hardly anyone else is.

In short, the very development of the American city has removed poverty from the living, emotional experience of millions upon millions of middle-class Americans. Living out in the suburbs, it is easy to assume that ours is, indeed, an affluent society.

This new segregation of poverty is compounded by a well-meaning ignorance. A good many concerned and sympathetic Americans are aware that there is much discussion of urban renewal. Suddenly, driving through the city, they notice that a familiar slum has been torn down and that there are towering, modern buildings where once there had been tenements or hovels. There is a warm feeling of satisfaction, of pride in the way things are working out: the poor, it is obvious, are being taken care of.

The irony in this is that the truth is nearly the exact opposite to the impression. The total impact of the various housing programs in postwar America has been to squeeze more and more people into existing slums. More often than not, the modern apartment in a towering building rents at $40 a room or more. For, during the past decade and a half, there has been more subsidization of middle- and upper-income housing than there has been of housing for the poor.

Clothes make the poor invisible too: America has the best-dressed poverty the world has ever known. For a variety of reasons, the benefits of mass production have been spread much more evenly in this area than in many others. It is much easier in the United States to be decently dressed than it is to be decently housed, fed, or doctored. Even people with terribly depressed incomes can look prosperous. There are tens of thousands of Americans in the big cities who are wearing shoes, perhaps even a stylishly cut suit or dress, and yet are hungry. It is not a matter of planning, though it almost seems as if the affluent society had given out costumes to the poor so that they would not offend the rest of society with the sight of rags.

Then, many of the poor are the wrong age to be seen. A good number of them (over 8,000,000) are sixty-five years of age or better; an even larger number are under eighteen. The aged members of the other America are often sick, and they cannot move. Another group of them live out their lives in loneliness and frustration: they sit in rented rooms, or else they stay close to a house in a neighborhood that has completely changed from the old days. Indeed, one of the worst aspects of poverty among the aged is that these people are out of sight and out of mind, and alone.

The young are somewhat more visible, yet they too stay close to their neighborhoods. Sometimes they advertise their poverty through a lurid tabloid story about a gang killing. But generally they do not disturb the quiet streets of the middle class.

And finally, the poor are politically invisible. It is one of the cruelest ironies of social life in advanced countries that the dispossessed at the bottom of society are unable to speak for themselves. The people of the other America do not, by far and large, belong to unions, to fraternal organizations, or to political parties. They are without lobbies of their own; they put forward no legislative program. As a group, they are atomized. They have no face; they have no voice.

Thus, there is not even a cynical political motive for caring about the poor, as in the old days. Because the slums are no longer centers of powerful political organizations, the politicians need not really care about their inhabitants. The slums are no longer visible to the middle class, so much of the idealistic urge to fight for those who need help is gone. Only the social agencies have a really direct involvement with the other America, and they are without any great political power.

Forty to 50,000,000 people are becoming increasingly invisible. That is a shocking fact. But there is a second basic irony of poverty that is equally important: if one is to make the mistake of being born poor, he should choose a time when the majority of the people are miserable too.

John Kenneth Galbraith develops this idea in *The Affluent Society,* and in doing so defines the "newness" of the kind of poverty in contemporary America. The old poverty, Galbraith notes, was general. It was the condition of life of an entire society, or at least of that huge majority who were without special skills or the luck of birth. When the entire economy advanced, a good many of these people gained higher standards of living. Unlike the poor today, the majority poor of a generation ago were an immediate (if cynical) concern of political leaders. The old slums of the immigrants had the votes; they provided the basis for labor organizations; their very numbers could be a powerful force in political conflict. At the same time the new technology required higher skills, more education, and stimulated an upward movement for millions.

Perhaps the most dramatic case of the power of the majority poor took place in the 1930's. The Congress of Industrial Organizations literally organized millions in a matter of years. A labor movement that had been declining and confined to a thin stratum of the highly skilled suddenly embraced masses of men and women in basic industry. At the same time this acted as a pressure upon the Government, and the New Deal codified some of the social gains in laws like the Wagner Act. The result was not a basic transformation of the American system, but it did transform the lives of an entire section of the population.

In the thirties one of the reasons for these advances was that misery was general. There was no need then to write books about unemployment and poverty. That was the decisive social experience of the entire society, and the apple sellers even invaded Wall Street. There was political sympathy from middle-class reformers; there were an elan and spirit that grew out of a deep crisis.

Some of those who advanced in the thirties did so because they had unique and individual personal talents. But for the great mass, it was a question of being at the right point in the economy at the right time in history, and utilizing that position for common struggle. Some of those who failed did so because they did not have the will to take advantage of new opportunities. But for the most part the poor who were left behind had been at the wrong place in the economy at the wrong moment in history.

These were the people in the unorganizable jobs, in the South, in the minority groups, in the fly-by-night factories that were low on capital and high on labor. When some of them did break into the economic mainstream—when, for instance, the CIO opened up the way for some Negroes to find good industrial jobs—they proved to be as resourceful as anyone else. As a group, the other Americans who stayed behind were not originally composed primarily of individual failures. Rather, they were victims of an impersonal process that selected some for progress and discriminated against others.

Out of the thirties came the welfare state. Its creation had been stimulated by mass impoverishment and misery, yet it helped the poor least of all. Laws like unemployment compensation, the Wagner Act, the various farm programs, all these were designed for the middle third in the cities, for the organized workers, and for the upper third in the country, for the big market farmers. If a man works in an extremely low-paying job, he may not even be covered by social security or other welfare programs. If he receives unemployment compensation, the payment is scaled down according to his low earnings.

One of the major laws that was designed to cover everyone, rich and poor, was social security. But even here the other Americans suffered discrimination. Over the years social security payments have not even provided a subsistence level of life. The middle third have been able to supplement the Federal pension through private plans negotiated by unions, through joining medical insurance schemes like Blue Cross, and so on. The poor have not been able to do so. They lead a bitter life, and then have to pay for that fact in old age.

Indeed, the paradox that the welfare state benefits those least who need help most is but a single instance of a persistent irony in the other America. Even when the money finally trickles down, even when a school is built in a poor neighborhood, for instance, the poor are still deprived. Their entire environment, their life, their values, do not prepare them to take advantage of the new opportunity. The parents are anxious for the children to go to work; the pupils are pent up, waiting for the moment when their education has complied with the law.

Today's poor, in short, missed the political and social gains of the thirties. They are, as Galbraith rightly points out, the first minority poor in history, the first poor not to be seen, the first poor whom the politicians could leave alone.

The first step toward the new poverty was taken when millions of people proved immune to progress. When that happened, the failure was not individual and personal, but a social product. But once the historic accident takes place, it begins to become a personal fate.

The new poor of the other America saw the rest of society move ahead. They went on living in depressed areas, and often they tended to become depressed human beings. In some of the West Virginia towns, for instance, an entire community will become shabby and defeated. The young and the adventurous go to the city, leaving behind those who cannot move and those who lack the will to do so. The entire area becomes permeated with failure, and that is one more reason the big corporations shy away.

Indeed, one of the most important things about the new poverty is that it cannot be defined in simple, statistical terms. If a group has internal vitality, a will—if it has aspiration—it may live in dilapidated housing, it may eat an inadequate diet, and it may suffer poverty, but it is not impoverished. So it was in those ethnic slums of the immigrants that played such a dramatic role in the unfolding of the American dream. The people found themselves in slums, but they were not slum dwellers.

But the new poverty is constructed so as to destroy aspiration; it is a system designed to be impervious to hope. The other America does not contain the adventurous seeking a new life and land. It is populated by the failures, by those driven from the land and bewildered by the city, by old people suddenly confronted with the torments of loneliness and poverty, and by minorities facing a wall of prejudice.

In the past, when poverty was general in the unskilled and semi-skilled work force, the poor were all mixed together. The bright and the dull, those who were going to escape into the great society and those who were to stay behind, all of them lived on the same street. When the middle third rose, this community was destroyed. And the entire invisible land of the other Americans became a ghetto, a modern poor farm for the rejects of society and of the economy.

It is a blow to reform and the political hopes of the poor that the middle class no longer understands that poverty exists. But, perhaps more important, the poor are losing their links with the great world. If statistics and sociology can measure a feeling as delicate as loneliness, the other America is becoming increasingly populated by those who do not belong to anybody or anything. They are no longer participants in an ethnic culture from the old country; they are less and less religious; they do not belong to unions or clubs. They are not seen, and because of that they themselves cannot see. Their horizon has become more and more restricted; they see one another, and that means they see little reason to hope.

Galbraith was one of the first writers to begin to describe the newness of contemporary poverty, and that is to his credit. Yet because even he underestimates the problem, it is important to put his definition into perspective.

For Galbraith, there are two main components of the new poverty: case poverty and insular poverty. Case poverty is the plight of those who suffer from some physical or mental disability that is personal and individual and excludes them from the general advance. Insular poverty exists in areas like the Appalachians or the West Virginia coal fields, where an entire section of the country becomes economically obsolete.

Physical and mental disabilities are, to be sure, an important part of poverty in America. The poor are sick in body and in spirit. But this is not an isolated fact about them, an individual "case," a stroke of bad luck. Disease, alcoholism, low IQ's, these express a whole way of life. They are, in the main, the effects of an environment, not the biographies of unlucky individuals. Because of this, the new poverty is something that cannot be dealt with by first aid. If there is to be a lasting assault on the shame of the other America, it must seek to root out of this society an entire environment, and not just the relief of individuals.

But perhaps the idea of "insular" poverty is even more dangerous. To speak of "islands" of the poor (or, in the more popular term, of "pockets of poverty") is to imply that one is confronted by a serious, but relatively minor, problem. This is hardly a description of a misery that extends to 40,000,000 or 50,000,000 people in the United States. They have remained impoverished in spite of increasing productivity and the creation of a welfare state. That fact alone should suggest the dimensions of a serious and basic situation.

Finally, one might summarize the newness of contemporary poverty by saying: These are the people who are immune to progress. But then the facts are even more cruel. The other Americans are the victims of the very inventions and machines that have provided a higher living standard for the rest of the society. They are upside-down in the economy, and for them greater productivity often means worse jobs; agricultural advance becomes hunger.

In the optimistic theory, technology is an undisguised blessing. A general increase in productivity, the argument goes, generates a higher standard of living for the whole people. And indeed, this has been true for the middle and upper thirds of American society, the people who made such striking gains in the last two decades. But the poor, if they were given to theory, might argue the exact opposite. They might say: Progress is misery.

As the society became more technological, more skilled, those who learn to work the machines, who get the expanding education, move up. Those who miss out at the very start find themselves at a new disadvantage. A generation ago in American life, the majority of the working people did not have high-school educations. But at that time industry was organized on a lower level of skill and competence. And there was a sort of continuum in the shop: the youth who left school at sixteen could begin as a laborer, and gradually pick up skill as he went along.

Today the situation is quite different. The good jobs require much more academic preparation, much more skill from the very outset. Those who lack a high-school education tend to be condemned to the economic underworld—to low-paying service industries, to backward factories, to sweeping and janitorial duties. If the fathers and mothers of the contemporary poor were penalized a generation ago for their lack of schooling, their children will suffer all the more. The very rise in productivity that created more money and better working conditions for the rest of the society can be a menace to the poor.

But then this technological revolution might have an even more disastrous consequence: it could increase the ranks of the poor as well as intensify the disabilities of poverty. At this point it is too early to make any final judgment, yet there are obvious danger signals. There are millions of Americans who live just the other side of poverty. When a recession comes, they are pushed onto the relief rolls. If automation continues to inflict more and more penalties on the unskilled and the semiskilled, it could have the impact of permanently increasing the population of the other America.

Even more explosive is the possibility that people who participated in the gains of the thirties and the forties will be pulled back down into poverty. Today the mass-production industries where unionization made such a difference are contracting. Jobs are being destroyed. In the process, workers who had achieved a certain level of wages, who had won working conditions in the shop, are suddenly confronted with impoverishment. This is particularly true for anyone over forty years of age and for members of minority groups. Once their job is abolished, their chances of ever getting similar work are very slim.

It is too early to say whether or not this phenomenon is temporary, or whether it represents a massive retrogression that will swell the numbers of the poor. To a large extent, the answer to this question will be determined by the political response of the United States in the sixties. If serious and massive action is not undertaken, it may be necessary for statisticians to add some old-fashioned, pre-welfare-state poverty to the misery of the other America.

Poverty in the 1960's is invisible and it is new, and both these factors make it more tenacious. It is more isolated and politically powerless than ever before. It is laced with ironies, not the least of which is that many of the poor view progress upside-down, as a menace and a threat to their lives. And if the nation does not measure up to the challenge of automation, poverty in the 1960's might be on the increase.

There are mighty historical and economic forces that keep the poor down; and there are human beings who help out in this grim business, many of them unwittingly. There are socio-logical and political reasons why poverty is not seen; and there are misconceptions and prejudices that literally blind the eyes. The latter must be understood if anyone is to make the necessary act of intellect and will so that the poor can be noticed.

Here is the most familiar version of social blindness: "The poor are that way because they are afraid of work. And anyway they all have big cars. If they were like me (or my father or my grandfather), they could pay their own way. But they prefer to live on the dole and cheat the taxpayers."

This theory, usually thought of as a virtuous and moral state-ment, is one of the means of making it impossible for the poor ever to pay their way. There are, one must assume, citizens of the other America who choose impoverishment out of fear of work. But the real explanation of why the poor are where they are is that they made the mistake of being born to the wrong parents, in the wrong section of the country, in the wrong indus-try, or in the wrong racial or ethnic group. Once that mistake has been made, they could have been paragons of will and morality, but most of them would never even have had a chance to get out of the other America.

There are two important ways of saying this: The poor are caught in a vicious circle; or, The poor live in a culture of poverty.

In a sense, one might define the contemporary poor in the United States as those who, for reasons beyond their control, cannot help themselves. All the most decisive factors making for opportunity and advance are against them. They are born going downward, and most of them stay down. They are victims whose lives are endlessly blown round and round the other America.

Here is one of the most familiar forms of the vicious circle of poverty. The poor get sick more than anyone else in the society. That is because they live in slums, jammed together under unhygienic conditions; they have inadequate diets, and cannot get decent medical care. When they become sick, they are sick longer than any other group in the society. Because they are sick more often and longer than anyone else, they lose wages and work, and find it difficult to hold a steady job. And because of this, they cannot pay for good housing, for a nutritious diet, for doctors. At any given point in the circle, particularly when there is a major illness, their prospect is to move to an even lower level and to begin the cycle, round and round, toward even more suffering.

This is only one example of the vicious circle. Each group in the other America has its own particular version of the experience. But the pattern, whatever its variations, is basic to the other America.

The individual cannot usually break out of this vicious circle. Neither can the group, for it lacks the social energy and political strength to turn its misery into a cause. Only the larger society, with its help and resources, can really make it possible for these people to help themselves. Yet those who could make the difference too often refuse to act because of their ignorant, smug moralisms. They view the effects of poverty—above all, the warping of the will and spirit that is a consequence of being poor—as choices. Understanding the vicious circle is an important step in breaking down this prejudice.

What shall we tell the American poor, once we have seen them? Shall we say to them that they are better off than the Indian poor, the Italian poor, the Russian poor? That is one answer, but it is heartless. I should put it another way. I want to tell every well-fed and optimistic American that it is intolerable that so many millions should be maimed in body and in spirit when it is not necessary that they should be. My standard of comparison is not how much worse things used to be. It is how much better they could be if only we were stirred.

Economic Opportunity Act of 1964:
Message to the Congress on Poverty

LYNDON B. JOHNSON

On March 16, 1964 President Johnson presented these proposals to combat poverty to the Congress of the United States.

WE ARE CITIZENS of the richest and most fortunate nation in the history of the world. One hundred and eighty years ago we were a small country struggling for survival on the margin of a hostile land. Today we have established a civilization of free men which spans an entire continent. With the growth of our country has come opportunity for our people—opportunity to educate our children, to use our energies in productive work, to increase our leisure—opportunity for almost every American to hope that through work and talent he could create a better life for himself and his family.

The path forward has not been an easy one. But we have never lost sight of our goal—an America in which every citizen shares all the opportunities of his society, in which every man has a chance to advance his welfare to the limit of his capacities. We have come a long way toward this goal. We still have a long way to go. The distance which remains is the measure of the great unfinished work of our society. To finish that work I have called for a national war on poverty. Our objective—total victory.

There are millions of Americans—one fifth of our people—who have not shared in the abundance which has been granted to most of us, and on whom the gates of opportunity have been closed. What does this poverty mean to those who endure it? It means a daily struggle to secure the necessities for even a meager existence. It means that the abundance, the comforts, the opportunities they see all around them are beyond their grasp. Worst of all, it means hopelessness for the young.

The young man or woman who grows up without a decent education, in a broken home, in a hostile and squalid environment, in ill health or in the face of racial injustice, that young man or woman is often trapped in a life of poverty. He does not have the skills demanded by a complex society. He does not know how to acquire those skills. He faces a mounting sense of despair which drains initiative and ambition and energy.

Our tax cut will create millions of new jobs—new exits from poverty. But we must also strike down all the barriers which keep many from using those exits. The war on poverty is not a struggle simply to support people, to make them dependent on the generosity of others. It is a struggle to give people a chance. It is an effort to allow them to develop and use their capacities, as we have been allowed to develop and use ours, so that they can share, as others share, in the promise of this Nation.

We do this, first of all, because it is right that we should. From the establishment of public education and land-grant colleges through agricultural extension and encouragement to industry, we have pursued the goal of a nation with full and increasing opportunities for all its citizens. The war on poverty is a further step in that pursuit.

We do it also because helping some will increase the prosperity of all. Our fight against poverty will be an investment in the most valuable of our resources: the skills and strength of our people. And in the future, as in the past, this investment will return its cost manyfold to our entire economy. If we can raise the annual earnings of 10 million among the poor by only $1,000 we will have added $14 billion a year to our national output. In addition we can make important reductions in public assistance payments which now cost us $4 billion a year, and in the large costs of fighting crime and delinquency, disease and hunger. This is only part of the story.

Our history has proved that each time we broaden the base of abundance, giving more people the chance to produce and consume, we create new industry, higher production, increased earnings, and better income for all. Giving new opportunity to those who have little will enrich the lives of all the rest. Because it is right, because it is wise, and because, for the first time in our history, it is possible to conquer poverty, I submit, for the consideration of the Congress and the country, the Economic Opportunity Act of 1964.

This Act does not merely expand old programs or improve

what is already being done. It charts a new course. It strikes at the causes, not just the consequences of poverty. It can be a milestone in our 180-year search for a better life for our people. The Act provides five basic opportunities:

It will give almost half a million underprivileged young Americans the opportunity to develop skills, continue education, and find useful work.

It will give every American community the opportunity to develop a comprehensive plan to fight its own poverty—and help them to carry out their plans.

It will give dedicated Americans the opportunity to enlist as volunteers in the war against poverty.

It will give many workers and farmers the opportunity to break through particular barriers which bar their escape from poverty.

It will give the entire Nation the opportunity for a concerted attack on poverty through the establishment, under my direction, of the Office of Economic Opportunity, a national headquarters for the war against poverty.

This is how we propose to create these opportunities:

First, we will give high priority to helping young Americans who lack skills, who have not completed their education or who cannot complete it because they are too poor. I, therefore, recommend the creation of a Job Corps, a work-training program, and a work-study program. A new national Job Corps will build toward an enlistment of 100,000 young men. They will be drawn from those whose background, health, and education make them least fit for useful work. Those who volunteer will enter more than 100 camps and centers around the country. Half of these young men will work, in the first year, on special conservation projects to give them education and useful work experience, and to enrich the natural resources of the country. Half of these young men will receive, in the first year, a blend of training, basic education and work experience in job training centers. These are not simply camps for the underprivileged. They are new educational institutions, comparable in innovation to the land-grant colleges. Those who enter them will emerge better qualified to play a productive role in American society.

A new national work-training program operated by the Department of Labor will provide work and training for 200,000 American men and women between the ages of 16 and 21. This will be developed through State and local governments and non-profit agencies. Hundreds of thousands of young Americans badly need the experience, the income, and the sense of purpose which useful full or part-time work can bring. For them such work may mean the difference between finishing school or dropping out. Vital community activities, from hospitals and playgrounds to libraries and settlement houses, are suffering because there are not enough people to staff them. We are simply bringing these needs together.

A new national work-study program operated by the Department of Health, Education, and Welfare will provide Federal funds for part-time jobs for 140,000 young Americans who do not go to college because they cannot afford it. There is no more senseless waste than the waste of the brainpower and skill of those who are kept from college by economic circumstance. Under this program they will, in a great American tradition, be able to work their way through school. They and the country will be richer for it.

Second, through a new community action program we intend to strike at poverty at its source—in the streets of our cities and on the farms of our countryside, among the very young and the impoverished old. This program asks men and women throughout the country to prepare long-range plans for the attack on poverty in their own local communities. These are not plans prepared in Washington and imposed upon hundreds of different situations. They are based on the fact that local citizens best understand their own problems, and know best how to deal with those problems. These plans will be local plans striking at the many unfilled needs which underlie poverty in each community, not just one or two. Their components and emphasis will differ as needs differ. They will be local plans calling upon all the resources available to the community—Federal and State, local and private, human and material. And when these plans are approved by the Office of Economic Opportunity, the Federal Government will finance up to 90 percent of the additional cost for the first two years.

The most enduring strength of our Nation is the huge reservoir of talent, initiative, and leadership which exists at every level of our society. Through the community action program we call upon this, our greatest strength, to overcome our greatest weakness.

Third, I ask for the authority to recruit and train skilled volunteers for the war against poverty. Thousands of Americans have volunteered to serve the needs of other lands. Thousands more want the chance to serve the needs of their own land. They should have that chance.

Fourth, we intend to create new opportunities for certain hard-hit groups to break out of the pattern of poverty. Through a new program of loans and guarantees we can provide incentives to those who will employ the unemployed. Through programs of work and retraining for unemployed fathers and mothers we can help them support their families in dignity while preparing themselves for new work. Through funds to purchase needed land, organize cooperatives, and create new and adequate family farms we can help those whose life on the land has been a struggle without hope.

Fifth, I do not intend that the war against poverty become a series of uncoordinated and unrelated efforts—that it perish for lack of leadership and direction. Therefore this bill creates, in the Executive Office of the President, a new Office of Economic Opportunity. Its Director will be my personal chief of staff for the war against poverty. He will be directly responsible for these new programs. He will work with and through existing agencies of the Government.

The Congress is charged by the Constitution to "provide * * * for the general welfare of the United States." Our present abundance is a measure of its success in fulfilling that duty. Now Congress is being asked to extend that welfare to all our people.

Approaches to the Reduction of Poverty: I

ROBERT J. LAMPMAN

Robert J. Lampman, Professor of Economics at the University of Wisconsin, presented this paper at a session of the American Economic Association meetings in December 1964 on "The Economics of Poverty."

THE GREATEST ACCOMPLISHMENT of modern economies has been the raising of living standards of the common man and the reduction of the share of the population in poverty. Contrary to the gloomy predictions of Malthus, production has increased faster than population and, unlike the expectations of Marx, inequality of income has not steadily increased. The growth in value of product per person is generally understood to arise out of more capital, economies of scale and specialization, better management and organization, innovation with regard both to end products and techniques of production, greater mobility of factors, and improved quality of labor. All of these in turn yield additional income which, in a benign spiral, makes possible more and higher quality inputs for further growth.

The process of growth has not meant simply higher property incomes. As a matter of fact, income from property has fallen as a share of national income. Neither has growth meant a widening of differential for skill in labor incomes. Rates of pay for the most menial of tasks have tended to rise with average productivity. Social policies in fields such as labor and education aimed at assuring opportunities for all have narrowed initial advantages of the more fortunate. Such policies, along with taxation, social insurance, and public assistance measures which redistribute income toward the poor have tended to stabilize if not reduce the degree of the income inequality.

A growth in productivity of 2 percent per person per year and a relatively fixed pattern of income inequality probably have combined to yield a net reduction in poverty in most decades of American history. However, the rate of reduction has undoubtedly varied with changes in the growth rate, shifts from prosperity to depression, changes in immigration, in age composition, and in differential family size by income level.

The Poverty Rate and the Poverty Income Gap · Using a present-day standard for poverty and even without recognizing the relativity of poverty over long periods, we would estimate that poverty had become a condition that afflicted only a minority of Americans by the second decade of this century. This situation was upset by the Great Depression of the 1930's but later restored by the booming economy of World War II. The postwar period has yielded a somewhat above average rate of growth in productivity and a reduction in poverty which probably is at least average for recent decades. The number of families in poverty (as marked off from nonpoverty by a $3,000 income at 1962 prices) fell from 12 million in 1947 to 9 million in 1963. This was a drop from 32 percent to 19 percent of families.

The rate of reduction one records or predicts will vary somewhat with the definition of poverty which he adopts. The Council of Economic Advisers adopted an income cut-off of $3,000 of total money income for families and $1,500 for unrelated individuals.[1] It is not inconsistent with those guidelines to make further modification for family size, using $3,000 as the mark for an urban family of four persons with variations of $500 per person and to set a lower mark for rural families. Such a procedure yields a slightly lower rate of reduction in the percentage of all persons in poverty than is suggested by the 32- to 19-percent drop shown above. This discrepancy is due to a shift in family size and the rural to urban migration during the postwar years.

It is possible that consideration of personal income as opposed to total money income, of average rather than one year's income, of assets and extraordinary needs as well as income, and of related matters would alter our understanding of how poverty has been reduced. It is clear that some of these considerations affect the number and the composition of the population counted as poor; and it is obvious that the rate of reduction would vary if we varied the poverty line over time.

These matters of definition are important to a refinement of the generalized goal of elimination of poverty to which President

1. *Annual Report* (1964), Chap. 2.

Johnson has called us. Economists can assist in reaching a national consensus on the specific nature of the goal, of ways to measure the distance from and rate of movement toward the goal.

At this point in time, poverty is clearly a condition which afflicts only a minority—a dwindling minority—of Americans. The recent average rate of change, namely, a fall in the percentage of families in poverty by one percentage point per year, suggests that the poverty problem is about twenty years from solution. This rate of reduction may be difficult to maintain as we get down to a hard core of poverty and a situation in which further growth will not contribute to the reduction of the poverty rate. My own view is that this rate is still highly responsive to changes in the growth rate and that it will continue to be so for some time ahead. The relationship between the two rates is a complex one and is influenced by such things as demographic change, changes in labor force participation, occupational shifts in demands for labor, and derived changes in property incomes and social security benefits. Some groups—notably the aged, the disabled, and the broken families—have poverty rates that appear to be relatively immune to growth in average income. One powerful drag on the responsiveness of the poverty rate to growth, which has now about run its course and will shortly reverse, is the aging and reduction in labor force participation of family heads.

While the size of the poverty population is dwindling, the size of what can be called the "poverty income gap" is diminishing. This gap—the aggregate amount by which the present poor population's income falls short of $3,000 per family or $1,500 per unrelated individual—is now about $12 billion, or 2 percent of GNP. As time goes on this gap will assuredly be less, both because of economic growth and because of scheduled increases in social insurance benefits. (Transfers now make up about $10 billion of the $25 billion income of the poor.) Projecting recent rates of change suggests that by 1975 the poor will be no more than 12 percent of the population and the poverty income gap will be as little as 1 percent of that year's GNP.

As I see it, the goal of eliminating poverty needs to have a time dimension and intermediate targets. I assume we want a rate of progress at least as fast as that of recent years. Further, it helps to think of the goal in two parts: the reduction of the poverty rate and the reduction of the poverty income gap. This means we want to work from the top down and from the bottom up, so to speak. The aim of policy should be to do each type of reduction without slowing the other and to do both with the least possible sacrifice of and the greatest possible contribution to other important goals.

Why Poverty Persists · As background to such strategic decisions, it is useful to categorize the causes of poverty in today's economy. But perhaps it is necessary first to brush aside the idea that there has to be some given amount of poverty. Most economists have long since given up the idea that a progressive society needs the threat of poverty to induce work and sobriety in the lower classes. Similarly, one can consign to folklore the ideas that some are rich only because others are poor and exploited, that if none were poor then necessary but unpleasant jobs would go undone, that the middle class has a psychological need to exclude a minority from above-poverty living standards, and that poverty is a necessary concomitant of the unemployment which necessarily accompanies economic growth.

Why, then, is it that there remains a minority of persons who are involuntarily poor in this affluent society? How does our system select the particular members for this minority? To the latter question we offer a three-part answer: (1) Events external to individuals select a number to be poor. (2) Social barriers of caste, class, and custom denominate persons with certain characteristics to run a high risk of being poor. (3) The market assigns a high risk of being poor to those with limited ability or motivations.

One cannot look at the data on who are the poor without sensing that many are poor because of events beyond their control. Over a third of the 35 million poor are children whose misfortune arises out of the chance assignment to poor parents. In some cases this poverty comes out of being members of unusually large families. Among the poor adults, about a third have either suffered a disability, premature death of the family breadwinner, or family dissolution. A considerable number have confronted a declining demand for services in their chosen occupation, industry, or place of residence. Some have outlived their savings or have lost them due to inflation or bank failure. For many persons who are otherwise "normal" poverty may be said to arise out of one or a combination of such happenings.

A second factor that operates in the selection of persons to be poor is the maintenance of social barriers in the form of caste, class, and custom. The clearest example of this, of course, is racial discrimination with regard to opportunities to qualify for and to obtain work. (It is perhaps worth emphasizing here that only a fifth of the present poor are nonwhite, and that only a minority of the nonwhites are presently poor.) Similar types of arbitrary barriers or market imperfections are observable in the case of sex, age, residence, religion, education, and seniority. They are formalized in employer hiring procedures, in the rules of unions and professional and trade associations, in governmental regulations concerning housing and welfare and other programs, and are informally expressed in customer preferences. Barriers, once established, tend to be reinforced from the poverty side by the alienated themselves. The poor tend to be cut off from not only opportunity but even from information about opportunity. A poverty subculture develops which sustains attitudes and values that are hostile to escape from poverty. These barriers combine to make events nonrandom; e.g., unemployment is slanted away from those inside the feudalistic walls of collective bargaining, disability more commonly occurs in jobs reserved for those outside the barriers, the subculture of poverty invites or is prone to self-realizing forecasts of disaster.

The third factor involved in selecting persons out of the affluent society to be poor is limited ability or motivation of persons to earn and to protect themselves against events and to fight their way over the barriers.[2] To the extent that the market is perfect one can rationalize the selection for poverty (insofar as earnings alone are considered) on the basis of the abilities and skills needed by the market and the distribution of those abilities and skills in the population. But we note that ability is to some extent acquired or environmentally determined and that poverty tends to create personalities who will be de-selected by the market as inadequate on the basis of ability or motivation.

2. For an insight into the relative importance of this factor see James N. Morgan, Martin H. David, Wilbur J. Cohen, and Harvey E. Brazer, *Income and Welfare in the U.S.* (1962), pp. 196–98.

Countering "Events" · Approaches to the reduction of poverty can be seen as parallel to the causes or bases for selection recounted above. The first approach, then, is to prevent or counter the events or happenings which select some persons for poverty status. The poverty rate could be lessened by any reduction in early death, disability, family desertion, what John Kenneth Galbraith referred to as excessive procreation by the poor, or by containment of inflation and other hazards to financial security. Among the important events in this context the one most relevant to public policy consideration at this time is excessive unemployment. It would appear that if the recent level of over 5 percent unemployment could be reduced to 4 percent, the poverty rate would drop by about one percentage point.[3] Further fall in the poverty rate would follow if—by retaining and relocation of some workers—long-term unemployment could be cut or if unemployment could be more widely shared with the nonpoor.

To the extent that events are beyond prevention, some, e.g., disability, can be countered by remedial measures. Where neither the preventive nor the remedial approach is suitable, only the alleviative measures of social insurance and public assistance remain. And the sufficiency of these measures will help determine the poverty rate and the size of the poverty income gap. It is interesting to note that our system of public income maintenance, which now pays out $35 billion in benefits per year, is aimed more at the problem of income insecurity of the middle class and at blocking returns to poverty than in facilitating exits from poverty for those who have never been out of poverty. The nonpoor have the major claim to social insurance benefits, the levels of which in most cases are not adequate in themselves to keep a family out of poverty. Assistance payments of $4 billion now go to 8 million persons, all of whom are in the ranks of the poor, but

3. Unemployment is not strikingly different among the poor than the nonpoor. Nonparticipation in the labor force is more markedly associated with poverty than is unemployment. However, it seems that about 1 million poor family heads experience unemployment during the year. (*Census Population Reports,* P-60, No. 39, Feb. 28, 1963, Tables 15 and 16.) If half of this group were moved out of poverty by more nearly full employment, then the poverty rate would be one percentage point lower. Another way to estimate this is as follows. The national income would be $30 billion higher than it is if we had full employment. And a $30 billion increase in recent years has generally meant a full percentage point drop in the percent of families in poverty.

about half of the 35 million poor receive neither assistance nor social insurance payments. One important step in the campaign against poverty would be to reexamine our insurance and assistance programs to discover ways in which they could be more effective in helping people to get out of poverty. Among the ideas to be considered along this line are easier eligibility for benefits, higher minimum benefits, incentives to earn while receiving benefits, ways to combine work-relief, retraining, rehabilitation, and relocation with receipt of benefits.

Among the several events that select people for poverty, the ones about which we have done the least by social policy are family breakup by other than death and the event of being born poor. Both of these could be alleviated by a family allowance system, which the United States, almost alone among Western nations, lacks. We do, of course, have arrangements in the Federal individual income tax for personal deductions and exemptions whereby families of different size and composition are ranked for the imposition of progressive rates. However, it is a major irony of this system that it does not extend the full force of its allowances for children to the really poor. In order to do so, the tax system could be converted to have negative as well as positive rates, paying out grants as well as forgiving taxes on the basis of already adopted exemptions and rates. At present there are almost $20 billion of unused exemptions and deductions, most of which relate to families with children. Restricting the plan to such families and applying a negative tax rate of, say, 20 percent, to this amount would "yield" an allowance total of almost $4 billion. This would not in itself take many people out of poverty, but it would go a considerable distance toward closing the poverty income gap, which now aggregates about $12 billion.

It would, of course, be possible to go considerably further by this device without significantly impairing incentives to work and save. First, however, let me reject as unworkable any simple plan to assure a minimum income of $3,000. To make such an assurance would induce many now earning less than and even some earning slightly more than $3,000 to forego earnings opportunities and to accept the grant. Hence the poverty income gap of $12 billion would far understate the cost of such a minimum income plan. However, it would be practicable to enact a system of progressive rates articulated with the present income tax schedule.[4] The present rates fall from 70 percent at the top to 14 percent at income just above $3,700 for a family of five, to zero percent for income below $3,700. The average negative tax rates could move, then, from zero percent to minus 14 percent for, say, the unused exemptions that total $500, to 20 percent for those that total $1,000 and 40 percent for those that total $3,700. This would amount to a minimum income of $1,480 for a family of five; it would retain positive incentives through a set of grants that would gradually diminish as earned income rose.

The total amount to be paid out (interestingly, this would be shown in the federal budget as a net reduction in tax collections) under such a program would obviously depend upon the particular rates selected, the definition of income used, the types of income-receiving units declared eligible, and the offsets made in public assistance payments. But it clearly could be more than the $4 billion mentioned in connection with the more limited plan of a standard 20 percent negative tax rate. At the outset it might involve half the poverty income gap and total about $6 billion. This amount is approximately equal to the total federal, state, and local taxes now paid by the poor. Hence it would amount to a remission of taxes paid. As the number in poverty fell, the amount paid out under this plan would in turn diminish.

Breaking Down Barriers · The approaches discussed thus far are consistent with the view that poverty is the result of events which happen to people. But there are other approaches, including those aimed at removing barriers which keep people in poverty. Legislation and private, volunteer efforts to assure equal educational and employment opportunities can make a contribution in this direction. Efforts to randomize unemployment by area redevelopment and relocation can in some cases work to break down "islands of poverty." Public policy can prevent or modify the forming of a poverty subculture by city zoning laws, by public housing and by regulations of private housing, by school redistricting, by recreational, cultural, and public health programs. It is curious that medieval cities built walls to keep poverty outside. Present arrangements often work to bottle it up inside cities or parts of cities and thereby encourage poverty to function as its own cause.

4. Cf. Milton Friedman, *Capitalism and Freedom* (1962), pp. 192–93.

Improving Abilities and Motivations · The third broad approach
to accelerated reduction of poverty relates to the basis for selection referred to above as limited ability or motivation. The
process of economic growth works the poverty line progressively
deeper into the ranks of people who are below average in ability
or motivation, but meantime it should be possible to raise the
ability and motivation levels of the lowest. It is interesting that
few children, even those of below average ability, who are not
born and raised in poverty, actually end up in poverty as adults.
This suggests that poverty is to some extent an inherited disease.
But it also suggests that if poor children had the same opportunities, including preschool training and remedial health care, as
the nonpoor (even assuming no great breakthroughs of scientific
understandings), the rate of escape from poverty would be
higher. Even more fundamentally, we know that mental retarda-
tion as well as infant mortality and morbidity have an important
causal connection with inadequate prenatal care, which in turn
relates to low income of parents.

A belief in the economic responsiveness of poor youngsters to
improved educational opportunities underlies policies advocated
by many educational theorists from Jeremy Bentham to James B.
Conant. And this widely shared belief no doubt explains the emphasis which the Economic Opportunity Act places upon education and training. The appropriation under that Act, while it
seems small relative to the poverty income gap, is large relative
to present outlays for education of the poor. I would estimate
that the half-billion dollars or so thereby added increases the
national expenditure for this purpose by about one-seventh. To
raise the level of educational expenditure for poor children—who
are one-fifth of the nation's children but who consume about a
tenth of educational outlay—to equal that of the average would
cost in the neighborhood of $3 billion. Such an emphasis upon
education and training is justified by the fact that families
headed by young adults will tend, in a few years, to be the most
rapidly increasing group of poor families.

Approaches to the Reduction of Poverty: II

HARRY G. JOHNSON

Harry G. Johnson, Professor of Economics at the University of Chicago, was a discussant of the foregoing paper delivered by Professor Lampman at the American Economic Asociation meetings in December 1964.

I WOULD LIKE to begin by suggesting that two other approaches [beside the economic]—those of the economic historian and of the social philosopher—might be useful in placing the current concern about poverty in perspective. From the point of view of economic history, it is, I think, significant that this is the second instance of presidential concern about poverty in this century, and that in both cases the economic conjuncture has been one of unusually high and prolonged unemployment, suggesting that poverty is a stagnation-correlated fashion. It is also worth noting that the maximum income required to be considered poor has been rising over the long run, which implies that poverty is a socially relative category and that it may be naïve to expect to make substantial permanent inroads on it. From the point of view of social philosophy, the poverty problem is largely a middle-class moral concern, and correspondingly programs for attacking poverty are conceived in middle-class terms and to a significant degree self-frustrating through concern for the preservation of middle-class values. Professor Robert Lampman has made the point that existing social security serves more to block regression into poverty than to open escape routes from it; I would add the observation that contemporary thinking about poverty is dominated by the notion of elevating the poor into the middle class—hence the stress now laid on education as the key to the poverty problem—and is both seriously handicapped and forced into deviousness by the requirement that this elevation be accomplished in ways consistent with middle-class morality.

To be specific, poverty is invariably defined in terms of inadequacy of income to support a minimum standard of decent living. One might therefore naïvely suppose that the solution to the poverty problem would be simply to arrange income transfers to the poor on an appropriate scale. Such payments of social conscience money would not seriously strain the resources of an economy as affluent as this one, and they would have the advantage of eliminating a large part of the administrative overhead required by existing and proposed assistance and welfare programs. It is true that they would generate some waste, by making poverty more eligible than work to some people and by encouraging various kinds of fraud; but waste is one of the main uses of resources that an affluent society can and does afford, and given our society's tolerance of organized crime and of sharp business practices, the anxiety to prevent or punish fraudulent poverty is something of an eccentricity. It is also arguable that the experience of a decent income would itself have a powerful educative influence in inculcating middle-class habits and ambitions. Yet the simple solution of arranging adequate transfer payments is universally rejected out of hand, on the grounds that it would "impair incentives to work and save."

I am not arguing that poverty should necessarily be tackled exclusively by income transfers, but only that income transfers are dismissed summarily by arguments that either rely on a mythology of free enterprise that is inconsistent with concern about poverty, or depend implicitly on assertions about economic behavior that require more empirical investigation than they have been accorded as yet. This is my main quarrel with Professor Lampman's paper, which is on the whole a very useful, compact, and well-organized treatment of the subject. Lampman brushes aside "the idea that there has to be some given amount of poverty," and consigns to folklore a number of rationalizations of this notion. But in his own discussion of the approach of countering "events" that cause poverty—and specifically of the problem of childhood poverty—he is led by the same folklore to produce a compromise negative tax rate plan that would preserve poverty though ameliorating it by reducing the poverty income gap. Lampman rejects "as unworkable any simple plan to assure a minimum income of $3,000." The term "unworkable" is a vague, practical-sounding adjective, commonly employed to close off dangerous thought. What Lampman means by it is the testable but untested empirical proposition that $3,000 would cause many people to cease work, combined with the personal judgment that the resulting cost would be politically unacceptable. I am skeptical about the empirical proposition; but even if it were true, a rough calculation from Lampman's figures, made by assuming that all the present private income of the poor would have to be replaced by public transfers, produces a total bill of $27 billion, or 4½ percent of GNP, as compared with the poverty income gap of $12 billion or 2 percent of GNP. Four and a half percent of GNP may well be politically unacceptable; but it is really small potatoes as war finance goes, if war on poverty is really what has been declared. Lampman's alternative negative tax scheme is equally dependent on an untested proposition about incentives to work. It also ignores the strong possibility that the preoccupation of parents with the earning of money—especially in broken homes —is an important factor in the perpetuation of poverty among the children of the poor. I would myself prefer to recommend an explicit system of family allowances. More generally, I believe that in many cases of poverty income transfers would be the most efficient solution.

In conclusion, I offer a few brief comments. First, I suspect that if poverty specialists referred to modern growth models rather than the classical models based on the iron law of wages, they might be surprised by the slowness rather than the speed of progress in overcoming poverty. Second, it would seem to me desirable to work out what the prevalence of poverty would be exclusive of the effects of existing programs, to determine how far progress in reducing poverty has been automatic and how far it has been due to social policy intervention in the economy. Third, I would place more emphasis than Lampman does on the factor of discrimination—against Negroes, against women, against the aged, and against the uneducated—as a cause of poverty. Fourth, I concur in Lampman's emphasis on the interaction of causal factors in poverty; but this leads me to place much greater emphasis on the importance of maintaining full employment for the reduction of poverty, on the grounds that a tight labor market is a powerful long-run solvent of discriminatory barriers to participation in the labor market at nonpoverty wages.

PART FIVE   Private Wants
and Public Needs

EVERYONE RECOGNIZES the need for ground rules governing the operation of the private economy. Governments—federal, state, and local—are generally counted on to enforce contracts, sanction private property, outlaw theft, regulate business, and intervene to some degree in the distribution of the yield of private economic activity. It would be wrong to suggest that there are no longer live issues surrounding the performance of these functions. The extent to which governments exert control on the individual is a source of recurrent debate; people do express their continuing interest in the distribution of income, particularly their share in the total tax burden and in the benefits (transfers) disbursed to individuals by the public sector. But if governments confined themselves to carrying out regulatory or housekeeping operations, controversy over the proper role of the public sector in the economy would be far milder than it is today. All production would have to pass the test of market demand. Goods which consumers would not buy would be unprofitable and not be produced. The nation's output would be produced and distributed by private enterprise, for private profit. Every man's employer (neglecting the handful of public employees busy regulating) would be just another private citizen, like himself. In any basic sense, ours would be a "free enterprise" system.

This is not the system we have. Alongside the private-enterprise sector there has grown up a *public sector* that supplies the community with a great many services. To provide these services the public sector now purchases over one-fifth of the Gross National Product—the market value of all goods and services produced by the economy. Whether these public purchases are from private firms who do the producing or whether the public sector employs resources to do its own producing, the consequence is clear: Much of the nation's production is directly determined not by consumer decisions but by government.

These facts will hardly surprise the contemporary observer. Yet the present-day importance of the public sector could hardly have been dreamed of fifty or even twenty-five years ago. In 1925, all public expenditures for goods and services comprised only 11 per cent of the Gross National Product.

Despite the rapid growth of government expenditure, there are contentions heard that the public sector has only begun to fill the need for public services. This remarkable expansion of the public sector and the popular pressures surrounding it have made government expenditures the center of controversy concerning the role of government and public policy. Are public expenditures too large? Too small? By what principles should we decide the magnitude of government expenditures? Is the scope of the existing expenditure programs too broad and an encroachment on private enterprise? Or is the public sector neglecting needs which it alone can effectively satisfy? On what criteria should governments decide whether to supply a service? The essays collected here debate these central questions.

The use of government expenditures for anti-cyclical purposes is not considered here. With respect to combating short-term fluctuations, one can say that these essays are concerned with the average level of government expenditures over the cycle; their variation or timing over the course of the business cycle is another matter. With respect to combating a deeper-seated tendency toward depression, measures designed to raise private expenditures, such as tax reductions and easy money, are roughly as effective as increased public expenditures. Similarly, with respect to inflationary tendencies, one has the option to cut private expenditures or public expenditures. Unemployment and inflation depend upon the intensity with which we use (or try to use) our resources, not primarily upon the sector (public or private) where the resources are employed or to which their output is sold. Once the total level of expenditures has been decided, the choice between public and private expenditure must be faced. That is what makes it essentially an economic problem.

E. S. P.

The Dependence Effect and Social Balance

JOHN KENNETH GALBRAITH

John Kenneth Galbraith, Professor of Economics at Harvard University, was formerly United States Ambassador to India. In The Affluent Society, *from which the following essay was taken, Galbraith examines the use to which this country puts its wealth.*

WEALTH IS not without its advantages and the case to the contrary, although it has often been made, has never proved widely persuasive. But, beyond doubt, wealth is the relentless enemy of understanding. The poor man has always a precise view of his problem and its remedy: he hasn't enough and he needs more. The rich man can assume or imagine a much greater variety of ills and he will be correspondingly less certain of their remedy. Also, until he learns to live with his wealth, he will have a well-observed tendency to put it to the wrong purposes or otherwise to make himself foolish.

As with individuals so with nations. And the experience of nations with well-being is exceedingly brief. Nearly all throughout all history have been very poor. The exception, almost insignificant in the whole span of human existence, has been the last few generations in the comparatively small corner of the world populated by Europeans. Here, and especially in the United States, there has been great and quite unprecedented affluence.

The ideas by which the people of this favored part of the world interpret their existence, and in measure guide their behavior, were not forged in a world of wealth. These ideas were the product of a world in which poverty had always been man's normal lot, and any other state was in degree unimaginable. This poverty was not the elegant torture of the spirit which comes from contemplating another man's more spacious possessions. It was the unedifying mortification of the flesh—from hunger, sickness, and cold. Those who might be freed temporarily from such burden could not know when it would strike again, for at best hunger yielded only perilously to privation. It is improbable that the

227

poverty of the masses of the people was made greatly more bearable by the fact that a very few—those upon whose movements nearly all recorded history centers—were very rich.

No one would wish to argue that the ideas which interpreted this world of grim scarcity would serve equally well for the contemporary United States. Poverty was the all-pervasive fact of that world. Obviously it is not of ours. One would not expect that the preoccupations of a poverty-ridden world would be relevant in one where the ordinary individual has access to amenities—foods, entertainment, personal transportation, and plumbing—in which not even the rich rejoiced a century ago. So great has been the change that many of the desires of the individual are no longer even evident to him. They become so only as they are synthesized, elaborated, and nurtured by advertising and salesmanship, and these, in turn, have become among our most important and talented professions. Few people at the beginning of the nineteenth century needed an adman to tell them what they wanted.

It would be wrong to suggest that the economic ideas which once interpreted the world of mass poverty have made no adjustment to the world of affluence. There have been many adjustments including some that have gone unrecognized or have been poorly understood. But there has also been a remarkable resistance. And the total alteration in underlying circumstances has not been squarely faced. As a result we are guided, in part, by ideas that are relevant to another world; and as a further result we do many things that are unnecessary, some that are unwise, and a few that are insane. . . .

THE LOW REPUTE OF PUBLIC PRODUCTION

Our concern for production is traditional and irrational. We are curiously unreasonable in the distinctions we make between different kinds of goods and services. We view the production of some of the most frivolous goods with pride. We regard the production of some of the most significant and civilizing services with regret.

In the general view it is privately produced production that is important, and that nearly alone. This adds to national well-being. Its increase measures the increase in national wealth.

Public services, by comparison, are an incubus. They are necessary, and they may be necessary in considerable volume. But
they are a burden which must, in effect, be carried by the private
production. If that burden is too great, private production will
stagger and fall.

At best public services are a necessary evil; at worst they
are a malign tendency against which an alert community must
exercise eternal vigilance. Even when they serve the most important ends, such services are sterile. "Government is powerless
to create anything in the sense in which business produces
wealth. . . ." [1]

Such attitudes lead to some interesting contradictions. Automobiles have an importance greater than the roads on which they
are driven. We welcome expansion of telephone services as improving the general well-being but accept curtailment of postal
services as signifying necessary economy. We set great store by
the increase in private wealth but regret the added outlays for
the police force by which it is protected. Vacuum cleaners to
insure clean houses are praiseworthy and essential in our standard
of living. Street cleaners to insure clean streets are an unfortunate
expense. Partly as a result, our houses are generally clean and our
streets generally filthy. In the more sophisticated of the conventional wisdom, this distinction between public and private
services is much less sharp and, as I have observed, it does not
figure in the calculation of Gross National Product. However, it
never quite disappears. Even among economists and political
philosophers, public services rarely lose their connotation of
burden. Although they may be defended, their volume and
quality are almost never a source of pride.

There are a number of reasons for these attitudes, but again
tradition plays a dominant role. In the world into which economics was born the four most urgent requirements of man were
food, clothing, and shelter, and an orderly environment in which
the first three might be provided. The first three lent themselves
to private production for the market; given good order, this
process has ordinarily gone forward with tolerable efficiency.
But order which was the gift of government was nearly always

1. Francis X. Sutton, Seymour E. Harris, Carl Kaysen, and James Tobin,
The American Business Creed (Cambridge, Mass.: Harvard University Press,
1956), p. 195.

supplied with notable unreliability. With rare exceptions it was also inordinately expensive. And the pretext of providing order not infrequently afforded the occasion for rapacious appropriation of the means of sustenance of the people.

Not surprisingly, modern economic ideas incorporated a strong suspicion of government. The goal of nineteenth century economic liberalism was a state which did provide order reliably and inexpensively and which did as little as possible else. Even Marx intended that the state should wither away. These attitudes have persisted in the conventional wisdom. And again events have dealt them a series of merciless blows. Once a society has provided itself with food, clothing, and shelter, all of which so fortuitously lend themselves to private production, purchase, and sale, its members begin to desire other things. And a remarkable number of these things do not lend themselves to such production, purchase, and sale. They must be provided for everyone if they are to be provided for anyone, and they must be paid for collectively or they cannot be had at all. Such is the case with streets and police and the general advantages of mass literacy and sanitation, the control of epidemics, and the common defense. There is a bare possibility that the services which must be rendered collectively, although they enter the general scheme of wants after the immediate physical necessities, increase in urgency more than proportionately with increasing wealth. This is more likely if increasing wealth is matched by increasing population and increasing density of population. Nonetheless these services, although they reflect increasingly urgent desires, remain under the obloquy of the unreliability, incompetence, cost, and pretentious interference of princes. Alcohol, comic books, and mouth wash all bask under the superior reputation of the market. Schools, judges, and municipal swimming pools lie under the evil reputation of bad kings.

Moreover, bad kings in a poorer world showed themselves to be quite capable, in their rapacity, of destroying or damaging the production of private goods by destroying the people and the capital that produced them. Economies are no longer so vulnerable. Governments are not so undiscriminating. In western countries in modern times economic growth and expanding public activity have, with rare exceptions, gone together. Each has served the other as indeed they must. Yet the conventional wisdom is far from surrendering on the point. Any growth in public services is a manifestation of an intrinsically evil trend. If the vigor of the race is not in danger, liberty is. And this may be threatened even by the activities of the local school board. The structure of the economy may also be at stake. In one branch of the conventional wisdom the American economy is never far removed from socialism, and the movement toward socialism may be measured by the rise in public spending. Thus even the most neutral of public services, for one part of the population, fall under the considerable handicap of being identified with social revolution.

Finally—also a closely related point—the payment for publicly produced services has long been linked to the problem of inequality. By having the rich pay more, the services were provided and at the same time the goal of greater equality was advanced. This community of objectives has never appealed to those being equalized. Not unnaturally, some part of their opposition has been directed to the public services themselves. By attacking these, they could attack the leveling tendencies of taxation. This has helped to keep alive the notion that the public services for which they pay are inherently inferior to privately produced goods.

While public services have been subject to these negative attitudes, private goods have had no such attention. On the contrary, their virtues have been extolled by the massed drums of modern advertising. They have been pictured as the ultimate wealth of the community. Clearly the competition between public and private services, apart from any question of the satisfactions they render, is an unequal one. The social consequences of this discrimination—this tendency to accord a superior prestige to private goods and an inferior role to public production—are considerable and even grave.

THE IMPERATIVES OF CONSUMER DEMAND

Both the ancient preoccupation with production and the pervasive modern search for security have culminated in our time in a concern for production. Increased real income provides us with an admirable detour around the rancor anciently associated with efforts to redistribute wealth. A high level of production has become the keystone of effective economic security. There remains, however, the task of justifying the resulting flow of goods. Production cannot be an incidental to the mitigation of inequality or the provision of jobs. It must have a *raison d'être* of its own. At this point economists and economic theory have entered the game. The result has been an elaborate and ingenious defense of the importance of production as such. It is a defense which makes the urgency of production largely independent of the volume of production. In this way economic theory has managed to transfer the sense of urgency in meeting consumer need that once was felt in a world where more production meant more food for the hungry, more clothing for the cold, and more houses for the homeless to a world where increased output satisfies the craving for more elegant automobiles, more exotic food, more erotic clothing, more elaborate entertainment—indeed for the entire modern range of sensuous, edifying, and lethal desires.

Although the economic theory which defends these desires and hence the production that supplies them has an impeccable (and to an astonishing degree even unchallenged) position in the conventional wisdom, it is illogical and meretricious and in degree even dangerous. . . .

In part [the defense by economists] will take the form of a purely assertive posture. "There is still an economic problem"; "We still have poverty"; "It is human nature to want more"; "Without increasing production there will be stagnation"; "We must show the Russians." But the ultimate refuge will remain in the theory of consumer demand. This is a formidable structure; it has already demonstrated its effectiveness in defending the urgency of production. In a world where affluence is rendering the old ideas obsolete, it will continue to be the bastion against the misery of new ones.

The theory of consumer demand, as it is now widely accepted, is based on two broad propositions, neither of them quite explicit but both extremely important for the present value system of economists. The first is that the urgency of wants does not diminish appreciably as more of them are satisfied or, to put the matter more precisely, to the extent that this happens it is not demonstrable and not a matter of any interest to economists or for economic policy. When man has satisfied his physical needs, then psychologically grounded desires take over. These can never be satisfied or, in any case, no progress can be proved. The concept of satiation has very little standing in economics. It is neither useful nor scientific to speculate on the comparative cravings of the stomach and the mind.

The second proposition is that wants originate in the personality of the consumer or, in any case, that they are given data for the economist. The latter's task is merely to seek their satisfaction. He has no need to inquire how these wants are formed. His function is sufficiently fulfilled by maximizing the goods that supply the wants.

The examination of these two conclusions must now be pressed. The explanation of consumer behavior has its ancestry in a much older problem, indeed the oldest problem of economics, that of price determination.[2] Nothing originally proved more troublesome in the explanation of prices, i.e., exchange values, than the indigestible fact that some of the most useful things had the least value in exchange and some of the least useful had the most. As Adam Smith observed: "Nothing is more useful than water; but it will purchase scarce anything; scarce anything can be had in exchange for it. A diamond, on the contrary, has scarce any value in use: but a very great quantity of other goods may frequently be had in exchange for it." [3]

In explaining value, Smith thought it well to distinguish between "value in exchange" and "value in use" and sought thus to reconcile the paradox of high utility and low exchangeability. This distinction begged questions rather than solved them and for another hundred years economists sought for a satisfactory formulation. Finally, toward the end of the last century—though it is now recognized that their work had been extensively anticipated—the three economists of marginal utility (Karl Menger, an Austrian; William Stanley Jevons, an Englishman; and John Bates Clark, an American) produced more or less simultaneously the explanation which in broad substance still serves. The urgency of desire is a function of the quantity of goods which the individual has available to satisfy that desire. The larger the stock the less the satisfactions from an increment. And the less, also, the willingness to pay. Since diamonds for most people are

2. The provenance of the theory of consumer behavior is sketched in Mr. I. D. M. Little's interesting article "A Reformulation of Consumer Behavior," *Oxford Economic Papers*, New Series, vol. 1, no. 1 (January 1949), p. 99.
3. *Wealth of Nations*. Smith did not foresee the industrial diamond.

in comparatively meager supply, the satisfaction from an additional one is great, and the potential willingness to pay is likewise high. The case of water is just the reverse. It also follows that where the supply of a good can be readily increased at low cost, its value in exchange will reflect that ease of reproduction and the low urgency of the marginal desires it thus comes to satisfy. This will be so no matter how difficult it may be (as with water) to dispense entirely with the item in question.

The doctrine of diminishing marginal utility, as it was enshrined in the economics textbooks, seemed to put economic ideas squarely on the side of the diminishing importance of production under conditions of increasing affluence. With increasing per capita real income, men are able to satisfy additional wants. These are of a lower order of urgency. This being so, the production that provides the goods that satisfy these less urgent wants must also be of smaller (and declining) importance. In Ricardo's England the supply of bread for many was meager. The satisfaction resulting from an increment in the bread supply —from a higher money income, bread prices being the same, or the same money income, bread prices being lower—was great. Hunger was lessened; life itself might be extended. Certainly any measure to increase the bread supply merited the deep and serious interest of the public-spirited citizen.

In the contemporary United States the supply of bread is plentiful and the supply of bread grains even redundant. The yield of satisfactions from a marginal increment in the wheat supply is small. To a Secretary of Agriculture it is indubitably negative. Measures to increase the wheat supply are not, therefore, a socially urgent preoccupation of publicly concerned citizens. These are more likely to be found spending their time devising schemes for the effective control of wheat production. And having extended their bread consumption to the point where its marginal utility is very low, people have gone on to spend their income on other things. Since these other goods entered their consumption pattern after bread, there is a presumption that they are not very urgent either—that *their* consumption has been carried, as with wheat, to the point where marginal utility is small or even negligible. So it must be assumed that the importance of marginal increments of all production is low and declining. The effect of increasing affluence is to minimize the importance of economic goals. Production and productivity become less and less important.

The concept of diminishing marginal utility was, and remains, one of the indispensable ideas of economics. Since it conceded so much to the notion of diminishing urgency of wants, and hence of production, it was remarkable indeed that the situation was retrieved. This was done—and brilliantly. The diminishing urgency of wants was not admitted. In part this was accomplished in the name of refined scientific method which, as so often at the higher levels of sophistication, proved a formidable bulwark of the conventional wisdom. Obvious but inconvenient evidence was rejected on the grounds that it could not be scientifically assimilated. But even beyond this, it has been necessary at times simply to close one's eyes to phenomena which could not be reconciled with convenience.

Economics took general cognizance of the fact that an almost infinite variety of goods await the consumer's attention. At the more elementary (and also the more subjective) levels of economic analysis it is assumed that, while the marginal utility of the individual good declines in accordance with the indubitable law, the utility or satisfaction from new and different kinds of goods does not diminish appreciably. So long as the consumer adds new products—seeks variety rather than quantity—he may, like a museum, accumulate without diminishing the urgency of his wants. Since even in Los Angeles the average consumer owns only a fraction of the different kinds of goods he might conceivably possess, there is all but unlimited opportunity for adding such products. The rewards to the possessors are more or less proportional to the supply. The production that supplies these goods and services, since it renders undiminished utility, remains of undiminished importance.

This position ignores the obvious fact that some things are acquired before others and that, presumably, the more important things come first. This, as observed previously, implies a declining urgency of need. However, in the slightly more sophisticated theory this conclusion is rejected. The rejection centers on the denial that anything very useful can be said of the comparative states of mind and satisfaction of the consumer at different periods of time. Few students of economics, even in the elementary course, now escape without a warning against the error of intertemporal comparisons of the utility from given acts of consumption. Yesterday the man with a minimal but increasing real income was reaping the satisfactions which came from a decent diet and a roof that no longer leaked water on his face. Today, after a large increase in his income, he has extended his consumption to include suede shoes and a weekly visit to the races. But to say that his satisfactions from these latter amenities and recreations are less than from the additional calories and the freedom from rain is wholly improper. Things have changed; he is a different man; there is no real standard for comparison. That, as of a given time, an individual will derive lesser satisfactions from the marginal increments to a given stock of goods, and accordingly cannot be induced to pay as much for them, is conceded. But this tells us nothing of the satisfactions from such additional goods, and more particularly from different goods, when they are acquired at a later time. The conclusion follows. One cannot be sure that the satisfaction from these temporally later increases in the individual's stock of goods diminishes. Hence one cannot suggest that the production which supplies it is of diminishing urgency.

A moment's reflection on what has been accomplished will be worth while. The notion of diminishing utility still serves its indispensable purpose of relating urgency of desire and consequent willingness to pay to quantity. At any given time the more the individual might have, the less would be the satisfaction he would derive from additions to his stock and the less he would be willing to pay. The reactions of the community will be the aggregate of the reactions of the individuals it comprises. Hence the greater the supply the less the willingness to pay for marginal increments and hence the demand curve familiar to all who have made even the most modest venture into economic theory. But, at the same time, the question of the diminishing urgency of consumption is elided. For, while the question of willingness to pay for additional quantities is based on a hypothesis as to behavior in face of these quantities at a given point of time, an increase in stock of consumers' goods, as the result of an increase in real income, can occur only over time. On the yield of satisfactions from this the economist has nothing to say. In the name of good scientific method he is prevented from saying anything. There is room, however, for the broad assumption—given the large and ever-growing variety of goods awaiting the consumer's attention—that wants have a sustained urgency. In any case, it can safely be concluded that more goods will satisfy more wants than fewer goods. And the assumption that goods are an important and even an urgent thing to provide stalks unchallenged behind, for have not goods always been important for relieving the privation of mankind? It will be evident that economics has brilliantly retrieved the dangers to itself and to its goals that were inherent in diminishing marginal utility.

There has been dissent. Keynes observed that the needs of human beings "fall into two classes—those needs which are absolute in the sense that we feel them whatever the situation of our fellow human beings may be, and those which are relative only in that their satisfaction lifts us above, makes us feel superior to, our fellows." While conceding that the second class of wants might be insatiable, he argued that the first were capable of being satisfied and went on to conclude that "assuming no important wars and no important increase in population the *economic problem* may be solved, or at least within sight of solution, within a hundred years. This means the economic problem is not—if we look into the future—*the permanent problem of the human race.*" [4] However, on this conclusion Keynes made no headway. In contending with the conventional wisdom he, no less than others, needed the support of circumstance. And in contrast with his remedy for depressions this he did not yet have.

THE DEPENDENCE EFFECT

The notion that wants do not become less urgent the more amply the individual is supplied is broadly repugnant to common sense. It is something to be believed only by those who wish to believe. Yet the conventional wisdom must be tackled on its own terrain. Intertemporal comparisons of an individual's state of mind do rest on doubtful grounds. Who can say for sure that the deprivation which afflicts him with hunger is more painful than the deprivation which afflicts him with envy of his neighbor's new car? In the time that has passed since he was poor his soul may have become subject to a new and deeper searing.

4. J. M. Keynes, *Essays in Persuasion,* "Economic Possibilities for Our Grandchildren," pp. 365–66. The italics are in the original. Notice that Keynes, as always little bound by the conventional rules, did not hesitate to commit the unpardonable sin of distinguishing between categories of desire.

And where a society is concerned, comparisons between marginal satisfactions when it is poor and those when it is affluent will involve not only the same individual at different times but different individuals at different times. The scholar who wishes to believe that with increasing affluence there is no reduction in the urgency of desires and goods is not without points for debate. However plausible the case against him, it cannot be proven. In the defense of the conventional wisdom this amounts almost to invulnerability.

However, there is a flaw in the case. If the individual's wants are to be urgent they must be original with himself. They cannot be urgent if they must be contrived for him. And above all they must not be contrived by the process of production by which they are satisfied. For this means that the whole case for the urgency of production, based on the urgency of wants, falls to the ground. One cannot defend production as satisfying wants if that production creates the wants.

Were it so that a man on arising each morning was assailed by demons which instilled in him a passion sometimes for silk shirts, sometimes for kitchenware, sometimes for chamber pots, and sometimes for orange squash, there would be every reason to applaud the effort to find the goods, however odd, that quenched this flame. But should it be that his passion was the result of his first having cultivated the demons, and should it also be that his effort to allay it stirred the demons to ever greater and greater effort, there would be question as to how rational was his solution. Unless restrained by conventional attitudes, he might wonder if the solution lay with more goods or fewer demons.

So it is that if production creates the wants it seeks to satisfy, or if the wants emerge *pari passu* with the production, then the urgency of the wants can no longer be used to defend the urgency of the production. Production only fills a void that it has itself created.

The point is so central that it must be pressed. Consumer wants can have bizarre, frivolous, or even immoral origins, and an admirable case can still be made for a society that seeks to satisfy them. But the case cannot stand if it is the process of satisfying wants that creates the wants. For then the individual who urges the importance of production to satisfy these wants is precisely in the position of the onlooker who applauds the efforts of the squirrel to keep abreast of the wheel that is propelled by his own efforts.

That wants are, in fact, the fruit of production will now be denied by few serious scholars. And a considerable number of economists, though not always in full knowledge of the implications, have conceded the point. In the observation cited earlier Keynes noted that needs of "the second class," i.e., those that are the result of efforts to keep abreast or ahead of one's fellow being "may indeed be insatiable; for the higher the general level the higher still are they." [5] And emulation has always played a considerable role in the views of other economists of want creation. One man's consumption becomes his neighbor's wish. This already means that the process by which wants are satisfied is also the process by which wants are created. The more wants that are satisfied the more new ones are born.

However, the argument has been carried farther. A leading modern theorist of consumer behavior, Professor Duesenberry, has stated explicitly that "ours is a society in which one of the principal social goals is a higher standard of living. . . . [This] has great significance for the theory of consumption . . . the desire to get superior goods takes on a life of its own. It provides a drive to higher expenditure which may even be stronger than that arising out of the needs which are supposed to be satisfied by that expenditure." [6] The implications of this view are impressive. The notion of independently established need now sinks into the background. Because the society sets great store by ability to produce a high living standard, it evaluates people by the products they possess. The urge to consume is fathered by the value system which emphasizes the ability of the society to produce. The more that is produced the more that must be owned in order to maintain the appropriate prestige. The latter is an important point, for, without going as far as Duesenberry in reducing goods to the role of symbols of prestige in the affluent society, it is plain that his argument fully implies that the production of goods creates the wants that the goods are presumed to satisfy.

The even more direct link between production and wants is provided by the institutions of modern advertising and salesman-

5. *Op. cit.*

6. James S. Duesenberry, *Income, Saving and the Theory of Consumer Behavior* (Cambridge, Mass.: Harvard University Press, 1949), p. 28.

ship. These cannot be reconciled with the notion of independently determined desires, for their central function is to create desires —to bring into being wants that previously did not exist. This is accomplished by the producer of the goods or at his behest. A broad empirical relationship exists between what is spent on production of consumers' goods and what is spent in synthesizing the desires for that production. A new consumer product must be introduced with a suitable advertising campaign to arouse an interest in it. The path for an expansion of output must be paved by a suitable expansion in the advertising budget. Outlays for the manufacturing of a product are not more important in the strategy of modern business enterprise than outlays for the manufacturing of demand for the product. None of this is novel. All would be regarded as elementary by the most retarded student in the nation's most primitive school of business administration. The cost of this want formation is formidable. In 1956 total advertising expenditure—though, as noted, not all of it may be assigned to the synthesis of wants—amounted to about ten billion dollars. For some years it had been increasing at a rate in excess of a billion dollars a year. Obviously, such outlays must be integrated with the theory of consumer demand. They are too big to be ignored.

But such integration means recognizing that wants are dependent on production. It accords to the producer the function both of making the goods and of making the desires for them. It recognizes that production, not only passively through emulation, but actively through advertising and related activities, creates the wants it seeks to satisfy.

The businessman and the lay reader will be puzzled over the emphasis which I give to a seemingly obvious point. The point is indeed obvious. But it is one which, to a singular degree, economists have resisted. They have sensed, as the layman does not, the damage to established ideas which lurks in these relationships. As a result, incredibly, they have closed their eyes (and ears) to the most obtrusive of all economic phenomena, namely modern want creation.

This is not to say that the evidence affirming the dependence of wants on advertising has been entirely ignored. It is one reason why advertising has so long been regarded with such uneasiness by economists. Here is something which cannot be accommodated easily to existing theory. More pervious scholars have speculated on the urgency of desires which are so obviously the fruit of such expensively contrived campaigns for popular attention. Is a new breakfast cereal or detergent so much wanted if so much must be spent to compel in the consumer the sense of want? But there has been little tendency to go on to examine the implications of this for the theory of consumer demand and even less for the importance of production and productive efficiency. These have remained sacrosanct. More often the uneasiness has been manifested in a general disapproval of advertising and advertising men, leading to the occasional suggestion that they shouldn't exist. Such suggestions have usually been ill received.

And so the notion of independently determined wants still survives. In the face of all the forces of modern salesmanship it still rules, almost undefiled, in the textbooks. And it still remains the economist's mission—and on few matters is the pedagogy so firm—to seek unquestioningly the means for filling these wants. This being so, production remains of prime urgency. We have here, perhaps, the ultimate triumph of the conventional wisdom in its resistance to the evidence of the eyes. To equal it one must imagine a humanitarian who was long ago persuaded of the grievous shortage of hospital facilities in the town. He continues to importune the passers-by for money for more beds and refuses to notice that the town doctor is deftly knocking over pedestrians with his car to keep up the occupancy.

And in unraveling the complex we should always be careful not to overlook the obvious. The fact that wants can be synthesized by advertising, catalyzed by salesmanship, and shaped by the discreet manipulations of the persuaders shows that they are not very urgent. A man who is hungry need never be told of his need for food. If he is inspired by his appetite, he is immune to the influence of Messrs. Batten, Barton, Durstine & Osborn. The latter are effective only with those who are so far removed from physical want that they do not already know what they want. In this state alone men are open to persuasion.

The general conclusion of these pages is of such importance for this essay that it had perhaps best be put with some formality. As a society becomes increasingly affluent, wants are increasingly created by the process by which they are satisfied. This may operate passively. Increases in consumption, the counterpart of increases in production, act by suggestion or emulation to create wants. Or producers may proceed actively to create wants through advertising and salesmanship. Wants thus come to depend on output. In technical terms it can no longer be assumed that welfare is greater at an all-round higher level of production than at a lower one. It may be the same. The higher level of production has, merely, a higher level of want creation necessitating a higher level of want satisfaction. There will be frequent occasion to refer to the way wants depend on the process by which they are satisfied. It will be convenient to call it the Dependence Effect.

We may now contemplate briefly the conclusions to which this analysis has brought us.

Plainly the theory of consumer demand is a peculiarly treacherous friend of the present goals of economics. At first glance it seems to defend the continuing urgency of production and our preoccupation with it as a goal. The economist does not enter into the dubious moral arguments about the importance or virtue of the wants to be satisfied. He doesn't pretend to compare mental states of the same or different people at different times and to suggest that one is less urgent than another. The desire is there. That for him is sufficient. He sets about in a workmanlike way to satisfy desire, and accordingly he sets the proper store by the production that does. Like woman's his work is never done.

But this rationalization, handsomely though it seems to serve, turns destructively on those who advance it once it is conceded that wants are themselves both passively and deliberately the fruits of the process by which they are satisfied. Then the production of goods satisfies the wants that the consumption of these goods creates or that the producers of goods synthesize. Production induces more wants and the need for more production. So far, in a major *tour de force*, the implications have been ignored. But this obviously is a perilous solution. It cannot long survive discussion.

Among the many models of the good society no one has urged the squirrel wheel. Moreover, the wheel is not one that revolves with perfect smoothness. Aside from its dubious cultural charm, there are serious structural weaknesses which may one day embarrass us. For the moment, however, it is sufficient to reflect on the difficult terrain which we are traversing. We find our concern for goods undermined. It does not arise in spontaneous consumer need. Rather, the dependence effect means that it grows out of the process of production itself. If production is to increase, the wants must be effectively contrived. In the absence of the contrivance the increase would not occur. This is not true of all goods, but that it is true of a substantial part is sufficient. It means that since the demand for this part would not exist, were it not contrived, its utility or urgency, ex contrivance, is zero. If we regard this production as marginal, we may say that the marginal utility of present aggregate output, ex advertising and salesmanship, is zero. Clearly the attitudes and values which make production the central achievement of our society have some exceptionally twisted roots. . . .

THE THEORY OF SOCIAL BALANCE

The final problem of the productive society is what it produces. This manifests itself in an implacable tendency to provide an opulent supply of some things and a niggardly yield of others. This disparity carries to the point where it is a cause of social discomfort and social unhealth. The line which divides our area of wealth from our area of poverty is roughly that which divides privately produced and marketed goods and services from publicly rendered services. Our wealth in the first is not only in startling contrast with the meagerness of the latter, but our wealth in privately produced goods is, to a marked degree, the cause of crisis in the supply of public services. For we have failed to see the importance, indeed the urgent need, of maintaining a balance between the two.

This disparity between our flow of private and public goods and services is no matter of subjective judgment. On the contrary, it is the source of the most extensive comment which only stops short of the direct contrast being made here. In the years following World War II, the papers of any major city—those of New York were an excellent example—told daily of the shortages and shortcomings in the elementary municipal and metropolitan services. The schools were old and overcrowded. The police force was under strength and underpaid. The parks and playgrounds were insufficient. Streets and empty lots were filthy, and the sanitation staff was underequipped and in need of men. Access to the city by those who work there was uncertain and painful and becoming more so. Internal transportation was overcrowded, unhealthful, and dirty. So was the air. Parking on the streets had to be prohibited, and there was no space elsewhere. These deficiencies were not in new and novel services but in old and established ones. Cities have long swept their streets, helped their people move around, educated them, kept order, and provided horse rails for vehicles which sought to pause. That their residents should have a nontoxic supply of air suggests no revolutionary dalliance with socialism.

The discussion of this public poverty competed, on the whole successfully, with the stories of ever-increasing opulence in privately produced goods. The Gross National Product was rising. So were retail sales. So was personal income. Labor productivity had also advanced. The automobiles that could not be parked were being produced at an expanded rate. The children, though without schools, subject in the playgrounds to the affectionate interest of adults with odd tastes, and disposed to increasingly imaginative forms of delinquency, were admirably equipped with television sets. We had difficulty finding storage space for the great surpluses of food despite a national disposition to obesity. Food was grown and packaged under private auspices. The care and refreshment of the mind, in contrast with the stomach, was principally in the public domain. Our colleges and universities were severely overcrowded and underprovided, and the same was true of the mental hospitals.

The contrast was and remains evident not alone to those who read. The family which takes its mauve and cerise, air-conditioned, power-steered, and power-braked automobile out for a tour passes through cities that are badly paved, made hideous by litter, blighted buildings, billboards, and posts for wires that should long since have been put underground. They pass on into a countryside that has been rendered largely invisible by commercial art. (The goods which the latter advertises have an absolute priority in our value system. Such aesthetic considerations as a view of the countryside accordingly come second. On such matters we are consistent.) They picnic on exquisitely packaged food from a portable icebox by a polluted stream and go on to spend the night at a park which is a menace to public health and morals. Just before dozing off on an air mattress, beneath a nylon tent, amid the stench of decaying refuse, they may reflect vaguely on the curious unevenness of their blessings. Is this, indeed, the American genius?

In the production of goods within the private economy it has long been recognized that a tolerably close relationship must be maintained between the production of various kinds of products. Just as there must be balance in what a community produces, so there must also be balance in what the community consumes. An increase in the use of one product creates, ineluctably, a requirement for others. If we are to consume more automobiles, we must have more gasoline. There must be more insurance as well as more space on which to operate them. Beyond a certain point more and better food appears to mean increased need for medical services. This is the certain result of the increased consumption of tobacco and alcohol. More vacations require more hotels and more fishing rods. And so forth. With rare exceptions—shortages of doctors are an exception which suggests the rule—this balance is also maintained quite effortlessly so far as goods for private sale and consumption are concerned. The price system plus a rounded condition of opulence is again the agency.

However, the relationships we are here discussing are not confined to the private economy. They operate comprehensively over the whole span of private and public services. As surely as an increase in the output of automobiles puts new demands on the steel industry so, also, it places new demands on public services. Similarly, every increase in the consumption of private goods will normally mean some facilitating or protective step by the state. In all cases if these services are not forthcoming, the consequences will be in some degree ill. It will be convenient to have a term which suggests a satisfactory relationship between the supply of privately produced goods and services and those of the state, and we may call it social balance.

The problem of social balance is ubiquitous, and frequently it is obtrusive. As noted, an increase in the consumption of automobiles requires a facilitating supply of streets, highways, traffic control, and parking space. The protective services of the police and the highway patrols must also be available, as must those of the hospitals. Although the need for balance here is extraordinarily clear, our use of privately produced vehicles has, on occasion, got far out of line with the supply of the related public services. The result has been hideous road congestion, an annual massacre of impressive proportions, and chronic colitis in the cities. As on the ground, so also in the air. Planes collide with disquieting consequences for those within when the public provision for air traffic control fails to keep pace with private use of the airways.

But the auto and the airplane, versus the space to use them, are merely an exceptionally visible example of a requirement that is pervasive. The more goods people procure, the more packages they discard and the more trash that must be carried away. If the appropriate sanitation services are not provided, the counterpart of increasing opulence will be deepening filth. The greater the wealth the thicker will be the dirt. This indubitably describes a tendency of our time. As more goods are produced and owned, the greater are the opportunities for fraud and the more property that must be protected. If the provision of public law enforcement services does not keep pace, the counterpart of increased well-being will, we may be certain, be increased crime.

The city of Los Angeles, in modern times, is a near-classic study in the problem of social balance. Magnificently efficient factories and oil refineries, a lavish supply of automobiles, a vast consumption of handsomely packaged products, coupled with the absence of a municipal trash collection service which forced the use of home incinerators, made the air nearly unbreathable for an appreciable part of each year. Air pollution could be controlled only by a complex and highly developed set of public services—by better knowledge stemming from more research, better policing, a municipal trash collection service, and possibly the assertion of the priority of clean air over the production of goods. These were long in coming. The agony of a city without usable air was the result. . . .

The case for social balance has, so far, been put negatively. Failure to keep public services in minimal relation to private production and use of goods is a cause of social disorder or impairs economic performance. The matter may now be put affirmatively. By failing to exploit the opportunity to expand public production we are missing opportunities for enjoyment which otherwise we might have had. Presumably a community can be as well rewarded by buying better schools or better parks as by buying bigger automobiles. By concentrating on the latter rather than the former it is failing to maximize its satisfactions. As with schools in the community, so with public services over the country at large. It is scarcely sensible that we should satisfy our wants in private goods with reckless abundance, while in the case of public goods, on the evidence of the eye, we practice extreme self-denial. So, far from systematically exploiting the opportunities to derive use and pleasure from these services, we do not supply what would keep us out of trouble.

The conventional wisdom holds that the community, large or small, makes a decision as to how much it will devote to its public services. This decision is arrived at by democratic process. Subject to the imperfections and uncertainties of democracy, people decide how much of their private income and goods they will surrender in order to have public services of which they are in greater need. Thus there is a balance, however rough, in the enjoyments to be had from private goods and services and those rendered by public authority.

It will be obvious, however, that this view depends on the notion of independently determined consumer wants. In such a world one could with some reason defend the doctrine that the consumer, as a voter, makes an independent choice between public and private goods. But given the dependence effect— given that consumer wants are created by the process by which they are satisfied—the consumer makes no such choice. He is subject to the forces of advertising and emulation by which production creates its own demand. Advertising operates exclusively, and emulation mainly, on behalf of privately produced goods and services.[7] Since management and emulative effects operate on behalf of private production, public services will have an inherent tendency to lag behind. Automobile demand which is expensively synthesized will inevitably have a much larger claim on income than parks or public health or even roads where no such influence operates. The engines of mass communication, in their highest state of development, assail the eyes and ears of the community on behalf of more beer but not of more schools. Even in the conventional wisdom it will scarcely be contended that this leads to an equal choice between the two.

---

7. Emulation does operate between communities. A new school or a new highway in one community does exert pressure on others to remain abreast. However, as compared with the pervasive effects of emulation in extending the demand for privately produced consumer's goods there will be agreement, I think, that this intercommunity effect is probably small.

The competition is especially unequal for new products and services. Every corner of the public psyche is canvassed by some of the nation's most talented citizens to see if the desire for some merchantable product can be cultivated. No similar process operates on behalf of the nonmerchantable services of the state. Indeed, while we take the cultivation of new private wants for granted we would be measurably shocked to see it applied to public services. The scientist or engineer or advertising man who devotes himself to developing a new carburetor, cleanser, or depilatory for which the public recognizes no need and will feel none until an advertising campaign arouses it, is one of the valued members of our society. A politician or a public servant who dreams up a new public service is a wastrel. Few public offenses are more reprehensible.

So much for the influences which operate on the decision between public and private production. The calm decision between public and private consumption pictured by the conventional wisdom is, in fact, a remarkable example of the error which arises from viewing social behavior out of context. The inherent tendency will always be for public services to fall behind private production. . . .

THE REDRESS OF BALANCE

Our next task is to find a way of obtaining and then of maintaining a balance in the great flow of goods and services with which our wealth each year rewards us. In particular, we must find a way to remedy the poverty which afflicts us in public services and which is in such increasingly bizarre contrast with our affluence in private goods.

The problem will not be settled by a resolve to spend more for schools and streets and other services and to tax accordingly. Such decisions are made every day, and they do not come to grips with the causes of the imbalance. These lie much deeper. The most important difference between private and public goods and services is a technical one. The first lend themselves to being sold to individuals. The second do not. In the evolution of economic enterprise, the things which could be produced and sold for a price were taken over by private producers. Those that could not, but which were in the end no less urgent for that reason, remained with the state. Bread and steel went naturally to private enterprise, for they could readily be produced and marketed by individuals to individuals. Police protection, sanitation, and sewer systems remained with public authority for, on the whole, they could not. Once the decision was taken to make education universal and compulsory, it ceased to be a marketable commodity. With the rise of the national state so did national defense. The line between public and private activity, as we view it at any given moment, is the product of many forces—tradition, ideological preference, and social urgency all play some part. But to a far greater degree than is commonly supposed, functions accrue to the state because, as a purely technical matter, there is no alternative to public management.

The goods and services which are marketable at a price have a position of elementary strategic advantage in the economy. Their price provides the income which commands labor, capital, and raw materials for production. This is inherent in the productive process. In the absence of social intervention, private production will monopolize all resources. Only as something is done about it will resources become available for public services.

The solution is a system of taxation which automatically makes a pro rata share of increasing income available to public authority for public purposes. The task of public authority, like that of private individuals, will be to distribute this increase in accordance with relative need. Schools and roads will then no longer be at a disadvantage as compared with automobiles and television sets in having to prove absolute justification.

However, even though the higher urgency of the services for social balance is conceded, there is still the problem of providing the revenue. And since it is income taxes that must be used, the question of social balance can easily be lost sight of in the reopened argument over equality. The truce will be broken and liberals and conservatives will join battle on this issue and forget about the poverty in the public services that awaits correction and the poverty of people which can only be corrected at increased public cost. All this—schools, hospitals, even the scientific research on which increased production depends—must wait while we debate the ancient and unresolvable question of whether the rich are too rich.

The only hope—and in the nature of things it rests primarily with liberals—is to separate the issue of equality from that of social balance. The second is by far the more important question.

The rational liberal, in the future, will resist tax reduction, even that which ostensibly favors the poor, if it is at the price of social balance. . . .

One final observation may be made. There will be question as to what is the test of balance—at what point may we conclude that balance has been achieved in the satisfaction of private and public needs. The answer is that no test can be applied, for none exists. The traditional formulation is that the satisfaction returned to the community from a marginal increment of resources devoted to public purposes should be equal to the satisfaction of the same increment in private employment. These are incommensurate, partly because different people are involved, and partly because it makes the cardinal error of comparing satisfaction of wants that are synthesized with those that are not.

But a precise equilibrium is not very important. For another mark of an affluent society is the opportunity for the existence of a considerable margin for error on such matters. The present imbalance is clear, as are the forces and ideas which give the priority to private as compared with public goods. This being so, the direction in which we move to correct matters is utterly plain. We can also assume, given the power of the forces that have operated to accord a priority to private goods, that the distance to be traversed is considerable. When we arrive, the opulence of our private consumption will no longer be in contrast with the poverty of our schools, the unloveliness and congestion of our cities, our inability to get to work without struggle, and the social disorder that is associated with imbalance. But the precise point of balance will never be defined. This will be of comfort only to those who believe that any failure of definition can be made to score decisively against a larger idea.

Public versus Private: Could Galbraith Be Wrong?

HENRY C. WALLICH

Henry C. Wallich is Professor of Economics at Yale University. His book The Cost of Freedom, *from which a part of this essay is taken, argues that we must not ask maximum efficiency of our economic system if we also value individual freedom.*

In addition to free advice about growth, the nation has received helpful suggestions of another sort, in a rather opposite vein. It has been argued that we have all the production we need and to spare, but that too much of our growth has gone into private consumption, too little into public. We are said to be wasting our substance on trivia while allowing urgent public needs to go uncared for. This view does not complain of inadequate growth. But it sees us riding in tail-finned, oversized automobiles through cities that are becoming slums, finds our children sitting glued to the latest TV models but lacking schools where they can learn to read properly, and generally charges us with putting private profligacy ahead of public provision.

The general doctrine that in the United States public needs tend to be underfinanced in relation to private I first heard many years ago from my old teacher Alvin Hansen. It has always seemed to me to possess a measure of appeal. Throughout this book, I have been at pains to argue that with rising wealth and industrialized living, the need for public services advances, and probably faster than living standards. In part this reflects simply the familiar fact that the demand for services tends to expand faster than the demand for goods. In part, the social conditions of modern life are also accountable for the growing need for government services. Private business is learning to meet many of these new needs—for instance in the field of insurance. It is not inconceivable that some day we shall become rich enough to be able to indulge increasingly a preference for privately supplied services. But at present, and as far ahead as one can see, the trend seems the other way. I would footnote this reference by observing that to recognize a rising trend in the need for public services and to claim that at present we have too little of them, are two different things. The more than doubling of federal and also of state and local expenditures since 1950 should drive home that distinction.

The thesis that public services are neglected and private consumption inflated with trivia has found its most eloquent interpretation in *The Affluent Society* by John Kenneth Galbraith, to whom we were previously indebted for important insights into the workings of American capitalism. Galbraith argues that this imbalance is nourished by advertising, which creates artificial wants. He sees it further accentuated by an obsession with production, which keeps us from realizing that our problems are not those of want, but of affluence. The imbalance is epitomized by our supposed tendency to limit public expenditures to what is strictly essential, while we apply no such criterion to private expenditures.

TOO MANY TRIVIA?

One may reasonably argue that Galbraith exaggerates the distorting influence of advertising. That would not alter the basic assumption on which his thesis rests—the assumption that there are better wants and worse wants. Scientific detachment notwithstanding, I find it extraordinarily difficult to disagree with this proposition. To rate an attendance at the opera and a visit to an (inexpensive) nightclub as equivalents, because the market puts a similar price on them, goes against my grain. So does the equation of a dollar's worth of education and a dollar's worth of chromium on an automobile. And a plausible case would probably be made, on the basis of the evolution of the species, that opera and education do represent more advanced forms of consumption.

But what consequences, if any, should be drawn from such judgment? It is one thing to be irritated by certain manifestations of our contemporary civilization—the gadgets, the chrome, the

tail fins and the activities that go with them. It is quite another—
and something of a *non sequitur*—to conclude from this that the
only alternative to foolish private spending is public spending.
Better private spending is just as much of a possibility.

And does this judgment yield a basis for trying to discourage
the growth of the less "good" expenditures? In a free society, we
obviously want to move with the utmost circumspection. It is
worth remembering that even Thorstein Veblen, who went to
some extreme in deriding the "leisure class" and its "conspicuous
consumption," did not take an altogether negative view of all
conspicuous waste. In *The Theory of the Leisure Class* he said,
"No class of society, not even the most abjectly poor, foregoes
all customary conspicuous consumption. . . . There is no class
and no country that has yielded so abjectly before the pressure
of physical want as to deny themselves all gratification of this
higher or spiritual need."

For fair appraisal of the case against trivia, we would also
want to know the approximate size of the bill that is being incurred for various frills and frivolities. Gadgets in cars and homes
have drawn the special ire of the critics. It is interesting to note,
therefore, that expenditures for all kinds of durable consumer
goods, including automobiles, run about 14 per cent of personal
consumption. The greater part of this, presumably, goes for the
essential parts of fairly essential equipment. What is left for orna-
ments and gadgets does not loom impressively large. After all,
not all the income in this country is spent by people for whom life
begins at $25,000. The median family income is $5,600. Would
the critics of the affluent society want to live on much less than
that?

Whatever our private feelings about the gadgetry in our life,
we probably do well not to stress them too hard. It is only too
easy for some members of a community to work themselves into
a fit of righteousness and to feel tempted to help the rest regulate
their existence. In an extreme form, and not very long ago, this
happened in the United States with the introduction of prohibition. Some of us may lean toward special taxation of luxuries,
but surely no one wants sumptuary legislation banishing from
our show windows and homes the offending contrivances. A new
puritanism directed against wasteful consumption, however un-

derstandable, would make no great contribution to an economy that requires incentive goods to activate competition and free markets. Neither would it be compatible with the freedom that we value.

ENDS AND MEANS

It is the positive side of the case—the asserted need for more public services—that must chiefly concern us. My contention here will be that to talk in terms of "public vs. private" is to confuse the issue. More than that, it is to confuse means and ends. The choice between public and private money is primarily a choice of means. The sensible approach for those who are dissatisfied with some of the ends to which private money is being spent, is to specify first what other ends are important and why. Having determined the ends, the next step is to look to the means. That is the order in which I propose to proceed here.

The critics are right in pointing out that new material needs have been carried to the fore by social and economic evolution—even though they mislabel them as public needs. In the good old days, when this was still a nation of farmers, most people had no serious retirement worries, there was no industrial unemployment problem, good jobs could be had without a college degree, most diseases were still incurable—in short, social security, education, and health care found primitive and natural solutions within the family and among the resources of the neighborhood. Today, these solutions are neither adequate nor usually even possible.

Mounting wealth and advancing technology have brought within reach the means of meeting these needs. We can afford to live better in every way—more creature comforts, more leisure, more attention to matters of the mind and spirit. At the same time we can take better care of retirement, of unemployment, of illness, of education, of the possibilities opened by research, than ever before.

There are indeed new needs. The citizen-taxpayer has his choice of meeting them, as well as all his other needs, in one of two ways. He can buy the goods or services he wants privately, for cash or credit. Or he can buy them from the government, for taxes.

The nation as a whole pays taxes to buy public services as it pays grocery bills to buy groceries. The tax burden may be heavier for some individuals than for others. But the nation as a whole has no more reason to complain about the "burden" of taxes than about the "burden" of grocery bills—and no more reason to hope for relief.

Of the two stores, the private store today still is much the bigger. The public store is smaller, but it is growing faster.

Each store has some exclusive items. The private store sells most of the necessities and all of the luxuries of life, and in most of these has no competition from the government side. The public store has some specialties of its own: defense, public order and justice, and numerous local services that the private organization has not found profitable. But there is a wide range of items featured by both stores: provision for old age, health services, education, housing, development of natural resources.

THE NEW NEEDS

The bulk of the new needs are in this competitive area. The fashionable notion is to claim them all for the public store and to label them public needs. The statistics say otherwise. They say in fact two things: First, the supply of this group of goods and services has expanded very rapidly in recent years; and second, they are being offered, in varying degrees, both by the private and the public suppliers. Let us run down the list.

Provision for old age is predominantly private. The average American family, realizing that while old age may be a burden, it is the only known way to achieve a long life, takes care of the matter in three ways: (1) by private individual savings—home ownership, savings deposits, securities; (2) by private collective savings—life insurance, corporate pension funds; and (3) by public collective savings through social security. Statisticians report that the two collective forms are advancing faster than the individual. The increases far exceed the rise in the Gross National Product of almost 80 per cent (in current prices) over the past ten years; they do not indicate either that these needs are neglected or that they are necessarily public in character.

Education: the bulk of it is public; but a good part, particularly of higher education, is private. Total expenditures for all education have advanced in the last ten years from $9.3 billion to $24.6 billion ($19.3 billion of it public). Education's share in the national income has advanced from 3.8 per cent to 5.8 per cent. The silly story that we spend more on advertising than on education is a canard, though with its gross of over $10 billion, advertising does take a lot of money.

Health expenditures are still mainly private. At considerable expense, it is now possible to live longer and be sick less frequently or at least less dangerously. In the past, most people paid their own doctors' bills, although health care for the indigent has always been provided by public action or private philanthropy. Since the war, the proliferation of health insurance has given some form of collective but private insurance to three-quarters of our 182 million people. This has greatly reduced pressure for a national health service along British lines. For the aging, whose health-care needs stand in inverse proportion to their capacity to pay or insure, public insurance has finally been initiated and needs to be expanded. The total annual expenditure on health is estimated at over $25 billion, a little more than on education. Of this, about $6 billion is public.

So much for the allegation that the "new needs" are all public needs. Now for some further statistics on the public store, which is said to have been neglected. Some of them could make an investor in private growth stocks envious. Research expenditures (mainly for defense and atomic energy) have gone from about $1 billion to over $8 billion in the last ten years. Federal grants to the states have advanced from $2.2 billion to $7 billion during the same period. Social-security benefits rose from $1 billion to over $10 billion. All in all, public cash outlays (federal and state) advanced from $61 billion to $134 billion over ten years, 57 per cent faster than the GNP.

For those who feel about public spending the way Mark Twain felt about whiskey, these figures may still look slim. (Mark Twain thought that while too much of anything was bad, too much whiskey was barely enough.) To others, the data may suggest that the advocates of more public spending have already had their way. Could their present discontent be the result of not keeping their statistics up-to-date? In one of his recent pamphlets, Arthur M. Schlesinger, Jr., claims that the sum of the many neglects he observes (including defense) could be mended by raising public expenditures by $10 to $12 billion. That is well below the increase in public cash outlays that actually did take place in one single fiscal year, from $118.2 billion in 1958 to $132.7 billion in 1959. In the three fiscal years 1957–59, these outlays went up more than $31 billion, though the advance slowed down in 1960. More facts and less indignation might help to attain better perspective.

Some parts of federal, state, and local budgets have expanded less rapidly than those cited—in many cases fortunately. The massive buildup in defense expenditures from the late 'forties to the 'fifties has squeezed other programs. Unfortunately, on the other hand, some programs that both political parties have favored— including aid to education, to depressed areas, for urban renewal —have been delayed unduly by the vicissitudes of politics. But the figures as a whole lend little support to the thesis that politicians don't spend enough, and that the government store is not expanding fast enough.

THE CITIZEN IN THE STORES

The two stores—private and public—work very hard these days to capture the business of the citizen-taxpayer. Here is what he hears as he walks into the private store:

"The principal advantage of this store," the private businessman says, "is that you can shop around and buy exactly what you want. If I don't have it I'll order it. You, the consumer, are the boss here. To be sure, I'm not in business for charity but for profit. But my profit comes from giving you what you want. And with competition as fierce as it is, you can be sure the profit won't be excessive."

If the proprietor has been to Harvard Business School, he will perhaps remember to add something about the invisible hand which in a free economy causes the self-seeking of competitors to work for the common good. He will also, even without benefit of business school, remember to drop a word about the danger of letting the public store across the street get too big. It might endanger freedom.

As the citizen turns this sales talk over in his mind, several points occur to him. Without denying the broad validity of the argument, he will note that quite often he has been induced to buy things he did not really need, and possibly to neglect other, more serious needs. Snob appeal and built-in obsolescence promoted by expensive advertising don't seem to him to fit in with the notion that the consumer is king. Looking at the brand names and patents and trademarks, he wonders whether most products are produced and priced competitively instead of under monopoly conditions. The invisible hand at times seems to be invisible mainly because it is so deep in his pocket.

Bothered by these doubts, the citizen walks across the street and enters the public store.

"Let me explain to you," says the politician who runs it—with the aid of a horde of hard-working bureaucrats doing the chores. "The principles on which this store is run are known as the political process, and if you happen to be familiar with private merchandising they may seem unusual, but I assure you they work. First of all, almost everything in this store is free. We simply assess our customers a lump sum in the form of taxes. These, however, are based largely on each customer's ability to pay, rather than on what he gets from the store. We have a show of hands from the customers once a year, and the majority decides what merchandise the store is to have in stock. The majority, incidentally, also decides how much everybody, including particularly the minority, is to be assessed for taxes.

"You will observe," the politician continues, "that this store is not run for profit. It is like a co-operative, run for the welfare of the members. I myself, to be sure, am not in politics for charity, but for re-election. But that means that I must be interested in your needs, or you would not vote for me. Moreover, there are some useful things that only I can do, with the help of the political process, and in which you and every citizen have an interest. For instance, everybody ought to go to school. I can make them go. Everybody ought to have old-age insurance. I can make that compulsory too. And because I don't charge the full cost of the service, I can help even up a little the inequalities of life.

"By the way," the politician concludes, "if there is any special little thing you want, I may be able to get it for you, and of course it won't cost you a nickel."

The citizen has some fault to find with the political process too. He notes that there is not even a theoretical claim to the benefits of an invisible hand. Majority rule may produce benefits for the majority, but how about the other 49 per cent? Nor is there the discipline of competition, or the need for profits, to test economy of operation. There is no way, in the public store, of adjusting individual costs and benefits. And the promise to get him some small favor, while tempting, worries him, because he wonders what the politician may have promised to others. The political process, he is led to suspect, may be a little haphazard.

He asks himself how political decisions get to be made. Sometimes, obviously, it is not the majority that really makes a decision, but a small pressure group that is getting away with something. He will remember that—after payments for major national security and public debt interest—the largest single expenditure in the federal budget is for agriculture, and the next for veterans. He may also recall that one of the first budgetary actions of the new Administration was to increase funds for agriculture by $3 billion.

THE EXPANDING BELT

Next, the citizen might consider the paralyzing "balance-of-forces" effect that often blocks a desirable reshuffling of expenditures. The allocation of public funds reflects the bargaining power of their sponsors, inside or outside the government. A classical example was the division of funds that prevailed in the Defense Department during the late 'forties. Army, Navy, and Air Force were to share in total resources in a way that would maximize military potential. By some strange coincidence, maximum potential was always achieved by giving each service the same amount of money. It took the Korean War to break this stalemate.

What is the consequence of the balance-of-forces effect? If the proponents of one kind of expenditure want to get more money for their projects, they must concede an increase also to the advocates of others. More education means more highways, instead of less; more air power means more ground forces. To increase a budget in one direction only is as difficult as letting out one's belt only on one side. The expansion tends to go all around. What this comes down to is that politicians are not very good at setting priorities. Increases in good expenditures are burdened with a political surcharge of less good ones.

The last-ditch survival power of federal programs is a specially illuminating instance of the balance of forces. If a monument were built in Washington in memory of each major federal program that has been discontinued, the appearance of the city would not be greatly altered. In contrast, when the Edsel doesn't sell, production stops. But the government is still reclaiming land to raise more farm surpluses and training fishermen to enter an occupation that needs subsidies to keep alive. Old federal programs never die, they don't even fade away—they just go on.

The citizen will remember also the ancient and honorable practice of logrolling. The unhappy fate of the Area Development bill illustrates it admirably. As originally proposed, the bill sought to aid a limited number of industrial areas where new jobs were badly needed. It got nowhere in the Congress. Only when it was extended to a large number of areas with less urgent or quite different problems, were enough legislators brought aboard to pass it. Because of the heavy political surcharge with which it had become loaded, President Eisenhower vetoed the bill. A bill was finally enacted early this year, long after aid should have been brought to the areas that needed it.

Finally, the citizen might discover in some dark corner of his mind a nagging thought: Any particular government program may be a blessing, but could their cumulative effect be a threat to freedom? He has heard businessmen say this so often that he has almost ceased to pay attention to it. He rather resents businessmen acting the dog in the manger, trying to stop useful things from being done unless they can do them. He is irritated when he hears a man talk about freedom who obviously is thinking about profit. And yet—is there any conclusive rebuttal?

THE CITIZEN'S FAILURES

The citizen would be quite wrong, however, if he blamed the politician for the defects of the political process. The fault lies with the process, or better with the way in which the process, the politician, and the citizen interact. The citizen therefore would do well to examine some of his own reactions and attitudes.

First, when he thinks about taxes, he tends to think of them as a burden instead of as a price he pays for a service. As a body, the nation's taxpayers are like a group of neighbors who decide to establish a fire department. Because none is quite sure how much good it will do him, and because each hopes to benefit from the contribution of the rest, all are prudent in their contributions. In the end they are likely to wind up with a bucket brigade.

But when it comes to accepting benefits, the citizen-taxpayers act like a group of men who sit down at a restaurant table knowing that they will split the check evenly. In this situation everybody orders generously; it adds little to one's own share of the bill, and for the extravagance of his friends he will have to pay anyhow. What happens at the restaurant table explains—though it does not excuse—what happens at the public trough.

Finally, in his reaction to public or free services, the citizen takes a great deal for granted, and seldom thinks of the cost. Public beaches mistreated, unmetered parking space permanently occupied, veterans' adjustment benefits continued without need —as well as abuses of unemployment compensation and public assistance—are some examples. This applies also, of course, to privately offered benefits, under health insurance, for instance. The kindly nurse in the hospital—"Why don't you stay another day, dearie, it won't cost you anything, it's all paid for by Blue Cross"—makes the point.

By removing the link between costs and benefits, the political process also reduces the citizen's interest in earning money. The citizen works to live. If some of his living comes to him without working, he would be less than rational if he did not respond with a demand for shorter hours. If these public benefits increase his tax burden so that his over-all standard of living remains unchanged, the higher taxes will reduce his work incentive. Why work hard, if much of it is for the government?

THE POLITICAL DOLLAR AT A DISCOUNT

These various defects of the political process add up to an obvious conclusion: the dollar spent by even the most honest and scrupulous of politicians is not always a full-bodied dollar. It often is subject to a discount. It buys less than it should because of the attrition it suffers as it goes through the process, and so may be worth only 90 cents or 80 cents and sometimes perhaps less. The private dollar, in too many cases, may also be worth less than 100 per cent. But here each man can form his own judgment, can pick and choose or refuse altogether. In the political process, all he can do is say Yes or No once a year in November.

The discount on the public dollar may be compensated by the other advantages of government—its ability to compel, to subsidize, to do things on a big scale and at a low interest cost. Whether that is the case needs to be studied in each instance. Where these advantages do not apply, the private market will give better service than the political process. For many services, there is at least some leeway for choice between the private and public store—health and retirement, housing, research, higher education, natural-resource development. Defense, on the other hand, as well as public administration, public works of all kinds, and the great bulk of education—while perhaps made rather expensive by the political process—leave no realistic alternative to public action.

The argument I have offered is no plea to spend more or less on any particular function. It is a plea for doing whatever we do in the most effective way.

The Role of Government in a Free Society

Milton Friedman is Paul Russell Snowden Professor of Economics at the University of Chicago. His book, Capitalism and Freedom, *from which this essay is taken, describes competitive capitalism as a necessary condition for political freedom and defines the role that government should play in a society dedicated to freedom.*

A COMMON OBJECTION to totalitarian societies is that they regard the end as justifying the means. Taken literally, this objection is clearly illogical. If the end does not justify the means, what does? But this easy answer does not dispose of the objection; it simply shows that the objection is not well put. To deny that the end justifies the means is indirectly to assert that the end in question is not the ultimate end, that the ultimate end is itself the use of the proper means. Desirable or not, any end that can be attained only by the use of bad means must give way to the more basic end of the use of acceptable means.

To the liberal, the appropriate means are free discussion and voluntary cooperation, which implies that any form of coercion is inappropriate. The ideal is unanimity among responsible individuals achieved on the basis of free and full discussion.

From this standpoint, the role of the market is that it permits unanimity without conformity; that it is a system of effectively proportional representation. On the other hand, the characteristic feature of action through explicitly political channels is that it tends to require or to enforce substantial conformity. The typical issue must be decided "yes" or "no"; at most, provision can be made for a fairly limited number of alternatives. Even the use of proportional representation in its explicitly political form does not alter this conclusion. The number of separate groups that can in fact be represented is narrowly limited, enormously so by comparison with the proportional representation of the market. More important, the fact that the final outcome generally must be a law applicable to all groups, rather than separate legisla-

tive enactments for each "party" represented, means that proportional representation in its political version, far from permitting unanimity without conformity, tends toward ineffectiveness and fragmentation. It thereby operates to destroy any consensus on which unanimity with conformity can rest.

There are clearly some matters with respect to which effective proportional representation is impossible. I cannot get the amount of national defense I want and you, a different amount. With respect to such indivisible matters we can discuss, and argue, and vote. But having decided, we must conform. It is precisely the existence of such indivisible matters—protection of the individual and the nation from coercion are clearly the most basic—that prevents exclusive reliance on individual action through the market. If we are to use some of our resources for such indivisible items, we must employ political channels to reconcile differences.

The use of political channels, while inevitable, tends to strain the social cohesion essential for a stable society. The strain is least if agreement for joint action need be reached only on a limited range of issues on which people in any event have common views. Every extension of the range of issues for which explicit agreement is sought strains further the delicate threads that hold society together. If it goes so far as to touch an issue on which men feel deeply yet differently, it may well disrupt the society. Fundamental differences in basic values can seldom if ever be resolved at the ballot box; ultimately they can only be decided, though not resolved, by conflict. The religious and civil wars of history are a bloody testament to this judgment.

The widespread use of the market reduces the strain on the social fabric by rendering conformity unnecessary with respect to any activities it encompasses. The wider the range of activities covered by the market, the fewer are the issues on which explicitly political decisions are required and hence on which it is necessary to achieve agreement. In turn, the fewer the issues on which agreement is necessary, the greater is the likelihood of getting agreement while maintaining a free society.

Unanimity is, of course, an ideal. In practice, we can afford neither the time nor the effort that would be required to achieve complete unanimity on every issue. We must perforce accept something less. We are thus led to accept majority rule in one

form or another as an expedient. That majority rule is an expedient rather than itself a basic principle is clearly shown by the fact that our willingness to resort to majority rule, and the size of the majority we require, themselves depend on the seriousness of the issue involved. If the matter is of little moment and the minority has no strong feelings about being overruled, a bare plurality will suffice. On the other hand, if the minority feels strongly about the issue involved, even a bare majority will not do. Few of us would be willing to have issues of free speech, for example, decided by a bare majority. Our legal structure is full of such distinctions among kinds of issues that require different kinds of majorities. At the extreme are those issues embodied in the Constitution. These are the principles that are so important that we are willing to make minimal concessions to expediency. Something like essential consensus was achieved initially in accepting them, and we require something like essential consensus for a change in them.

The self-denying ordinance to refrain from majority rule on certain kinds of issues that is embodied in our Constitution and in similar written or unwritten constitutions elsewhere, and the specific provisions in these constitutions or their equivalents prohibiting coercion of individuals, are themselves to be regarded as reached by free discussion and as reflecting essential unanimity about means.

I turn now to consider more specifically, though still in very broad terms, what the areas are that cannot be handled through the market at all, or can be handled only at so great a cost that the use of political channels may be preferable.

GOVERNMENT AS RULE-MAKER AND UMPIRE

It is important to distinguish the day-to-day activities of people from the general customary and legal framework within which these take place. The day-to-day activities are like the actions of the participants in a game when they are playing it; the framework, like the rules of the game they play. And just as a good game requires acceptance by the players both of the rules and of the umpire to interpret and enforce them, so a good society requires that its members agree on the general conditions that will govern relations among them, on some means of arbitrating different interpretations of these conditions, and on some device for enforcing compliance with the generally accepted rules. As in games, so also in society, most of the general conditions are the unintended outcome of custom, accepted unthinkingly. At most, we consider explicitly only minor modifications in them, though the cumulative effect of a series of minor modifications may be a drastic alteration in the character of the game or of the society. In both games and society also, no set of rules can prevail unless most participants most of the time conform to them without external sanctions; unless that is, there is a broad underlying social consensus. But we cannot rely on custom or on this consensus alone to interpret and to enforce the rules; we need an umpire. These then are the basic roles of government in a free society: to provide a means whereby we can modify the rules, to mediate differences among us on the meaning of the rules, and to enforce compliance with the rules on the part of those few who would otherwise not play the game.

The need for government in these respects arises because absolute freedom is impossible. However attractive anarchy may be as a philosophy, it is not feasible in a world of imperfect men. Men's freedoms can conflict, and when they do, one man's freedom must be limited to preserve another's—as a Supreme Court Justice once put it, "My freedom to move my fist must be limited by the proximity of your chin."

The major problem in deciding the appropriate activities of government is how to resolve such conflicts among the freedoms of different individuals. In some cases, the answer is easy. There is little difficulty in attaining near unanimity to the proposition that one man's freedom to murder his neighbor must be sacrificed to preserve the freedom of the other man to live. In other cases, the answer is difficult. In the economic area, a major problem arises in respect of the conflict between freedom to combine and freedom to compete. What meaning is to be attributed to "free" as modifying "enterprise"? In the United States, "free" has been understood to mean that anyone is free to set up an enterprise, which means that existing enterprises are not free to keep out competitors except by selling a better product at the same price or the same product at a lower price. In the continental tradition, on the other hand, the meaning has generally been that enterprises are free to do what they want, including the fixing of prices, division of markets, and the adoption of other techniques to keep out potential competitors. Perhaps the most difficult specific problem in this area arises with respect to combinations among laborers, where the problem of freedom to combine and freedom to compete is particularly acute.

A still more basic economic area in which the answer is both difficult and important is the definition of property rights. The notion of property, as it has developed over centuries and as it is embodied in our legal codes, has become so much a part of us that we tend to take it for granted, and fail to recognize the extent to which just what constitutes property and what rights the ownership of property confers are complex social creations rather than self-evident propositions. Does my having title to land, for example, and my freedom to use my property as I wish, permit me to deny to someone else the right to fly over my land in his airplane? Or does his right to use his airplane take precedence? Or does this depend on how high he flies? Or how much noise he makes? Does voluntary exchange require that he pay me for the privilege of flying over my land? Or that I must pay him to refrain from flying over it? The mere mention of royalties, copyrights, patents; shares of stock in corporations; riparian rights, and the like, may perhaps emphasize the role of generally accepted social rules in the very definition of property. It may suggest also that, in many cases, the existence of a well specified and generally accepted definition of property is far more important than just what the definition is. . . .

In summary, the organization of economic activity through voluntary exchange presumes that we have provided, through government, for the maintenance of law and order to prevent coercion of one individual by another, the enforcement of contracts voluntarily entered into, the definition of the meaning of property rights, the interpretation and enforcement of such rights, and the provision of a monetary framework.

ACTION THROUGH GOVERNMENT ON GROUNDS OF
TECHNICAL MONOPOLY AND NEIGHBORHOOD EFFECTS

The role of government just considered is to do something that the market cannot do for itself, namely, to determine, arbitrate, and enforce the rules of the game. We may also want to do through government some things that might conceivably be done through the market but that technical or similar conditions render it difficult to do in that way. These all reduce to cases in which strictly voluntary exchange is either exceedingly costly or practically impossible. There are two general classes of such cases: monopoly and similar market imperfections, and neighborhood effects.

Exchange is truly voluntary only when nearly equivalent alternatives exist. Monopoly implies the absence of alternatives and thereby inhibits effective freedom of exchange. In practice, monopoly frequently, if not generally, arises from government support or from collusive agreements among individuals. With respect to these, the problem is either to avoid governmental fostering of monopoly or to stimulate the effective enforcement of rules such as those embodied in our antitrust laws. However, monopoly may also arise because it is technically efficient to have a single producer or enterprise. I venture to suggest that such cases are more limited than is supposed but they unquestionably do arise. A simple example is perhaps the provision of telephone services within a community. I shall refer to such cases as "technical" monopoly.

When technical conditions make a monopoly the natural outcome of competitive market forces, there are only three alternatives that seem available: private monopoly, public monopoly, or public regulation. All three are bad so we must choose among evils. Henry Simons, observing public regulation of monopoly in the United States, found the results so distasteful that he concluded public monopoly would be a lesser evil. Walter Eucken, a noted German liberal, observing public monopoly in German railroads, found the results so distasteful that he concluded public regulation would be a lesser evil. Having learned from both, I reluctantly conclude that, if tolerable, private monopoly may be the least of the evils.

If society were static so that the conditions which give rise to a technical monopoly were sure to remain, I would have little confidence in this solution. In a rapidly changing society, however, the conditions making for technical monopoly frequently change and I suspect that both public regulation and public monopoly are likely to be less responsive to such changes in conditions, to be less readily capable of elimination, than private monopoly.

Railroads in the United States are an excellent example. A large degree of monopoly in railroads was perhaps inevitable on technical grounds in the nineteenth century. This was the justification for the Interstate Commerce Commission. But conditions have changed. The emergence of road and air transport has reduced the monopoly element in railroads to negligible proportions. Yet we have not eliminated the ICC. On the contrary, the ICC, which started out as an agency to protect the public from exploitation by the railroads, has become an agency to protect railroads from competition by trucks and other means of transport, and more recently even to protect existing truck companies from competition by new entrants. Similarly, in England, when the railroads were nationalized, trucking was at first brought into the state monopoly. If railroads had never been subjected to regulation in the United States, it is nearly certain that by now transportation, including railroads, would be a highly competitive industry with little or no remaining monopoly elements.

The choice among the evils of private monopoly, public monopoly, and public regulation cannot, however, be made once and for all, independently of the factual circumstances. If the technical monopoly is of a service or commodity that is regarded as essential and if its monopoly power is sizable, even the short-run effects of private unregulated monopoly may not be tolerable, and either public regulation or ownership may be a lesser evil.

Technical monopoly may on occasion justify a *de facto* public monopoly. It cannot by itself justify a public monopoly achieved by making it illegal for anyone else to compete. For example, there is no way to justify our present public monopoly of the post office. It may be argued that the carrying of mail is a technical monopoly and that a government monopoly is the least of evils. Along these lines, one could perhaps justify a government post office but not the present law, which makes it illegal for anybody else to carry mail. If the delivery of mail is a technical monopoly, no one will be able to succeed in competition with the government. If it is not, there is no reason why the government should be engaged in it. The only way to find out is to leave other people free to enter.

The historical reason why we have a post office monopoly is because the Pony Express did such a good job of carrying the mail across the continent that, when the government introduced transcontinental service, it couldn't compete effectively and lost money. The result was a law making it illegal for anybody else to carry the mail. That is why the Adams Express Company is an investment trust today instead of an operating company. I conjecture that if entry into the mail-carrying business were open to all, there would be a large number of firms entering it and this archaic industry would become revolutionized in short order.

A second general class of cases in which strictly voluntary exchange is impossible arises when actions of individuals have effects on other individuals for which it is not feasible to charge or recompense them. This is the problem of "neighborhood effects." An obvious example is the pollution of a stream. The man who pollutes a stream is in effect forcing others to exchange good water for bad. These others might be willing to make the exchange at a price. But it is not feasible for them, acting individually, to avoid the exchange or to enforce appropriate compensation.

A less obvious example is the provision of highways. In this case, it is technically possible to identify and hence charge individuals for their use of the roads and so to have private operation. However, for general access roads, involving many points of entry and exit, the costs of collection would be extremely high if a charge were to be made for the specific services received by each individual, because of the necessity of establishing toll booths or the equivalent at all entrances. The gasoline tax is a much cheaper method of charging individuals roughly in proportion to their use of the roads. This method, however, is one in which the particular payment cannot be identified closely with the particular use. Hence, it is hardly feasible to have private enterprise provide the service and collect the charge without establishing extensive private monopoly.

These considerations do not apply to long-distance turnpikes with high density of traffic and limited access. For these, the costs of collection are small and in many cases are now being paid, and there are often numerous alternatives, so that there is no serious monopoly problem. Hence, there is every reason why these should be privately owned and operated. If so owned and operated, the enterprise running the highway should receive the gasoline taxes paid on account of travel on it.

Parks are an interesting example because they illustrate the difference between cases that can and cases that cannot be justified by neighborhood effects, and because almost everyone at first sight regards the conduct of national parks as obviously a valid function of government. In fact, however, neighborhood effects may justify a city park; they do not justify a national park, like Yellowstone National Park or the Grand Canyon. What is the fundamental difference between the two? For the city park, it is extremely difficult to identify the people who benefit from it and to charge them for the benefits which they receive. If there is a park in the middle of the city, the houses on all sides get the benefit of the open space, and people who walk through it or by it also benefit. To maintain toll collectors at the gates or to impose annual charges per window overlooking the park would be very expensive and difficult. The entrances to a national park like Yellowstone, on the other hand, are few; most of the people who came stay for a considerable period of time and it is perfectly feasible to set up toll gates and collect admission charges. This is indeed now done, though the charges do not cover the whole costs. If the public wants this kind of an activity enough to pay for it, private enterprises will have every incentive to provide such parks. And, of course, there are many private enterprises of this nature now in existence. I cannot myself conjure up any neighborhood effects or important monopoly effects that would justify governmental activity in this area.

Considerations like those I have treated under the heading of neighborhood effects have been used to rationalize almost every conceivable intervention. In many instances, however, this rationalization is special pleading rather than a legitimate application of the concept of neighborhood effects. Neighborhood effects cut both ways. They can be a reason for limiting the activities of government as well as for expanding them. Neighborhood effects impede voluntary exchange because it is difficult to identify the effects on third parties and to measure their magnitude; but this difficulty is present in governmental activity as well. It is hard to know when neighborhood effects are sufficiently large to justify particular costs in overcoming them and even harder to distribute the costs in an appropriate fashion. Consequently, when government engages in activities to overcome neighborhood effects, it will in part introduce an additional set of neighborhood effects by failing to charge or to compensate individuals properly. Whether the original or the new neighborhood effects are the more serious can only be judged by the facts of the individual case, and even then, only very approximately. Furthermore, the use of government to overcome neighborhood effects itself has an extremely important neighborhood effect which is unrelated to the particular occasion for government action. Every act of government intervention limits the area of individual freedom directly and threatens the preservation of freedom indirectly.

Our principles offer no hard and fast line how far it is appropriate to use government to accomplish jointly what it is difficult or impossible for us to accomplish separately through strictly voluntary exchange. In any particular case of proposed intervention, we must make up a balance sheet, listing separately the advantages and disadvantages. Our principles tell us what items to put on the one side and what items on the other and they give us some basis for attaching importance to the different items. In particular, we shall always want to enter on the liability side of any proposed government intervention its neighborhood effect in threatening freedom and give this effect considerable weight. Just how much weight to give to it, as to other items, depends upon the circumstances. If, for example, existing government intervention is minor, we shall attach a smaller weight to the negative effects of additional government intervention. This is an important reason why many earlier liberals, like Henry Simons, writing at a time when government was small by today's standards, were willing to have government undertake activities that today's liberals would not accept now that government has become so overgrown.

ACTION THROUGH GOVERNMENT ON PATERNALISTIC GROUNDS

Freedom is a tenable objective only for responsible individuals. We do not believe in freedom for madmen or children. The necessity of drawing a line between responsible individuals and others is inescapable, yet it means that there is an essential ambiguity in our ultimate objective of freedom. Paternalism is inescapable for those whom we designate as not responsible.

The clearest case, perhaps, is that of madmen. We are willing neither to permit them freedom nor to shoot them. It would be nice if we could rely on voluntary activities of individuals to house and care for the madmen. But I think we cannot rule out the possibility that such charitable activities will be inadequate, if only because of the neighborhood effect involved in the fact that I benefit if another man contributes to the care of the insane. For this reason, we may be willing to arrange for their care through government.

Children offer a more difficult case. The ultimate operative unit in our society is the family, not the individual. Yet the acceptance of the family as the unit rests in considerable part on expediency rather than principle. We believe that parents are generally best able to protect their children and to provide for their development into responsible individuals for whom freedom is appropriate. But we do not believe in the freedom of parents to do what they will with other people. The children are responsible individuals in embryo, and a believer in freedom believes in protecting their ultimate rights.

To put this in a different and what may seem a more callous way, children are at one and the same time consumer goods and potentially responsible members of society. The freedom of individuals to use their economic resources as they want includes the freedom to use them to have children—to buy, as it were, the services of children as a particular form of consumption. But once this choice is exercised, the children have a value in and of themselves and have a freedom of their own that is not simply an extension of the freedom of the parents.

The paternalistic ground for governmental activity is in many ways the most troublesome to a liberal; for it involves the acceptance of a principle—that some shall decide for others—which he finds objectionable in most applications and which he rightly regards as a hallmark of his chief intellectual opponents, the proponents of collectivism in one or another of its guises, whether it be communism, socialism, or a welfare state. Yet there is no use pretending that problems are simpler than in fact they are. There is no avoiding the need for some measure of paternalism. As Dicey wrote in 1914 about an act for the protection of mental defectives, "The Mental Deficiency Act is the first step along a path on which no sane man can decline to enter, but which, if too far pursued, will bring statesmen across difficulties hard to meet without considerable interference with individual liberty." [1] There is no formula that can tell us where to stop. We must rely on our fallible judgment and, having reached a judgment, on our ability to persuade our fellow men that it is a correct judgment, or their ability to persuade us to modify our views. We must put our faith, here as elsewhere, in a consensus reached by imperfect and biased men through free discussion and trial and error.

CONCLUSION

A government which maintained law and order, defined property rights, served as a means whereby we could modify property rights and other rules of the economic game, adjudicated disputes about the interpretation of the rules, enforced contracts, promoted competition, provided a monetary framework, engaged in activities to counter technical monopolies and to overcome neighborhood effects widely regarded as sufficiently important to justify government intervention, and which supplemented private charity and the private family in protecting the irresponsible, whether madman or child—such a government would clearly have important functions to perform. The consistent liberal is not an anarchist.

Yet it is also true that such a government would have clearly limited functions and would refrain from a host of activities that are now undertaken by federal and state governments in the United States, and their counterparts in other Western countries. It may help to give a sense of proportion about the role that a liberal would assign government simply to list some activities currently undertaken by government in the U.S. that cannot, so far as I can see, validly be justified in terms of the principles outlined above:

1. Parity-price-support programs for agriculture.
2. Tariffs on imports or restrictions on exports, such as current

1. A. V. Dicey, *Lectures on the Relation between Law and Public Opinion in England during the Nineteenth Century*, 2d. ed. (London: Macmillan & Co., 1914), p. li.

oil import quotas, sugar quotas, etc.

3. Governmental control of output, such as through the farm program or through prorationing of oil as is done by the Texas Railroad Commission.

4. Rent control, such as is still practiced in New York, and more general price and wage controls such as were imposed during and just after World War II.

5. Legal minimum wage rates, or legal maximum prices, such as the legal maximum of zero on the rate of interest that can be paid on demand deposits by commercial banks, or the legally fixed maximum rates that can be paid on savings and time deposits.

6. Detailed regulation of industries, such as the regulation of transportation by the Interstate Commerce Commission. This had some justification on technical monopoly grounds when initially introduced for railroads; it has none now for any means of transport. Another example is detailed regulation of banking.

7. A similar example, but one which deserves special mention because of its implicit censorship and violation of free speech, is the control of radio and television by the Federal Communications Commission.

8. Present social security programs, especially the old-age and retirement programs compelling people in effect (a) to spend a specified fraction of their income on the purchase of retirement annuity and (b) to buy the annuity from a publicly operated enterprise.

9. Licensure provisions in various cities and states which restrict particular enterprises or occupations or professions to people who have a license, where the license is more than a receipt for a tax which anyone who wishes to enter the activity may pay.

10. So-called "public-housing" and the host of other subsidy programs directed at fostering residential construction such as FHA and V.A. guarantee of mortgage, and the like.

11. Conscription to man the military services in peacetime. The appropriate free-market arrangement is volunteer military forces; which is to say, hiring men to serve. There is no justification for not paying whatever prices is necessary to attract the required number of men. Present arrangements

are inequitable and arbitrary, seriously interfere with the freedom of young men to shape their lives, and probably are even more costly than the market alternative. (Universal military training to provide a reserve for wartime is a different problem and may be justified on liberal grounds.)

12. National parks, as noted above.
13. The legal prohibition on the carrying of mail for profit.
14. Publicly owned and operated toll roads, as noted above.

This list is far from comprehensive.

PART SIX

The Battle

Against

Unemployment

PROSPERITY IS RIVALED only by peace as the key political issue in the United States. Unemployment and recession hit people hard in their pockets and pocketbooks and threaten their freedom of action and security. Sustained economic expansion throughout the Kennedy-Johnson Administration was advanced by President Johnson as a strong argument for a Democratic vote in 1964. In contrast, after the 1960 election, former Vice President Richard M. Nixon expressed his feeling that the high unemployment of the 1960 recession had cost him the Presidency. Public action to curb unemployment lies in the sphere of political economy—both political values and economic analysis are essential ingredients in decision-making. Without assuming a set of social values, an economist cannot tell the nation what to do. Nevertheless economic analysis does have much light to throw on the issues.

While the selections that follow reach different conclusions on matters of fact and value, they all follow the spirit of social scientific inquiry. These essays also reflect the spirit of the Employment Act of 1946, which declared, "it is the continuing policy and responsibility of the Federal Government . . . to promote maximum employment, production, and purchasing power." The Employment Act committed the federal government to a policy of combating unemployment. The conclusion that social action to curb unemployment is necessary and desirable is neither trite nor self-evident. Thirty-five years ago most economists believed that the private enterprise system, functioning competitively, had an automatic tendency to balance supply and demand in the aggregate at the right level. Wide fluctuations in economic activity and excessive unemployment were generally interpreted as either inevitable features of a growing economy or the results of government interference in economic life. Such views pointed toward a hands-off policy of neutrality for the government.

The Great Depression had a permanent impact on attitudes toward public policy against unemployment. At the depths of the depression, one-fourth of the nation's labor force was unemployed; and the unemployment rate did not fall below 14 percent throughout the 1930s. No individual escaped the impact of this great collapse and no individual could combat it on his own. With the sole exception of the Civil War, no episode in our nation's history has so strained the very fabric of American society. The public refused to accept this deep and persistent depression as inevitable; nor could it be convinced that the depression was attributable to the errors of the government. The call for social action was insistent and persuasive; it was answered by the innovations of the New Deal. Meanwhile, at a theoretical level, the great British economist John Maynard Keynes dealt a mortal blow to Say's Law, the doctrine that supply creates its own demand; he thereby destroyed the logical foundation for faith in the basic stability of the private economy. Thus, the battle of public policy against unemployment took shape in the 1930s.

The battle was resumed under the banner of the Employment Act after 1946. The postwar employment record is far superior to that of earlier years. Indeed, in the first postwar decade, unemployment rates of 4 percent and lower were the rule, broken only during and immediately after two brief recessions. From late 1957 to 1964, however, unemployment was not significantly below 5 percent at any time; it averaged nearly 6 percent. This backsliding in our performance has been the subject of much discussion and investigation.

Beginning in 1961, however, the American economy experienced a long, sustained expansion of business activity, which dramatically reversed the trend toward frequent recessions in the 1950s. From the low point of the 1960–61 recession to the end of 1965, output grew by 30 percent.

The advances in economic performance have been matched by advances in economic policy. Measures to stabilize the economy have played an important role in supporting the economic upswing. Early in the Kennedy Administration, substantial increases in federal spending, required principally for defense and space, had an expansionary influence; then tax reduction became the principal expansionary instrument. Depreciation rules for taxation were liberalized in 1962; then a 7-percent tax credit on business investment in machinery and equipment was enacted; the Revenue Act of 1964 reduced personal income taxes by one fifth, on the average, and corporate income taxes by nearly one tenth. And finally, excise tax-cut legislation was enacted in 1965. Meanwhile, the Federal Reserve has avoided the increases in long-term interest rates and the tightening of credit that have typically accompanied the rising financial demands of an economic expansion.

As a result, there is increasing agreement that the government can contribute positively and decisively to the strength of prosperity in a free economy. There is less fatalism about the rhythm of the business cycle and more determination to head off threats of recession or of an unsuitable boom.

But our problems are far from solved. While unemployment has improved to the extent that gains in production have exceeded the rise in our productive capacity, about 4½ percent of the labor force still remain jobless. And our record of price stability has yet to be tested in an environment of full utilization. Much work remains ahead of us to achieve complete victory in the battle against unemployment.

A. M. O.

The Costs of Unemployment

SENATE SPECIAL COMMITTEE

ON UNEMPLOYMENT PROBLEMS

*This selection is from the 1960 report of the Senate Special
Committee on Unemployment Problems; Senator Eugene J. Mc-
Carthy of Minnesota served as chairman.*

WHETHER MEASURED by economic and material loss or by human
suffering and wasted skills, the cost of unemployment is high.
Unused natural resources remain to be used in the future. But
work, the creative activity of man, once wasted can never be
recovered; what might have been produced is lost. The damage
to individuals and to society from unemployment often cannot
be repaired.

THE ECONOMIC COST TO THE INDIVIDUAL AND HIS FAMILY

Nine out of ten workers in the United States are members of
families with responsibility for the support of other members.
Nearly half of the 44 million families in the United States in 1957
were supported by the efforts of one wage earner; 45 percent
had two or more wage earners; 5 percent had income exclusively
from pensions, investments, or social welfare assistance.

The financial problems of the families of the unemployed have
never been fully or accurately studied, but a number of State
unemployment bureaus have made intensive studies of spending
patterns before and during unemployment. A sampling of unemployment compensation beneficiaries in Oregon in 1958 showed
that 37 percent of the beneficiaries interviewed were heads of
families for whom unemployment benefits were the only re-

ported regular family income. Another 17 percent lived alone and were totally dependent upon unemployment compensation. Twenty-one percent were normally the chief wage earners in families which had, however, other wage earners.

Many families in the United States are dependent upon the earnings of two or more members or have adjusted their standards of living to the earnings of two or more members. Loss of job by any member contributing to the income of the family forces economic and social adjustment for everyone; in some cases it may even endanger family welfare.

Loss of jobs by the many individuals who do not qualify for unemployment insurance benefits usually means a complete loss of income, but even those who are eligible for benefits suffer a drastic reduction in income. In 1959, for example, unemployment insurance benefits averaged about $30 a week; very few of the unemployed who received unemployment benefits received more than half of their previous income.

Unemployment benefits for many are quickly exhausted. During the 1958 business downturn about two-thirds of the unemployed received benefits, but in the last part of 1959 fewer than half the unemployed collected benefits. Family incomes during these periods must, of course, be supplemented from other sources. Other members of the family may be able to get jobs, small family-farm production may be increased, or tenants may be taken into the family home.

Social security payments are particularly important as a source of income for older workers who become unemployed. Persons between 65 and 72 years old cannot collect these pensions if they continue to work, except at relatively low pay, but if they lose their jobs they become eligible at once. Old age and survivors insurance is important as a source of family income only if the recipient is a member of a family. Since many pension recipients live with their children or other relatives, some pensions do help support unemployed relatives.

Family investments and savings, including insurance policies, are another source of income during times of stress. According to a Michigan study introduced into the record during the committee hearings in Detroit,

About 44 percent of the unemployed heads of families reported that they had some savings which they used in the emergency. Although the extent of the savings drawn is not known, reliance upon savings was by far the most important measure taken. . . . This fact indicates the extent to which thrift and self-responsibility are relied upon to meet unemployment emergencies.

Measures taken to adjust to loss of income, according to the same study, were, in the order of importance: use of savings, reductions in buying, getting help from relatives, piling up bills, and borrowing money. Some families moved to cheaper quarters, were able to have another member of the family go to work, or sought relief from a public welfare agency. The average family took two of these measures. The major areas for economizing were clothing, recreational and community activities, food, insurance, living quarters, and postponement of medical or dental care.

The effects of unemployment are felt long after the unemployed person has gone back to work. Accumulated debts have to be repaid, neglected health problems attended to, and depleted savings replenished. In most cases it takes a family a long time to regain the financial position it held before unemployment.

THE SOCIAL EFFECTS OF UNEMPLOYMENT

Many serious social problems follow directly from unemployment. In some areas of chronic unemployment these problems are as bad now as they were during the depression of the 1930's. The social effects of unemployment vary considerably according to the age, length of unemployment, the economic level of the unemployed, and other factors, but there is a common pattern of unfortunate consequences.

Unemployment is, of course, the greatest hazard for people in the lowest social and income groups, whose members often hold short-term jobs and are subject to layoffs. The family's normal standard of living is low, and family life is often disorganized and unstable. Children generally leave school at an early age and the delinquency rate is high. One witness before the committee observed:

Except in those cases where there is obvious personal disability in either or both parents, the social scientist is reluctant to accept this as a normal situation. The cultural environment that is often the result of the unemployment situation also becomes a cause of unemployment as the employer sifts through the applications for the "right kind" of employee. This is obviously a vicious circle. This acts as a barricade to the normal aspirations of American people to move up into the broad middle class. The basic sociological question is whether we must necessarily and always have a residual category of people at the bottom of the social structure.

Unemployment also has serious effects upon citizens who consider themselves members of the middle class. For them unemployment carries a suggestion of failure, even though it may be the result of forces beyond the control of anyone in the family. Persons responsible for support of the family suffer loss of prestige and status. Members of the family are inclined to withdraw from participation in community and neighborhood activities, unions, lodges, and similar groups. One witness in Evansville, Ind., described the reaction in his own words:

I know all morning you have heard quite a bit about the financial status of the unemployed, but I would like to say a few words about the emotional status. . . . There is a social aspect to unemployment that arises from the ties and bonds of group relations and friends and neighbors and so on. Everybody wants to be recognized socially, and while I was unemployed, emotional problems did arise; for instance, with my friends, they knew I was unemployed and knew I could not afford to entertain, they didn't think I could afford it, and rather than ask us to go places with them, they wanted to save us the embarrassment and that leaves quite a problem of being under the pressure that we were under. I say "we"—my whole family was involved. It made us wonder if we were actually forsaken by our friends or if this was true friendship to ignore us.

The effect on the children of the unemployed is most distressing. Their health, security, educational opportunities, and entire future are endangered. In one county in West Virginia the school superintendent reported that one out of three pupils in a school enrollment of 22,374 came from a family in which the person who normally supported the family was unemployed; in the month of October 1959, 24.8 percent of the school lunches were free or sold at a reduced price. . . .

In another survey of 11 schools, the family head of 39 percent of the children was unemployed. Children in one school were weighed in November and again at the start of their Christmas vacation to measure the effect of the school's hot lunch program. The net gain of between 3 and 5 pounds per pupil was completely wiped out during the Christmas vacation when the children had to eat at home. . . .

An unemployed mine worker summarized his life and future this way:

The biggest majority of us never had an opportunity to get an education, so then we had to go into the mines at an early age—15, 16 years old. The biggest part of us are married and if we should leave here now and go to the city, what confronts us? If you're over 35 you can't get a job. And if a man's got a family and he goes to the city, what job can he get if he doesn't have any skill?

The director of the welfare department of St. Louis County in Minnesota reported:

In all too many families the stress of unemployment tends to separate rather than to mold the family into a smoother functioning unit. . . . The most important reaction is that there seems to be an increase in the hostile reaction toward one another and also toward society . . . the wife blames the husband for being out of work. . . . In many instances the roles become reversed. In many of these situations, the family is never able fully to recover, to the detriment of themselves and the community.

During fiscal year 1959, the Federal Government donated 700 million pounds of surplus foods to needy persons; in September 1959, more than 4 million persons in family units received donated commodities.

The problems of the underemployed are similar to those of the unemployed. In 1958, one-fourth of the 44 million families in the United States had annual cash incomes of less than $3,000; nearly one-fifth had incomes of less than $2,500.

Unemployment affects communities as well as families. If plants are closed, wages in other industries may be cut, retail sales drop, and plans to improve businesses and community facilities are often canceled. Property values generally decline and tax rates rise.

Many communities have made great efforts to solve their own problems. The adversity of unemployment often creates a common understanding and a community willingness to work together. This determination to rehabilitate a community was manifested strongly in the cooperative efforts of business, labor, and civic leaders in communities such as Evansville, Ind., and Scranton, Pa. In spite of the best efforts, however, the obstacles in most cases are too great for the community to overcome alone. One community leader in Pennsylvania expressed both the spirit of his community and the nature of the problem in these words:

It is an amazing thing that the unemployment, bad as it is, has not sapped or destroyed the spirit of the people in a community like this. . . . They are fighting and fighting very hard. . . . There is a great resource here in spirit and pride. There are institutions already built up, and I don't think we can today just casually walk away from them and abandon them and say we can put a steel mill or a factory in a field some place and the community will build up around it. . . . What sort of community will that be? . . . Which is easier to do, to build a community or to build an industry? . . . And which are the things that have the roots, the industrial plants or the people? . . . And these communities had their days when they were raw young communities without traditions . . . and now they are mature and can make a tremendous contribution to stability and to decency and to the morality of citizens, and do things for family life that a settled community can do, it is a shame if we just abandon them. . . . You probably will have to change a great deal of thinking, but I think we should not rule out some subsidies on a Government level to industries which will come into a place like this.

The economic and social costs of unemployment deserve far greater attention than they have received. Present measures to deal with unemployment and its consequences at the local, State, and Federal governmental levels are seriously inadequate.

The Gap between Actual and
Potential Output

ARTHUR M. OKUN

This article is adapted from a paper which appeared in the 1962
Proceedings of the Business and Economic Statistics Section of
the American Statistical Association. The technical statistical anal-
ysis in the original article is omitted here.

"How much output can the economy produce under conditions
of full employment?" The concept and measurement of potential
GNP are addressed to this question. It is a question with policy
significance because the pursuit of full employment (or "maximum employment" in the language of the Employment Act) is
a goal of policy. And a target of full employment of labor needs
to be linked to a corresponding target of full-employment output,
since policy measures designed to influence employment operate
by affecting aggregate demand and production. How far we
stand from the target of full-employment output is important
information in formulating fiscal and monetary policy. Thus,
quantification of potential output offers one of the guides to
stabilization policy and one indicator of its success.

The quantification of potential output—and the accompanying
measure of the "gap" between actual and potential—is at best an
uncertain estimate and not a firm, precise measure. While there
are more precise measures of economic performance, they are not
fully substitutable for the concept of potential output. To appraise the vigor of an expanding economy, it is important and
enlightening to study customary cyclical measures, such as advance over previous peak levels or recession trough levels. But
these measures do not tell us how far we have to go to meet our
targets, unless we are prepared to assume that each peak is like
any other one and all troughs are likewise uniform. The record
of the past decade testifies to the dramatic differences among
cyclical peaks in levels of resource utilization.

The evaluation of potential output can also help to point up the enormous social cost of idle resources. If programs to lower unemployment from 5½ to 4 percent of the labor force are viewed as attempts to raise the economy's "grade" from 94½ to 96, the case for them may not seem compelling. Focus on the "gap" helps to remind policy-makers of the large reward associated with such an improvement.

THE 4-PERCENT UNEMPLOYMENT RATE

Potential GNP is a supply concept, a measure of productive capacity. But it is not a measure of how much output could be generated by unlimited amounts of aggregate demand. The nation would probably be most productive in the short-run with inflationary pressure pushing the economy. But the social target of maximum production and employment is constrained by a social desire for price stability and free markets. The full-employment goal must be understood as striving for maximum production without inflationary pressure; or, more precisely, as aiming for a point of balance between more output and greater price stability, with appropriate regard for the social valuation of these two objectives.

It is interesting and perhaps surprising that there seems to be more agreement that a 4-percent unemployment rate is a reasonable target under existing labor-market conditions than on any of the analytical steps needed to justify such a conclusion. Economists have never developed a clear criterion of tolerable price behavior or a quantitative balancing of conflicting objectives which could be invoked to either support or attack the target of a 4-percent rate. Indeed, I should expect that many economists who agree on the 4-percent target would disagree in estimating how prices and wages would behave if we were on target. Nor can the 4-percent rate be said to meet Beveridge's criterion for full employment—that job vacancies should be equal to the number of unemployed. We simply have no count of job vacancies and could not possibly translate Beveridge's goal into any available measure of unemployment.

Having said what the 4-percent unemployment rate is not, I shall now state that it is the target rate of labor utilization underlying the calculation of potential GNP in this paper. The statistical and methodological problems would not be altered if a different rate were selected; only the numbers would be changed.

In estimating potential GNP, most of the facts about the economy are taken as they exist: technological knowledge, the capital stock, natural resources, the skill and education of the labor force are all data, rather than variables. Potential differs from actual only because the potential concept depends on the assumption—normally contrary to fact—that aggregate demand is exactly at the level that yields a rate of unemployment equal to 4 percent of the civilian labor force. If, in fact, aggregate demand is lower, part of potential GNP is not produced; there is unrealized potential or a "gap" between actual and potential output.

The failure to use one year's potential fully can influence future potential GNP: to the extent that low utilization rates and accompanying low profits and personal incomes hold down investment in plant, equipment, research, housing, and education, the growth of potential GNP will be retarded. Because today's actual output influences tomorrow's productive capacity, success in the stabilization objective promotes more rapid economic growth.

THE MEASUREMENT PROBLEM

As it has been defined above, potential output is observed only when the unemployment rate is 4 percent, and even then must be viewed as subject to random variation. At any other time, it must be regarded as a hypothetical magnitude. The observed actual measures of labor utilization tell us by a simple arithmetic calculation how much employment would have to increase, given the labor force, to make the unemployment rate 4 percent. But they do not offer similar direct information on other matters that might make labor input at full employment different from its observed level: (1) how average hours worked per man would be altered if the level of aggregate demand were consistent with full employment; (2) how participation rates in the labor force—and hence the size of the labor force—would be affected under conditions of full employment.

Nor do the data directly reveal what aggregate labor productivity would be under full-employment conditions. There are many reasons why productivity might be altered in the aggregate; the added workers, changed average hours, possible alterations in the sectoral distribution of employment, higher utilization rate of capital, and altered efficiency in the use of employees all could make a difference in productivity at full employment.

Ideally, the measurement of potential output would appraise the various possible influences of high employment on labor input and productivity and evaluate the influences step by step, developing quantitative estimates for each adjustment to produce the desired measure of potential. While I shall discuss the steps individually below, the basic technique I am reporting consists of a leap from the unemployment rate to potential output rather than a series of steps involving the several underlying factors. Strictly speaking, the leap requires the assumption that, whatever the influence of slack economic activity on average hours, labor-force participation, and manhour productivity, the magnitudes of all these effects are related to the unemployment rate. With this assumption, the unemployment rate can be viewed as a proxy variable for all the ways in which output is affected by idle resources. The measurement of potential output then is simplified into an estimate of how much output is depressed by unemployment in excess of 4 percent.

THE ESTIMATES

Even though the rate of unemployment has changed through time and even though the economy has not experienced an unemployment rate as low as 4 percent since the mid-1950s, we can make some reasonable statistical judgments about the hypothetical path of output at a constant 4-percent unemployment rate. Our estimates are based on the relationship between the actual path of real gross national product through time and the accompanying movements in the unemployment rate. It is not surprising that we find the unemployment rate declining in periods when output is rising rapidly. And we find the unemployment rate rising when real GNP declines. We also experience a rising unemployment rate typically when output is constant, since the growth through time of productivity and of the labor force reduces the fraction of the civilian labor force needed to produce the same output.

These qualitative relationships can be turned into numerical estimates by standard statistical techniques. The data for the past decade indicate:

1. A rise in real GNP of about 3½ percent per year—nearly 1 percent a quarter—is required merely to keep the unemployment rate constant over time.

2. At a given time, each extra 1 percent of real GNP means a decrement, on the average, of about one-third of a percentage point in the unemployment rate. Thus, when the unemployment rate is 5 percent, we estimate that an addition of 3 percent in real GNP would have been required to yield a 4-percent unemployment rate.

It should be emphasized that these are average and approximate, rather than exact, relationships. Indeed, they suggest two different rules for estimating potential GNP and, hence, the gap between potential and actual. One rule calls for a 3½-percent trend line to represent potential GNP; the data suggest that this line can be anchored at the level of actual output in mid-1955, when the unemployment rate was in fact very close to 4 percent. The gap is then the distance between that potential line and the actual level of real GNP. The other rule says: subtract 4 percent from the actual unemployment rate (U); then triple that remainder ($U - .04$) and multiply the result by actual GNP expressed in billions of dollars. If you have followed instructions, you now have an estimate of the gap. To put it into a formula:

$$\text{Gap} = 3 \cdot (U - .04) \cdot \text{actual GNP (in billions of dollars)}$$

Potential GNP is, of course, the sum of the gap and actual GNP. The two rules agree reasonably well, but they occasionally show differences that are not negligible. The smooth path of potential GNP generated by the 3½-percent trend line usually makes more sense when differences arise. Hence, this path is illustrated in the accompanying figure.

THE STEPS

The findings above assert that a reduction in unemployment, measured as a percentage of the labor force, is associated with a much larger than proportionate change in output. To appraise and evaluate this finding, it is necessary to inspect the steps which were leaped over in the statistical relationships between output and unemployment. Clearly, the simple addition of 1 percent of a given labor force to the ranks of the employed would increase employment by only slightly more than 1 percent: $\frac{100}{100 - U}$ percent to be exact. If the workweek and productivity were unchanged, the increment to output would be only that 1+ percent. The 3-percent result implies that considerable output gains in a period of rising utilization rates must stem from one or all of the following: induced increases in the size of the labor force, longer average weekly hours, and greater productivity.

Labor-force Size · Participation in the labor force as we measure it consists of either having a job or actively seeking a job. The resulting measures of labor force are not pure reflections of supply; they are affected by job availability. In a slack labor market, people without a job may give up when they are convinced that jobhunting is a hopeless pursuit. They then may be viewed as having left the labor force though they stand ready and eager to work. Furthermore, there are secondary or passive members of the labor force who will not actively seek employment but would accept gainful employment if a job came looking for them. This latter group suffers little or no personal hardship in not having work, but the output they would contribute in a fully employed economy is a relevant part of the nation's potential GNP.

There may be induced changes in the labor force in the opposite direction: e.g., the loss of a job by the breadwinner of a family might increase the measured labor force by leading his wife and teen-age children to seek work. The prewar literature debated the probable net effects of these opposing influences on participation rates. However, the postwar record has convincingly delivered the verdict that a weak labor market depresses the size of the labor force.

The Workweek · A weak labor market also shortens the workweek by creating more part-time employment and reduced overtime. Taking into account the normal secular decline in hours worked per man, there is a clear relationship between movements in average hours and in output. When output has been rising rapidly, average hours have expanded—or, at least, have not contracted. On the other hand, periods of low growth or decline in GNP mean more rapid declines in average hours per man.

Gross National Product, Actual and Potential, and the Unemployment Rate

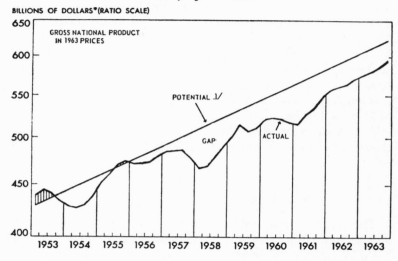

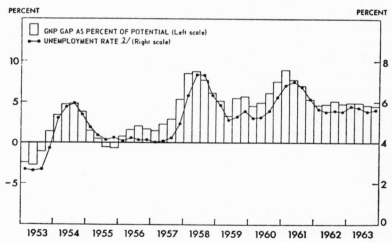

° Seasonally adjusted annual rates.

¹ 3½ percent trend line through the middle of 1955.

² Unemployment as a percent of the civilian labor force; seasonally adjusted.

SOURCES: Department of Commerce, Department of Labor, Council of Economic Advisers.

Productivity · The record clearly shows that manhour productivity is depressed by low levels of utilization, and that periods of movement toward full employment yield considerably above-average productivity gains. The implications and explanations of this phenomenon are intriguing. Indeed, many *a priori* arguments have been made for the reverse view—that depressed levels of activity will stimulate productivity through pressure on management to cut costs, through a weeding-out of inefficient firms and low quality workers, and through availability of more and higher quality capital per worker for those employees who retain their jobs. If such effects exist, the empirical record demonstrates that they are swamped by other forces working in the opposite direction.

LABOR AS A FIXED COST

The positive relationship between output and labor productivity suggests that much of labor input is essentially a fixed cost for fairly substantial periods. Thus high output levels permit the spreading of labor overheads, and low production levels raise unit fixed costs of labor. At times, we may take too seriously our textbook examples which view labor as a variable factor, with only capital costs as fixed. Even the most casual empiricism points to an overhead component in labor costs. There are many reasons why employment may not be easily variable:

1. *Contractual commitments* may tie the hand of management in a downward direction—employees may have guaranteed annual wages, supplementary unemployment compensation, rights to severance pay, and so forth, as well as actual contracts for a term of employment.

2. *Technological factors,* in a broad sense, may also be important. A firm plans on a division of labor and degree of specialization attuned to "normal" operations. If operations fall below normal, there may be marked indivisibilities which prevent the firm from curtailing its employment of specialists, clerical and sales personnel, and supervisors at the same rate as its output. In particular, where there are idle plants and machines, labor is needed merely to maintain the excess capacity and keep it available on a standby basis.

3. *Transactions costs* associated with laying off labor and

then, in the future, doing new hiring may be another influence retarding the adjustment of labor input to fluctuations in sales and output.

4. *Acquired skills* that existing employees have learned on the job may make them particularly valuable to the firm so that it pays to stockpile underemployed labor rather than run the risk of having to hire untrained men when business conditions improve.

5. *Morale factors* may also make layoffs undesirable.

All of these factors could help explain why slack economic activity is accompanied by "on-the-job underemployment," reflected in depressed levels of manhour productivity. Firms obviously do lay off labor in recession but they do so reluctantly. Their problems may be mitigated, in part, by the presence of voluntary quits which permit a downward adjustment of employment without layoffs. In part, the impact of slack on manhour productivity may be reduced by shortening average hours to spread the work and the wage-bill without a cut in employment. But these appear to be only partial offsets.

Thus far, I have ignored the dependence of labor productivity on plant and equipment capacity. The entire discussion of potential output in this paper has, in effect, assumed that idle labor is a satisfactory measure of all idle resources. In fact, measures of excess capacity in industrial plant and equipment do show a close relationship to unemployment—idle men are accompanied by idle machines. But the correlation is not perfect and operating rates in industry should be considered along with employment data as an indicator of the gap between potential and actual output. Obviously, if capital were fully employed while there was much unemployed labor, this would hold down the productivity gains that could be obtained through full employment of labor. Robert Solow did use capital-stock data together with unemployment data in fitting a production function for 1929 to date. His estimates of potential output for the post-Korean period agreed remarkably well with those I am reporting.

IN SUMMARY

Still, I shall feel much more satisfied with the estimate of potential output when data and analysis have advanced to the point where the estimate can proceed step by step and where the capital factor can explicitly be taken into account. Meanwhile, the measure of potential must be used with care and any specific figure must be understood as the center of a range of plausible estimates. But the general picture emerging from the analysis of potential GNP and the gap is clear.

In the first place, it reminds us that the economy loses ground if it stands still. Unless the growth of output keeps pace with our ever-expanding potential, the unemployment rate tends to rise. The nation needs continually to set new records in production and sales. Its economy needs to grow bigger and better than ever before—because its labor force, capital stock, technology, and managerial and organizational resources are always getting bigger and better.

Second, the gap analysis points out that measures of unemployment understate the economic cost and the economic problem of a slack economy. The unemployment rate misses the submerged part of the iceberg associated with depressed rates of participation in the labor force, the shrinkage of the workweek through part-time jobs and the loss of overtime, and the sag in labor productivity. Thus, if we are to meet our targets of full utilization, we need expansionary measures that are large in relation to excess unemployment. According to the estimates above, the demand for goods and services must rise relatively about three times as much as we can expect unemployment to fall.

Finally, we can recognize that excessive unemployment has been associated with a tremendous economic cost since 1957. The figure above indicates that the United States could have produced a total of nearly $200 billion more output from 1958 to 1963, if demand had been maintained at levels consistent with a 4-percent unemployment rate. This is two-thirds of the amount spent for national defense in the period and far more than the expenditure for public education. It is fair to conclude that tolerance of idle resources has been America's outstanding extravagance and waste in recent years.

The Bottleneck in Labor Skills

CHARLES C. KILLINGSWORTH

When the Senate Subcommittee on Employment and Manpower, chaired by Senator Joseph Clark, conducted hearings in the fall of 1963, one expert witness was Charles C. Killingsworth, University Professor of Labor and Industrial Relations at Michigan State University. This selection is condensed from his testimony.

AUTOMATION, especially in its advanced forms, fundamentally changes the man-machine relation. Such a change is not unprecedented in economic history. The assembly line, as it replaced earlier techniques, helped to create literally millions of simple, repetitive jobs that could be learned in a few hours or a few days. Anybody who had two hands, two eyes, and a capacity to endure monotony could do the work.

The economic environment today is so different from that of 40 or 50 years ago that simply more of the same kinds of technological change that we experienced in the first half of the century would have a different impact now. But automation differs in some respects from most of the earlier technological changes.

One major difference is the much broader applicability of automation. The steam engine had a number of uses, but mainly in factories and in transportation. The cotton gin, the spinning jenny, the linotype, and others had a substantial impact, but each in only one industry. Computer technology in particular seems likely to invade almost every area of industrial activity.

A related difference is that automation appears to be spreading more rapidly than most major technological changes of the past. It is difficult if not impossible to measure the diffusion of technology in quantitative terms, of course. But I find these facts suggestive: About a century was required for the general adoption of the steam engine in those activities where it could be employed; the comparable timespan for electric power was about 50 years. The first automatic accounting systems were installed in banks some 7 or 8 years ago. Today, about half of the banks are in the process of converting to this system. When the first large-scale computers were introduced early in the 1950s, there were estimates that only about 10 or 15 of them would ever be needed in the entire United States. Today, nearly 4,000 fully transistorized computers are in use, and the number on order is about double that, so that in 2 or 3 years we will have about three times as many in use as we have today.

Today we have the electric eye, the iron hand, the tin ear, and the electronic brain. We also have the know-how to tie them together in self-regulating systems that can perform an enormous variety of jobs. There are two major results. One is a great reduction in the number of simple, repetitive jobs where all you need is your five senses and an untrained mind. The other result is a great increase in the number of jobs involved in designing, engineering, programming and administering these automatic production systems. Industry needs many more scientists, engineers, mathematicians, and other highly trained people, and many fewer blue-collar workers. Between 1957 and 1962 in manufacturing, production workers declined by nearly a million, while nonproduction workers increased by about a third of a million. The net change was a reduction of about 600,000 in employment.

Not all of the increase in white-collar employment in manufacturing was due to automation, of course, and not all of the newly hired employees were scientists and engineers. But the changing composition of employment was partly due to automation. Moreover, what happened from 1957 to 1962 was the continuation of a postwar trend in the ratio between production and nonproduction workers in manufacturing. Throughout the 1920's, the ratio fluctuated between narrow limits at around 19 or 20 percent. The great depression and World War II temporarily affected the ratio; at the outset of the depression, the blue-collar workers were laid off before the white-collar workers were, and in the war salesmen and clerks were drafted while blue-collar workers were added. By about 1951, the prewar ratio of about one white-collar worker to four blue-collar workers had been reestablished. But as automation gathered momentum during the 1950s, the ratio continued to change. It is now at about 26 percent and the trend is still strongly upward. Generally, the most highly automated industries have the highest ratio of white-collar workers. In chemicals and petroleum, for example, the ratio is 40 percent.

Let me preface my own analysis with a brief restatement of my argument to this point. The fundamental effect of automation on the labor market is to "twist" the pattern of demand—that is, it pushes down the demand for workers with little training while pushing up the demand for workers with large amounts of training. The shift from goods to services is a second major factor which twists the labor market in the same way. There are some low-skilled, blue-collar jobs in service-producing industries; but the most rapidly growing parts of the service sector are health care and education, both of which require a heavy preponderance of highly trained people.

I have already presented some figures showing the changing patterns of demand for labor. These changing patterns of demand would not create labor market imbalance, however, unless changes in the supply of labor lagged behind. We turn now to the figures which show that such a lag has in fact developed.

The table shows the relationship between rates of unemployment and levels of education of males 18 and over in 2 years—1950 and 1962.

Unemployment and Education, for Males, 18 and over,
April 1950 and March 1962

Years of school completed	Unemployment rates 1950	1962	Change 1950–62
0 to 7	8.4%	9.2%	+ 9.5%
8	6.6	7.5	+13.6
9 to 11	6.9	7.8	+13.0
12	4.6	4.8	+ 4.3
13 to 15	4.1	4.0	− 2.4
16 or more	2.2	1.4	−36.4
All groups	6.2	6.0	− 3.2

The overall unemployment rate was substantially the same in both years—6.2 percent in 1950 and 6.0 percent in 1962. But there was a redistribution of unemployment between these two years. The unemployment rates at the top of the educational attainment ladder went down, while the rates at the middle and lower rungs of the ladder went up substantially. The most significant figure in this table, I think, is the one showing the very large decrease in the unemployment rate of college graduates.

It is important to note that all of the improvement in the unemployment situation in 1962, as compared with 1950, was concentrated in the elite group of our labor force—the approximately 20 percent with college training. In all of the other categories, which have about 80 percent of the labor force, unemployment rates were substantially higher in 1962 than in 1950. These figures, I contend, substantiate the thesis that the patterns of demand for labor have been twisted faster than the patterns of supply have changed, and that as a result we had a substantially greater degree of labor market imbalance in 1962 than in 1950.

But these figures do not fully reveal the power of the labor market twist. The "labor force" enumeration includes (with minor exceptions) only those who say that they have jobs or that they have actively sought work in the week preceding the survey. Those who have been out of work so long that they have given up hope and are no longer "actively seeking" work—but who would take a job if one were available—are simply not counted either as unemployed or as a member of the labor force. The percentage of a given category of the total population that is "in the labor force" (under the foregoing definition) is expressed as the "labor force participation rate." It seems probable that worsening employment prospects for a particular group over a long period would force down the labor force participation rate —i.e., would squeeze a number of people out of the labor market altogether, in the sense that they would give up the continuing, active search for jobs. Conversely, it seems probable that improving employment prospects would tend to pull more people into the labor market and thus to raise the labor force participation rate. These two trends are indeed observable since 1950. The squeezing out of people at the lower end of the educational ladder and the pulling in of people at the upper end is another manifestation of the labor market twist.

Bear in mind that the unemployment rates for the lower educational attainment groups (those with 80 percent of the men) are now higher than in 1950, and that the unemployment rate for college graduates is now substantially lower than in 1950. Also bear in mind that the labor force participation rate figures strongly suggest a large and growing "reserve army"—which is not counted among the unemployed—at the lower educational levels, and that there is no evidence of any such reserve of college-trained men. Finally, bear in mind the differences between the lower end of the educational scale and the upper end in responsiveness to overall decreases in the unemployment rate.

When you put all of these considerations together, I believe that you are ineluctably led to the conclusion that long before we could get down to an overall unemployment rate as low as 4 percent, we would have a severe shortage of workers at the top of the educational ladder. This shortage would be a bottleneck to further expansion of employment. I cannot pinpoint the level at which the bottleneck would begin to seriously impede expansion; but it seems reasonable to believe that we could not get very far below a 5-percent overall unemployment level without hitting that bottleneck.

The Case for High-pressure Economics

ALVIN H. HANSEN

*Alvin H. Hansen is Lucius N. Littauer Professor (Emeritus) of
Political Economy at Harvard University and is generally regarded
as the dean of American Keynesian economists. This selection is
taken from his book* The American Economy, *published in 1957.*

THE AMERICAN ECONOMY has undergone a considerable remodel-
ing during the last quarter-century. I begin with what I regard
as by far the most important single factor. It is a new factor,
never before experienced in American history. And it is this.
We have not had a major depression since 1938. Nearly two
decades without a serious downturn. We had, indeed, a minor
dip in 1949 and again in 1954—light jolts but no serious depression. And we have had virtually continuous full employment
since 1941. Now this is something distinctly new, and we would
do well to take a good look at this strange and quite novel
experience.

I repeat, we have had virtually full employment and booming
prosperity for sixteen years. Past experience has been quite
different. Throughout our history every eight or nine years we
have experienced serious depression and widespread unemployment. Indeed our economy was for a hundred years the most
violently fluctuating economy in the world. And in the 1930s
we had prolonged depression and seemingly endless stagnation.

THE MISSING LINK: ADEQUATE DEMAND

What is the essence of the American economic revolution of
the last fifteen years? The miracle of production? The economy
already had that *potential* back in the thirties, though the steam
was unfortunately lacking. Now, however, we have seen what
the economy can do under the pressure of *adequate aggregate
demand*. We now have acquired at least some confidence in
the government's responsibility for the maintenance of prosperity

and full employment. When the British Conservative Government, under Churchill, announced its assumption of continuing responsibility for high employment in 1944, that Act was regarded as a new venture of government, and so indeed it was. The Employment Act of 1946 set much the same goal for the United States. But it was not until President Eisenhower's statement with respect to the firm determination of his Administration to use the full powers of the government to prevent depression that general bipartisan acceptance of this program was achieved. It is indeed a revolution in men's thinking. And this revolution is in no small part the result of the vigorous economic controversies which have filled the pages of economic journals, and from there spilled out into the public forums, during the last two decades.

Now someone will say that the miracle of production which we have witnessed during the upsurge of the last fifteen years could never have occurred without the resourcefulness of private enterprise, the technical know-how, the technological innovations, and the capital formation necessary to implement the new technique. This is indeed unquestionably true, and it is a fact that should be stressed again and again. Yet even with respect to these factors it is important to note that the cause-and-effect relations are closely intertwined. The government has made a major contribution to ensure adequate aggregate demand. The upsurge related thereto has stimulated population growth, which in turn has contributed to the upsurge. The war and the postwar upsurge have served to stimulate new techniques, and these in turn reinforce the upsurge. And finally, investment in new capital (together with corporate and individual savings to finance it) is a consequence, no less than a cause, of a high and growing national income.

Thus the American economic revolution of the last quarter-century constitutes a laboratory experiment in which the flow of events has tested on a broad front the Keynesian diagnosis and the Keynesian policies.

The problems of a highly developed economy are different, as we have seen, from those of an economy in the earlier stages of industrial development. The advanced industrial society, having attained a high level of technology together with entrepreneurial know-how and worker skills, has equipped itself with a vast accumulation of fixed capital. The underdeveloped economy is capital-poor; the advanced country is capital-rich.

No one will deny that the developed economies of Western Europe and North America have reached, after 150 years of technological progress and capital accumulation, a high level of productive capacity. These countries have, moreover, within them the seeds of continued growth. Yet the output of the United Kingdom fell far below her potential throughout the two interwar decades, and in the United States the economy performed disastrously below her capacity for more than a decade before Pearl Harbor. How long must an economy fail notoriously to perform before it is generally admitted that something is seriously lacking?

Now it was Keynes' central thesis that the element that was woefully lacking was *adequate aggregate demand.* The classicals had argued that all that was needed was technology and capital, that the economy itself would automatically generate adequate demand. The interwar experience in the United Kingdom and the deep depression in the United States demonstrated, as conclusively as facts can, that the classical thesis, whatever may have been true of the early days of capitalism, was no longer valid.

But facts convinced no one. Facts alone can never destroy a theory. As James B. Conant has aptly put it, men strive desperately "to modify an old idea to make it accord with new experiments." An outworn theory will not be abandoned until it has been superseded by a better one. "It takes," says Conant, "a new conceptual scheme to cause the abandonment of an old one." [1]

In his *General Theory of Employment, Interest and Money,* Keynes challenged the view that the modern economic system can be *depended* upon to make automatically the adjustments needed to ensure full use of productive resources. The thing that private enterprise can certainly do efficiently and well is to *produce.* The thing that it cannot be *depended* upon to do well is to ensure adequate aggregate demand.

Just as the decade before the Second World War deepened the conviction that the classicals were wrong, so the last fifteen

1. James B. Conant, *On Understanding Science,* Yale University Press, 1947, pp. 89, 90.

years have strengthened the conviction that Keynes was right with respect to his positive program. Governments throughout Western Europe, and in the United States, have on an unprecedented scale augmented aggregate demand beyond that generated by private enterprise. And all over the free world, but especially in the United States, we have witnessed what the economy can do when it is put under pressure. Government expenditures, government borrowing, government guarantees and lending operations, government policies in the area of social security, agriculture, public power, rural electrification, securities regulation, deposit insurance, and monetary, banking, and fiscal policies have provided much of the *fuel* needed for the full use of the productive capacity created by technology and capital accumulation.

THE PROBLEM OF INFLATION

Operating under pressure the American economy has performed a miracle. The output response to adequate aggregate demand has surprised everyone, and, what is to many still more surprising, it has not led to any such destructive inflation as was feared. Clearly we are not out of the woods in this matter, but the experience of recent years is reassuring. One thing at least is certain. Our economy is equipped with three powerful safeguards against peacetime inflation: (1) our prodigious capacity to increase production when under pressure; (2) our capacity, both corporate and individual, to save at high-income levels; (3) our demonstrated capacity at responsible fiscal and monetary management. There remains the problem of wages and collective bargaining. This requires, there can be no doubt, statesmanlike action. At all events, I think it is fair to say that experience thus far indicates that the alarmists may well have beaten the drums a little too loudly, and I am happy to note recently a little softer note in the discussion of this very important problem.

A high degree of stability in the value of money must be an important consideration of public policy. Yet we are, I fear, in considerable danger of making a fetish of rigid price stability. This fetish could easily become a serious obstacle to optimum growth and expansion. If we are going to be frightened away

by every slight increase in prices, we are likely to fall far below
the growth of which we are potentially capable.

We use the term "inflation" far too loosely. The word "inflation" is used to describe the astronomical price increases experienced by Germany after the First World War, and the same
word is applied to the comparatively moderate increases in
prices in American history. The phrase "inflationary pressures"
has often become, I suggest, virtually synonymous with "expansionary forces." Brakes are thereby applied, and output is
sacrificed to rigid price stability.

I should like to propose a new definition—one, I hope, which
might have some operational value for monetary policy. I suggest that we need a new concept which I propose to call "pure
inflation," and I propose to set this concept over against the
concept of "price adjustments to output changes." "Pure inflation" (and I emphasize the word "pure"), I should say, is a
condition in which prices rise without any appreciable increase
in output.

Countries which have suffered in the past from the evils of
inflation have typically experienced large price increases with
no substantial increase in output. Indeed, in cases of hyper-
inflation, output has often actually decreased.

There are, to be sure, degrees of pure inflation. And I should
like to suggest, to help clarify our thinking, the following general observation. I suggest that at no time in our history, nor
indeed in that of any other country, can it be shown that price
increases have injured the economy and the general welfare if
in the period in question the increase in aggregate output has
exceeded percentagewise the increase in prices.

Frederick Mills, of the National Bureau of Economic Research, surveying eighty years of cyclical movements in our
history, has shown that, in periods of expansion, for every 1 percent increase in output we have had $8/10$ percent increase in
prices—a 5 to 4 ratio. Professor Mills' short-run ratios of output increases to price increases might, of course, develop against
the background either of a long-run downtrend in prices or a
long-run uptrend.

I repeat, one does not encounter the condition of inflation in
any meaningful sense so long as percentage increases in aggregate output exceed by some margin the percentage increases in

the price level.

I should be prepared, in special circumstances, however, to go a bit farther. There are times when a tremendous forward push is urgently needed, when a choice has to be made between permitting a price increase substantially greater than my rule suggests or else foregoing the needed increase in aggregate output.

Consider, for example, the situation in 1946 after the removal of price and wage controls and the cut in wartime taxes. Having chosen to remove the main restraints on consumption (and I assume that political realism forbade any other choice), what then? The only way remaining to keep aggregate demand in check would have been drastic monetary restraint on investment. Would this have been desirable policy? I think not. A rapid transition to full peacetime production required massive investment in plant, equipment, and inventories to make good the accumulated shortages caused by the war. It was a choice of the lesser evil. It did indeed mean a price increase percentage-wise considerably greater than the increase in aggregate output. But the massive investment laid the groundwork for a large increase in output later and contributed greatly to the slowing-down of the price movement by 1948.

Following the Second World War we had, as we all know, a considerable price rise. There are those who regard this as simply due to war and postwar mismanagement. I cannot agree. Granted that the controls had to be removed and that taxes had to be cut—that, politically speaking, they could not be continued for a year or so longer—then I think it follows that some considerable price rise was inevitable. This is true because of the accumulated backlog of unfulfilled demand and of postwar shortages. The closets were empty, the shelves were bare; consumers' stocks and business inventories had to be replenished. Under these circumstances price stability could not have been achieved unless indeed we had been prepared to cut employment and income sufficiently to reduce demand to the level of the then available flow of consumers' goods. And a severe cut of this character would have been necessary even though there had been no widespread holdings of liquid savings, since people were quite prepared, in view of the backlog of demand for clothing, household furnishings, automobiles, etc., to spend all of their current income. Any net investment in excess of corporate net saving would under these circumstances have created inflationary pressures.

The path we chose was much to be preferred. It brought indeed a considerable rise in prices, but it gave us full employment and it stimulated a tremendous outpouring of goods which already by the middle of 1947 had drenched the inflationary fires.

Periods of rapid growth have usually also been periods of moderate price increases. In the usual case the price system tends to respond in this manner to rapid expansion. It is not probable that we can achieve in the next twenty years anything like the growth of which we are capable, without some moderate increases in wholesale and consumer prices.

Economists generally tend to exaggerate the evils of moderate price increases. The accumulated savings, it is said, are eaten into. Inflation, it is said, tends to eliminate the sturdy middle class, and it concentrates income in the hands of the lucky few.

These things have indeed always happened in the great astronomical inflations. And conclusions based on these undoubted facts are then erroneously applied to such price increases as we have experienced in the United States during the last half-century.

The alleged evils which are typically cited are, in fact, based on abstractions that have no relevance to conditions as we actually find them in the United States. We have indeed experienced a considerable price upheaval both in the first quarter and again in the second quarter of the current century. But private property continues firmly in the saddle. Savings per family (after correcting for price changes) are more than twice as large as in 1925. Urban home ownership has increased from 45 to 55 percent. Farm ownership has increased from 58 percent to 75 percent. The middle class is stronger than ever before in our history. There is less inequality in the distribution of income. Adjustments in social-security benefits can be made and have been made when price changes occur.

In this connection it is well to remember that nothing eats so dangerously into family savings as deflation and unemployment. On the other hand, even the considerable price increases we have had since the end of the Second World War have not wiped out family savings. According to the Home Loan Bank Board, the accumulated savings, per family, in life insurance, savings accounts, United States savings bonds, and savings and loan associations have risen from $2,500 in 1944 to $4,200 in 1954, an increase (after correction for consumer price changes) of 10 percent in real purchasing power. I do not say that we might not have done better had not the aftermath of the war brought the price increases. But I do say we have not suffered the serious effects on family savings that are so often quite irresponsibly alleged.

Thus I conclude that if in the pursuit of rigid price stability we permit, and even foster, a considerable amount of unemployment, we shall then fail to achieve the growth of which we are capable. If, fearful of short-run instability, we fail to place the economy under the pressure of an aggregate demand adequate to produce full employment, we shall not even discover what our potentialities for growth are. Under these circumstances we could gradually drift into a condition of stagnation.

The Case against High-pressure Economics

HENRY C. WALLICH

Henry C. Wallich, who coined the phrase "high-pressure economics," criticizes it in an article entitled "Postwar United States Monetary Policy Appraised," which was written for the American Assembly in 1958. Mr. Wallich is professor of economics at Yale University and was a member of the Council of Economic Advisers from 1959 to 1961.

AGAINST THE SPECTRE of unemployment in a low-pressure economy, the defenders of [price stability] can raise the equally serious vision of inflation in an economy running at high pressure. Unemployment hurts a limited number of people severely, but for the most part temporarily. Inflation hurts large numbers, usually less severely, but the damage done to savings and relative income position tends to be permanent. If inflation should ultimately lead to severe depression we shall end up with the worst of both worlds. Yet it must be conceded that the public seems to enjoy most of the manifestations of inflation and, unlike unemployment, does not regard it as an evil demanding immediate redress.

Finally, the partisans of [price stability] can argue that full employment and growth are not indivisible. It is at least conceivable that an economy running at a slightly lower rate of employment and output for a time may in the end enjoy the same or a larger average rate of growth as would a high pressure economy. If a low pressure economy grows at the same rate as a high pressure economy, it will not lose very much by leaving an extra one or two percent of its labor force unused. At an annual growth rate of four percent, the loss of output from one percent unemployment will be the equivalent of three months' growth. At this rate, the low pressure economy would fall behind the high pressure economy only very little.

Whether or not the same rate of growth can be expected in the two economies depends principally on the kind of pressure prevailing in the high pressure system. It may be the kind that results from high investment financed by bank credit, creating large profits and imposing "forced savings" on the consumer by preventing him from consuming as much as he would like. This kind of inflationary pressure probably accelerates growth, at least for a while. The inflationary pressure may also be of the type known as cost push, however. In that case, consumption rather than investment will be the expanding force. Whether growth can much accelerate in this type of situation is doubtful, and what will happen eventually if inflation should gain momentum or be brought to a sudden halt is quite obscure. The recent inflation in the United States has had many of the earmarks of cost-push inflation, although it has also featured an expansion of investment.

It is on the longer-run consequences of inflation that the defenders of stable prices must fundamentally rest their case. In the short run all sorts of good things can be promised and performed by the high pressure economy—fuller employment, more output, more growth. What will happen in the long run?

The United States has no experience of a prolonged inflation consciously felt as such. Prolonged upward price movements have occurred—from 1896 to 1940, or even from 1933 to the present. But when those who think inflation is relatively harmless point to these periods as evidence, they overlook one basic distinction: those price increases were not viewed by the public as a continuing process. An inflation that is expected to continue, one that everybody tries to stay ahead of, is a new phenomenon. Consequently, we cannot appeal to experience in trying to forecast the long-run results of inflation. We depend upon surmises. That is the great uncertainty in the debate over inflation.

It has been argued that permanent inflation must inevitably accelerate from a creep to a run. As its victims learn to defend themselves, by obtaining quicker wage and salary adjustment or through escalation, the beneficiaries must move their own demands ahead faster and faster to preserve their gains. Galloping inflation, however, is obviously unsustainable; it must end in collapse or it will be stopped in some other, probably drastic manner.

This chain of reasoning is plausible but not compelling. If inflation is fought vigorously, it may well be held to a permanent or intermittent creep. Perhaps the best one can say is that acceleration constitutes a serious risk.

But even if it does not accelerate, continuing inflation will, in the view of those who oppose it, do increasing harm. The distortion of investment decisions, the discouragement of saving, the compulsion to speculate, the misallocation of resources, the strengthening of the monopoly position of firms owning old and low cost equipment—all are familiar dangers that have been pointed out many times. The inherent instability of an economy in which everything is worth what it is only because it is expected to be worth more next year; the fluctuations in the value of "inflation hedges" produced by the uncertain speed of the inflation; the need to concentrate all efforts on staying ahead of the game—all this does not add up to a satisfactory picture of a stable and rapidly growing economy. And, as the moralistically inclined may feel tempted to add, a society in which all contracts and financial promises are made with the afterthought that they will be partly cancelled by inflation, does not offer a morally-elevating picture either.

Few of the critics of inflation would claim that they can foresee its ultimate consequences. It may lead to collapse into deep depression, or simply to more inflation with stagnating growth. Or more likely, it will lead to price controls imposed under the pressure of impatient citizens and politicians. The immediate sacrifices that a policy of stable prices demands seem preferable to any of these.

I have presented here what I believe to be the main points of view in the debate over the objectives of policy, a debate that has gained urgency ever since the recent boom seemed to open a chasm between the objectives of price stability on one side and growth and full employment on the other. In this debate, the inflationists enjoy one great advantage: in the short run, they are usually right. More can be got out of an economy over a few months or years by running it at high pressure instead of at low. The chickens take some time to come home to roost—if they do come.

The supporters of stable prices labor under a corresponding difficulty. Theirs is a long-run case, in a world where experience consists of a succession of short runs. At best they can argue that the period during which inflation may help growth has become shorter, because everybody is watching the price index.

Inflation anticipated holds fewer promises and far more threats than inflation noted only after the event. Their case could be proved only, if at all, over a prolonged period and at great ultimate cost. One may hope that this form of proof will never have to be supplied. But one must realize also that so long as it has not, the inflationists will always have a plausible argument.

Functional Fiscal Policy for the 1960s

In the Wicksell Lectures, delivered in Sweden in 1961, Professor Samuelson covered a wide range of topics relating to "Stability and Growth in the American Economy." In this selection he comments on American fiscal policy.

DEFICIT FOLKLORE VS. ECONOMICS

THE REAL BARRIER to optimal fiscal policy is not procedural or administrative. It is ideological. If the American people, Congress, and the President all had a desire for the requisite pattern of expenditure and taxing—and the implied budget deficits (and surpluses!)—then without any structural reforms our present system could be more nearly optimally stabilizing. It is simply a matter of fact, though, that Americans attach great ideological importance to that particular arbitrary magnitude which is called the administrative budget. The American public simply cannot stomach budgetary deficits of the size sometimes needed for stability, high employment and growth. Or, what is really an indistinguishable variant, the American public cannot be persuaded or persuade itself that such sizable deficits are truly needed and feasible.

Foreigners may find this surprising. Economists may find it shocking. They may point out that a year is an arbitrary unit and that since the budget cannot be balanced in every day or every month, there is no particular merit in trying to balance it in the arbitrary astronomical cycle involved in one swing of the earth around the sun. Why not balance it over some other cycle, say the business cycle? Or over the nineteen year cycle of Easter? Or over a decade?

And why balance the so-called administrative budget? It differs from, and is inferior to, the cash budget, which nets out purely bookkeeping items that involve no flow of funds between government and the public. But why jettison one shibboleth only to take on another? The cash budget itself is inferior as a measure of the government's current impact on the economy to the budget on national income account, which takes into consideration the accruals of corporate tax liability as they occur and become a crucial factor in corporate spending decisions. While the administrative budget is probably the least meaningful and useful of these three budget concepts, none of them takes into account public capital formation and the increase in assets that is taking place in the governmental sector. It has long been argued that America should adopt some form of a capital budget which will distinguish between current and capital items and will bring to attention the public assets that offset the public debt.

An informed economist knows that no single concept of the budget can do justice to the qualitative and quantitative aspects of fiscal policy. No single one can be set up in advance as the desirable goal to be "balanced" in any year, month, business cycle, or decade. Changing the focus of attention from one concept to another one may minimize the economic harm resulting from ideological attitudes. Or changing from focussing upon one concept to spreading attention over several may serve to blunt and confuse ideological preoccupations. In principle, though, there is only one correct rule about budget balance—Smith's Law (not from Adam Smith but Professor Warren Smith of the University of Michigan). It goes as follows:

Smith's Law. There is only one rule about budget balancing, and it is that the budget should never be balanced.

Never? Well, hardly ever. Economic conditions will generally call for either a surplus or a deficit. Only in the transition as the budget is passing from the black to the red (or from the red to the black) should the budget be fleetingly in balance.

Avoiding Inflation or Deflation · My nine-year-old boy asked me recently "Why should there be taxes? Why not just print money to pay for the goods government needs?" He is a dangerous character. The next thing I know he will be questioning capital punishment, the law of gravity, and my own infallibility. But in nine more years he will have learned the facts of life and come to regard his question as a foolish one. Imagine questioning the inevitability of taxes, or death!

It will take another nine years of advanced study in economics before he comes to appreciate the wisdom of his question and the proper answer to it. As given by A. P. Lerner, that answer would go roughly as follows.

Never tax just for the sake of taxing. Tax primarily to reduce the pressure of excessive dollar demand for society's current limited resources, which are limited because of their scarcity in relationship to government and private bids for them. If the sum of private and public dollar demand is sufficiently great, you should legislate taxes great enough to produce a large and persistent budget surplus. If the total of dollar demand is chronically low relative to the value of total resources available at current prices, economic prudence requires you to legislate tax rates low enough to result in a budget deficit. Such a deficit, which results from the indicated pattern of public expenditure and taxes, can be counted on to produce expansionary stimulus needed to offset the deflationary pressures in the economic system. This government stimulus is not more expansionary nor more inflationary than would be an equivalent billions of dollar increase in spontaneous family expenditure on consumption or spontaneous pickup in investment spending.

Budget balance is itself irrelevant. Such a point of balance could be much too inflationary at certain times and deflationary at others. The effects of a budget balance with public expenditure and taxes both high cannot be expected to be the same as an equivalent balance achieved when low taxes match low expenditures. While a nine-year-old might be forgiven for not realizing it, we should know that financing substantial public expenditures by the printing of new money would probably be swelling the total value of dollar spending beyond the likely surplus of private saving over private investment. So we tax just enough to avoid such an inflationary gap, financing the algebraic difference by nothing so crude as the printing of Treasury currency, instead relying upon optimal debt management and central banking credit creation.

I had a teacher who was seven times nine years old but the doctrine of *de mortuis nihil nisi bonum* forbids me to reveal his name, which is just as well since he was always something of an unknown soldier. He used to say pithily: "A dollar of expenditure is a dollar of taxes." A glance at public accounts will show there to be billions of exceptions to that theorem. His doctrine is wrong today; and it was obsolete before it had been enunciated, which is something of a *tour de force*. The history of capitalism, and perhaps of the Darwinian ascent of man, is a history of deficits outweighing surpluses. This is not a matter of mankind living beyond its means but rather up to them. . . .

NARROWING THE GAP

We are not now living up to our potential. So America could achieve very rapid short-term growth just by getting unemployment down from 5½ percent to 4 percent, and excess capacity down from say 20 percent to 10 percent.

Popular discussion, particularly in liberal circles, has quite naturally put the greatest emphasis on achieving rapid (near-term) growth through restoring full employment. To move nearer to full employment, an increase in consumption, investment, or government spending is needed.

Expanding Government Expenditures · So liberals often propose that more be spent on urban renewal, conservation, health and other programs, both because such programs are desired for their own sake and also because (like digging ditches and filling them up again) such government expenditure programs result in increased money and real income, with multiplier effects on consumption and perhaps investment spending, and regardless of whether such programs have any direct bearing on our growth potential.

Expanding Consumption · The same people urge that tax rates be reduced so that consumption spending, particularly of the lower-income ready-spenders, be increased. Such consumption itself adds to the increase in GNP, and in addition can be expected to have secondary effects of a multiplier kind on further consumption and perhaps investment. . . .

Expanding Investment · Fiscal policy could also be directed toward direct stimulus to investment. President Kennedy early proposed an *investment tax credit* to induce greater net capital formation. This concession to business met a cold reception from businessmen for reasons that lie outside economics: after a long legislative struggle, such an investment tax credit was passed, involving reduced rates and no longer involving extra credit for firms which expanded their investments from earlier levels.

More *rapid depreciation,* which had made some headway in Eisenhower's 1954 tax act, was scheduled to go into effect in 1962. Such measures, to the degree that they permit depreciation more rapid than actual decline in economic value as a result of obsolescence and physical wear, represent an interest-free loan to business with the favorable feature that the loan has to be paid back only if business subsequently has taxable income. Like the investment credit, it should provide some extra funds available for investment and increase the incentive to use other funds for investment. Since I am adding quiet remarks, I ought to say softly that the competitive race between the various developed countries of the world to give the fastest depreciation rates has gone beyond the point where true economic depreciation is recognized by the tax authorities; it is now at the point where loopholes have been deliberately created in tax systems alleging to tax (money and not real) earnings, with the design of giving a bribe and bait to expand investment and employment. It is like the case of our municipalities, which vie with each other to give greater tax concessions in order to lure firms away from other areas.

In America we have a double layer of income taxation. Ford Motors is taxed in its earning at a marginal rate of 52 percent, regardless of how much it pays out in dividends; then whatever is paid out in dividends is taxed to the person who receives the dividends at essentially his regular marginal rate of personal income tax. A *reduction in the corporate tax rate* to below 52 percent might be expected to have some favorable effect upon capital formation. Thus, if managers insist on a 10 percent yield after taxes before they will build a plant and if the pre-tax yield is now only 20 percent, they will not build that plant. However, if the corporate tax rate were cut from 52 percent down to below 50 percent, that investment project would now become worthwhile. Moreover, as firms accumulate more money because of the rate reduction, they may bid down the postulated 10 percent after-tax yield needed to induce certain kinds of risky investment.

Liberals argue that it is inequitable to help owners of property too much. They also argue that, with investment so sluggish in the American economy of recent years, there will be an inelastic stimulus to investment from such tax reductions. On the other hand, more conservative people argue that since it is investment that has been so disappointing in recent years, tax reduction should be specially directed toward it—either as a matter of equity, or because its marginal social worth is so great, or because of a presumed elasticity of its response.

Leaving ethical judgments to the side, my observation of the behavior of decision makers and of their cash positions and opportunities suggests to me that in the short run there is not a great deal of potency in corporation tax reduction. In the longer run, combined with a vigorous full-employment program and taking into account the international balance constraint on credit ease, there may be merits in such programs in accelerating the "deepening of capital" so helpful for a growth program.

PUBLIC THRIFT

For half a dozen years I have been preaching the doctrine that a mixed-enterprise economy can raise its rate of capital formation, and hence the growth rate of potential GNP, by supplementing private thrift by public thrift. Just as people decide their day-to-day decisions about consuming and nonconsuming in the marketplace for goods, for bonds and saving accounts and for equities, so they may voluntarily come together at the political polls and vote for an additional rate of capital formation to be brought about through government action. I do not have in mind here merely that people may vote for durable dams, school buildings, and other forms of social capital, even though such programs may well be desirable for their own sakes and for growth. What I mean is that we may all democratically vote that our full-employment mix of output should be shifted toward more capital formation and less consumption by a package of the following devices:

1. *Expansionary monetary policies* by the central bank and other credit agencies are needed to make credit more available and cheaper to potential investors. With effective interest rates low, investment projects which previously didn't pay unless they yielded (say) a 10 percent equity yield, now will be profitable to carry through. Then 9 percent projects can be made to be profit-

able by further credit-expansion programs, thereby causing the stimulus to growth coming from technical change to be supplemented by greater "induced capital deepening" than would otherwise have been the case.

2. *Austere fiscal policies* will also be necessary whenever Step 1's monetary ease induces so much private investment as to open up an inflationary gap of excessive dollar spending. By raising or maintaining tax rates high enough relative to needed government expenditure on current and capital goods and on welfare transfers, we can lower the share of total income accruing to private persons and firms, thereby causing the reduction in consumption needed to release the scarce resources in our postulated full-employment economy that are needed for the induced investment programs. The two-step program for growth has not even been tested yet because it was never able to get off the ground: Step 1, involving militant monetary expansion, has never taken place because our international deficit would not permit us to have really low short-term and long-term interest rates. Hence, we have no real evidence as to the potency or impotence of easy money to induce capital formation of a deepening kind.

While the factual issue is still open, from the viewpoint of policy in the early 1960s the verdict is clear. So long as we cannot introduce Step 1 of the new-look program, Step 2 is clearly undesirable and the whole program must be for some time soft-pedaled. It would be too dramatic to say that we are in an era of stagnation. Perhaps it will sound better if we say that we *may* be in one of the slack periods of the so-called Kuznets long waves, which at 15- to 25-year intervals seem to appear in American annals of the last 75 years (in construction data, population and immigration data, in various measures involving the scale of economic resources *and their degree of intensity* of utilization).

We no longer regard such swings as immutable facts of nature, like the inevitable plagues that man could do nothing about before the age of penicillin, sulpha, medical care, and public health. Fiscal and monetary policies can ameliorate, moderate, and perhaps even compensate fully for such tendencies toward sluggish investment opportunities. But until we regain freedom of domestic monetary policy or experiment further with unconventional credit policies—such as helpful guarantees that reduce riskiness of domestic investment without sending funds abroad to get higher yields in London and other money markets —we must welcome anything which increases public or private consumption.

CONCLUSION

Ours, for the most part, are the happy problems that come with affluence. We have made strides toward solving many of them, and shall be making further strides these next few years. But we do not make progress by being complacent or by sticking to ancient orthodoxies. That reasoning suggested long ago and events of the last few years have amply confirmed.

Moreover, we still have one non-economic obstacle to overcome. I refer to Americans' ideological repugnance for continuing budgetary deficits. It must be evident to any attentive listener that my diagnosis of recent economic history has the implication that the United States *may* be in prudent need of sizable deficits in the administrative budget for at least the next few years of the 1960s and perhaps even longer. As the lungs need air, the heart needs blood and the stomach needs food—and not as a drunkard needs drink, an addict needs dope, and a diabetic needs insulin—a modern economy may in some epochs need chronic deficits and a growing public debt (and in other epochs need a chronic surplus, i.e., a chronic overtaxation to release resources to investment needs and to curtail inflation and to reduce the public debt). I say this in all seriousness even though scarcely one in a hundred of our opinion makers can yet comprehend my meaning. But here too I am optimistic that rationality will win out over habit.

The Influence of Monetary Policy on Economic Stability

BOARD OF GOVERNORS,

FEDERAL RESERVE SYSTEM

This official explanation of how monetary policy works is part of the Board of Governors' publication, The Federal Reserve System: Purposes and Functions. *Ralph A. Young, adviser to the Board, supervised the staff efforts in preparing the publication.*

RESERVE BANKING policy attempts to provide a financial climate conducive to sustainable growth in output, employment, and consumption under conditions of relative stability in the average level of prices and of long-run balance in our international payments. However, these objectives cannot be attained through reliance on monetary policy alone. Their accomplishment also depends on fiscal and other governmental policies and on policies of private institutions and organizations.

The posture of Federal Reserve monetary policy at any moment—whether restrictive or expansive—is a reaction to prevailing economic conditions. Monetary policy functions restrictively when inflationary tendencies are present. In other circumstances it functions expansively or assumes a posture somewhere between stimulation and restraint. To help avoid the dangers of economic downturn, reserve banking works to prevent speculative or otherwise unsustainable expansion of bank credit.

The diagram on the following page shows in a simplified way how actions taken by the Federal Reserve System influence total spending and thereby contribute to the ultimate objectives of high employment, maximum production, and stable prices.

The Federal Reserve carries out its responsibility for the public interest by influencing the reserves of member banks. As the diagram shows, that is where the initial impact of reserve banking policy falls. As banks respond to changes in the avail-

FLOW OF FEDERAL RESERVE INFLUENCE

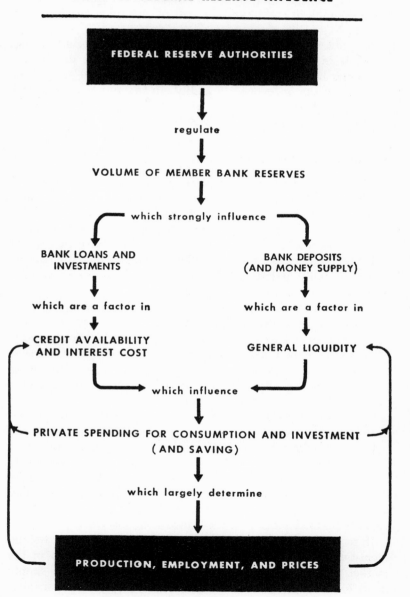

ability of reserve funds by altering their lending and investment policies, reserve banking comes to influence the supply of money, the availability of credit, and the cost of money in various credit markets.

Some observers stress the influence of reserve banking in terms of its effects on the money supply, others emphasize the impact of changes in the availability and cost of credit, and still others stress its effects on over-all liquidity. In the functioning of the economy each of these modes of influence has a role, and in the discussion that follows each is taken into account.

REACTIONS OF COMMERCIAL BANKS

What is the reaction of commercial banks to changes in the supply of reserves? For example, what is their reaction to limitations on reserves in a period of strongly expanding demand for bank loans? When they are in this situation and therefore under reserve pressure, banks are more reluctant to make new loans and interest rates on the loans they do make tend to rise, as compared with periods when their reserves are rising rapidly as the result of reserve banking policy.

In a period in which policy is limiting bank credit expansion, a bank that seeks to expand its loans rapidly may have to obtain funds by selling Government or other securities (mainly short-term) in the market, by permitting its holdings of maturing issues to run off, or by drawing down balances with, or borrowing from, other banks. Discounting at Reserve Banks, is primarily for meeting passing contingencies and is not, in the U.S. banking system, a source of funds to individual banks for financing permanent loan expansion.

If a bank sells securities, lets maturing issues run off, or draws down its balance with another bank, its action will necessarily affect other banks. In the case of security sales, for example, the buyer is likely to draw down his account at another bank to make payment. Consequently, banks as a group cannot expand their total loans and investments in this way.

If many banks try to obtain additional reserves by selling securities, the amount of short-term paper or securities in the market will be increased significantly. This increased supply tends to lower prices and to raise yields on all such paper. Similar market pressures may result if banks, in order to build up their reserves, allow maturing issues to run off or draw upon balances with correspondents.

At the lower prices and higher yields, Government and other short-term securities will be more attractive. In order to buy them, nonbank investors may use temporarily idle deposits or they may even be induced to economize on cash balances held for current payments. When banks sell short-term paper to other investors and use the proceeds to make loans, ownership of deposits may shift from holders of idle balances to borrowers who are spenders and will shortly disburse the proceeds. To the extent that this occurs, the velocity of existing deposits will increase. In this process, the volume of money transactions increases as the existing supply of money is used more actively.

As banks see their short-term securities or secondary reserves declining, however, they become increasingly reluctant to reduce these securities or reserves further in order to make additional loans. This leads banks to raise interest rates on loans and to adopt more selective loan standards.

In addition, as market interest rates rise—a development that is reinforced by bank sales of securities—security prices decline and sales of securities may involve book losses. Banks are influenced to some extent by potential capital losses on the securities in their portfolios, and they hesitate to sell securities at a loss. Income tax considerations and strict earnings calculations, however, may moderate or even negate the deterrent effect of such losses on continued sales of securities.

At times when monetary policy aims at stimulating bank credit expansion to help counteract recessionary tendencies in the economy, banks will find their reserve funds increasing quite rapidly. In using these funds, they are likely first to repay any outstanding indebtedness to the Reserve Banks, particularly if loan demands are weak or declining as might be expected under the conditions assumed. After they have reduced their borrowings, banks will begin to purchase short-term securities, thereby rebuilding their secondary reserve positions and reinforcing any tendency already existing in the market toward declining interest rates. They will also begin to relax their loan policies and this, together with reduced interest rates, may actively encourage the extension of bank loans that were postponed or that were not encouraged by lenders under the earlier conditions of credit restraint.

EFFECTS OF CHANGES IN THE MONEY SUPPLY

Changes in bank reserve availability influence changes in the money supply. What is the response of the economy to changes in the rate at which the supply of money is growing, under the influence of monetary policy?

At each level of income and interest rates, there will be an amount of money that the public wishes to hold for transactions, or for precautionary or speculative purposes. Suppose that actions taken by the Federal Reserve fail to provide the desired amount of money. In that event some reaction is likely to be registered both in spending and in interest rates.

In an attempt to reestablish its desired level of balances, the public may spend less, or it may sell off financial assets (or purchase fewer of them), with a consequent rise in interest rates. As interest rates rise in this situation, they too influence decisions to spend and to save. Also, the rise in interest rates affects the demand for money balances, as it leads people to accommodate themselves to smaller cash balances.

On the other hand, a volume of money in excess of what the public wishes to hold leads to increased spending and lending and to reductions in interest rates.

Demand for Cash · In assessing the effect on economic activity of changes in the money supply, it is important to recognize that there is no simple automatic measure of the appropriate relationship between the amount of money outstanding and the level of economic activity. A given volume of money, for example, can be associated with either higher or lower levels of total spending—that is, can finance more or fewer transactions—depending on how often it is used. The rate of turnover, or velocity, of money indicates how much work each unit of money does in financing transactions.

Cash balances are held by private sectors of the economy for a variety of reasons. A large part of their total represents working balances, that is, amounts of demand deposits and currency held for financing regular transactions. The size of such balances varies in part with the time lag between receipts and expenditures. For example, the time that elapses between pay dates is one factor affecting the size of cash balances. People who are paid every week have smaller cash balances, on the average, than those who are paid monthly. The size of the cash balance also varies with income. The higher a person's income and expenditures, the larger his cash balance for transactions is likely to be.

Cash balances are held for other reasons too. They may represent saving out of income, as a store of value for precautionary reasons—to gain flexibility in choice and timing of purchases, to provide against a rainy day, or to anticipate future expenditures or investments. In other instances they may be held as a store of value for speculative reasons, with the expectation of buying in case of a sharp decline in security, real estate, or commodity prices.

The size of the cash balances that businesses and individuals find it desirable to hold depends in part on the level of interest rates. When interest rates are low, the holder sacrifices relatively little in holding cash rather than an asset that earns interest. The higher the level of interest rates, the greater the sacrifice in holding idle cash instead of an interest-bearing financial asset. The form in which contingency or speculative balances are held —whether it be in demand deposits that bear no interest or in interest-earning assets—is highly sensitive to the rate of interest paid.

Several types of assets are close substitutes for cash in its store-of-value function. These include savings and time deposits at commercial banks, deposits at mutual savings banks, shares in savings and loan associations, and U.S. Government savings bonds. Short-term market instruments, especially obligations of the U.S. Government, such as Treasury bills, are also close substitutes for cash because they are generally convertible into cash with relatively small risk of capital loss. Such assets possess high, though varying, degrees of liquidity. A backlog of these "near money" assets, together with some holdings of cash, gives the individual consumer or enterprise greater discretion in making its decisions to spend.

Use of Cash in Relation to Monetary Policy · Efforts of reserve banking policy to curb inflationary spending by limiting expansion of the money supply are generally accompanied by more active use of cash balances by the public. Some individuals and businesses may increase their spending by drawing upon their own existing cash balances or by converting financial assets into cash. As interest rates rise in this situation, others will be induced to put their idle balances to work in interest-earning assets. Such an addition to the flow of available credit tends to offset somewhat the credit-restraining effects of anti-inflationary monetary policy.

As incomes rise in an expansionary period, however, people will feel a growing need for transactions cash, and it will become increasingly inconvenient for them to economize on existing holdings. For this reason many economists believe that a rise in velocity in this situation will approach a definable limit. Another reason is that there are limits to the increases in interest rates that nonbank financial institutions can offer to induce the public to economize on cash holdings. Institutions are limited in bidding for funds because when they pay higher interest rates this affects the cost of their lending, and as lending costs rise borrowing becomes less attractive to businesses and individuals. Therefore, the ability of institutions to attract funds and to use them profitably is reduced.

When economic activity is declining, efforts to stimulate spending by encouraging expansion of the money supply may be accompanied by a less active use of cash balances. The expansionary effects of additions to bank reserves and the supply of money may be weakened, in other words, by a rise, however activated, in the public's desire to hold cash and by an accompanying decline in the velocity of money. As a result, countercyclical monetary action, even though aggressive, may not be accompanied by a commensurate rise in spending.

With the changing use of cash balances a potential countervailing force to monetary policy, it is necessarily incumbent on the monetary authorities to pay close attention to money velocity and to weigh its strength carefully in determining possible actions.

EFFECT OF CHANGES IN CREDIT CONDITIONS

Changes in interest rates and other credit conditions associated with countercyclical variations in the supply of money and credit influence economic developments through their effect on decisions to borrow and spend or to save and lend.

How Lenders and Savers Are Affected · Commercial banks' willingness to lend and the terms they offer are strongly influenced by monetary policy because it has a direct impact on their reserve positions. Other lenders, such as finance companies and mortgage companies, obtain part of their funds by borrowing from commercial banks. At times when credit expansion is under restraint, these lenders find that funds are less readily available and more expensive than in times of credit ease. As the volume of their borrowing is restricted and its cost rises, nonbank lenders may find it necessary to curtail their lending. They will also tend to charge customers higher rates of interest on loans. . . .

The flow of lendable funds in the over-all credit market depends to a large extent, however, on the saving of consumers, who make funds available to the market directly or through intermediary financial institutions. . . . How much total consumer saving will respond in given circumstances to changes in interest rates is a matter of some uncertainty. Nevertheless, changes in interest rates do have discernible effects on the distribution of the flow of consumer saving among various financial investments and also, to a degree, on the distribution of total consumer saving between financial investments and investments in capital goods.

How Business Borrowing and Spending Respond · The effect on borrowing and on spending of changes in credit conditions and costs will not be uniform among businesses and individuals. The effect will vary with—among other things—the reliance that is placed on credit by the potential borrowers, with the borrower's financial position and credit standing, and with his income and profit expectations.

In periods of restraint on the pace of monetary expansion, potential business borrowers will be discouraged in a number of ways. The pressure on banks to restrict the growth of their loan portfolios will lead them to ask some borowers to accept smaller loans and some to accept shorter maturities. In other instances banks may ask customers to postpone their borrowing altogether. And any rise in bank lending rates may also discourage some potential borrowers from seeking loans. Customers who want to borrow are likely to seek accommodation elsewhere, but these sources—nonbank financial institutions and the credit market generally—will also be under pressure as a result of the general excess of demand at current levels of interest rates.

The net effect of receding ease and eventual tightening of credit markets is likely to be some curtailment of spending by business. Forward inventory commitments, and later the actual purchases, may be curbed; and there may also be a slowing down in planned spending for plant and equipment.

These curtailments in spending may not affect the majority of businesses or the full amount of many loans, but they will affect some borrowers and the amounts involved in some loans. In other words, marginal borrowing will be restrained. The result usually is a smaller increase in spending than transactors would have wanted under more favorable credit conditions, rather than an actual contraction in spending. For this reason, the brake on business spending is difficult to observe.

The sensitivity of business spending and borrowing to changes in interest rates and other credit terms varies widely. The ability and willingness to accumulate inventories, for example, may be significantly affected for some enterprises by a rise in bank lending rates, while for others, whose inventory costs are smaller or whose financial position is stronger, such a rise may have little deterrent impact. In certain fields such as industrial and commercial construction, public utilities, and railroads, where there are large fixed investments, long-term interest rates are a particularly significant cost factor. In such fields comparatively small increases in interest rates can result in postponement of borrowing to finance capital outlays. Even in fields where interest costs incurred for financing fixed investment may be less important, as in retail and wholesale trade, some business units may be induced to cut back on their reliance on longer-term borrowing when interest rates rise, and other borrowers may be deterred from adding to such debt. . . .

Businesses borrow in the expectation that the return from the use of borowed funds will exceed interest costs by a significant margin. When the margin is large and when it is fairly well assured, moderate increases in interest rates may have little effect on the willingness of a business to borrow. But when the margin is smaller or when the return is less certain, a rise in interest rates discourages borrowers.

A rise in interest rates increases the cost of long-term borrowing and influences the utilization of productive resources through changes in the relationship between prices of existing capital assets and the cost of producing new assets. These changes direct some activity away from production of long-lived, slowly depreciating capital goods and thereby free resources for an immediate increase in output of consumer goods or of producers' equipment to make consumer goods. In the fixed-capital area these changes, together with changes in the outlook for profits and risks due to the altered credit and monetary situation, shift the balance of business decisions toward holding or buying old assets, and adapting such assets to new uses, as compared with producing new ones.

The relationship between capitalized values of existing assets and costs of producing new ones is indicated below. The illustration pertains to an office building with a net income from rent of $100,000 a year.

If the current interest rate for such investment, with allowance for risk, were 6 percent, the capitalized value of the existing property would be more than the cost of constructing a new building with the same earning prospects. An investor in this type of real estate would build a new structure instead of buying an existing building, other things being equal.

Estimated cost of constructing a new building:	$1,500,000
Capitalized market value of an existing building with earnings from rent (net of all current costs and depreciation) of $100,000:	
If current interest rate, with allowance for risk, is 6 percent:	1,666,667
If current interest rate, with allowance for risk, is 7 percent:	1,428,571

On the other hand, if the relevant interest rate were 7 percent, it would not pay to build a new structure and the decision would go the other way. The economic resources that would have gone into constructing the new building would then be available for other uses.

How Consumer Borrowing and Spending Respond · Consumers make use of both short- and long-term credit. They use short- and intermediate-term credit to finance purchases of durable goods, home improvements, and a variety of services. Most of their long-term borowing takes the form of residential mortgages.

Various types of institutions extend short- and intermediate-term credit to consumers on fairly standardized terms and charge rates that are relatively inflexible and high in relation to open market rates of interest. The interest rate that a consumer-financing institution pays for the funds it borrows is only one of the cost elements in the finance charge to consumers, but it does have an influence on the institution's willingness to lend.

General credit tightness or ease will be transmitted to consumer credit through changes in the strictness or leniency of credit standards applied by institutions granting such credit. The variation of credit standards affects the volume of new credit extended, and this in turn affects the volume of consumer credit that is outstanding.

Even though the mortgage market is less highly organized than are markets for government and corporate obligations, and interest rates on mortgages are less sensitive to shifts in supply or demand pressures than are rates on other securities, the financing available for home purchases is considerably affected by credit conditions and interest rates.

Some lending institutions increase or decrease sharply the proportion of lendable funds they are willing to place in mortgages when interest rates on competing investment media fall or rise significantly. This tendency may be especially pronounced for Government-underwritten mortgages—FHA-insured or VA-guaranteed—because administrative ceilings on their contract rates make their actual market rates less flexible than those on other media.

As the availability of residential mortgage funds fluctuates, potential borrowers may encounter more or less difficulty in qualifying for mortgage loans. Borrowing to buy houses is typically long-term and repayable in monthly instalments. The ability of a potential borrower to qualify for a mortgage usually depends on the relationship of the monthly payment to his income. The standards that lenders apply in this respect depend in large measure on the availability of mortgage funds, and these standards become more stringent as the amount of funds available for lending declines.

In addition, any increase in interest rates on mortgages adds to the monthly payment. Thus marginal borrowers are no longer able to qualify on the basis of existing loan standards regarding the relation of the monthly mortgage payment to monthly income. In periods when over-all demand for goods and services is tending to be excessive, limitations on the pace of monetary expansion and on the availability of credit, together with increases in interest costs, tend to discourage house building or to encourage preferences for lower priced houses. In periods of economic slack and credit ease, increases in loanable funds and lower interest rates encourage residential construction. . . .

As the flows of spending, investing, and saving in the economy change in response to monetary policy and also to other circumstances, the reserve banking authorities are in a position to adapt current policies to these developments. If spending is tending to react too strongly or too weakly to policy shifts, the stance of policy can be altered. The gradualness with which policy has its effect, together with the inherent flexibility of monetary instruments, enables the reserve banking authorities to adapt to changing circumstances. At the same time, policy needs to be sensitive to, and also to anticipate, current economic tendencies and what they are likely to mean for the near-term future. Through these efforts the timing of policy is made consonant with the evolving course of the economy.

PART SEVEN

Changing Patterns
in Foreign Trade
and Payments

UNTIL RECENTLY the relationships between the United States economy and foreign economics have commanded little attention in this country. Although public interest periodically turned to the tariff issue and, after the war, the question of foreign aid emerged as a matter of some concern, foreign trade and the balance of payments seemed to take care of themselves. Neither did trade or payments considerations exert much influence on domestic economic policy.

This situation changed markedly in the late 1950's with the development of two serious challenges to the economic relations of the United States with the rest of the world: a continuing deficit in the United States balance of payments and the growth of the European Common Market into the largest trading unit in the world economy with its trade-diverting effects on some United States exports. These new developments were accompanied by the re-emergence of the problem of international liquidity, widely discussed in the early thirties but well-nigh forgotten afterwards. This problem took on greater urgency as the stepped-up pace of international transactions called for a new look at the international monetary system. These outstanding issues of international economic policy—their nature, their ramifications, and their possible solutions—are the subject of these essays.

B. B.

The United States as World Trader, Investor, and Banker

COUNCIL OF ECONOMIC ADVISERS

The Council of Economic Advisers reports to the President of the United States on the conditions and prospects of the nation's economy and helps him formulate economic policy. This description of the United States position in the world economy appeared in the 1963 Annual Report of the Council.

THE UNITED STATES is by far the largest producing nation in the world, accounting for more than 40 percent of total industrial production of the free world. Its 188 million inhabitants place it fourth among nations in population, and its unequalled level of per capita income makes it the world's largest domestic market and largest source of savings.

AS TRADER

The basic purpose of our foreign trade is to exchange goods produced efficiently in the United States for goods which we can produce relatively less efficiently or not at all. International trade lowers costs and raises standards of living both at home and abroad. Foreign trade accounts for a much larger part of transactions of the U.S. economy than is generally appreciated. Even though our merchandise exports are only about 4 percent of total gross national product (GNP), they amount to nearly 9 percent of our total production of movable goods. For some products, overseas demand is exceptionally important; it provides over half the market for such diverse U.S. products as rice, DDT, and tracklaying tractors. Imports by the United States provide materials essential for production and also permit Americans variety and diversity in their consumption. Crucial products like nickel and cobalt come almost entirely from foreign sources.

U.S. exports and imports are a major part of world trade. In the first three quarters of 1962, U.S. merchandise imports were nearly 14 percent of total world imports. For some countries and some commodities, of course, the U.S. market is far more important than this average share implies. For example, U.S. coffee imports are usually over half of total world imports of coffee.

U.S. citizens pay large sums for services provided by foreigners —transportation of goods and persons, food and lodging for American tourists and businessmen traveling abroad, interest, dividends, and profits on the funds of foreigners invested in American enterprise or securities. In addition, the United States spends overseas nearly $3 billion (gross) a year for its own military defense and, indeed, for the defense of the entire free world. This expenditure is made in part directly by the U.S. Government and in part by more than one million U.S. servicemen and their dependents stationed abroad.

The United States is also a major supplier of goods and services, accounting in 1961 for nearly 18 percent of total world exports of merchandise, for nearly one-fourth of world exports of manufactures, and for nearly one-third of world exports of capital goods. It is a principal exporter of many agricultural goods, especially cotton, wheat, tobacco, soybeans, and poultry, and it exports large amounts of military equipment to its allies—some on a grant basis, some for cash payment.

The very size of the United States in the world economy lends to its economic activity and its economic policies special importance and interest abroad. Its rate of unemployment, economic growth, and commercial and financial policies are closely charted and carefully watched throughout the world.

AS SAVER AND INVESTOR

A nation as large and wealthy as the United States is naturally an important source of savings for the entire world, and national savings move abroad both as private investment and as official foreign aid. Its advanced technology invites emulation abroad, and the profitability of duplicating American technology draws American savers and investors beyond domestic borders. Its need for foreign resources to supply American production attracts private U.S. development capital. In addition, the United States has accepted heavy responsibility for the economic development of emerging nations, which require public as well as private capital.

Private long-term investment abroad by U.S. residents has risen markedly in the past decade, from an annual average of $0.9 billion in 1952–55 to $2.5 billion in 1958–61. Much of this increase has gone to Europe.

The U.S. Government provided $3.2 billion to foreign countries and international lending institutions in the first three quarters of 1962—in the form of development loans, Export-Import Bank export credits, sales for local currencies, commodity and cash grants, technical assistance, and contributions to international institutions. This was 12 percent more than in the corresponding period in 1961. U.S. foreign aid to the developing nations has risen markedly since 1954, and under new programs, notably the Alliance for Progress in Latin America, U.S. economic assistance is expected to continue to be high. Total aid expenditures are, however, still below those reached in the late 1940's under the Marshall Plan to assist European recovery.

Both private investment outflows and government aid are appropriate for a high-output, high-saving country such as the United States, and both are expected to yield considerable economic and political returns in the long run. Government and private lending and equity investment add substantial amounts each year to the net foreign assets of the United States, which have risen steadily in the past decade. But in the short run, both also aggravate the U.S. balance of payments deficit. To reduce the impact of the foreign aid program on the balance of payments, a large part of foreign aid expenditure has been tied to the purchase of goods and services in the United States. In the first three quarters of 1962, 76 percent of government grants and capital outflows resulted in no direct dollar outflow, compared with 64 percent two years earlier. Recent changes in the tax treatment of earnings on foreign investments were designed to achieve more equitable tax treatment between U.S. investment at home and abroad. They should reduce the outflow of investment funds to the extent that these funds were attracted by various tax privileges available in several other countries, and should also increase the repatriation of foreign earnings. Thus these changes should improve the U.S. payments position, at least in the short run when improvement is crucially needed.

Though foreign aid and investment absorb only a small part of U.S. savings, the United States is providing a substantial part of the total flow of savings across national boundaries, especially of the flow to the developing nations. The Development Assistance Committee (DAC) of the 20-nation Organization for Economic Cooperation and Development (OECD) estimates that the United States in 1961 supplied 57 percent of official foreign aid and 44 percent of private long-term investment flow from DAC members to the less developed countries.

AS BANKER

Since the end of World War I, and especially in the past 15 years, the U.S. dollar has emerged as the principal supplement to gold as an international store of value and medium of exchange. The important position of the United States as a market for goods and as a source of goods and savings, its well-developed, extensive, and efficient financial markets, and its long-standing policy of buying gold from, and selling it to, foreign monetary authorities at a fixed price have all made the U.S. dollar an attractive form in which to hold international reserves. Foreign monetary authorities hold more than $12 billion—over one-quarter of their total gold and foreign exchange reserves—in liquid dollar assets, mostly in the form of U.S. Treasury bills and deposits in American banks. In addition, foreign private parties hold $8 billion in dollar assets, and international institutions nearly $6 billion.

These large outstanding claims on the United States indicate the importance attached by the rest of the world to the dollar as an international currency, and the significance of the United States as an international banking center. For a number of years, the deficit in the U.S. balance of payments was financed to a large extent by increases in foreign dollar holdings which enabled foreign governments and nationals to acquire earning assets and at the same time add to their liquid resources. In recent years, about one-fourth to one-half of our over-all deficit has been settled in gold, but the growth in dollar holdings abroad has continued on a significant scale. The rise in dollar holdings has been an important element in the growth of international liquidity.

But these large balances also make the dollar peculiarly vulnerable. A decline of confidence in the dollar, resulting in widespread conversion of dollars into gold, would create a serious problem for the international payments system and for the economic progress of the free world. Therefore, satisfactory progress in reducing the U.S. payments deficit is essential at this time.

The United States still holds large gold and foreign exchange reserves. Last summer the President reaffirmed U.S. determination to defend the existing parity of the dollar and indicated the country's willingness to use its entire gold stock, if necessary, to do so. In addition to the $16 billion in gold and convertible currencies held by the United States, stand-by arrangements have been entered into with a number of individual countries, and the United States has extensive drawing rights on the International Monetary Fund. The Fund itself was strengthened in October when a special borrowing arrangement, supplementing the Fund's resources by as much as $6 billion, came into force.

Competitiveness of American Manufacturing in World Markets

This essay is an abridged version of a paper entitled "Recent Developments of American Industry and Prospects for the Future," which was submitted to the United States Congress Joint Economic Committee in September, 1962.

THE MEANING OF "COMPETITIVENESS"

FOR THE individual producer, competitiveness, broadly defined, means the ability to sell, to compete on the market. But since international trade is determined by relative rather than absolute advantages, this concept does not fit well into classical comparative-cost theory. If exchange rates are free to fluctuate, shifts in demand-and-supply conditions do not make a country more (or less) competitive but rather change her trade pattern; goods that might have been imported before will now be exported, and vice versa. On the other hand, under fixed exchange rates, we can say that a country has become more or less competitive if, as a result of cost-and-price developments or other factors, her ability to sell on foreign and domestic markets has improved or deteriorated.

Still, while we can speak about changes in competitiveness in regard to all commodities produced in a particular country, at a given point of time we can only say that a country's producers are more or less competitive with respect to certain commodities or commodity groups (e.g., steel) than are other producers; and superior (or inferior) competitiveness cannot relate to *all* goods produced. At the same time, statistical difficulties hinder a comparison of prices and wages in absolute terms, and more meaning can be attached to comparing changes over time.

Changes in the competitive position of the seven largest exporters of manufactures (United States, Belgium-Luxembourg, France, Western Germany, Italy, Japan, and the United Kingdom) over the period 1953–61 will be our concern in the following investigation. It is restricted to manufactured goods because export subsidies, food disposal programs, and other discriminatory measures distort competitive conditions in the trade of agricultural products.

CHANGES IN THE SHARES OF MANUFACTURING EXPORTS

The relative shares of the countries under consideration in their combined exports of manufactured goods have undergone substantial changes over the period 1953–61. Given the approximate doubling of the volume of manufactured exports from the seven countries taken together, Italian and Japanese exports expanded approximately fourfold and German exports nearly threefold. At the same time, Belgium and France roughly maintained their shares as of 1953, while the increase of exports was less than one third in the case of the United States and the United Kingdom.

Correspondingly, the export share of the United States fell from 31.4 per cent in 1953 to 24.4 per cent in 1961. About one third of this decrease can be explained by the relative decline of exports to traditional United States markets, Latin America and Canada; the deterioration of the American competitive position accounts for the remainder.

Competitiveness is effected by changes in relative prices as well as by nonprice factors (shortening of delivery dates, development of new capacity, introduction of new products, etc.). Although nonprice factors undoubtedly play an important role in changes of trade patterns, we limit our discussion to the relationship of developments in costs and prices and export shares where quantitative comparisons can be made.

PRICE COMPETITION

The importance of cost-price factors has often been discounted in the past. It was argued, for example, that the decline of the

United States export share in the world market for manufactures could not be attributed to changes in relative prices, since the cost-of-living index and the general wholesale price index did not show larger increases in the United States than elsewhere.

But these indexes are inappropriate for the problem at hand, because both include goods and services that do not enter into international trade. Instead, comparison should be made between changes in the cost and price of manufactured goods, on the one hand, and the volume of manufacturing exports, on the other. This can be done by linking changes in labor and material costs to price changes in manufacturing and, by examining the relationship between changes in relative prices and exports.

Up to 1959 the increase of United States labor costs in manufacturing had been surpassed solely in the United Kingdom; and not until 1961 did Germany overtake the United States, partly as a result of the appreciation of the German mark in February, 1961. Elsewhere, labor costs per unit of output were generally lower in 1961 than in 1953. But labor costs in manufacturing as a whole imperfectly indicate changes in competitiveness, by reason of the existing differences in regard to the export shares of the various industries and their labor costs in individual countries.

Among manufacturing industries, comparisons of labor costs in the basic metal industry are of special interest. Basic metals are of importance not only because of their significance in international trade but also by reason of the fact that these provide raw materials for the machinery and transport industries, which account for about one half of world exports of manufactures.

Between 1953 and 1960, labor costs in the basic metals industries rose by 20 per cent in the United States, while in the other countries under consideration these costs fell or—as in Germany and Japan—showed a small increase. The greater than average rise of labor costs in the United States metals industries has been due to the fact that while wage increases in these industries exceeded the average rise of wages in manufacturing, their productivity advance was less than for manufacturing as a whole.

The largest increases in labor costs and prices have taken place in steel. In the period 1953–61, average steel prices rose by 29 per cent in the United States and accounted for about 70 per cent of the increase of the price index of industrial raw materials. Correspondingly, raw-material prices in the United States rose faster than in any other industrial country. Higher steel prices greatly contributed to the price increase of machinery and transport equipment and thereby had a detrimental effect on the export possibilities of the latter industries. At the same time, the United States, a former net exporter of steel, has become a net importer, while exports from the Common Market countries with relatively stable prices have risen.

PRICES AND EXPORTS IN MANUFACTURING INDUSTRIES

Reference was made above to the statistical difficulties encountered in the international comparison of the absolute level of prices and wages. Such comparisons can be made with regard to rolled steel products, however. Table 1 indicates that in all major

TABLE 1. *Steel Export Prices by Products*
(U.S. dollar per metric ton)

	May 30, 1953			January 1, 1961		
	European Coal and Steel Community	United Kingdom	United States	European Coal and Steel Community	United Kingdom	United States
Merchant bars	93	96	105	100	113	134
Sections	93	105	104	94	109	132
Plate	115	127	104	99	115	127
Sheet (cold rolled)	147	128	134	148	145	157

categories, American steel was competitive with steel of foreign origin in 1953 but that in 1961 steel prices in the United States exceeded foreign prices by 5 to 40 per cent. This has led to the United States' becoming a net importer of steel.

For individual industries other than steel, changes in prices, export volumes, and export shares in the period 1953–61 are shown in Table 2. The pattern of price changes is, by and large, uniform in the machinery and transport equipment industries. Japan and Italy showed the most favorable developments in all cases, with Germany following; price rises in the United Kingdom were greater than average, and the largest increases were experienced in the United States. Japan and Italy experienced the largest drop in prices in the chemical and textile industries, too, except that

TABLE 2. *Prices and Exports in Selected Manufacturing Industries*

	Index of export (E) or wholesale (W) prices, 1961 (1953 = 100)	Index of export volume, 1961 (1953 = 100)	Export shares (per cent) 1953	1961
I. Electrical machinery:				
United States (W)	123	137	36.3	25.9
Belgium	✿	✿	4.2	3.6
France	✿	✿	7.4	8.6
Germany (E)	109	339	17.7	27.7
Italy (W)	103	416	2.5	4.5
Japan (W)	105	2140	1.0	9.1
United Kingdom (E)	121	131	30.9	20.6
II. Nonelectrical machinery:				
United States (W)	132	126	44.6	34.1
Belgium	✿	✿	1.9	2.3
France	✿	✿	5.6	6.3
Germany (E)	127	231	20.3	27.4
Italy (E)	104	390	3.1	5.9
Japan (E)	93	590	1.2	3.0
United Kingdom (E)	126	155	23.3	21.0
III. Transport equipment:				
United States (W)	118	130	36.8	24.8
Belgium	✿	✿	3.1	3.1
France	✿	✿	7.9	11.1
Germany (E)	96	459	13.3	25.8
Italy (E)	81	641	2.9	6.7
Japan (W)	90	447	3.6	6.4
United Kingdom (E)	118	131	32.4	22.1
IV. Chemicals:				
United States (W)	103	209	34.3	32.2
Belgium (W)	105	149	6.7	4.6
France (W)	81	275	11.9	11.6
Germany (E)	86	337	20.0	25.4
Italy (E)	60	618	3.7	5.9
Japan (E)	66	477	2.5	3.5
United Kingdom (E)	95	195	20.9	16.8
V. Textiles:				
United States (W)	97	107	16.1	12.5
Belgium (W)	93	163	9.2	10.4
France (W)	77	160	15.7	14.4
Germany (E)	88	218	7.3	10.5
Italy (E)	81	219	9.4	12.4
Japan (E)	86	312	11.2	22.3
United Kingdom	107	71	31.1	17.5
VI. Manufactured goods:				
United States	121	131	31.4	24.4
Belgium	95	187	7.8	6.9
France	97	217	10.9	11.2
Germany	109	281	16.0	24.1
Italy	80	446	3.9	6.7
Japan	95	382	4.3	8.1
United Kingdom	114	130	25.7	18.6

✿ Not available.

successive devaluations lowered the French index of textile prices below that of the two former countries. Again, price increases were above average in the United Kingdom and the United States.

Turning to the export performance of national industries, a correspondence between changes in prices and in exports is evident. Among steel-using industries, the exports of electrical machinery grew particularly in Japan, Italy, and Germany (in this order), and the smallest price rises were also experienced in these countries. At the same time, corresponding to a price increase of 23 and 21 per cent between 1953 and 1961, the export shares of American and British industries declined by about one third.

Similar conclusions apply to nonelectrical machinery, except that here Japanese prices actually fell and the rise of prices in Germany slightly exceeded that in the United Kingdom. But given the lag between the ordering and delivery of machinery, the rise of the German export-price index, resulting from the appreciation of the mark in February, 1961, could have had little effect on export sales in the same year. Again, the highest rate of expansion of exports was experienced in Japan and Italy, where the most favorable price developments have taken place, while the brunt of the loss was borne by the United States, which exhibited the largest price increases.

The fall of the price of transport equipment in Japan, Italy, and Germany was accompanied by a more than fourfold increase in the value of exports originating in these countries, while world exports only doubled. At the same time, the United States and the United Kingdom—whose prices increased equally by 18 per cent—lost one third of their share in the world market.

These results indicate that not only the pattern of price changes but also shifts in export shares have been largely identical in the steel-using industries. Some differences are experienced in the case of chemicals and textiles, however. In chemicals, the largest gains were in Italy and Japan, where prices fell most, while Belgium, the United States, and the United Kingdom exhibited an increase in relative (and in the first two cases, also in absolute) prices and a fall in market shares. France does not fit the pattern in the case of textiles, however. Although, as a result of two devaluations, prices expressed in dollars fell most in France, French exports increased less than the average. But the export shares of

Germany and Japan—where prices also fell considerably—increased, and in the United Kingdom—the only country where textile prices rose—exports fell in relative and in absolute terms.

Similar results are obtained if we consider manufactured goods as a whole. Between 1953 and 1961, export prices of United States manufactures rose by 21 per cent, as against a 14 per cent rise in the United Kingdom and small price increases and declines elsewhere. It is small wonder that in the same period the United States share in world exports declined from 31.4 to 24.4 per cent and that of the United Kingdom from 25.7 to 18.6 per cent.

PROSPECTIVE CHANGES IN COMPETITIVENESS

While a decline of United States competitiveness characterized the 1950's, there are indications for an improvement in the competitive position of American industry. In recent years cost-inflationary pressures have developed in Europe, while in the United States strong pressures for wage increases outrunning the rise of productivity are not apparent at the present time. The origin of these differences can be found in the conditions of the labor market here and abroad.

The unemployment of over 5 per cent in the United States weakens the bargaining power of the labor unions, while serious labor shortages have developed in most of Europe. In each of the Common Market countries, a fall in unemployment has been accompanied by a continuing increase in jobs in recent years. The labor shortage is most acute in Germany, where the number of jobs is six times the number of unemployed. Even in Italy, with an unemployment of 1,100,000, shortages have developed in skilled labor.

The continuing tightness of European labor markets gives promise of further improvements in the relative position of the United States. A comparison of conditions in the United States and Germany offers an especially sharp contrast. During the 1950's the increase of the labor force was larger in Germany than in the United States; but in the coming decade the United States labor force is expected to rise at a yearly rate of 1.5 per cent, whereas the natural increase of the working population will be nil in Germany. The high unemployment provides a further reserve in the United States, while German unemployment is negligible and the importation of foreign workers possessing the necessary skills becomes increasingly difficult.

Various factors may reduce the gains expected from the continuation of cost-inflationary pressures in Europe, however. A reduction of unemployment to 4 per cent in the United States would give rise to greater pressures for wage increases, and an inflationary settlement or a marked price increase in a key industry can again create an inflationary psychology. Also, in the absence of multilateral reductions in duties on manufactures, the elimination of internal tariffs in the Common Market will lead to discrimination against American exports. It should be noted in this connection that while the 10 to 20 per cent discrimination existing in the second half of 1961 represents only an approximately 1 to 3 per cent price differential to the detriment of United States manufactures, the average degree of discrimination will rise to about 12-13 per cent by 1967. The prospects for our exports will thus depend to a large extent on economic policies followed here and abroad, and on the successful implementation of the Trade Expansion Act of 1962.

The U.S. Trade Position and the
Common Market

IRVING B. KRAVIS

*Irving B. Kravis is Professor of Economics at the University of
Pennsylvania. He was one of the panelists appearing before a Congressional subcommittee who contributed papers to the compendium* Factors Affecting the United States Balance of Payments.

It is widely appreciated that the terms upon which the United
States has participated in world trade during the past century
have been favored by unique features of U.S. geography and economic structure. There is reason to fear that some of these past
sources of strength may be eroding, owing partly to the continuing revolution in transportation and communication and partly to
economic changes both in the United States and in other important industrial countries.

In particular, the economic structure of Western Europe has
been moving closer to that of the United States. The United States
thus is being made less unique; it is being confronted with
keener competition and with a more nearly equal concentration
of economic and political power.

The European Economic Community (EEC) or the Common
Market has accelerated these developments—some more clearly
than others. It may not be amiss, therefore, to try to assess the
impact of the Common Market upon the United States against
this general background of changing relative positions. This approach shifts attention somewhat from the usual emphasis on the
dangers of trade diversion that are created by the rapid elimination of trade barriers within the Common Market and the estab-

lishment of a common tariff wall around it. Aside from the fact that trade diversion has already been so widely discussed, there are several reasons for favoring this line of attack.

In the first place, the extent of trade diversion itself will depend largely upon the policy choices made by the EEC and these will in turn be influenced by the whole constellation of political and economic power relationships between the EEC and other countries, particularly the United States. This is the more likely since the common external tariff itself cannot be regarded as unduly protective by American standards. Tariff comparisons are notoriously difficult, but it is probably significant that at the rates prevailing in 1960 the average U.S. duty was higher than the common external tariff for 47 out of 74 chapters of the Brussels classification for which data were calculated by the Committee for Economic Development. Taken in conjunction with the trade-creating effects of the fillip to economic growth given by the Common Market, adverse overall effects on U.S. exports to the Common Market countries will not necessarily follow *automatically* from the existence of the Common Market. Adverse effects may, however, result from the future commercial and economic policies of the Common Market.

Secondly, a discussion of the effects of the Common Market which is concentrated upon trade diversion stresses competition for EEC markets and may omit the important question of competition between EEC and U.S. firms for American and third markets. After all, U.S. exports to the Six account for only about 15 percent of U.S. commodity exports, and they are, of course, small relative to total sales in the domestic market. Furthermore the more basic issues of relative competitiveness are important also in the contest for EEC markets.

ADVANTAGES OF THE UNITED STATES IN WORLD TRADE

The historical advantages of the United States in world trade may be listed as follows:

1. By the happy accident of geography the United States had an abundant supply of the materials which constituted the essential requisites of an industrial civilization. Coal and iron were linked by cheap water transport. There were ample supplies of wood. Copper, lead, and zinc were found in quantities adequate

not only to supply the United States but also to export to other countries. Abundant supplies meant that materials were cheap and gave a corresponding advantage to manufactured goods.

2. Not only was there a supply of abundant metals but there was also a vast expanse of land variegated with respect to climate and soil. Elsewhere in the world where favorable climate and soil are found, the man-land ratio is generally much higher, and therefore less agricultural output is available for export. Almost from the beginning of the Nation until this day, the United States has thus been a major exporter of agricultural products. It is true that the proportion of our exports made up by agricultural products has been much smaller in recent decades than in the 18th and 19th centuries but it nevertheless remains a fact that agricultural exports account for one-fourth of the total nonmilitary exports of the United States.

3. The United States has been a capital-rich country. The availability of cheap or free land made labor expensive from the beginning, and placed a premium on mechanization. Rough comparisons suggest that in the early or middle 1950's the amount of physical capital per worker used by U.S. enterprises was well over twice as great as that used by the leading countries of Western Europe, while the amount of equipment used per worker was almost twice as great. While the connection between factor intensities and comparative advantage may not be as simple as was once thought, the abundance of capital in the United States has undoubtedly been an important source of advantage for the United States in world competition. At the minimum a plentiful supply of capital made it easier for American firms to take advantage of the opportunities for large-scale production and made resources more readily available for research and development.

4. The American economy has had the advantage of bold and imaginative entrepreneurs. The combination of a rich and unexploited continent and a high degree of equality of economic opportunity stimulated a vigorous competitive race. While the visible hand of the entrepreneur engaged in self-aggrandizement not infrequently seemed to operate with greater strength than the invisible hand supposedly promoting the public interest, the ruthless entrepreneurs of the 19th century did serve to bring about the rapid economic development of the country. They left a heritage of vigor in the adaptation to changing conditions that still

permeates American business leadership.

These are the basic factors, but there are two more elements, arising in part at least from some combination of the above, that ought to be mentioned separately.

5. The presence of a domestic market that was both large in size and rich in its capacity to absorb new and high quality products strengthened the export position of the United States. The large American market, combined with the availability of capital and the pressures of competition, stimulated American firms to exploit the advantages of mass production at an earlier date and more extensively that foreign firms. It was the low costs of large size plants that gave the United States the opportunity to enter world markets for many manufactured goods. This was true for standard items such as apparel and farm implements which were produced in other countries by handicraft or small scale manufacturing industries. In addition, however, the wealth of the American market made it possible to cater to a demand for costly and high quality products by developing mechanized methods for their production. This applied not only to consumer durables but also to the improved machines and materials that were required for their production. Countries whose markets would not support the large-scale output of these products imported them from the United States. In a later stage they imported the improved machines and materials.

6. The movement toward the efficiency of mass production may be regarded as part of a broader search for cheaper methods of production and better or new products. In the 19th century, the "build a better mousetrap" motivation stimulated a flow of new inventions that were quickly inserted into the economic process. As research and development problems became more complicated, teams of specialists working with expensive equipment began to be developed in virtually every large firm. The result was that the American economy had a significant margin of technological superiority, and in many lines of production U.S. exports depended not so much upon the ability to quote favorable prices as upon the ability to offer qualities, designs, or basic products that could not be obtained elsewhere.

CHANGES IN THE AMERICAN POSITION

Basic forces operating both in the United States and the world at large seem to be weakening at least a number of these sources of strength in the American position. Let us take them one by one.

1. The advantage of cheap natural materials has been reduced by a number of factors. First of all the voracious appetite of the American industrial machine has chewed up significant portions of the original deposits of many ores. The once rich Mesabi range no longer yields huge quantities of rich ore but mainly the lower grade taconite. Iron ore, like copper, lead, and zinc which the United States once exported to other countries, must now be imported. The new sources of supply—Labrador, South America, Africa, and Asia—are often exploited by international companies in which entrepreneurs from different countries participate, and American buyers have no favored position vis-a-vis buyers from England, Germany, or other countries. Secondly, oil and natural gas have replaced coal as the lowest cost fuel and the availability of cheap Middle East oil has given our chief industrial rivals an important if sometimes embarrassing (for the coal-producing countries among them) opportunity to offset the advantage of cheap energy enjoyed by American manufacturers. Third, the advance of technology has reduced the relative advantage derived from having a domestic supply of raw materials. Part of this has been accomplished by the continuing revolution in transport which has been reducing the time and cost required to move heavy materials. Another part stems from the increasing economy in the use of natural materials in industry; according to one estimate, for example, natural inputs declined from 25 percent of the gross value of manufacturing output in the world's industrial areas in 1938 to 17.6 percent in 1955. An example of this tendency that has adversely affected the competitive position of an American industry is the reduction in the amount of coke required in the operation of blast furnaces; since coke is more expensive in Europe, the change is more favorable for Europe than for the United States.

On the other hand, the American economy has been a leader in the development of synthetic materials including such important products as artificial fibers, synthetic rubber, and plastics. To the extent that the latest variants of these products continue to be available first and most cheaply in the United States an off-setting advantage with respect to materials is enjoyed by the United States. The possession and extent of such an advantage turns upon technological leadership, discussed below.

2. The potential advantages of the United States in world agricultural markets are frustrated by governmental supports and controls. Although the U.S. Government is scarcely an exception to the almost universal tendency of governments to subsidize and protect agriculture, U.S. agriculture would probably be able to enlarge its export surplus in a free world market. In the world as it actually is, the trend toward increased output behind tariff and quota barriers threatens to limit further the ability of American agriculture to export its products.

3. The U.S. advantages derived from the possession of large amounts of capital have also tended to diminish. One reason—which is of recent origin and may prove to be temporary—is that many of the main competitors of the United States (Germany, France, and Japan, but not the United Kingdom) have increased their stocks of capital at a faster rate than the United States. The impact of the differential in growth rates is not, however, nearly so immediate as a different factor which operates so as to minimize the effect of the abundance of capital in the United States. The shrinkage of distance by phone and plane has increased the mobility of capital. The riskiness of investment in Western Europe has been greatly reduced by political stability, rapidly growing markets, strong currencies, and increased familiarity with European laws and business practices. The $18 billion outflow of private long-term capital from the United States during the past decade (exclusive of reinvested earnings) is the equivalent of 2 percent of the value of reproducible wealth of the United States and perhaps one-fifth that of a country such as Germany, France, or England. (Of course only about one-fourth has gone to Western Europe and a much smaller fraction to any one country, and the comparison with the wealth of these countries is intended only to give an impression of the magnitude of the outflow.)

4. Not only capital but also entrepreneurship has become more mobile; modern technology has expanded the geographical span of control to encompass the world. Thus two-thirds of the long-term private capital outflow of the past decade has been in the

form of direct investment. Direct investment is accompanied by American entrepreneurship, production know-how, and product design.

5. The increase in incomes in Western Europe and elsewhere has greatly expanded the size of the market and thus the opportunities for mass production of standard products such as apparel, of more costly items such as automobiles, and finally of the improved materials and machines required to produce the higher quality goods. This can be clearly seen in the automobile industry. One of the keys to the new-found ability of the Europeans to meet U.S. competition is a market now large enough to obtain an economical scale of output. In other parts of the world, such as Latin America, where the same techniques of production are available and wage rates are even lower than in Europe, automobile production costs are still high; the market in these places simply is not large enough to obtain the volume necessary for economical output. The dependence of the European automobile industry upon American materials and machines is also being reduced. Originally, a leading German automobile producer bought sheet steel from the United States because the desired quality was scarce in Europe. Now supplies are improving in Europe and prices are lower, and the German company's business may be kept only by special price concessions on the part of the American mill or as a result of a desire on the part of the auto manufacturer to maintain diverse sources of supply.

6. A number of factors have operated in the postwar period to minimize the effect upon international trade of the technological superiority enjoyed by U.S. industry. Shortly after the war, the U.S. Government, for good reasons, encouraged the export of American techniques to other countries. Thus the latest machinery and methods of production were incorporated in foreign plants often built with U.S. funds. In addition, the policies of foreign governments operated to offset the technological advantages enjoyed by the United States. In the first place, certain American companies which were permitted to sell in European markets found themselves holding large sums of inconvertible currencies. Although they had been accustomed to supplying their international operations from American sources, they thus found it desirable to cultivate European sources of supply. In some cases, this involved teaching European suppliers to meet the quality

requirements and design specifications that formerly had been available only from American sources. Secondly, many American firms found that they could overcome the barriers of tariffs, exchange controls, and Government purchasing policies only by establishing branches, subsidiaries, or licensees in Europe and elsewhere. More recently, of course, such moves into Europe have been motivated by more purely economic factors, such as higher profit margins, tax advantages, low labor costs, and closer proximity to the market, although tariffs and other Government policies still play a role. In any case, these establishments have the advantage of American know-how. According to a British estimate made about a half-dozen years ago, 25 to 30 percent of company-financed research in the United States was directly available to Britain through branches of American firms, and the resources this represented were greater than those spent by British industry as a whole upon research.

The effect of foreign affiliates upon U.S. exports and the U.S. balance of payments is not clear. There is some indication of a negative correlation between the expansion of U.S.-owned manufacturing production abroad and U.S. exports for given industries. Even if this is more firmly established, it is still possible that foreign affiliates stimulate U.S. exports through purchases of capital equipment, materials, complementary products (to fill out lines) and components more than they hurt them. In addition, it is claimed that foreign producers rather than U.S. home companies would win the foreign markets if the U.S. producers did not establish the foreign affiliates. This argument may have long-run validity, but it is weakened at the moment by the fact that the economies of the continental European countries have been working at capacity; it is not apparent therefore that the European producers would have been able to expand to take the business now enjoyed by the American affiliates. Finally, it is pointed out that the foreign affiliates held the balance of payments by giving rise to a stream of dividends, profits, and royalties, but this contention is set aside by some who stress the short-run effects of the immediate investment outlays upon the balance of payments.

Whether inevitable or induced by governmental policies or by the profit seeking responses of individual companies, it seems more probable that the effect of oversea affiliates and licensing will be adverse for the U.S. trade balance. They certainly appear likely to accelerate the speed with which knowledge of advanced U.S. methods is spread throughout the rest of the world.

Of course, these factors work both ways. European affiliates have been established in the United States and there are American companies that have been licensed to produce European and other foreign designs that are superior to those available in the United States. Nevertheless, an increase in the speed with which new products or methods are transferred is more advantageous for less advanced countries than for those that are in the forefront of technological development.

However, the diffusion of knowledge is scarcely likely to become instantaneous, and it would be of interest to know whether the United States is maintaining its past superiority in developing new methods and products. Research and development expenditures of the United States, it is known, are still many times that of other industrial countries, but it is not known whether the difference is narrowing or not. The importance of this question arises from the fact that the monopoly that an innovating country enjoys on a new product is almost always temporary; even without foreign affiliates or licensees, as knowledge of the new product spreads it is sooner or later successfully imitated abroad. In many cases it will turn out that the innovating country does not enjoy a long-run comparative advantage in producing the new product; thus it sees today's exports become tomorrow's imports. This has happened to a long list of American products from sewing machines to transistors. Furthermore, it is possible that the speed with which innovations are imitated or replaced by superior innovations may be increasing.

If the technological gap between the United States and other industrial countries is, indeed, narrowing, an important source of a demand for dollars is being weakened and the maintenance of our trade position being made more precarious. It is extremely difficult to assess what is happening in this area. One can point to important innovations that have recently come from other countries, but the importation of improved methods is not new. Thus, if one cites the recent import of the oxygen processes for steelmaking from Austria, Germany, or Sweden, it is possible to point to the earlier imports of the bessemer and open hearth processes from England and somewhat later, the extrusion process of squeezing cold steel into desired shapes from Italy. In one area, however, U.S. basic research and development work should be far ahead of that of other countries if the returns are at all proportionate to the investments that have been made—viz., atomic science. If this work begins to produce an economic return the margin of U.S. technological leadership may be strengthened.

More generally, rapid growth in output appears to favor innovation, and a maintenance of the recently developed superiority in the rates of growth of the Six and of Japan would not augur well for the United States. Full use of capacity in the United States with the consequent stimulus to investment (foreign as well as domestic financed) and innovation would, on this account at least, be beneficial to the trade balance.

POLITICAL FACTORS

No account of the American position in international trade, however short, would be complete without reference to the way in which it has been fortified by political factors. The relatively small importance of international trade to the American economy and the dispersion of retaliatory power among a fairly large number of trading partners left the United States free to use its great political power to limit or withdraw access to the domestic market whenever foreign producers made inroads that were damaging to American interests. Although the broader political compulsions to which the United States was subjected, especially after the beginning of the cold war, caused this power to be used rather sparingly, the very threat of its use reduced the incentives of foreign producers to make the investment required in many lines of industry to cultivate the U.S. market.

In the last few years, however, the situation has been changing. First, the balance-of-payments difficulties of the United States have for the first time in generations placed it in a position where a sensitive economic nerve was exposed to the good will of other countries. Second, the rise in relative economic power of other countries cannot be ignored. For example, the real gross national product of the five major members of the Common Market expanded from something like 40 percent of that of the United States in 1950 to 55 percent in 1960, and if the United Kingdom is added the change is from 60 percent in 1950 to 75 percent in

1960. The coalescence of other countries into trading blocs, of which the Common Market is the prime example, has enhanced the significance of these changes. Indeed the formation of these blocs may have a more lasting significance than the difference between EEC and U.S. rates of growth since the probability of survival is higher for the Common Market than for the growth gap.

THE IMPACT OF THE COMMON MARKET

The forces working against the U.S. trade position thus arise fundamentally from changes in the technology of transportation and communications and from basic changes in the economic structure of Western Europe. Western Europe has been the chief beneficiary of the enhanced geographical mobility of the elements that historically have been primarily sources of American advantage in international trade. Furthermore, Western Europe proceeds toward Americanization from an internal dynamic as well as from external effects flowing from the United States. As incomes rise, costly and high quality products begin to find domestic markets. Domestic industries arise to cater to these demands, and supplying industries develop to produce the improved materials and the new machines necessary to make the new goods.

These changes were flowing at full tide before the advent of the Common Market at the beginning of 1958, and the new organization has probably added to them only marginally. It is easy to exaggerate the purely economic impact of the Common Market upon its members. The Six were growing rapidly before they joined together as well as afterwards; indeed in the 4 years preceding the Common Market (1953–57) industrial production in the six countries combined expanded by 40 percent and their trade with one another by 78 percent, while in the 4 ensuing years (1957–61) the corresponding percentages were 30 and 64, respectively. The real threat posed by the organization of the Common Market for the trade position of the United States is the greater concentration of economic and political power than had previously existed, particularly since there are built-in factors that may cause this power to be used in ways that will be harmful to American exports.

Before turning to these political aspects, however, let us examine briefly the respects in which the advent of the Common Market brings or accelerates economic changes that weaken the U.S. trade position.

In the first place, the Common Market institutions may have had some effect in producing more rational practices with respect to certain raw materials than might otherwise have been followed. The complete elimination of tariffs and other restrictions on intracommunity trade in coal and steel, achieved under the European Coal and Steel Community (ECSC), reduced transport costs by rationalizing channels of distribution. In coal, for example, mines near national boundaries began to serve areas determined by economic rather than political factors. There are some signs also that the European Communities (i.e., the ECSC, EEC, and Euratom) aided by pressure from the Italians (who have no coal and depend upon cheap oil from external sources), will hasten the process of relaxing restrictions against the import of oil so as to obtain cheap energy supplies despite unfavorable effects on coal. Belgium has surely gone farther in closing down high cost coal mines than she would have been able to do without the political and economic support of the ECSC. Of course, there are some offsetting policies which tend to raise material costs, but these affect mainly tropical products from French-associated areas in Africa and are probably less important in their overall impact upon materials costs than the policies relating to coal and steel.

Secondly, the Common Market has dramatized the European market and made it more attractive to American capital and enterprise. The Common Market thus has tended to accelerate the process by which American enterprise, technology, and capital rather than American goods move across the ocean.

Third, the formation of the Common Market seems to have provided a stimulus to the growth of large size firms. A wave of mergers, affiliations, and understandings has probably led to larger size and lower cost plants, and has increased the degree of product specialization in plants of a given size. It has led also to larger firms which are more strongly placed with respect to research, finance, and foreign marketing than the smaller ones they replaced. The extent and significance of merger movement in the Common Market are difficult to assess. It is conceivable that what is going on is merely an adjustment by business to the new situation created by the prospect of free trade within the

Community. If so, the policy of live and let live, which seems to have characterized Western European business psychology to a greater degree than that of the United States, may soon reassert itself. It is possible that this attitude was as responsible as the inherent limitations of a market of the size of say England or France or Germany for the existence of smaller scale plants than in America. Of course, the EEC has taken steps to implement the anti-cartel provisions of the Rome Treaty, but whether European business will become imbued with a new competitive spirit either through self- or official-inspiration is far from clear. In any case, at the moment there has been a clear gain in efficiency from the rationalization movement that has taken place.

Fourth, the formation of the Common Market has made a contribution to the rate of growth, and thus created a greater market and a greater opportunity for the mass production of standard items and for the large scale production of more costly goods that were almost an American monopoly. In TV and radio, for example, the European market is already on a par with that of the United States in the quality of the product which it can absorb; in most other consumer durables, however, it is 10 to 30 years behind the United States. Of course, the expansion of the European market has been a boon to American exports thus far; it has offset any tendency for trade diversion to hurt U.S. exports. Indeed, U.S. exports to the Common Market have expanded more rapidly than U.S. exports as a whole since 1957 or 1958. However, the European boom can hardly last forever, and when the domestic absorption of European output slackens, U.S. producers may feel the full impact of the new capacities of European firms to produce goods in varieties, qualities, and quantities which formerly could be obtained only in the United States. Many American businessmen fear just this. They feel that their European competitors have been satisfied to follow the price leadership of American firms in the American and sometimes in other markets; this enables European firms, in view of their lower costs, to enjoy high profit margins on their foreign business at a time when their plants are occupied with domestic orders anyway. Of course, if the European countries succeed in maintaining full employment economies with only mild and infrequent recessions further European inroads on markets held by the United States will depend upon the longer-run growth of European capacity.

Finally, the agricultural policy of the Common Market threatens to increase the degree of self-sufficiency of the area by stimulating the expansion of internal production. New export surpluses such as French wheat have already appeared, and if high internal prices are added to the system of variable levies giving preference to Community products, the United States which has been exporting over $1 billion of agricultural products to the Common Market may find itself reduced to the position of a residual supplier especially for grains. Unlike the other factors we have listed, this one involves competition between United States and European producers only for the markets of the Community itself. To the extent that it will affect competition for other markets, it will be unfavorable to the EEC because it will tend to raise the level of costs.

With the possible exception of the last factor, the adverse influences upon U.S. trade that we have discussed thus far have stemmed from economic changes. The most important consequences of the Common Market for the U.S. trade position are, however, likely to flow from a new political fact: For the first time in many decades the United States is faced in the Western World with an almost equal aggregation of economic and political power. The uncoordinated, sometimes conflicting, and often offsetting policies pursued by six governments are being replaced by coordinated decisions reached in Brussels. Even without the addition of new members, the decisions are taken on behalf of countries whose combined importance in world trade already equals or exceeds that of the United States and who provide a significant fraction of the U.S. export surplus. The bargaining power of the Common Market, already substantial, will of course be further increased if Great Britain and other new members and associates are admitted. As the geographical scope of the Common Market is expanded, it will embrace an increasingly diversified area and will become more self-sufficient and less dependent upon external trade than the individual member countries have been. Thus, like the United States, the new entity will have considerable leeway for deciding upon more or less liberal policies.

How will this power be used? Some parts of the answer seem clear. In the first place, the power of the Common Market is likely to be used to retaliate promptly and fully in response to any adverse actions taken in trade matters by another country, including the United States. This has recently been illustrated by the action of the Council of Ministers of the EEC in raising the common external tariff on a half-dozen product groups in reprisal for U.S. increases under the GATT escape clause in the duties on carpets and glass. This type of response may be expected not only because of the natural tendency for partners to support an aggrieved member (Belgium, in the carpet and glass case) against an outsider, but also because of the psychology underlying commercial policy in Western Europe. In the latter connection, it is not much of an exaggeration to describe the postwar history of the dismantlement of trade barriers in Western Europe as a story of careful horsetrading in which no concession was given without extracting one of equal value. In the past, however, retaliatory action by European countries against American protective measures has been infrequent and never so prompt and forthright; countries almost always awaited the negotiation of compensatory concessions from the United States to replace the ones that had been withdrawn. The past patience of European countries may, of course, be attributable to the fact that their quantitative restrictions against American goods were still in effect, and as long as this was the case they could not feel quite so ill treated by U.S. actions. However, it may also have been due in part to the absence of a mechanism such as the Common Market which has the power to retaliate effectively and without the fear of the consequences that a small country acting alone would have.

A second factor affecting the use of the power that the EEC has is the inherent tendency of any large area composed of diverse interests to reconcile conflicts over the resolution of domestic difficulties by shifting as much of the burden of adjustment to outsiders as possible. This is evident in U.S. commercial policy. For example, the extensive protection accorded by the United States to its textile industry, including high tariffs and new legislation authorizing the establishment of import quotas, reflects pressures arising from the failure of domestic consumption of textile products to expand as rapidly as productivity, with the result that employment levels have been declining. In the short history of the Common Market, there are already a number of illustrations of this tendency to resolve difficulties by cutting off the outsider. These include instances of troubles caused by shortages as well as those caused by surpluses. The most important case involving a surplus, which related to coal, developed in the late 1950's. The desirability of a reduction in imports from the United States and other third countries was virtually the only point on which the Six could agree in their prolonged and difficult negotiations on means of meeting the coal crisis. Analogous action was taken in a number of cases involving shortages; for example, last spring the European Commission recommended to the Dutch Government that it permit the normal volume of potato exports to member countries and restrict exports to third countries.

Even if it seems reasonable to suppose that the Common Market will retaliate when the occasion arises and shift the burden of adjustments to third countries when internal difficulties develop, there remains a large and important area of doubt about the way in which the Community will wield the great power which its size and importance confers upon it. Although the Rome Treaty contains a clause stating that the member countries intend to follow a liberal commercial policy (art. 110), the commitment is quite general and could conceivably be subordinated to other objectives of the Six. At the risk of some oversimplification, one might say that there are two schools of thought within the Community on this matter. One school, for which the French are the spokesmen on many issues, takes the view that the Community represents, among other things, a club for the mutual benefit of the member countries at the expense of outsiders. This position has been generally opposed by the Dutch and also by the Germans, both of whom tend to prefer more liberal trading policies for the Community. Of course, the difference is one of degree, albeit an important one, because some element of tariff discrimination in favor of fellow members is the essence of a customs union. While it is true that the conception of the EEC goes far beyond a mere customs union, it is also true that the most immediate practical attraction of the EEC to participants and would-be participants is its customs union feature.

The Threat to the Dollar

ROBERT TRIFFIN

Robert Triffin is Pelatiah Perit Professor of Political Science at Yale University. In this article (published originally in 1961) and in his books Europe and the Money Muddle *and* Gold and the Dollar Crisis, *he reviews the contemporary international monetary scene and provides suggestions for changes in the world monetary system.*

THERE ARE two ways to go broke: a slow one and a fast one. The slow way is to go on, year after year, spending more money than you earn. But if you are rich to begin with, you won't go broke very fast that way. You will pay for your overspending by depleting your bank balance and other assets and by getting loans from people who trust your capacity to repay them later.

A much faster way to go broke is to finance too much of your overspending by short-term borrowing. Even if you stop overspending, you may then still run into serious trouble if your IOU's are suddenly presented to you for repayment at a time when your bank balance has fallen too low to cover them. If you still have other, longer-term assets in sufficient amount, you will remain perfectly solvent, but you will be confronted, nevertheless, with what is called a liquidity crisis.

This, in a nutshell, is the United States' problem today and the reason why our dollar is facing a serious threat in the international exchange markets. We have, over the past decade, spent, lent, and given away about $20 billion more than we earned and covered the difference by cash payments in gold ($6 billion) and also by short-term IOU's ($14 billion), which foreign central banks, private banks, and individuals were, until recently, quite glad to invest in, since the dollar was regarded as safer than any other currency, and even, for the time being, as safe as gold itself.

The Eisenhower Administration woke up belatedly to the problem when gold prices suddenly flared up on the London free market last October and when U.S. gold losses shot up in the following weeks to a rate of between $400 million and $500 million per month. A wind of panic blew over Washington officialdom, and hurried steps were taken or planned "to restore overall balance in our foreign transactions."

Although the exact measures adopted may not have been the wisest ones, their objective was highly laudable. We should, of course, steer away from the slow road to bankruptcy. The trouble is that we have not given much evidence so far of any clear understanding of the liquidity, as opposed to solvency, crisis that constitutes the real and most urgent threat to the dollar and of the measures needed to combat this far greater danger.

We might well regain full equilibrium in our overall balance of payments—we are indeed far closer to that goal already than the Eisenhower Administration seemed to suspect—and yet be faced by massive demands for conversion into gold of the short-term debts inherited from our former deficits. Such massive liquidation by foreigners of their present dollar holdings would certainly become less likely as we gave evidence of our determination and ability to put a stop to our persistent deficits of the last decade. It would still exist, however, and might be triggered at any time by speculative rumors—justified or unjustified—or, more simply, by interest-rate differentials between New York and other financial centers, primarily in Western Europe. As long as such a threat is allowed to persist, we may find ourselves unable to manage our own credit and interest-rate policies, in the best interests of our economy, without running the risks of large gold outflows from our shores and, ultimately, of a totally unnecessary devaluation of the dollar, disastrous to us and to the rest of the world as well.

Even if we chose to close our eyes to this danger, another major crisis would in time develop from the very success of our efforts to redress our own balance-of-payments position. The elimination of our deficits would indeed dry up at the source two thirds of the annual supply of monetary reserves on which the rest of the world has come to depend for the maintenance of international currency convertibility in an expanding world economy.

The present crisis of the dollar is in fact inextricably bound up with the ill-fated attempt to dig up and dust off an international monetary system which collapsed nearly half a century ago, during World War I, and which must be thoroughly overhauled in order to adapt it to present-day needs and conditions.

This international monetary system is theoretically based on the old, pre-1914 gold standard. In the decade following World War I, the "world gold shortage" was a frequent subject for discussion among academic economists and the main topic on the agenda of a long series of international conferences which culminated in the marathon debates of the Gold Delegation of the defunct League of Nations. The "gold shortage" was temporarily solved in the meantime by the growing use of two national currencies, sterling and the dollar, as international world reserves, along with the gold, in short supply. This, however, could not be more than a makeshift. It ended, disastrously, in the early 1930s with the successive devaluations of both of these currencies and the consequent collapse of the world monetary system.

In the decade following World War II, the basic role played by gold in our international monetary system was all but forgotten. A new slogan came to dominate academic discussions and governmental policies: the slogan of the "world dollar shortage." These policies were eminently successful. They accelerated the reconstruction of war damage and the expansion of the underdeveloped economies, and stimulated a rate of growth in world trade and world production unprecedented in duration and magnitude in the history of the world.

Yet they, too, were built upon the same make-shifts as in the 1920s. They, too, threatened to end in the early 1960s in a new collapse of world trade and world currencies similar to that of the early 1930s.

This grim parallel has its roots in a common and age-old problem: the routine and inertia which tie man to his past and make him unable or unwilling to effect in time the adjustments necessary to the successful performance, and ultimate survival, of his economic, social, and political institutions in a fast-changing world.

A simple comparison may be helpful at this stage. We all know too well the need which we have to carry some amount of currency in our pockets and to keep a checking account at our bank in order to bridge the gap between paydays and to be able to pay for our groceries and other purchases. The amounts of currency and deposits which we have to hold for this purpose bear some obvious, even though fairly loose, relation to the level of our income and expenditures. In very much the same way, countries must hold, generally in their central bank, international reserves to bridge seasonal and other inevitable and unpredictable gaps between their receipts from and payments to other countries. The amounts of reserves required for this purpose also hold an obvious, although equally loose, relation to the turnover of trade and production.

Now, imagine how little trade and production could have grown in the United States over the last century if the only means of payment available to all of us, as a group, had been the number of gold coins that could be minted from the haphazard growth of gold mining in California and Colorado. This, fortunately, was never the case, either here or in any other country. Paper currency and bank deposits played, throughout, a large and growing role, alongside declining amounts of gold, silver, and other minor coin, in the national monetary system of every country. Even in the heyday of the gold standard, the total monetary gold stock of the United States, for instance—both in the form of gold coin and central gold reserves—fell from about 30 per cent of the overall means of payment of the country in 1860 to about 8 per cent in 1914. The provision of an adequate, but noninflationary, volume of money for our expanding economy already depended then, as it still does today, upon the soundness and resiliency of our banking institutions and credit policies, rather than on any blind enslavement to the much-vaunted automatic discipline of the so-called—or miscalled—gold standard.

The basic problems which deposit banking has long been able to solve within national borders, under the guidance of national monetary authorities, still remain largely unsolved, however, as far as international payments are concerned. Or, rather, since the world has to go on, they have been solved after a fashion, but only through a succession of makeshifts and at the cost of recurrent international crises manifesting themselves in the form of widespread deflation, currency devaluations, and trade and exchange restrictions.

Under the so-called full-fledged gold standard, prevalent in the last third of the nineteenth century and until World War I, gold was used exclusively, or nearly exclusively, by most central banks as international reserves and as the ultimate means of settlement for temporary imbalance in all major countries' international transactions. The enormous gold discoveries of the mid-nineteenth century had made possible for a while the adoption of such a system, but the maintenance of adequate gold reserves by central banks the world over was fed in addition, even then, by the gradual replacement of gold coin by currency and deposits in the countries' national monetary circulation. But this latter process was bound to come to an end and did with the world-wide demonetization of gold in the 1920s and early 1930s. The world gold shortage has been with us ever since, although its timing and acuity have also been vitally affected by the vast price disturbances arising from wartime and post-war inflation and from the Great Depression of the 1930s.

Over the whole period from 1914 through 1959, new gold production outside the Soviet bloc has fed considerably less than half of the average increase in the world's monetary reserves. In the fifteen years from 1914 through 1928, it accounted for only 38 per cent of reserve increases, another 30 per cent of which was derived from the withdrawal of gold coin from active circulation, and the remaining 32 per cent from the growing use of major *national* currencies—primarily sterling in those days—as *international* reserves by central banks, alongside gold itself. This custom had spread under the prodding of British currency experts and the spur of the interest that central banks could earn on such foreign exchange investments—but not, of course, on the gold kept in their vaults. Together with the flight of hot money from the war-torn and inflation-wrecked continent of Europe, it helped the British restore the pound to its pre-war parity in 1925, while Continental currencies sank excessively in value under the impact of speculative money flights from the Continent to London.

This soon proved a very mixed blessing for Britain. The overvaluation of sterling or the undervaluation of other European currencies handicapped British exporters in relation to their main competitors in world markets. Europe boomed while Britain suffered from economic stagnation and unemployment. Britain, moreover, felt impelled to tighten credit and interest rates in order to attract or retain foreign funds in London and avoid unsustainable gold losses. Such monetary policies were bound to aggravate the deflationary pressures already at work on the British economy. They became, in any case, powerless to stem the flow when the later stabilization of currency conditions on the Continent triggered a massive repatriation of the funds which had previously sought refuge in London.

Continental central banks reluctantly agreed to support sterling for a while by moderating their own conversions of sterling funds into gold. This merely postponed the day of reckoning. The collapse of a bank in Vienna unleashed a new wave of currency speculation which led to further withdrawals of funds from London. On a fateful day in September, 1931, Britain threw in the sponge. The collapse of the most powerful currency that the world had ever known spelled the collapse of the international gold exchange standard itself and ushered in a long period of exchange chaos in the world's monetary relations.

A grim parallel could easily be drawn between the rise and fall of the sterling exchange standard after World War I on the one hand, and on the other the rise of the dollar exchange standard after World War II and the difficulties which we are facing today. Foreign funds have, ever since 1931, sought a haven in New York rather than in London. These speculative movements played a role in the consolidation of exchange rates—mostly in 1949—at levels which appear now to have undervalued European currencies with respect to the dollar. Our economy has grown, for the last ten years, at a snail's pace in contrast to the rates of growth experienced by most European countries. The repatriation of European funds which had previously sought refuge here initiated a gold outflow of more than $2 billion in 1958.

This drain was slowed down to $1 billion in 1959 and to a mere trickle in the first half of 1960 under the impact of a drastic stiffening of interest rates in this country. It again assumed dramatic and even alarming proportions, however, in the second half of last year. This was primarily, at first, the result of the lower interest rates and the darkening Wall Street outlook brought about here by an incipient recession coupled with booming activity and a tightening of interest rates in Europe. Incredible bungling by some of our Treasury officials during the September meetings of the International Monetary Fund poured oil on the fire by allowing a flare-up of gold prices in the London market, which unleashed a wave of speculative gold buying by Americans as well as foreigners. Our gold losses jumped from an average of only $25 million a month during the first half of 1960 to more than $200 million a month in the third quarter, $300 million in October, and $500 million in November; that is, to an annual rate of nearly $6 billion a year, just about equal to the amount which antiquated and ill-conceived legislative provisions leave us as "free gold" reserves.

Fortunately, other countries have as great a stake as we have in helping the United States ward off a devaluation of the dollar, which would once more usher in a long period of chaos in exchange rates, such as followed the 1931 sterling devaluation, and benefit mostly the two largest gold-producing countries in the world, South Africa and the U.S.S.R. Time is running short, however, and we are each day living more and more dangerously on the edge of the precipice.

The most feasible and constructive way to ward off the international monetary breakdown which a dollar collapse would entail would be to enlarge and streamline the present methods of operation of the International Monetary Fund. This could be done in two stages.

All that the first stage would require would be a mere declaration by the Fund that it stands ready to accept reserve deposits from its member central banks, just as our Federal Reserve System accepts reserve deposits from commercial member banks in this country. Under the rules of the Fund, such deposits would carry a gold-exchange guarantee, making them extremely attractive to central banks. They would be as safe as gold itself and as usable for payments anywhere in the world. Their conversion into any currency needed for payment would be effected most simply, efficiently, and economically by drawing a check on the paying country's account and depositing it in the account of the country whose currency was purchased.

The Fund, moreover, would be in a position to pay interest on these deposits out of the earnings derived from investment of the assets transferred to it by members in exchange for such deposits. The advantages of interest-earning, gold-guaranteed deposits with the Fund over both sterile gold holdings and exchange-risky balances in national currencies should be sufficient to induce most countries to exchange voluntarily for Fund deposits the bulk of their present foreign exchange holdings and possibly even some portion of the reserves which they now retain in gold.

Countries other than the United States and the United Kingdom would constitute, initially, the bulk of their deposits with the Fund by transferring to it the dollar and sterling balances which they now hold as part of their monetary reserves. The United States and the United Kingdom would, as a consequence, owe these balances to the Fund rather than to several scores of foreign central banks. The Fund would hardly wish to liquidate precipitously its holdings of such balances at the risk of precipitating a monetary crisis in the United States or the United Kingdom, and should not, in any case, be allowed to do so. Its right to demand repayment should be limited to a pre-agreed annual ceiling and should, even then, be exercised only insofar as is useful for the conduct of its own operations. In view of the vast expansion of its resources which the proposed reform would entail, it could, on the contrary, be expected to seek to expand, for several years to come, its dollar and sterling investments, thus giving us a further and useful breathing spell to bring about, in as smooth a manner as possible, the needed readjustments in our overall balance of payments.

The United States and the United Kingdom would, in this manner, recoup the freedom of monetary management—particularly in relation to their interest-rate policies—which is now so severely handicapped by the fear of the gold losses that would accompany the liquidation of foreign-owned short-term dollar and sterling balances. As for the other countries, they should also welcome the opportunity of exchanging their over-bloated dollar and sterling balances for equivalent Fund deposits. They now hold large amounts of such balances in preference to gold because of the interest earnings which they carry. They do, however, expose themselves thereby to the exchange losses which would be entailed in a dollar or sterling devaluation, to say nothing of the risks of blocking or inconvertibility. Deposits with the Fund should offer them the same incentive of interest earnings—although at a slightly reduced rate—while giving them the full gold guarantees which automatically attach to all transactions with the International Monetary Fund.

The second stage of my plan would require a modification of the Fund's Charter, but a very simple and unobjectionable one. The present system of arbitrary and rigid quota subscriptions to the Fund's capital should be dropped and replaced by minimum deposit requirements with the Fund. That is to say, all countries would undertake to hold, in the form of deposits with the Fund, an agreed proportion of their total monetary reserves. They would remain free to convert into gold, if they wished, any amounts accruing to their Fund deposit over and above this agreed minimum.

Such an obligation would adjust automatically and continuously each country's actual lending to the Fund according to its contributive capacity and to the need of the Fund for the currency of the particular country. It would do away with a system under which the Fund is now flooded with national currency capital subscriptions in bahts, kyats, bolivianos, and other currencies for which it has no earthly use and under which 90 per cent of its lending has in fact been made in dollars, thus aggravating our reserve losses, rather than in the currencies of the countries which were actually accumulating large reserve surpluses in their international transactions.

These proposals have been amply scrutinized and discussed in recent months, here and abroad, by academic, financial, and government experts. They obviously raise a host of questions which cannot be fully examined in this brief article. The real obstacle to action does not lie in their technical details, which could easily be modified in the course of negotiations, but in their long-run political implications. There is no denying the fact that such a reform of the International Monetary Fund could be interpreted as a first step toward the setting up of a supranational monetary authority to which central banks and governments are understandably reluctant to yield any portion of their cherished national sovereignty and independence.

Whatever one's views are in relation to this broad issue, it should be obvious that none of the measures proposed here would restrict the present real sovereignty of any country any more than it is already restricted. These measures would substitute, in a limited area, collective, mutually debated, and agreed limitations on national monetary sovereignties for the much harsher, haphazard, and often disastrous limitations now imposed upon them by chance events and by the uncoordinated use of sovereignty by several scores of so-called independent countries, with little or no regard to their compatibility and their impact on others.

Clearly, the world cannot tolerate much longer an international monetary system which has become so utterly dependent for its functioning on such accidental sources of reserve supplies as these:

1. Gold digging in a country—South Africa—whose economic life might be paralyzed tomorrow by the eruption of racial warfare.

2. Mr. Khrushchev's policies about U.S.S.R. gold sales to the West, which were responsible for more than a third of monetary gold increases in both 1958 and 1959 and whose abrupt cessation in 1960 contributed, at least in part, to the recent explosion of gold prices in London.

3. The perpetuation of our balance of payments deficits and the continued acceptance of dollar IOU's as monetary reserves by other countries; such gold and dollar losses by us have accounted for about two thirds of foreign countries' reserve increases over the last ten years and cannot continue much longer without undermining confidence in the dollar and its acceptability as a reserve currency.

I have no doubt, therefore, that future events will push us inevitably toward a basic reform of our present international monetary system. The real question at issue is not whether the proposals outlined here, or other broadly similar ones, will be adopted in the end. It is whether political leadership in the United States and the other free countries will prove sufficiently enlightened and dynamic to adopt them in time or whether they will have to be forced upon us by new crises and upheavals such as we experienced thirty years ago, during the first years of the worst international depression that the world has ever known.

PART EIGHT

The Goal of
Economic Growth

THE ECONOMIC growth of this country was, until recently, a
matter of little popular interest. There was continual concern
over the growth of *market demand* in relation to the growth of
productive capacity: inflation was feared if demand grew too
rapidly, unemployment was feared if demand grew too slowly.
But the growth of *productive capacity* itself was not a source of
worry. The nation's capacity to produce grew steadily decade
after decade. The adequacy of the rate of growth, which had
made this nation the most prosperous in the world, was not
questioned.

The lack of popular concern over growth was reflected in
government policy. We had no public policy toward the rate of
growth. Many government activities, especially investments in
the public sector, made a vital contribution to growth. Yet no
branch of government ever took measures explicitly to alter the
growth of the private economy where the great bulk of the goods
and services are produced. Our public policies sought mainly to
make the private economy efficient, equitable, and stable. Clearly
an economy can achieve all these goals and yet not grow; pursuit
of these goals did not necessarily stimulate growth. If the legislation, expenditures, taxes, and monetary operations by which
government pursued these goals sometimes affected the rate of
growth, this effect was typically a by-product. Government
policies expressly designed to alter the growth of the private
economy were not contemplated.

Now attitudes and public policy give signs of changing. After
a brief postwar spurt ending about 1952, capacity has grown at
an average annual rate of 3.7 percent. This is a respectable rate
by our historical standards: it exceeds slightly our growth rate
between 1900 and 1929, and it is far better than the dismal years
of the Great Depression and World War II. But many people are
no longer content with our average peacetime growth rate. They

are calling growth a public responsibility. Government measures to raise the rate of growth are being proposed. President Kennedy declared 4½ percent annual growth in this decade a goal of public policy.

Yet the idea of accelerating our economic growth has, quite properly, raised many questions and controversies. Do we, the richest nation in the world, need to be richer? What benefits could faster growth confer that we cannot have now through better use of our existing resources? Is the control of our growth a proper function of government? Can government avoid affecting the rate of growth?

There are other questions. In view of past trends here and abroad, how fast can we hope to grow over the next decade? Is Russia likely to catch up?

Finally, what are the means of economic growth? Which are best? What have economists learned about how to grow and what is being done to implement this knowledge?

E. S. P.

Growth Through Taxation

JAMES TOBIN

James Tobin contributed this essay in 1960 to The New Republic *shortly before becoming a member of the Council of Economic Advisers under President Kennedy. He has since returned to Yale University, where he is Sterling Professor of Economics.*

THE OVERRIDING issue of political economy in the 1960's is how to allocate the national output. How much to private consumption? How much for private investment in plant and equipment? For government investment and public services? For national defense? For foreign aid and overseas investment? Though our productive capacity is great and is growing, the demands upon it seem to be growing even faster.

The allocation of resources among competing uses is *the* central and classical theoretical problem of economics. Likewise it is the inescapable central practical problem of a Soviet-type planned economy, or of any economy under the forced draft of total war. Only recently has allocation of the output of the peacetime American economy begun to emerge from economics texts into the political arena, as a challenge and opportunity for democratic decision and governmental action. Public economic policy and debate have long been dominated by other concerns: unemployment, inflation, inequality. The composition of national output has been an unintended byproduct rather than a conscious objective of economic policy.

The importance of accelerating economic growth brings the question of allocation to the fore. Can we as a nation, by political decision and governmental action, increase our rate of growth? Or must the rate of growth be regarded fatalistically, the result of uncoordinated decisions and habits of millions of consumers, businessmen, and governments, uncontrollable in our kind of society except by exhortation and prayer? The communists are telling the world that they alone know how to mobilize economic resources for rapid growth. The appeal of free institutions in the underdeveloped world, and perhaps even their survival in the West, may depend on whether the communists are right. We cannot, we need not leave the outcome to chance.

USING OUR CAPACITY FOR GROWTH

How can an increase in the rate of growth of national output be achieved? The answer is straightforward and painful. We must devote more of our current capacity to uses that increase our future capacity, and correspondingly less to other uses. The uses of current capacity that build up future productive capacity are of three major types: (1) *Investment:* replacement and expansion of the country's stock of productive capital—factories, machines, roads, trucks, school buildings, hospitals, power dams, pipelines, etc. (2) *Research,* both in basic science and in industrial application, by government, private industry, and non-profit institutions, leading sooner or later to more efficient processes and new products. (3) *Education* of all kinds augmenting the skill of the future labor force. The competing uses of current capacity are: (1) *Unemployment:* failure to employ current capacity to the full, letting potential production be lost through unemployment. (2) *Consumption,* where most of our resources are engaged, providing us with the goods, services, and leisure that constitute the most luxurious standard of living the world has known.

Since 1953 the economy has been operating at an average unemployment level of over 5% of the labor force. A society geared to the objective of growth should keep the average unemployment rate down to 3%. Reduction of unemployment to this level could increase Gross National Product from the current labor force and capital stock by about 20 billion dollars. But this increase in output will contribute to economic growth only if it is used in substantial part for investment, research, and education; it will make no contribution if it is all consumed.

To stimulate growth we must somehow engineer two shifts in the composition of actual and potential national output. One is from private consumption to the public sector, federal, state, and local. Domestic economic growth is, of course, not the only reason for such a shift. Increased defense, increased foreign aid, increased public consumption are possibly equally urgent reasons.

The second shift of resources that must be engineered is from private consumption to private investment. About three quarters of Gross National Product is produced with the help of business plant and equipment. Faster growth of output requires a more rapidly expanding and more up-to-date stock of plant and equipment. Every $1.00 increase of GNP requires in the neighborhood of $1.50 new plant and equipment investment. Thus to raise the rate of growth two percentage points, say from 3% to 5% per annum, the share of plant and equipment investment in current GNP must rise by three percentage points, e.g., from 10% to 13%.

Between 1953 and 1959 potential GNP rose from 365 to an estimated 500 billion dollars. Some of the potential increase went to waste in unemployment. Of the realized increase, 69% went into consumption, 13% into government activity, and 18% into investment.

Unfortunately these calculations *understate* the effective growth of consumption relative to government and investment. The reason is that the prices of goods and services needed for government activity and private investment rose relative to the prices of consumption goods and services. For example, the services of government employees (teachers, policemen, clerks, etc.) rose in price 34% while consumer prices rose 9%. Although we managed to increase government expenditure for such services by 13 billion dollars, 11 billion dollars of the increase was simply the higher cost of the volume of services we were already getting in 1953 and only 2 billion represented a real expansion of such services. When account is taken of this and other unfavorable relative price changes, some 92% of the growth in output "in constant dollars" went to consumption; *government activity actually diminished;* private investment got 16% of the increase in GNP, and *none of this increase was for plant and equipment.*

This suggests we will probably have to continue to do some running just to stay in the same place. Even if we resolve to increase to 25% the government share of that output, and to

18% the investment share, the likely price increases in those sectors would nullify part of those increases.

POLICY MEASURES FOR GROWTH

Policy to accelerate growth must be double-edged. On the one hand, it must stimulate the desired government and private expenditures. On the other hand, it must discourage consumption. Here are some major constituents of a program for growth:

1. Increased expenditure by federal, state, and local governments for education, basic and applied research, urban redevelopment, resource conservation and development, transportation and other public facilities.

2. Stimulus to private investment expenditures by:

(a) Federal Reserve and Treasury policy to create and maintain "easy money" conditions, with credit readily available and interest rates low, especially in long-term capital markets.

(b) Improvement of averaging and loss-offset provisions in taxation of corporate income, in order to increase the degree to which the tax collector shares the risk of investment as well as the reward.

(c) The privilege of deducting from corporate net income for tax purposes a certain percentage of a corporation's outlays for plant and equipment to the extent that these outlays exceed a specified minimum. The specified minimum would be the sum of depreciation and (on the assumption that the tax rate is 52%) 48% of net income before tax. To qualify for the tax concession, a corporation would have to be investing more than its normal gross profits after tax. The concession, and the minimum requirement for eligibility for it, are designed to encourage greater corporate saving, the full investment of internal funds, and, most important, the undertaking of investment financed by outside saving obtained from the capital market. An analogous proposal to encourage non-corporate saving and investment is suggested below.

If these measures were adopted, a reduction in the basic corporate income tax rate, advocated by many as essential to growth, would be neither necessary nor equitable. Indeed the strength of these measures might be greater if the rate were increased.

3. Restriction of consumption, by:

(a) Increase in personal income tax at all levels, accompanied by permission to deduct a certain amount of saving from income subject to tax. Like present deductions for charity, medical care, etc., the saving deduction would be claimed at the taxpayer's option, with the burden of proof on him. A schedule of "normal" saving for taxpayers of various incomes and family circumstances would be established, and only saving in excess of a taxpayer's "normal" would be eligible for deduction. A scheme of this kind seems to be the most feasible equitable way to use the tax instrument to favor saving at the expense of consumption.

(b) Improvements in the social security system—e.g., raising retirement benefits and relating their amount, above a common minimum, to cumulated covered earnings—should be introduced on a quasi-contributory basis. Since the payroll tax contributions then precede the benefits, the funds accumulate and can be an important channel of national saving.

(c) Increases in state and local taxes—property or sales or income as the case may be—to keep pace with the share of these governments in the necessary expansion of the public sector.

(d) Limitation, to a reasonable proportion of sales, of the privilege of deducting advertising and promotional expenses from corporate income subject to tax. No observer of the American scene doubts that advertising is excessive. From the economic point of view, it absorbs too large a share of the nation's resources itself, and at the same time it generates synthetic pressures for ever-higher consumption.

RESTRAINING THE INCREASE OF CONSUMPTION

Increased taxation is the price of growth. We must tax ourselves not only to finance the necessary increase in public expenditures but also to finance, indirectly, the expansion of private investment. A federal budget surplus is a method by which we as a nation can expand the volume of saving available for private investment beyond the current saving of individuals and corporations. The surplus must, to be sure, be coupled with measures to stimulate investment, so that the national resolution to save actually leads to capital formation and is not wasted in unemployment and unrequited loss of consumption. It is only superficially paradoxical to combine anti-inflationary fiscal policy with an expansionary monetary policy. The policies outlined above must be combined in the right proportions, so that aggregate demand is high enough to maintain a 3% unemployment rate but not higher. There are several mixtures which can do that job; of them we must choose the one that gives the desired composition of aggregate demand. If the overwhelming problem of democratic capitalism in the '30's and even the '50's was to bring the business cycle under social control, the challenge of the '60's is to bring under public decision the broad allocation of national output. Fortunately the means are at hand. They are techniques well within the peacetime scope of government. We can do the job without the direct controls of wartime—priorities, rationing, price and wage controls.

The means are at hand; to use them we will need to muster more wisdom, maturity, leadership, and sense of national purpose than we displayed in the '50's. A program which allows an increase of per capita consumption of about 1% a year would scarcely be a program of austerity. Indeed it would not even feel austere if the growth of gross output per head were held to 1½% per annum. We are used to institutions that let us realize in increased consumption about two-thirds of increases in output. But let people earn the incomes associated with a 2½% rise in output per capita, and the measures necessary to keep their consumption from rising faster than 1% may seem burdensome sacrifices. Our communist competitors have an advantage. Since they do not pay out such increases in output as personal incomes in the first place, they do not have the problem of recapturing them in taxes or saving. That problem we cannot escape in a free society. Unless we master it, we shall not fare well in the competition for economic growth and national survival.

Economic Growth as a National Goal

HERBERT STEIN AND EDWARD F. DENISON

Herbert Stein is Director of the research staff of the Committee for Economic Development. Edward F. Denison is an economist at the Brookings Institution. Both organizations sponsor research on current economic problems. This essay was part of a longer contribution to the American Assembly symposium on American goals in the 1960's.

THE AMERICAN ECONOMY works well. It produces the highest income per capita ever known, and a rate of growth that raises real income per capita by half from one generation to the next. This income, and its increase, are widely distributed. Economic advance has produced a revolutionary reduction in the hours and burdens of work. Americans have great freedom to use their resources and incomes as they choose. The system is highly responsive to the demands of the people, producing with exceptional efficiency, inventiveness and adaptability the particular goods and services for which a private or public demand is expressed. Unemployment remains a problem, but one so reduced in magnitude since the 1930's as to be qualitatively different.

America and the civilization to which it belongs stand at an historic turning point. They confront a critical danger and inspiring opportunities. The danger is indicated by the phrase "cold war." Among the opportunities are to help the billion people of the under-developed world realize their aspirations, to reduce nationalist and racialist limitations upon man's freedom and horizons, and to push back the frontiers of human knowledge in many directions. Neither avoidance of the danger nor realization of the opportunities *requires* that the American economy work better, although better economic performance would make both objectives easier to attain. Insofar as movement toward these more important goals depends upon the availability of economic resources, the American economy as it is and is likely to be can provide them. It would be tragic if the United States should fall prey to the danger or fail to grasp the opportunities because of preoccupation with the idea that it is not rich enough and needs to become richer faster.

NATIONAL PRODUCTION AND NATIONAL NEEDS

From 1929 to 1957 the total production of goods and services in the United States increased at an average rate of 2.93 per cent per annum. We estimate that if unemployment is kept to about 4 per cent of the labor force, the annual rate of growth from 1957 to 1970 would be 3.27 per cent, and from 1957 to 1980 would be 3.24 per cent. At the estimated rate of growth GNP would be about $709 billion in 1970 and $972 billion in 1980 [at 1957 prices].

This estimate of future growth assumes that no special measures are taken to accelerate growth other than the reduction of unemployment. It is based on an analysis of the probable contribution to growth that will be made by several factors—the number, hours of work, educational attainment and age-sex composition of the labor force, the stock of capital, the increase of knowledge, and others. It assumes, among other things, that the 1970 labor force will be about 19 per cent larger and average annual full-time working hours about 5 per cent shorter than in 1960; that the educational attainment of the labor force will increase sharply; that the capital stock will grow at about the rate indicated by past ratios of saving to national product under prosperous conditions.

Estimates of future growth under conditions of high employment have been made by other students. Some project growth rates similar to ours, others project higher rates. The difference generally lies in the weight given to the relations observed in the long period 1929–57 as compared with a shorter more recent period, especially 1947–1950 or the postwar period inclusive of those dates. This shorter period may be interpreted as evidence that a "New Era" began after the war, in which various factors, notably the advance of technology, will hereafter generate a more rapid rate of growth than previously experienced. Alternatively, since this short period was one of quite low unemployment, it may be interpreted as evidence that high employment by itself makes a very large contribution to the growth rate.

In the space available here we cannot discuss and defend the points of difference between our estimates and others. We would only say that we believe the longer period to be more reliable than a selected shorter period, in the absence of clearer evidence than now exists of a persistent change in some relationship.

The most obvious question to ask about the projected rate of growth is: Will it be enough? In one sense of course the answer is No. The growth of production is the source from which desires for goods and services are satisfied. These desires appear limitless. However fast production may grow, some desires will be left unsatisfied, and many will wish that growth were faster.

However, the rate of growth will not be increased by wishing. Steps will have to be taken to increase it. By and large these steps will involve some cost to someone—otherwise we could assume that they would already have been taken. (Remember that we are discussing the problem of raising the rate of growth above that which would otherwise result at high employment—whatever that rate may be.) The question then is not whether faster growth is desirable but whether it is sufficiently desirable to justify any particular step that might be taken to achieve it.

This question may be concretely illustrated as follows. We estimate that if annual hours of work were to remain at their 1957 level, rather than to decline at the rate we project, our annual rate of growth from 1957 to 1970 would be 3.6 per cent instead of 3.3 per cent. Faster growth is a good thing and reduction of hours of work is a good thing. The question is whether increasing the rate of growth is more important than reducing hours of work. Similar questions can be asked about increasing immigration, or employment of women, or expenditures for education, or taxes for public investment, or tax changes to promote private investment, or expenditures for research.

When the question is put in this way it becomes obvious that the authors of this paper cannot responsibly pretend to answer it. We can try to illuminate the benefits of more rapid growth and indicate the costs of achieving it. But whether the benefits are worth the costs can be answered only by those affected or by

those making the decisions. The costs and benefits are not re-
ducible to any common terms that permit their objective measurement and comparison. In the end the decision will have to
reflect subjective judgments, and insofar as they are collective
decisions they will have to reflect some concensus of subjective
judgments.

Whether a collective decision about the rate of growth should
be made, through government, is in our opinion a real and serious
question. The alternative view is that the desirable rate of
growth and the correct means to achieve it are those that would
emerge from private decisions. These would inevitably be affected by the action of government in discharging its important
functions. But these functions do not include the explicit determination of the rate of growth. We believe that there is much to be
said for this position, and we trust that it will receive due weight
in public discussion of growth. We do not examine this position
here only because it seems more fruitful to use our limited space
to indicate what choices are available in the economic system if
collective choices are to be made.

How much is growth worth? · If our economy grows at the rate
we project, 3.3 per cent per annum, total output (Gross National
Product) will be about $710 billion in 1970. If it grows at 4 per
cent per annum, GNP in 1970 will be about $780 billion. The
value of the higher rate of growth is $70 billion of output in
1970 and corresponding amounts in other years.

How much is this $70 billion worth? Obviously, the answer will
depend upon what the $70 billion consists of and what wants it
satisfies. If it includes critical defense expenditures, the ca-
loric intake necessary for sustaining the population, the capital
assistance that would set the underdeveloped world on the road
to growth, then the $70 billion will be of the utmost importance.
But anyone can think of possible uses of $70 billion that would be
of little importance.

One can conceive of all possible uses of output being ranked
in an endless descending series from the most important to the
less important, to those of no importance at all, to those of negative value. Ideally, with $710 billion of GNP we would go down
from the top of this list through the $710 billion most important
uses. If we had another $70 billion of GNP we would take the

next most important $70 billion of uses, all of which would be less valuable than any of the first $710 billion. The value of the additional $70 billion would be much less than 10 per cent of the value of the first $710 billion.

It may be that the actual American selection of uses of output does not conform to this pattern. Possibly we select more or less at random from the most important, less important, and unimportant uses. In this case the additional $70 billion of output might be as valuable, dollar for dollar, as the first $710 billion.

There might even be a systematic bias in the process, which causes the less important needs to be satisfied before the more important. If so, the needs satisfied by the additional $70 billion of output would be much more important, on the average, than those satisfied by the first $710 billion.

The importance of more rapid growth depends critically upon how well we allocate our output among our needs. This simply means that if we can count on devoting our expected output to satisfying our most urgent needs, additional output will be only as valuable as the satisfaction of our less urgent needs.

As the authors see it, the key current question about the allocation of output relates to the division between private and public uses. There may be limits upon the amount of public expenditure that keep critical public needs from being met, even though much less important private needs are met. Suppose, for example, that we cannot or will not spend more than 20 per cent of the gross national product for public purposes. If the gross national product in 1970 is $710 billion we can have only $142 billion of public expenditures, even though this may leave unmet many public needs more important than the needs satisfied by some of the $568 billion of private expenditures. The value of raising the GNP would then lie in the additional public expenditures it would permit.

It should be understood that in this paper we have made no evaluation of the need for additional public expenditure. Here we are concerned only to explore the implications for economic growth on the hypothesis that a very large increase of public expenditure is necessary.

There are two main possibilities to be considered. One is that we cannot raise tax rates above their present levels, at least without serious effects upon economic growth. The other is that we *will* not raise tax rates. In either case the yield of the existing tax rates sets a limit to public expenditure, and the only way to raise that expenditure would be to increase the yield of the existing tax rates by increasing the rate of economic growth.

Granted a willingness to raise tax rates, it must be recognized that certain patterns of tax increase might tend to retard the rate of growth. But substantial additions to revenue can be obtained without such an effect. This might involve some combination of (a) increases in the beginning rate of individual income tax (now 20 per cent), (b) a broadening of the income tax base by reduction of exemptions and exclusions and (c) increased taxation of consumption. Such taxation would be burdensome, but this burden is simply that which is implicit in any decision to sacrifice private consumption for public expenditures.

Whether higher public expenditures financed by higher taxes will retard the rate of economic growth depends not only on the character of the taxes but also on the character of the expenditures. If the expenditure increase is heavily weighted with public investment, research, education, and defense programs with a large research content, and if the taxation impinges almost entirely on private consumption, the net effect may be a higher rate of growth.

Even if taxes can be increased without adverse effects upon growth the public and its government representatives may be unwilling to impose the additional taxes. In this case a higher rate of growth would be needed to permit more public expenditures by increasing the yield of the existing tax system.

The authors believe that there are unnecessary obstacles to an increase or decrease of federal taxes. Sharp disagreement over the proper distribution of tax burdens, exaggerated impressions of the consequences of the level and structure of taxes, the complexity of the tax system—all these make a tax increase or decrease excessively difficult. As a result, government expenditures tend to be adjusted to the yield of the existing tax system, even though the best level of expenditure might be higher or lower.

Too much should not be made of this point. At least in this century, no President has been unable to get an increase of taxes when he asked for it to finance expenditures that he described as essential to a vital national interest. Nevertheless, the tendency to regard the yield of the existing tax system as a limit to public expenditures is, we believe, a potentially dangerous obstacle to sound public policy. No law of history assures us that we can get safely through the twentieth century with the yield of the tax system we inherited from the Revenue Acts of 1950 and 1954. The American people should recognize this.

A more rapid rate of economic growth would reduce the importance of this obstacle. But we are doubtful of the possibility of circumventing this obstacle by raising the rate of growth. Many of the steps that might be taken to increase the rate of growth would themselves require higher taxes. Is it likely that, being unable to raise taxes to pay for important public expenditures, we would be able to raise taxes to stimulate growth so that we could pay for these same expenditures? We think not, but we are not experts on what the American people can be persuaded to do. In any case we believe it would be a serious mistake to leave the American people with the impression that the rate of economic growth can be raised to whatever figure is necessary to make the yield of the existing tax system cover all desired public expenditures.

The argument to this point may be summarized as follows: If the national product is wisely used, the contribution of a higher rate of economic growth would be the satisfaction of less critical needs, not of the most critical needs. But the less critical needs are still worth satisfying, and should not be disregarded. They motivate a large part of the work done in this country.

If this country does not allocate its output to the most important uses, it cannot be sure that any specified rate of growth or level of output will satisfy its critical needs. In this case there are two possibilities. One is to increase the rate of growth, which would probably increase the likelihood that important needs would be met. The other is to become more intelligent in recognizing and responding to vital needs. The latter is essential whatever is done about the former. If we are not wise in the use of our resources, we cannot expect the abundance of our resources always to compensate.

The Competition of Soviet Growth · Up to this point we have been discussing the value of more rapid growth as a means of satisfying private or public needs for goods and services. In the present state of the world, rapid growth of the American economy may have an additional value.

Let us postulate this situation. The Soviet economy is now growing at a percentage rate higher than ours. If this should continue, the absolute annual growth of the Soviet economy will overtake our growth (it may already have done so). Although there are strong reasons to believe that the Soviet Union will be unable to maintain a growth rate faster than ours once it has achieved a comparable level of technical efficiency, let us nonetheless assume that it will do so. Suppose further that, despite this, the United States is able to maintain an adequate military establishment, provide for necessary public services and sustain a rate of growth of private income that is satisfactory to the American people individually. Would we then regard our rate of growth as adequate?

This is an extremely difficult question to answer. It requires us to project our imaginations into a totally new economic, political and psychological situation. We, our allies, neutral nations, and the Soviet bloc are all deeply affected by the vision of the United States as by far the world's richest and economically strongest country. It is hard to conceive a world in which this would not be true.

But it seems possible that a change to a situation in which the Soviet economy is generally recognized to be growing faster than ours, not only in percentages but also absolutely, not in spurts but steadily, and is approaching ours in total size, could have profound consequences. It could greatly strengthen the confidence of the Russians in their own system, increase the attraction of the Communist system for the independent, underdeveloped countries, worry our allies about their reliance upon us, and weaken our own morale.

These consequences might not follow. Certainly they are paradoxical on their face. They imply that in order to increase the attraction of our system to populations with average per capita incomes of $100 we, with per capita incomes of $2,000, must become still richer faster. They imply that even though we fully discharge our real obligations to our allies, they will lose confidence in us because we do not choose to raise our personal consumption more rapidly. They imply that the rest of the world will not evaluate us by the standards we choose for ourselves but will compel us to be measured by standards made in Moscow.

Moreover no one really knows what the standards are in the production race upon which world opinion is said to hinge. We do not know whether the Soviet GNP is now one-third of ours or two-thirds of ours, because the composition of their GNP is so different from ours. And it is not clear whether the race is in GNP at all, or in steel production, or in butter consumption per capita. Each side presumably wants to race on its own track and to persuade the world that it is the right track. The outcome may depend as much on the persuasion as on the running.

Nevertheless the possibility described cannot be ignored. Accelerating our pace in the production race is probably a positive factor for our national security. How important a factor it is, the authors cannot pretend to say. This is a question the American people will have to decide on the advice of people more expert than we in the politics and psychology of the cold war. If they should decide that it is important, this would, in our opinion, be the strongest reason for a collective decision to increase the rate of growth.

The costs of accelerating growth must also be considered. We do not do *everything* that might promote our national security. Especially, we want to promote our national security in the most efficient way. Somehow we must judge whether a cost of x spent in accelerating growth will yield more in national security than the same cost spent for weapons, or for foreign aid, or for space exploration, or for many other things that affect our military, political and psychological position in the cold war. Again this is a question that the authors cannot answer. . . .

CHOOSING AMONG GOALS

Economic growth is a good thing, and it is tempting to elevate any good thing to the state of a goal of national policy. The main point of our paper is that the establishment of such a goal is wise only if the benefits of the "good thing" are worth its costs. We have neither invented nor discovered the costs. In fact, we suppose that consciousness of these costs has weighed in the decisions not to undertake the measures that might have given us more rapid growth in the past.

We should refer here to one kind of benefit and one kind of cost that we have not mentioned but that may be very important. There may be value in having a "national goal" aside from the benefits of achieving any particular goal and almost without regard to what the goal is. The goal may be inspiring, give "point" to life, and serve as a common bond holding the society together. This may be a benefit even though at the present stage of history our psychological need would be better served by a goal less materialistic and less parochial than the growth of the American economy.

There is a limit to the number of goals that the American people or any people can pursue, the number of crusades they can engage in. There is a limit to our supply of leadership for "pointing the way" and to the supply of attention and followership. In this sense, any goal is proposed at the expense of others that are or might have been advanced, and the cost of elevating accelerated economic growth to the front rank of goals is that something else is deprived of that position. The number of goals calling for our attention is large—to help set the under-developed world on the path of economic progress, to reduce the barriers of nationalism and racialism, to strengthen our national security, to improve the lives we lead with our immense flow of goods and services, to set a floor of economic security and welfare for all. We need not feel guilty of negativism or passivity if we decide that accelerating growth is not one of our most critical needs.

In closing, the authors repeat what was said at the outset. We do not, in this paper, attempt to decide what the public attitude toward the rate of growth should be. This is a question that the people must decide, referring to the kinds of considerations discussed here but also in the end expressing their own values, their own views of what is worth what.

Public Responsibility for Growth and Stability

PAUL A. SAMUELSON

Paul A. Samuelson is Professor of Economics at the Massachusetts Institute of Technology. A widely known theorist, he frequently testifies at Congressional hearings on government economic policy. The present essay, originally entitled "The New Look in Tax and Fiscal Policy," appeared in Federal Tax Policy for Growth and Stability, *a compendium of contributions by panelists before a subcommittee of the Joint Economic Committee in 1956.*

THERE IS much talk about taxes. When I flick on the dial of my radio in the morning, I hear a Congressman quoted on how our high level of taxes is ruining the Nation. Scratch the barber who cuts my hair and you find a philosopher ready to prescribe for the Nation's monetary ills.

This is as it should be. We expect sweeping statements in a democracy. Yet such sweeping statements have almost no validity from a scientific point of view. Campaign oratory aside, the more assuredly a man asserts the direction along which salvation is alone to be found, the more patently he advertises himself as an incompetent or a charlatan.

The plain truth is this, and it is known to anyone who has looked into the matter: The science of economics does not provide simple answers to complex social problems. It does not validate the view of the man who thinks the world is going to hell, nor the view of his fellow idiot that ours is the best of all possible tax systems. Quite the contrary, economists would indeed be useless if any sensible man could quickly infer for himself simple answers to the big policy questions of fiscal policy. No need then to feed economists while they make learned studies of the obvious. It is precisely because public policy in the tax and expenditure area is so complex that we find it absolutely indispensable to invest thousands of man-years of scholarly time in scholarly economic research in these areas.

COMPETING GOALS

Turning now to the goals of any tax system, we can ask: What tax structure will give us the most rapid rate of growth? What tax system will give us the highest current standard of living? What tax structure will make our system most immune to the ups and downs in employment and prices that make American families insecure? What tax structure will realize most closely the community's sense of fairness and equity? What tax structure will maximize the efficiency with which we produce what our citizens most want?

Upon careful thought it will be obvious that there cannot exist a tax system which will simultaneously maximize these five quite different goals of social life.

It is easy to see that high current living standards and rapid growth of our ability to produce are conflicting ends: you have only to look at a collectivized society like the Soviet Union, which decides to sacrifice consumption levels of the current generation in favor of a crash program of industrialization; you have only to reflect that historically in the slums of Manchester working families might have lived longer in the 19th century if England and the other nations had during the industrial revolution slowed down their rates of material progress; you have only to consider the problem of conserving scarce exhaustible natural resources to realize that every society must all the time be giving up higher future resource potentials in favor of keeping current generation consumption, as high as it is.

You can imagine a society that decides to devote its income in excess of the bare physiological existence level 100 per cent to capital formation. You can imagine it—but there never has been such a society. Nor would any of us want to live in such a one. It should be obvious, therefore, that no sane person would ever seek a tax program which literally maximized our rate of economic growth. It is just as obvious that no sane person would want to maximize present living levels if this meant eating up all our capital on a consumption bender that would leave us an impoverished nation.

There is no need to go through all the other pairs of the five listed goals to show their partial incompatibility. If we are willing to frame a tax system that strongly favors thrifty men of wealth, we may thereby be able to add to our rate of current growth; if we encourage a gentle rate of inflation, we may be able to increase the profits in the hands of the quick-reacting businessman, perhaps thereby stepping up our rate of growth. So it goes, and one could easily work through the other permutations and combinations.

But not all of our five goals are necessarily competing. Some when you realize them, help you to realize the others. If we succeed in doing away with the great depressions that have dogged the economic record, we may thereby add to our rate of growth. If we shape a graduated tax system that enables lower income groups to maintain minimum standards of life, we may ease the task of stabilizing business activity. If we replace distorting taxes by less distorting alternatives, the fruits of the resulting more efficient production can add to our current consumption and to our rate of progress in capital formation.

I shall not prolong the discussion of the degree to which the diverse goals of tax policy are competing or complementary. For we can formulate proper policies without having to measure these important, but complicated, relationships.

IMPLEMENTING COMMUNITY PREFERENCES

Upon being told by the economist that it is absurd for Congress to aim at the most rapid rate of growth possible and that it is equally absurd for Congress to aim at the highest possible current level of consumption, the policymaker may be tempted to say: "I understand that. Won't you therefore as an economist advise us as to just what is the best possible compromise between these extremes?"

A good question but, unfortunately, not one that the expert economist can pretend to give a unique answer to. If he is honest, he must reply: "The American people must look into their own hearts and decide on what they consider to be the best compromise rate of growth."

Just because I have advanced degrees in economics and have written numerous esoteric works in the field, I am not thereby empowered to let my personal feelings, as to how much the present generation ought to sacrifice in favor of generations to come, become a prescription for society. It would be as presumptuous for me to offer such specific advice as to let my family's notions about dental care determine how much the typical American family ought to spend on toothpaste. But it is legitimate for me as an economist to say this: *Whatever rate of capital formation the American people want to have, the American system can, by proper choice of fiscal and monetary programs, contrive to do.* This can be shown by an example.

Suppose the vast majority of the American people look into the future or across the Iron Curtain at the rate of progress of others. Suppose they decide that we ought to have a more rapid rate of capital formation and technological development than we have been having recently. Then the economist knows this can be brought into being (a) by means of an expansionary monetary policy that makes investment funds cheaper and easier to get. Admittedly, such an expanded investment program will tend, if it impinges on an employment situation that is already full and on a price level that is already stationary, to create inflationary price pressures and over-full employment—unless something is done about it. What would have to be done about this inflationary pressure? Clearly (b) a tight fiscal policy would be needed to offset the expansionary monetary policy: By raising taxes relative to expenditure, we would reduce the share of consumption out of our full employment income, releasing in this way the real resources needed for investment.

From these remarks it will be clear that economic science is not only neutral as to the question of the desired rate of capital accumulation—it is also neutral as to the ability of the economy to realize any decided-on rate of capital formation.

I repeat: With proper fiscal and monetary policies, our economy can have full employment and whatever rate of capital formation and growth it wants.

I want to cap the daring doctrine that an economy can have the rate of capital formation it wants with a doctrine that may seem even more shocking. Naturally, I cannot here develop all of the underlying reasoning, nor give all the needed qualifications. But I do in advance want to stress the earnestness with which I put it forward, and to underline that it does spring from careful use of the best modern analyses of economics that scholars here and abroad have over the years been able to attain.[1] The doctrine goes as follows:

1. [Samuelson has elsewhere described that analysis as a *neoclassical synthesis* of modern income determination theory and the truths of classical capital theory. *Editor.*]

A community can have full employment, can at the same time have the rate of capital formation it wants, and can accomplish all this compatibly with the degree of income redistribution taxation it ethically desires.

This is not the place to give a detailed proof of the correctness of this general proposition. It will suffice to illustrate it with two extreme examples.

In the first, suppose that we desire a much higher rate of capital formation but stipulate that it is to be achieved by a tax structure that favors low-income families rather than high-income. How can this be accomplished? It requires us to have an active expansionary policy (open-market operations, lowering of reserve requirements, lowered rediscount rates, governmental credit agencies of the FHA and RFC type if desired) which will stimulate investment spending. However, with our taxes bearing relatively lightly on the ready-spending poor, consumption will tend to be high at the same time that investment is high. To obviate the resulting inflationary pressure, an increase in the overall tax take with an overly balanced budget [*i.e.*, budgetary surplus] would be needed.

Alternatively, suppose the community wants a higher level of current consumption and has no wish to make significant redistributions away from the relatively well-to-do and toward the lower income groups. Then a tighter money policy that holds down investment would have to be combined with a fiscal policy of light taxation relative to expenditure. But note that in this case, as in the one just above, any qualitative mix of the tax structure can be offset in its effects by appropriate changes in the overall budget level and in the accompanying monetary policy.

A SOBERING PUBLIC RESPONSIBILITY

Modern societies necessarily are pursuing monetary and fiscal policies. These policies interact with private thrift to shape the pattern of high employment consumption and investment. Hence it is these public policies that determine to an important degree how fast society builds up its capital. This power over the community's rate of capital formation should constitute a sobering responsibility for the voters in any modern democracy.

Policies for Economic Growth

COUNCIL OF ECONOMIC ADVISERS

The Council of Economic Advisers consults with the President on matters of economic policy before the executive branch of the Federal Government. At the time this statement was prepared its members were Walter W. Heller, chairman, Kermit Gordon, and James Tobin. In this essay, which appeared in its Annual Report for 1962, the Council discusses the contribution that national policy measures can make to economic growth.

THE GROWTH of the U.S. economy results primarily from decisions taken by individuals, families, and firms. However, all levels of government—Federal, State and local—have a role in the promotion of economic growth. It is no part of that role to force on unwilling households and business firms any particular rate of growth in their own individual activities. But if, as a Nation, we desire a higher rate of growth, there are two consequences for government policy. First, in those areas of economic activity traditionally allotted to some level of government, public expenditures must provide services which contribute to the growth of potential output and which satisfy the needs that accompany increasing income and wealth. Second, public policy—notably in the fields of taxation, education, training, welfare, and the control of money and credit—inevitably stimulates or retards the growth potential of the private economy, even if no such result is consciously intended. Accelerated economic growth requires coordinated policy at all levels of government to facilitate the increase of productivity and the expansion of capacity. . . .

Economic growth is the product of growth in the labor force and growth in productivity. Productivity is preserved and increased primarily through acts of investment: investment in the improvement of human resources, in the creation of new technical and managerial knowledge, in the development of natural resources, and in the formation of physical capital. In the case of investment in human capital and in research and development, the link between expenditure and yield is difficult to measure, but there can be little doubt that the return is substantial. In regard to investment in plant and equipment and the development of natural resources, there is more statistical evidence available. No one of these investments can make its full contribution to the objective of accelerated growth without the others. Each of them is necessary; there is good reason to believe that together they can be sufficient, if vigorously pursued.

INVESTMENT IN HUMAN RESOURCES

Americans have long spoken of foregoing consumption today in order to invest in their children's education and thus in a better tomorrow. For an economy, just as for an individual, the use of the word *invest* in this connection is clearly justified, since it is precisely the sacrifice of consumption in the present to make possible a more abundant future that constitutes the common characteristic of all forms of investment. That devoting resources to education and health is, in part, an act of investment in human capital explains why programs in the area of education and health are economic growth programs. This kind of investment has a long and remarkable history. Rough estimates, which take into account differences in the length of the school year and in school attendance, suggest that the stock of equivalent school years in the labor force rose more than sixfold between 1900 and 1957. The annual rate of growth of the stock of education was more than 3 percent, or about twice the rate of growth of the labor force itself.

Failure to pursue vigorous educational and health policies and programs leads to smaller increases in output in the long run; it is also associated with higher expenditures in the short run. If we fail to invest sufficiently in medical research, we lose not only what stricken individuals might have produced had they been well, but also the use of the resources and funds currently devoted to their care. Failure to invest sufficiently in education means that we will lose the additional output that would be possible with a better educated labor force; it may also mean the perpetuation of social problems necessitating public expenditures. Recognition of the costs of inadequate investment in social welfare is one of the reasons for the Administration's concern to strengthen family services in the public welfare field.

It is a waste of resources to restrict health and education to those who can afford them. Moreover, in addition to each person's interest in his own health and education, there is a public interest in everybody's health and education. The well-being of each citizen contributes to the well-being of others. As a result, we have organized programs to help the population to obtain a quality education, to require attendance in schools, to help ourselves and others to obtain needed medical care, to require that certain medical precautions, such as vaccinations, be taken by everyone.

Education · Estimates made by private scholars suggest that about one-half of the growth in output in the United States in the last 50 years has resulted from factors other than increases in physical capital and man-hours worked. Education is one of the "other factors." Even without allowance for the impact of education on invention and innovation, its contribution appears to account for between one-fourth and one-half of that part of the increase of output between 1929 and 1956 not accounted for by the increased inputs of capital and labor. Education is of vital importance in preparing the skilled labor force demanded by new investment and new technology.

Education's contribution to output is reflected by the well-documented fact that income—a measure of each individual's contribution to production—tends to rise with educational attainment. Of course, not all differences in money income are the result of education. Differences in native ability as well as parental economic and social status are also reflected. Nevertheless, a substantial proportion of the increase in income at increasing levels of education may be attributed to that education.

In 1930, $3.2 billion (3.3 percent of GNP in current prices) was spent for all schools at all levels of education. In 1960, expenditures had risen to about $24.6 billion (5.0 percent of GNP). In turn, in 1930, 29.0 percent of the population 17 years old graduated from high school. By 1958 this was true for 64.8 percent. Similarly, in higher education the number of earned degrees conferred rose from 140,000 in 1930 to 490,000 in 1960.

Though significant progress has been made, substantial opportunities and needs for investment in education still exist. There is a pressing need to improve curricula and teaching methods, make education more readily available to students of merit by reduction of financial barriers, expand facilities and staff to meet rising enrollments, improve the quality and productivity of our teaching staffs and increase their salaries, and narrow the gap in opportunities available to students in different parts of our country. These problems must be met—and met quickly—at all levels of government and at all levels of education if our standards of education are to keep abreast of our needs.

Health · U.S. economic growth in the twentieth century has been associated with better health of the population as a whole as well as an increase in per capita expenditures on health and medical care. Public and private expenditures on health care increased from $3.6 billion, or 3.5 percent of GNP, in 1929 to $26.5 billion, or 5.4 percent of GNP, in 1960. This has been accompanied by a sharp increase in life expectancy and a reduction in death rates from communicable diseases.

At the same time that economic growth has contributed to an improvement in the health of our people, better health has contributed to economic growth. Better health makes possible an increase in the size of the labor force and in the effectiveness of effort on the job.

Further improvements in health would yield significant economic, as well as human, benefits. On an average day in 1960, 1.3 million employed persons—2 percent of civilian employment—were absent from work because of illness or accident. The days of work lost because of illness far exceeded the days of work lost because of industrial disputes; in fiscal year 1960, "currently employed" persons lost a total of 371 million days from work as a result of illness or injury, while the loss from industrial disputes in 1960 totaled 19 million days.

Public support for medical research, the most basic of investments in better health, has been growing. In fiscal year 1962, total expenditures will exceed a billion dollars, of which 60 percent is supported by the Federal Government. Further expansion of research activities, where funds can be wisely spent and where qualified research personnel exist, is desirable both for humanitarian and economic reasons. Much of the necessary research is carried on by doctors of medicine. More rapid expansion of the number of physicians is required to insure that patient care needs, teaching needs, and research needs can all be met. This will be true even if needed improvements are made in the organization and financing of medical care. The Administration has presented a program to authorize Federal grants for the construction of medical, dental, osteopathic, and public health teaching facilities, project grants to plan for new facilities and improved educational programs, and scholarship aid to students.

Eliminating Racial Discrimination · Although significant reductions in discriminatory barriers have been accomplished in recent years, important problems remain. Many nonwhite families are trapped in a vicious circle: Job discrimination and lack of education limit their employment opportunities and result in low and unstable incomes; low incomes, combined with direct discriminations, reduce attainable levels of health and skill and thus limit occupational choice and income in the future; limited job opportunities result in limited availability of vocational education and apprenticeship training. Unless action is taken, today's training practices, affecting tomorrow's employment possibilities, will help to perpetuate inequitable employment patterns.

Our economy loses when individuals who are capable of acquiring skills are denied opportunities for training and are forced into the ranks of the unskilled, and when individuals with education, skill, and training face discriminatory hiring practices that result in their employment in low productivity jobs.

Discrimination is reflected in the distribution of income and in disparities in the levels of education attained by white and nonwhite groups. Nonwhite families had a median money income of $3,233 in 1960. Although this represents a remarkable advance over the figure of $2,099 for 1947 (in 1960 prices), the magnitude of the problem still remaining is indicated by the fact that in 1960 the median income for white families was $5,835.

In 1947, 11 percent of the nonwhite population 14 years of age and over was illiterate; by 1959, this percentage had dropped to 7.5, with declines registered in every age group. The figure was, however, considerably higher than the 1.6 percent illiterate in the white population.

In December 1961 nonwhite workers made up less than 12 percent of the labor force, but accounted for 22 percent of the total unemployed and 24 percent of those unemployed 15 weeks or more.

Economic growth will be furthered by the adoption of nondiscriminatory policies and practices to insure that all Americans may develop their abilities to the fullest extent and that these abilities will be used. The Department of Justice, the President's Committee on Equal Employment Opportunities, and the U.S. Commission on Civil Rights are already acting vigorously. They should be joined in the campaign by all parts of our population and all units of government, business, and labor.

INVESTMENT IN TECHNOLOGICAL PROGRESS

Technological knowledge sets limits on the productivity of labor and capital. As the frontiers of technology are pushed ahead, industrial practice and productivity follow, sometimes pressing close on the best that is known, sometimes lagging behind, with the gap varying from industry to industry and from firm to firm. A stimulus to economic growth can come either from increasing the rate at which the frontiers are advancing or from bringing the technology actually in use closer to the frontiers.

Research and Development · The advance of technological knowledge depends on the amount and effectiveness of the human and material resources devoted to research and development. The limited data available suggest that within industries and between industries there is a positive correlation between research effort and productivity growth. However, some of the most important developments affecting the productivity of a firm or industry may originate from research done by equipment and material suppliers, or from basic research done by government and the universities. The benefits of research activity are often widely shared.

Expenditures on research and development in 1960 totaled about $14 billion. In 1961 the total was probably in the neighborhood of $15 billion, nearly three times the expenditures in 1953, and almost a third as large as business expenditures on fixed capital. Between 1953 and 1960, research and development as a percentage of GNP in current prices doubled from 1.4 percent to 2.8 percent.

Research and development cover a wide range of activities aimed at increasing the stock of scientific and technical knowledge. As we move from basic research to applied research and to development, the goals become more closely defined in terms of specific practical objectives, the predictability of the results increases, and the benefits become less diffuse. More than 90 percent of research and development spending is for applied research and development—most of it for development. Slightly less than 10 percent is for basic research.

Approximately three-fourths of the Nation's total research and development effort is performed by industry, and over half of this is financed by the Federal Government. Profit considerations naturally lead private firms to concentrate on developing and improving marketable products. Even here, supplementary government support can pay off handsomely. Estimates suggest that hybrid corn research, of which perhaps one-third was publicly supported, yielded a substantial return to society over and above the returns to farmers and seed producers.

Less than one-third of all basic research is done by industry. Government, the universities, and other nonprofit institutions, although doing only one-fourth of total research, do most of the Nation's basic research. Such research seldom results directly or immediately in new products and processes. But in the long run, basic research is the key to important advances in technology. Fundamental inventions like the transistor—an outgrowth of basic research in solid-state physics—may revolutionize large sectors of industry and have a tremendous ultimate effect on productivity.

The Federal Government plays a much larger role in financing than in performing research. It is estimated that in 1961 the Government paid for about two-thirds of the total national research effort including, in addition to work done in government laboratories, almost 60 percent of the research undertaken in industry-run laboratories and over 70 percent of the research done by universities. About 70 percent of government research and development spending is accounted for by the Department of Defense. The Atomic Energy Commission and National Aeronautics and Space Administration together account for nearly 20 percent.

In addition to its direct contributions to research and development spending, the Federal Government has stimulated private research and development activity. The science information services of the National Science Foundation, the Atomic Energy Commission, the Office of Technical Services of the Department of Commerce, and other government agencies contribute to the over-all efficiency of national research and development. Federal tax law encourages research and development by making such costs fully deductible in the year they are incurred. The Small Business Act encourages spending on research and development, including cooperative research, by small companies. Moreover, the Federal Government makes an important contribution to the training of future research scientists and engineers through its support of education and basic research in the universities.

STRENGTHENING RESEARCH AND DEVELOPMENT. During the 1950's, the number of professional scientists and engineers in the United States increased at an annual rate of approximately 6 percent. Total resources allocated to research and development grew at an even faster rate because a rising proportion of all scientists and engineers were engaged in research, and because supporting personnel, equipment, and material per research scientist increased. During the 1960's, these trends will continue, but one limit to growth will be the supply of scientists and engineers in certain fields. Future investment in research will be limited largely by the quantity and quality of earlier investment in education.

Overemphasis on current research and development activity should not be permitted to erode the underlying educational base. Just as research is investment for the economy, education is investment for research. The needs for educational expansion stressed earlier in this chapter include urgent requirements for laboratories, laboratory equipment, and other science teaching facilities.

A greater share of research and development resources and talent should be devoted to basic research and prototype development and experimentation in fields which promise major advances in civilian technology. Military research helped to create such important discoveries as isotope medicine, the computer, and the jet engine. The important impact on civilian technology of these offspring of military research suggests that high returns might be achieved if sights were set higher in nonmilitary research. Since the risks of basic research and experimental development are very great, and since the rewards for success are not confined to single firms or even industries, there is a case for public support to attract additional resources into this work.

In a number of industries, firms which are highly efficient in production and marketing may be too small to undertake an efficient research and development program. In others, a research tradition is lacking, or research is discouraged because the benefits tend to diffuse beyond the market grasp of individual firms. In agriculture, all these conditions are present, and the high returns to society from government support of research suggest that comparable programs to increase research in certain manufacturing industries might be highly desirable.

More Effective Use of Existing Technology · (1) In some industries there are legal obstacles to technical change. The housing construction codes of many localities provide a prominent example. In principle, these codes protect the public from shoddy construction; in practice, they often prevent the use of new materials, designs, and techniques which are superior to the old, and a lack of uniformity among codes in different localities discourages mass production of certain prefabricated housing components. With respect to construction codes in particular, the Housing and Home Finance Agency should continue to encourage the adoption of performance standards for codes and should strengthen its programs of testing and evaluation.

(2) American labor has a remarkable record of acceptance of new technology; but understandable resistance to the displacement of labor by new equipment has occasionally developed when opportunities for retraining and re-employment were not clearly visible. The Federal Government can help considerably, first, by pursuing effective policies to maintain full employment, and second, by expanding and improving its programs in job training and retraining.

(3) The process of technological change would be smoother if society knew better how to reap the rewards and reduce the costs. Research in the social, behavioral, and managerial sciences can lead to more efficient use of resources and to quicker grasp of the opportunities afforded by technological progress.

(4) Innovation is facilitated by a flow of information about new technical developments. Since many firms, especially small ones, are not in a position to follow new technological developments closely, the Government can play a useful role by providing business with relevant information and analysis.

(5) The Panel on Civilian Technology, composed of a group of distinguished scientists, engineers, businessmen, and economists, has been brought together under the joint auspices of the office of the President's Special Assistant for Science and Technology, the Department of Commerce, and the Council of Eco-

nomic Advisers. The panel is examining opportunities for stimulating civilian research and development as well as for more effective use of existing technology. It has begun to address itself particularly to those sectors of our economy where major social and economic benefits could be expected to accrue from technological advances.

(6) By eliminating monopolistic and collusive barriers to the entry of new business and by maintaining the spur of competition to innovation and the utilization of technology, antitrust enforcement tends to create conditions which encourage economic growth.

INVESTMENT IN PLANT AND EQUIPMENT

Between the resourcefulness of the labor force and the ideas of the laboratory on one side and the satisfaction of consumption needs on the other, the indissoluble link is the economy's stock of plant and machinery. Our own history and the experience of other industrial countries alike demonstrate the connection between physical investment and growth of productive capacity. Without investment in new and renewed plant and equipment, skills and inventions remain preconditions of growth; with it, they become ingredients.

Investment as a Source of Growth · Investment in fixed capital leads to increased capacity both by equipping new members of the labor force with capital up to existing standards and by providing greater amounts for all workers. Since 1929, the stock of privately owned plant and equipment (in constant prices) has grown relative to private man-hours worked by nearly 80 percent and by nearly 50 percent relative to the private labor force. Nearly all of the latter increase has taken place during the postwar period. Between 1929 and 1947, the rate of investment was sufficient only to provide enough capital—although more modern capital—to keep pace with a growing labor supply. No increase in capital per worker occurred. Since 1947, the rate of growth in the ratio of capital stock to labor supply has been approximately 2.7 percent a year, but there is a perceptible difference between the growth records of the first and second halves of the postwar period. From 1947 to 1954, the amount of capital per worker increased by 3.5 percent a year; in contrast, the annual increase from 1954 to 1960 averaged only 1.9 percent.

The importance of investment in the growth process is suggested by the parallel movement of the growth of potential output per man and the growth of capital per man (Table 1). Both

Table 1.—Growth in Business Potential Capital-labor and Output-labor Ratios, 1929–60

[Percent per year]

Item	1929 to 1947	1947 to 1960	1947 to 1954	1954 to 1960
Capital stock per worker [1]	0.0	2.7	3.5	1.9
Output per worker [2]	1.5	2.8	3.3	2.1

1. Business capital stock is built up from private purchases of plant and equipment, with allowance for retirements; excludes religious, educational, hospital, other institutional, and farm residential construction.

2. Business output is gross national product minus product originating in general government, government enterprises, households and institutions, the rest of the world, and services of existing houses.

SOURCE: Council of Economic Advisers.

ratios grew more rapidly after 1947 than before, and more rapidly between 1947 and 1954 than subsequently. In general, the experience since 1929 supports the belief that the more rapidly the capital stock grows relative to the labor force, the greater will be the growth in potential output per worker, provided that other necessary conditions are met.

Though there was no increase in capital per worker between 1929 and 1947, there was a slow increase in productivity which must be attributed to technical progress and to improvement in the quality of both labor and capital. When, as in subsequent years, investment was more rapid, there was an accompanying acceleration of productivity gains. These gains were not simply the result of the separate contributions of the advance of knowledge, the improved skills of the working population, and the rise in capital per worker, but came in large part from the interaction of all three.

Investment in new equipment serves as a vehicle for technological improvements and is perhaps the most important way in which laboratory discoveries become incorporated in the production process. Without their embodiment in new equipment, many new ideas would lie fallow. Conversely, the impact of a dollar's investment on the quality of the capital stock depends on how rapidly increases in knowledge have taken place. This interaction between investment and technological change permits each worker to have not only more tools, but better tools as well.

The slower rate of growth of the capital stock in recent years provides one explanation for the accompanying slower growth of labor productivity and potential output. The proportion of output devoted to investment, and the rate of growth of the capital stock itself, are measures of the diversion of current resources to the creation of future capacity. During the period 1947–54, expenditures on business fixed investment averaged 11.0 percent of GNP and the stock grew at an annual rate of 4.2 percent (valued in 1961 prices). In the period 1955–60, 9.8 percent of GNP was invested and the capital stock grew at an annual rate of 3.2 percent. The ratio of investment to potential GNP is even more relevant; in this case, the ratios are 10.9 percent and 9.4 percent for the two periods. This difference of 1.5 percent in the fraction of potential GNP invested represents nearly $45 billion of additional capital.

Policies to Encourage Investment · (1) ADEQUATE LEVELS OF DEMAND. The single most important stimulant to investment is the maintenance of full utilization of capacity. The historical record shows that when output falls below its potential the rate of growth of the capital stock declines. Expected profit from investment is strongly influenced by the expected demand for the output that the new capital will help produce, even if the investment is meant largely for cost reduction rather than capacity expansion. Estimates of future demand are colored by the experience of the present and the recent past. During periods of economic slack, estimates of future demand are relatively pessimistic, and many projects are foregone which would appear profitable under conditions of high demand.

There is a tendency to think of profitable investment opportunities for the whole economy as exhaustible: the more of them that are used up in any one year, the fewer remain. There may be some validity to this view for a single industry, which can mistakenly expand its capacity beyond the possibilities of future market demand. But for the entire economy, what appears as unavoidable excess capacity is in fact avoidable deficiency of demand. There are, and always will be, unsatisfied wants for a higher standard of living, though the demand for any particular product may perhaps be satiated.

It is true that, with any given level of technology, a higher rate of investment can occur only through the acceptance of investment opportunities of lower profitability. But appropriate tax and monetary measures can make even these investments sufficiently attractive. And technical progress can have the same effect. To equip a more rapidly growing labor force also demands a larger volume of investment relative to potential GNP. Fortunately, if actual output is held close to a rising potential output, faster labor force growth will open opportunities for additions to plant and equipment which would be economically unattractive if the labor supply situation were tighter. Thus a higher ratio of investment to output can be more easily maintained. When excess capacity already exists, however, profitability is low for that reason alone, and the growing labor force appears as a threat, instead of the stimulus to investment it really is.

In addition to serving as an indicator of future profits, the level of aggregate demand, through its impact on current profits, plays an important role in providing finance for investment. A policy that sustains near-capacity operations goes beyond strengthening the profitability of investment; it insures an ample supply of low-cost internal funds, which itself encourages investment.

(2) MONETARY AND CREDIT POLICY. The open market operations of the Federal Reserve and the debt-management operations of the Treasury exert a powerful influence on supply conditions in credit markets. If economic growth were the only end to be served, the sole object of monetary and credit policy would be to assure an adequate flow of funds to finance the needed capital formation at interest rates appropriate to the basic profitability of investment.

Use of monetary techniques for growth purposes must, of course, be limited by the demands placed on them by other national objectives. In the present situation, for example, monetary policy has a role to play in the attainment of recovery from recession and in the restoration of balance of payments equilibrium. Policies for growth and recovery are complementary, since any policy that stimulates investment will simultaneously stimulate aggregate demand. This situation, however, will not always prevail. When excessive demand threatens inflation, stability and growth goals will tend to push monetary policy in opposite directions. At such times, the importance of economic growth would suggest the major use of other measures—principally budgetary surpluses—to achieve stability. For when demand is strong enough to generate pressure on existing capacity, and only then, rapid growth requires that enough resources be withheld from other uses to make a sustained high rate of investment possible without inflation. Under these circumstances, a surplus in the Federal budget plays the constructive role of adding to national saving and making resources available for investment. The role of a policy of monetary ease at full employment is then to insure that the resources freed by a tight fiscal policy are indeed used for investment and not wasted in unemployment.

The current balance of payments problem puts additional constraints on the use of monetary policy to promote recovery and growth. If low interest rates encourage foreign borrowing in the U.S. and a large outflow of funds seeking higher yields abroad, monetary policy may have to be more restrictive than domestic objectives alone would dictate. We need monetary techniques that can serve both masters at once. But difficult decisions of balance between conflicting objectives may sometimes be unavoidable.

(3) TAX POLICY. Every tax system is the product of particular needs and economic conditions; no tax system can be neutral in its effects on the ways in which households and business firms earn and spend their incomes. If faster economic growth is desired, revision of the tax structure is called for, to permit a higher rate of investment once full use of resources is achieved.

The Administration's program encompasses two complementary approaches to this objective. The first is an investment tax credit equal to 8 percent of investment in eligible machinery and equipment; the second is revision of the guidelines for the tax lives of properties subject to depreciation.

The investment credit will stimulate investment by reducing the net cost of acquiring depreciable assets, thus increasing expected profitability. The increase will vary inversely with the expected life of the asset. For an asset with a service life of 10 years and an after-tax yield of 10 percent before the credit, the investment credit will increase the expected rate of return by about one-third. The increase in net yield will be greater for less durable equipment and smaller for more durable equipment.

Investment decisions are also influenced by the availability of funds. The investment tax credit will increase by some $1.5 billion the flow of cash available for investment under conditions anticipated for 1962.

Since the credit applies only to newly acquired assets, the entire incentive effect is concentrated on the profitability of new capital and no revenue is lost in raising the profitability of assets already held by business firms. It is an efficient way of encouraging re-equipment and modernization of productive facilities, as well as the expansion of capacity. The credit will thus help to accelerate economic growth and improve our competitive position. It will also increase the attractiveness of investment at home relative to direct investment abroad. In both ways the credit will help to ease our balance of payments problem.

Revision of tax lives for depreciable property is desirable as a matter of equity to reflect more accurately the influence of obsolescence on economic lives of capital assets. Present guidelines were established 20 years ago on the basis of replacement practices of the depressed prewar years. Depreciation, designed to reflect the loss in value of plant and equipment over time, is a function not alone of "wear and tear," but also of technological progress, changes in the relative costs of economic inputs, competitive conditions, and consumer tastes and demand. Through its favorable effects on cash flows, expected rates of return, and risk, liberalized depreciation will tend to stimulate investment.

Attention to Federal income tax adjustments to stimulate investment must not be allowed to obscure the role of State and local tax policies and practices in economic growth. The tax collections of these governments are nearly half as large as Federal collections.

The power to tax under this governmental system is shared by thousands of separate jurisdictions. Improved coordination among them will improve economic efficiency. Identical tax sources are frequently utilized by two, three, and even four layers of government without appropriate cooperation. Taxing authorities occasionally use their powers in ways that capriciously affect decisions concerning the location of plants and disrupt normal competition. The result may be a misallocation of resources and economic loss.

The Congress has recognized the need for better intergovernmental coordination. It has provided for the creation of the Advisory Commission on Intergovernmental Relations to foster "the fullest cooperation and coordination of activities between the levels of government." The Advisory Commission, composed of representatives of the executive and legislative branches of all levels of government, has already made important recommendations for the coordination of local taxes by the States and for improved tax coordination and cooperation between Federal and State governments.

INVESTMENT IN NATURAL RESOURCES

Economic growth is not simply a matter of growth in the size and skills of the labor force, in the quantity and quality of capital goods, and in the productivity of the processes by which these inputs are combined. It is equally a matter of turning more and more of the earth's endowment of natural wealth—soil, sunlight, air, water, minerals, plant and animal life—to the purposes of man. America's position has generally been one of natural plenty, but we cannot complacently assume that the abundance of the past will also characterize the future.

But neither is there any reason to suppose that resource limitations will in the foreseeable future place serious limits on the growth of the economy. Technological change, substitution of abundant and cheap raw materials for scarce and expensive ones, investment in improved resource management and conservation, and increased reliance on imports all provide important offsets to the effects of increasing scarcity on the real cost of obtaining resource inputs. Taken together, these factors tend to keep the economy growing along the path of least resistance so far as its resource requirements are concerned. If the various offsets to increasing scarcity are not fully effective, resources can be obtained by digging and drilling deeper, utilizing lower grade deposits, constructing dams and better waste treatment facilities, and other measures involving higher costs. But the necessity to devote more labor and capital to these tasks would constitute a drag on the economy, tending to cancel some of the efforts we make to stimulate growth.

The Historical Record · A rough judgment as to the probable consequences of continued depletion of resources in the future can be derived by examining the record of the past. The long-term trend of raw materials prices relative to the prices of finished products is a useful, though by no means ideal, indicator of the effectiveness of the offsets to natural scarcity.

From 1900–04 to 1955–57—the last period for which data are available—the over-all index of raw-materials prices increased by 25½ percent, an average rate of increase just over 0.4 percent per year. The most striking feature of the record, however, is not this slow but visible trend toward increasing costs as our resource endowment has been exploited more intensively but the varying patterns of price movement shown by different commodities and by the same commodity at different times.

The lessons to be drawn from such past trends are these: First, it is likely that increasing resource scarcity has had only a negligible retarding effect on economic growth during the present century. Rising real costs of obtaining some resources have been largely compensated by declining costs of obtaining others. Second, the historical record does not indicate that more rapid economic growth will simply result in our "running out of resources" more quickly. On the contrary, past investments have permitted resources to be extracted more efficiently and used more efficiently.

Public policy has contributed to this success by limitation of economic waste, the development and adoption of improved methods in agriculture, forestry, and other fields, the unified development of river valleys, and a variety of other measures. Finally, the opportunity to obtain raw materials from abroad has been important in the past and will be increasingly important in the future.

Water Resources · There is wide agreement that one of the most serious resource problems facing the United States at present and in the immediate future is the development of water resources. The use of water has been increasing rapidly as a result of population growth, higher living standards, increasing urbanization, rapid growth of industries that are heavy users of water, increases in the amount of land under irrigation, and other factors. In the Eastern United States and the Pacific Northwest, the problem presented by these trends can be met for the next few decades by an adequate and appropriately timed program of investment in (1) multiple purpose water resource development which, in addition to other benefits, permits the collection and storage of water for use as needed and (2) facilities for treatment of industrial and municipal wastes. In some of the dry regions of the West, however, the opportunities for further development of water resources will be exhausted within the next two decades. Barring major scientific breakthroughs, the continued economic development of these regions will soon come to depend upon how effectively an almost fixed supply of water is used to satisfy the most important of the various industrial, agricultural, and municipal needs for water.

It is certain that additional investment to increase the quantity and to improve the quality of the supplies of water will be a major part of any solution to the problem. Pollution control, in particular, will require major investment expenditures in the coming decades. Additional research and development in methods of conserving and augmenting water supplies, including desalinization, weather modification, reduction of evaporation losses, cheaper and more effective waste treatment and more efficient use of water in industry and agriculture may produce high returns.

Since expensive investments must be undertaken to increase the quantity and quality of water supplies, it is appropriate that the costs be reflected in prices charged industrial and agricultural users. The burdens of scarcity on the economy cannot be entirely eliminated by using scarce capital to augment the supply of scarce water. But the burden can be minimized by a proper balance between investments in increased supply on the one hand, and price increases to eliminate inefficient use on the other.

Agricultural Land · The problem of agricultural land stands in sharp contrast to the problem of water resources. Whereas in the latter the problems requiring attention are those posed by increasing scarcity, in the former they are problems of adjusting to abundance.

The Department of Agriculture currently has plans for a long-range land use adjustment program. This program has three major facets: transfer of cropland to grass; transfer of cropland to forest; and greater emphasis on wildlife and recreational development in the small watershed programs. As the program develops, it will be possible for supply management to place less emphasis on temporary diversion of acreage from the production of specific crops.

The present problems of U.S. agriculture, which reflect in part the fact that the pace of technological progress in agriculture exceeds the rate of growth in demand for farm products, should not blind us to the important lessons to be drawn from the record. When strong policy measures are taken well in advance, technological progress affords an escape from increasing scarcity. Indeed, it is technology that largely determines which portions of the environment are regarded as resources and which are not. Research not only makes possible the more effective use of existing resources, as in the case of agriculture, but may create important new ones. The record of agriculture also illustrates, however, the long lag between the decision to act and the appearance of the benefits. Careful and continuing analysis of present and future resource needs, coupled with readiness to act when the indications of potential difficulties become persuasive, is the best hope for success in meeting the resource requirements of rapid economic growth.

INVESTMENT IN PUBLIC SERVICES

Accelerated economic growth will require increased public investment, just as it will require increased private investment. Without additional plant and equipment, governments at all levels will be unable to meet the increased demands for public services that arise both as a consequence of measures taken to stimulate growth and as a consequence of growth itself. If a high and rising educational level of the labor force is sought as a means to speed economic growth, additional investment in school and college buildings, furnishings, and laboratory equipment will be required. Demands for transportation of both people and goods will increase as a result of economic growth; meeting these demands will require additional investment in urban public transportation systems, airports, roads and highways.

Failure to make adequate investments in the physical basis of public services inevitably retards economic growth. In some cases, the connection is fairly easy to trace; inadequate investment in highways will bring an increase in congestion, with consequent declines in the productivity of trucks and truck drivers, and rising transportation costs. In other cases, the process by which a shortage of basic public services tends to retard the growth of output is less obvious, but no less real; education is an important example. As has been noted above, an inadequate effort to solve the water pollution problem will be paid for in higher costs of obtaining water of adequate quality—unless it is paid for by a decline in the health of the population and decreased productivity in water-using industrial processes. Inadequacy of public services also has effects on economic welfare that are not reflected in aggregate economic statistics. Commuters are well aware of the sacrifice of time that results from inadequate urban transportation systems. The sacrifice of recreational opportunities resulting from failure to make sufficient provisions for public parks as cities expand is another example.

The task of meeting the transportation, recreation, education, housing, and other needs of growing metropolitan areas poses a major challenge to our existing forms of political organization at the State and local level. Public facilities serving the needs of individual political jurisdictions within an urban area are often less efficient than they would be if they had been designed for all, or a large part, of the area. For example, lack of effective and well coordinated land use planning and zoning regulation has resulted in locational patterns of residential, commercial, and industrial developments that intensify transportation problems. Improved planning and coordination can increase the efficiency of public services and make cities better places in which to live. Progress can be achieved through continued Federal assistance to States and local bodies for the planning of urban area development, comprehensive urban renewal programs within cities, public improvement programs, and specific public improvements.

Although the Federal Government is making an important contribution to the solution of problems whose significance extends beyond the boundaries of political units at lower levels, it must be remembered that civil government is basically a State and local responsibility.

INVESTMENT IN HOUSING

The higher standard of living made possible by economic growth results from increased output of a wide variety of goods and services. Among these is one item which, by virtue of its economic importance, its great influence on the general quality of life, and the unique character of the capital investment required to expand its supply, deserves special attention in a discussion of economic growth. This item is housing.

The value of the current services supplied by the Nation's residential structures—the total of rents paid plus the imputed rental value of owner-occupied dwellings—accounted for 13.1 percent of personal consumption expenditures in 1961, or 8.5 percent of GNP. Another 4.1 percent of GNP was accounted for by residential nonfarm construction—the total expenditures on replacing, improving, and adding to the nonfarm portion of the stock of residential structures. That stock itself represents roughly one-fourth of our national wealth, about twice the share accounted for by producers' durable equipment.

These figures are, in part, a statistical image of the importance of the basic human need for shelter. To a greater extent, however, they reflect the fact that better housing is among the most important benefits that economic progress can confer. A dwelling that provides adequate protection against the elements may nevertheless be a serious hazard to the mental and physical health of its occupants, if it is overcrowded, lacking in hot and cold running water or plumbing facilities, or structurally unsound. A better home provides a healthier, safer, and more comfortable living environment; it affords greater opportunities for recreation, aesthetic enjoyment, and peace and quiet.

Few, if any, Americans actually lack a roof over their heads. But about one-fifth of the Nation's housing units are classified as "dilapidated" or else lack one or more of the basic plumbing facilities. Like the poverty that it reflects, substandard housing is a burden borne to a disproportionate extent by a few groups in the society; the aged, the nonwhite, the poorly educated, and families without a male breadwinner. The burden is perhaps most regrettable when it renders ineffective the measures society takes to promote equality of opportunity. The child who has no decent place in which to study can hardly take full advantage of the free education that is provided to him.

A sharp rise in the rate of household formation will occur in the latter part of this decade, reflecting the high birth rates of the middle and late 1940's. It is all the more important, therefore, that substantial progress in improving the average quality of the

Nation's housing be made in the early part of the decade, when the need to increase its quantity will be less urgent. The enactment in the last session of Congress of the Administration-sponsored Housing Act of 1961 was a major step toward meeting the Nation's housing needs. In addition to extending and expanding existing programs for public housing, housing for the elderly, college housing, and farm housing, the Act provides for major new programs of FHA-insured loans to finance construction and rehabilitation of housing for moderate income families, and long-term FHA-insured home repair loans. These new types of loans are eligible for purchase by FNMA. Other important provisions make Federal assistance available to States and localities for various measures in the field of urban affairs, including planning, loans, and demonstration grants for mass transportation projects, and acquisition of land for permanent open-space uses, such as parks. Additional funds were authorized to finance the construction of community facilities. Finally, a series of provisions make additional assistance available for households and businesses displaced by urban renewal programs or other government actions.

The concern here has been the source of rising productive potential and the policies that can strengthen them. Granted continued prosperity, we can have slower growth or faster growth. There is substitution between the composition of output in the present and the level of output in the future. Just as a single individual can increase his consumption possibilities in the future by present saving, so can a whole society provide more fully for its future by using present resources for acts of investment in the broadest sense. No absolute reduction in current consumption need occur; it is only necessary that consumption grow less rapidly than total output for a time. Indeed, future levels of consumption will be higher than they could otherwise be—the cost is primarily in postponement. Happily, for an advanced society like ours, much of what is described from this point of view as investment can also be seen as present enjoyment of some of the delights of civilization: widespread education, good health, and the search for knowledge.

PERHAPS NO policy issue in recent times has stirred as much controversy as the U.S. foreign aid program. Each year the Congress —and the public at large—cast a thoroughly jaundiced eye at this "temporary" program of assistance to the less developed world. Each year we have had a round of appraisals and reappraisals, lamentations about the folly of "give-aways," and protestations about the corruptibility of man. Nevertheless, in spite of occasional frayed nerves in Washington and the near-exhaustion of the alphabet as the foreign aid agency is periodically "re-born" under a new set of initials (ECA, FOA, MSA, ICA, AID), foreign aid has consistently enjoyed the support of a bipartisan majority in Congress and seems firmly imbedded in our national budget. It is thus fair to inquire why we continue to subject ourselves to the annual ritual of the "numbers game" on Capitol Hill, yet invariably emerge determined to honor what has become a basic national commitment.

Any attempt to answer this question must be based on the understanding that foreign aid constitutes a novel response to a novel, post World War II phenomenon. Never before has the world witnessed the virtually simultaneous emergence of a large number of new, and for the most part poor, nation-states all clamoring for a measure of "economic independence" to go along with their recently acquired political independence. Once colonial rule—in no small measure responsible for initially stirring up these traditional societies into an awareness of the possibilities of economic progress—could no longer be blamed for the slow pace of economic advance, the attention of virtually all the governments of Africa, Asia, and Latin America has been turned by necessity to the achievement of this overriding objective. As a consequence, century-long traditions of apathy and resignation have yielded, at least in the cities and at the governmental level, to an ever-growing consciousness of international disparities and an ever-growing faith in the attainability of change.

What do the developing countries bring to the task they have thus set themselves? Precious little in the way of material resources. Per capita incomes in the poorest 57 nations of the globe encompassing 82 per cent of its people typically fluctuate between several hundred dollars for Latin America and $50–$60 for some of the more heavily populated countries of Asia and the Far East —this compared with a 1962 per capita income of $2400 in the United States. Consequently, saving rates are low, typically at less than 5 per cent of national income,[1] capital is scarce, the educational structure inadequate and illiteracy high. Accidents of nature have here and there treated some region kindly by bestowing it with mineral or oil deposits or with the climatic conditions favorable to growing a particular type of primary commodity. But even in such regions, the impact of rich natural resources on the general well-being of the society is usually severely limited. More pervasive is the poor quality of the soil in the preponderant agricultural sectors of these societies and the seeming inability to produce enough to keep the law of diminishing returns at bay on the tired land.

The one "resource" usually in abundant supply in the less developed world is people, but so many and growing at such rapid rates (as mortality rates fall without a compensating decline in fertility) that a large percentage remain unemployed or underemployed. A vicious circle gets underway as a burgeoning population consumes more than it contributes productively, pulling per capita income down further. Consequently, savings rates cannot be easily raised, little capital information to equip the swelling labor force can take place, and the vicious circle repeats itself. One of the few ways to help break out of it is to be able to call on other countries to make a portion of their own resources available in the form of loans and grants, thus alleviating the shortage of capital in the developing economy.

But why should all this be of concern to the developed countries, in particular the United States? It could be argued that the West, having been primarily responsible for casting traditional societies adrift through the introduction of science, tech-

1. As compared with 15 per cent for the United States.

nology, and all the attendant acquisitive virtues, had to take some responsibility for seeing the ship to safe harbor. Alternatively, it could be said that it is but in the natural order of things for the "have-not" nations to be assisted by the "haves," as overall levels of affluence continue to rise. Finally, the concern may be simply a general manifestation of a variety of more or less specific political and economic objectives which can, for now at least, be conveniently summarized under the umbrella of "enlightened national self-interest."

We have never really taken the time to reexamine our national objectives in this light. In fact, we have virtually "backed into" our role as principal provider of economic assistance to the developing countries without ever really taking stock of the nature and dimensions of the task. Perhaps the reason is that we are by nature a businesslike people not much given to contemplation of the long-run implications of particular policies. Having rolled up our national sleeves to do a clearly definable job under the Marshall Plan, we simply transferred our experience expecting once again to reach certain objectives over a certain limited period of time.

Perhaps our unwillingness to define either the objectives or the time period involved stems from an uneasy feeling in the back of our minds that the answers are not necessarily pleasant: that the job we have taken on is vastly more difficult, more costly and more elusive than anything we have ever committed ourselves to before. The controversial nature of the foreign aid program, the perennial need to fight for its life, reassert its usefulness, mollify its critics, and alter its institutional frame may to a large extent be placed at the doorstep of the inadequate, sometimes fuzzy, often wishful thinking on this subject.

Our national motivations for participating—in fact, taking the leadership—in this novel act of international income redistribution, the criteria and instruments for allocating aid among the large number of recipient countries in the light of our national objectives, and the economic significance of foreign aid and its potential impact on the performance of recipient countries, are the subjects of the following essays.

G. R.

The Poor Nations

BARBARA WARD

Barbara Ward, of The Economist *of London, has written and lectured widely on problems of the newly emerging countries. This paper is selected from her book* The Rich Nations and the Poor Nations, *published in 1962.*

How ARE we to define the 'poor' nations? The phrase 'under-developed' is not very satisfactory for it groups together very different types of under-development. India and Pakistan, for instance, are heirs of a great and ancient civilization and have many of the other attributes—in art, literature, and administration—of developed states, even though they are also very poor. Other areas—one thinks of the Congo—are developed in virtually no sense at all. I think, therefore, that perhaps the most satisfactory method of defining poverty at this stage is to discuss the question simply in terms of per-capita income—the average income available to citizens in the various countries. If you fix the level of wealth of 'wealthy' communities at a per-capita income of about $500 a year, then eighty per cent of mankind lives below it. It is chiefly among the privileged nations living round the North Atlantic that we find levels of annual income above the 500-dollar mark. Indeed, in the United States or Canada, it is three and four times above the minimum. Australia and New Zealand also belong to this group. In the Communist bloc, Czechoslovakia is moving up into it, and so is Russia. In fact, it is a marginal question whether they should not now be included among the rich. But what is certain is that the mass of mankind live well below the income level of $500 per head a year; and in some countries—one thinks particularly of India—per-capita income may be as low as $60. Yet between 400 and 500 million people live in India—something like two-fifths of all the poor people in the uncommitted world. So the gap between rich and poor is tremendous and, as we have already noticed, it is tending to widen further.

What is the cause of this? Why is there this great blanket of poverty stretched across the face of the globe? Before we attempt an answer, we should, I think, remember that ours is the first century in which such a question can even be put. Poverty has been the universal lot of man until our own day. No one asked fundamental questions about a state of affairs which everyone took for granted. The idea that the majority could have access to a little modest affluence is wholly new, the break-through of whole communities to national wealth totally unprecedented.

To return to our question: the contrast between the wealth of the West and the poverty of nearly everybody else does have some puzzling features. For centuries, for millennia, the East had been the region of known and admired wealth. It was to the Orient that men looked when they spoke of traditional forms of riches: gold and diamonds, precious ointments, rare spices, extravagant brocades and silks. In fact, for over a thousand years, one of the great drives in the Western economy was to open trade with the wealthier East. And one of the problems facing that trade—as far in the past as in the days of imperial Rome—was the West's inability to provide very much in return. It is hard to sell bear rugs to merchants at Madras, especially during the monsoon. Nor is the contrast between the East's endowment and the relative poverty of the West simply a matter of history. Today, for instance, Indonesia seems obviously better endowed in a whole range of ways than are some European countries—one might perhaps pick Norway.

In spite of these puzzles, there are some underlying physical causes which explain why some countries have been left behind in the world's present thrust towards greater wealth. Many of the tropical soils have been submitted to millennia of leaching under the downpour of heavy rains and are precarious soils for agriculture. Nor is the climate of tropical regions precisely designed for work. When the temperature rises to ninety degrees and the humidity to ninety per cent, you do not feel like rushing out and solving one of the first problems in Euclid. Even less do you want to cut a tree—favourite occupation of Victorian gentlemen—or dig a ditch.

Wherever the monsoon is the rain-bringing force, there is an underlying element of instability in farming. The concentration of rain in a few months creates expensive problems of control and storage. Rivers vary from raging torrents to dry beds. And if the monsoons fail in India or South-east Asia, then there is quite simply no agriculture because there is no water.

Another fact making for poverty is that the great tropical belt stretching round the world has only limited sources of energy: no coal and not too much oil outside the Middle East, Venezuela, and Indonesia. One must conclude, therefore, that certain original differences exist in the actual endowment of resources in the advancing Northern Hemisphere and the relatively stagnant South. Nonetheless, I think the profound reason for the contrast of wealth and poverty lies in the fact that the various revolutions which have swept over the face of the Western world in the last hundred years exist at only a chaotic or embryonic stage among the poorer states.

The biological revolution of more rapid growth in population is on the way in these areas. But the other vast changes—an intellectual revolution of materialism and this-worldliness, the political revolution of equality, and above all the scientific and technological revolution which comes from the application of savings and the sciences to the whole business of daily life—are only beginning the process of transforming every idea and institution in the emergent lands. The revolution of modernization has not yet driven these states into the contemporary world. The greatest drama of our time is that they will be swept onwards. But we are still uncertain over the form these revolutions will finally take. Everywhere they have started; nowhere are they yet complete; but the trend cannot be reversed. The modernizing of the whole world is under way.

Millennia ago, hunting and food-gathering began to give way before the advance of settled agriculture. So today the transformation of society by the application of reason, science, and technology is thrusting the old static subsistence economies to the backwaters of the world. In the wealthier lands, the first stage of this transformation has been completed in the emergence of the modern, wealthy, reasonably stable, technologically adept capitalist state. In the poorer lands, the first stage only has opened. The contrast between world wealth and world poverty largely turns upon this lag in time.

Now we must examine the impact of change upon emergent

lands—and we should remember again the distinction between poorer lands such as India which are at the same time rich in culture, history, and tradition, and tribal lands, whether in Africa, Australia, or Latin America, which lack even the rudiments of a developed tradition. The biological revolution brought about by a sudden acceleration of the birth-rate could not take place in these countries until colonial rule abolished local wars and until modern medical science and modern sanitation began to save babies and lengthen life. That these changes were introduced *before* the establishment of a modern economy is one of the most fateful differences between East and West, and one to which we will return. But until the second half of the nineteenth century most of these lands still followed the old millennial pattern of a population rising to the limits of production and then falling back into violence, struggle, and death where the limits were surpassed.

Now let us turn to a second force: the new revolutionary emphasis on work and effort devoted to the things of *this* world, the drive of interest devoted to changing and bettering man's physical environment. In traditional or tribal societies, this force is, in the main, lacking. Very largely, the material organization of life and, above all, the natural sequence of birth and death, of the seasons, of planetary change, have been taken as given: they were not the subject of speculative activity. In primitive tribal society one can say that nature is very largely accepted as impenetrable by reason. It can be propitiated. It can be worked on by human will through magic. A flood may be diverted by drowning a male child. But no one connects the precipitation of rain at the head of the watershed with the expected annual flow and devises earthworks to avert disaster. Life is lived in the midst of mystery which cannot be manipulated, beyond very narrow limits, in answer to human needs.

The chief aims of these societies were not this-worldly in our modern sense. Take, for instance, the significant Victorian phrase 'making good.' We understand it in terms of making money, of achieving material success in the broadest sense. In pre-modern society no such meaning could possibly have been attached to any activity thought of as being 'good.' In tribal society, approved behaviour implies strict observance of tribal laws and customs. In archaic civilization, the good man, the man of wisdom, is the man who observes the rules and duties of his way of life: the rich man, in magnificence, affability, and alms-giving; the poor man, in work and respect. No group, except the despised merchant, devotes his life to accumulation. And even the merchant tends, as he did in China, to turn his wealth into land and leave the life of capital-formation behind as soon as his fortune permits the change. Such societies incline of their very nature to be backward-looking, to preserve rather than to create, and to see the highest wisdom in the effort to keep things as they are. Under these conditions no underlying psychological drive impels people to work and accumulate for the future. Wisdom is to wait on Providence and follow in the ways of your forefathers, ways of life compatible with great serenity, great dignity, profound religious experience, and great art, but not with the accumulation of material wealth for society as a whole.

The lack of a third revolution—equality—has worked in the same sense. There was no concept of equality in traditional society. As one knows from still-existing tribal societies, leadership lies with the old men of the tribe. There is no way for the 'young men' to claim equality. They simply have to wait for the years to pass. Seniority (as in the American Senate) also ensures that the leaders are men who respect the backward-looking traditions of the group and have a vested interest in the unequal prestige conferred by advancing years. It is the inescapable recipe for extreme conservatism.

When tribal society is left behind, the values supported by the leaders are still conservative. They are fixed by an inviolate upper order. Save in times of immense upheaval, the peasant does not reach the throne. King, warrior, landlord form a closed order to which recruitment is in the main by birth.

Another facet of equality—a vital facet for economic growth—was lacking: since there was no national community as we understand it, competitive drives based on national equality were also absent. The tribe is a sort of tiny nation, a nation in embryo, but it cannot exercise the same economic influence as the modern nation because it is too small to be a significant market. In any case, tribal agriculture is devoted to subsistence, not to exchange.

The larger post-tribal political units were, in the main, dynastic or imperial units—one thinks of such loose structures as the India of the Guptas or of China's gigantic bureaucracy—in which there was little interconnection between the scattered cities and the great mass of people living their isolated, subsistence village lives. Certainly there was not enough economic and social coherence to define a market in such terms that a merchant would feel himself in competition with other vigorous national markets and could operate with driving energy to defend national interests against the rival national interests of others. The competitive 'equality' of Western Europe's commerce was wholly absent. As one sees again and again in human history—or in daily life—people do not begin to act in new ways until they have formulated the idea of such ways in their minds. The idea of the nation was immensely reinforced—but also in part created—by the rivalry of commercial interests in Western Europe.

Now we turn to the last and most pervasive of the revolutions, the crucial revolution of science and saving. There is virtually no science in tribal society. There is a good deal of practical experience, skilled work, and early technique. It seems possible, for instance, that primitive farming developed as a result of close observation of nature's cycle of seed and harvest and its imitation in fertility rites and religious festivals. But the idea of controlling material things by grasping the inner law of their construction is absent.

In great traditional civilizations such as India and China, there certainly was enough intellectual ferment for a vast scientific break-through to be theoretically possible. Many of the most acute minds in those societies devoted themselves to systematic thought for generations. In the Eastern Mediterranean, among the Chaldeans and the Egyptians, some of the basic mathematical tools of science had been forged long before the Christian era. Yet the break-through never came.

Primitive and archaic societies match their lack of scientific *élan* by an equal lack of sustained saving. Every society saves something. Saving is, after all, not consuming. If everything were consumed, men would be reduced to hunting and fishing—and even these occupations require rods and spears. But in settled agricultural societies, seed-corn is set aside for the next harvest and men do the hedging and ditching and field-levelling needed to carry production forward year by year. Probably such saving for maintenance and repair—and more occasionally by land-clearing and irrigation, for expansion—does not surpass four or five per cent of national income in any year.

The savings which make possible a general change in the techniques of productivity—more roads, more ports, more power, more education, more output on the farms, new machines in the factories—must rise dramatically above the five-per-cent level. Economists fix a level of about twelve to fifteen per cent of national income as the range needed to cover all possible increases in population, some increase in consumption, and a high, expanding level of investment. And no traditional society ever reached this level.

One reason for this fact takes us back to the revolution of equality. The merchant in the Orient never achieved decisive political influence. There were no city corporations, no charters based on autonomous rights. As a result, the merchant never achieved full security either. The government of kings and emperors was a government above the law, depending upon the monarch's whim. There is a brilliant phrase used by one of the young gentlemen of the East India Company to describe the uncertainties of the commercial calling in India. He describes the monarch and his tax-gatherers as bird's-nesters who leave a merchant to accumulate a nestful of eggs and then come to raid them all. One can well understand that under such conditions the stimulus to sustained capital accumulation is fairly marginal. On the contrary, the tendency is to put money that is earned from trade—and a great deal of money was earned—either into hoards of currency that can be hidden or else into jewels which are easily transportable and easily hid. But neither of these reserves makes for the expansion of productive enterprise.

In short, the chief point that distinguishes tribal and traditional society is that all the internal impulses to modernization have been largely lacking. And yet today these societies are everywhere in a ferment of change. How has this come about? Where did the external stimulus come from? There is only one answer. It came, largely uninvited, from the restless, changing, rampaging West. In the last 300 years, the world's ancient societies, the great traditional civilizations of the East, together with the pre-Iberian civilizations of Latin America and the tribal societies of Africa, have all, in one way or another, been stirred up from outside by the new, bounding, uncontrollable energies of the Western powers which, during those same years, were undergoing concurrently all the revolutions—of equality, of nationalism, of rising population, and of scientific change—which make up the mutation of modernization.

Towards the close of the nineteenth century a spurt of population began throughout India and the Far East. But this spurt had a different consequence from the comparable increase in the West. Western lands were relatively under-populated—North America absolutely so—when the processes of modernization began. The growth in numbers was a positive spur to economic growth; it brought labourers into the market and widened the market. At the same time the new machines, the new developing economy based on rising productivity, expanded the possibilities of creating wealth in a way that more than outstripped the growth in population. But in the Far East, in India, where population was already dense, the effect of the colonial impact was to increase the rate of the population's growth without launching a total transformation of the economy. More births, longer lives, sent population far beyond the capabilities of a stumbling economy. Today the grim dilemma has appeared that population is so far ahead of the means of satisfying it that each new wave of births threatens in each generation to wipe out the margin of savings necessary to sustain added numbers. The West, where growth in population acted as a spur to further expansion, has not faced this dilemma, and in the East it is not yet clear how so grave a dilemma *can* be faced.

Colonial rule brought in the sense of a this-worldly concern for the advantages of material advance by the simplest and most direct route—the 'demonstration effect.' The new merchants, the new administrators, lived better, lived longer, had demonstrably more materially satisfying lives. The local people saw that this was so and they began to wonder why and whether others might not live so too. Above all, the local leaders saw vividly that the new scientific, industrial, and technological society enjoyed almost irresistible power. This, too, they naturally coveted.

At the same time, the colonial system did set in motion some definite beginnings in the processes of technical change and economic growth. There was some education of local people in the new techniques of Western life. Some merchants in the old societies, the Compradors in China, for instance, or the Gujaratis in India, began to exercise their talents as entrepreneurs in a new, settled, commercial society. Some of the preliminaries of industrialization—railways, ports, roads, some power—the preliminaries we call 'infrastructure'—were introduced to the benefit of the new colonial economy. Some export industries expanded to provide raw materials for the West. Virtually nothing was done about basic agriculture; but plantation systems did develop agricultural products—tea, pepper, ground-nuts, jute—for the growing markets of Europe.

Above all, the new political ideas streamed in. Western education gave an *élite* a first look at Magna Charta. In their schoolbooks in India the sons of Indians could read Edmund Burke denouncing the depradations of Englishmen in India. The new sense of equality, inculcated by Western education, was reinforced by the daily contrast between the local inhabitants and the colonial representatives who claimed to rule them. Personal equality fused with the idea of national equality, with the revolt educated men increasingly felt at being run by another nation. The whole national movement of anti-colonialism was stirred up by Western ideas of national rights and national independence, and by the perpetual evidence that the rights were being denied.

The important point to remember, however, if one wishes to grasp the present contrast between the rich nations and the poor, is that all these changes, introduced pell-mell by colonialism, did not really produce a new and coherent form of society, as they had done in the West. There was no 'take-off,' to use Professor Rostow's phrase, into a new kind of society. The colonial impact introduced problems that seemed too large to be solved, or, at least, problems that offered immense difficulty to any solution. Take, for instance, the problem of population. You could not deny medicine; you could not resist sanitation; yet all the time life lengthened, the birth-rate went on going up, and you could almost watch population beginning to outstrip resources that were not growing in proportion because saving and capital formation were still inadequate. Yet the rising population continuously made saving more difficult.

This small level of saving meant that all economic developments under colonialism—or semi-colonialism—were on too small a scale to lead to a general momentum. China is a good example. After the Opium Wars the British compelled the crumbling Manchu Empire to open its ports to Western trade. In the so-called treaty ports, quite a rapid rate of economic and industrial expansion took place. Europeans brought in capital. Some Chinese entrepreneurs joined them. International trade soared. The customs, also under European control, grew to be an important source of revenue. Plans for building railways were prepared. Meanwhile, however, the desperate, over-crowded countryside where the bulk of the people lived slipped steadily down into deeper ruin. Little economic activity could spread beyond the Westernized areas; for there were no markets, no savings, no initiative—only the dead weight of rural bankruptcy.

The same patchiness affected social life and education. All over Asia the educational system began to produce an *élite* who believed in Western ideas of law, Western ideas of liberty, of constitutional government. But behind them there was little general change among the people at large and, above all, no trace of change in the vast number—eighty or more per cent of the population—who lived on the land where the old, unchanged, subsistence agriculture went on as before. And so there came about what one can only call a kind of dual society, in which the scattered growing-points of a modern way of life were restrained almost to the pitch of immobility by enormous forces of inertia inherent in the old framework of society.

Throughout the uncommitted world, in the traditional societies of China and India, in large parts of Latin America, and in the primitive emergent countries of Africa, old and new remained locked in a kind of battle, stuck fast in an apparently unbreakable deadlock. And how to break out of it; how to get the forces of modernization flowing through all of society; how to change leadership; how to get the new cadres in education; how to stimulate massive saving; how to get agriculture transformed: all these urgent and irresistible problems of the new society still wait to be answered.

This is a fact which the West cannot ignore. Most of the dilemmas of the under-developed areas have been stirred up by Western impact. Yet I think it is not entirely untrue to say that the Western powers are not looking very hard to find answers to these dilemmas. And this, I think, is for a very good reason. They have largely forgotten about their own transition. They are not conscious of the fact that a hundred years ago, even fifty years ago, many of them were struggling with just these problems of changing leadership, of developing new social groups, giving rights to new classes, finding methods of achieving greater saving, and securing a technological break-through on a massive scale. We take our development so much for granted that we hardly understand the dilemmas of those who have not yet travelled so far.

Foreign Economic Aid: Means and Objectives

MILTON FRIEDMAN

Milton Friedman, Professor of Economics at the University of Chicago, is widely recognized as the distinguished leader of the so-called "Chicago School" of economics. He has written extensively, especially in the monetary field. This article first appeared in the Summer, 1958, issue of the Yale Review.

FOREIGN ECONOMIC aid is widely regarded as a weapon in the ideological war in which the United States is now involved. Its assigned role is to help win over to our side those uncommitted nations that are also underdeveloped and poor. According to this view, these nations are determined to develop economically. They will seek to do so, with or without our help. If we do not help them, they will turn to Russia. It is, therefore, in our own interest to help them to achieve their aims. And the way to help them is to make capital and technical assistance available largely free of charge, the cost to be borne by the United States and, we hope, those of its allies who are in a comparable stage of development.

This argument confuses two very different issues. One is the *objectives* toward which United States policy should be directed. The other is the *means* that are appropriate for the achievement of those objectives. I share fully the views of the proponents of foreign economic aid about objectives. It is clearly in our national interest that the underdeveloped nations choose the democratic rather than the totalitarian way of life. It is clearly in our national interest that they satisfy their aspirations for economic development as fully as possible in a democratic framework. And our national interest coincides with our humanitarian ideals: our fundamental objective is a world in which free men can peaceably use their capacities, abilities, and resources as effectively as possible to satisfy their aspirations. We cannot long hope to maintain a free island in a totalitarian world.

But this agreement about objectives does not settle the question of means. Is foreign economic aid as it has been administered, or as it is proposed that it should be administered, well adapted to secure these great objectives? This question is begged in most current discussion. Once the objectives are stated, it is generally simply taken for granted that foreign economic aid is an appropriate means, if not indeed the only appropriate means, to achieve these objectives. This conclusion seems to me fundamentally mistaken. Though foreign economic aid may win us some temporary allies, in the long run it will almost surely retard economic development and promote the triumph of Communism. It is playing into our enemies' hands, and should be abolished. Instead we should concentrate on promoting world-wide economic development through means that are consonant with the American tradition itself—strengthening of free market domestic economies in the less-developed nations, the removal of obstacles to private international trade, and the fostering of a climate favorable to private international investment.

To avoid confusion, it will be well to emphasize at the outset that this article is concerned solely with one particular category of United States expenditures on foreign aid—*economic aid*—and with one class of arguments for such expenditures—their value in promoting the economic development of other countries.

The sum listed in the Federal budget as spent for economic aid is only a small part of the total recorded expenditures for foreign aid. In the fiscal year ending June 30, 1957, total expenditures for foreign aid were nearly four billion dollars. Of this total, nearly two and a half billion dollars was for so-called "military aid"—primarily the transfer of military equipment to various United States allies. Another billion went for so-called "defense support"—expenditures in or payments to other countries (notably South Korea, Nationalist China, and South Vietnam) to finance activities that are regarded as contributing to their military effort. In addition, the President is empowered to make payments to certain countries, principally in the Middle East, the purpose of which is to induce the recipient countries to support particular policies that are thought to be in our interest—these are, in essence, straight military or political subsidies. Finally, about half a billion dollars went for so-called "economic aid" which includes both technical assistance (Point IV help) and funds for the economic development of recipient countries to which no direct military or political strings are attached.

At first glance, one may wonder why this relatively small budget category stirs up so much controversy. Part of the answer is that the figures cited are somewhat misleading. The generally more favorable attitude of Congress toward direct and indirect military aid understandably leads the Administration to classify as much as possible under these two headings. In addition, what in form is straight military aid may in effect be equivalent to economic aid, and it is often difficult to distinguish between the two. If country A would in any event have devoted a given sum to the purchase of military equipment and the United States pays for it instead, the country has available that sum for other purposes; the effect may be precisely the same as if the corresponding sum had been granted country A in straight economic aid. But more than this: it is on the enlargement of economic aid that advocates of greater public spending have concentrated their attention. In article and speech enlargement has been pressed by such men as Chester Bowles, Paul Hoffman, Walter Reuther, and Adlai Stevenson. In their recent book *A Proposal*,[1] Professors Millikan and Rostow of the Massachusetts Institute of Technology have urged that the United States should commit itself over a five-year period to put up some ten billion dollars for world economic development. And there is powerful support in the United Nations for setting up a special fund, SUNFED, for this purpose. In short, economic aid is neither so small nor so unimportant as current budgeted expenditures on it might suggest. On the contrary, it is the storm center of the whole debate about how this country can help other countries develop.

The case for military aid and defense support clearly rests on a very different range of considerations than the case for economic aid. Military aid and defense support are to be attacked or defended in terms of their contribution, first, to our effective military strength and, second, to the achievement of our direct political objectives. I can see no objection to them in principle; any criticism of them, or defense of their expansion, must rest on the severely practical grounds that, dollar for dollar, they yield less, or more, strength than alternative modes of expenditure. The one serious danger of confusion between these categories and economic aid is that the argument for economic aid which this article considers is sometimes used as a rationalization to permit straight military or political subsidies to be made under a different label. We shall be concerned with neither these types of expenditure nor this use of the argument for economic aid.

Economic aid proper raises much broader and certainly very different issues. These issues deserve far more public debate than they are getting. We are on the verge of committing ourselves to a policy which in my view can only have disastrous consequences for our country and our way of life. And we are doing so not after thoughtful and thorough consideration of the issues involved, but almost by inadvertence, by proceeding along what seems the line of least resistance.

Two questions must be answered in judging government economic aid. First, is it likely in fact to promote the economic development of the countries to whom aid is granted? Second, do its political effects in those countries promote democracy and freedom?

The second question, though not much discussed, is easy to answer and admits of little dispute. As it has so far been administered, our aid program has consisted predominantly of grants or loans or provision of personnel or material directly to the governments of recipient countries for specified projects regarded as contributing to economic development. It has thereby tended to strengthen the role of the government sector in general economic activity relative to the private sector. Yet democracy and freedom have never been either attained or maintained except in communities in which the bulk of economic activity is organized through private enterprise.

This problem has of course been recognized and partly explains why some grants or loans have been made to private enterprises in the recipient countries rather than directly to governments. Last year, John B. Hollister, on the occasion of his retirement as head of the International Cooperation Administration, proposed that a much enlarged fraction of total funds be channeled to private enterprises. This modification, which aroused strong opposition and is not likely to be carried far, would reduce the tendency of the aid program to strengthen the government sector. It would, however, not eliminate it. We are hardly likely to make funds available to enterprises in poor standing with their governments or for projects opposed by governments. The final result will therefore be much the same.

Many proponents of foreign aid recognize that its long-run political effects are adverse to freedom and democracy. To some extent, they plead special extenuating circumstances. For example, the group in power in a particular country may for the time being be in a shaky political position, yet its overthrow may mean the assumption of power by anti-democratic forces. And economic aid may help such a government over its temporary political crisis. Their main reply, however, is that economic progress is a prerequisite to freedom and democracy in underdeveloped countries, and that economic aid will contribute to this outcome and thereby on balance promote political freedom. This makes the crucial question, even for political effects, the first, namely, the economic effects of economic aid.

The belief that foreign aid effectively promotes economic development rests in turn on three basic propositions: first, that the key to economic development is the availability of capital; second, that underdeveloped countries are too poor to provide the capital for themselves; third, that centralized and comprehensive economic planning and control by government is an essential requisite for economic development.

All three propositions are at best misleading half-truths. Additional capital is certainly essential for development. And of course the more capital the better, *other things being the same*. But the way in which capital is provided will affect other things. The Pharaohs raised enormous sums of capital to build the Pyramids; this was capital formation on a grand scale; it certainly did not promote economic development in the fundamental sense of contributing to a self-sustaining growth in the standard of life of the Egyptian masses. Modern Egypt has under government auspices built a steel mill; this involves capital formation; but it is a drain on the economic resources of Egypt, not a contribution to economic strength, since the cost of making steel in Egypt is very much greater than the cost of buying it elsewhere; it is simply a modern equivalent of the Pyramids except that maintenance expenses are higher. Such modern monuments are by no means the exception; they are almost certain to be the rule when funds are made available directly or indirectly to governments that are inevitably under pressure to produce the symbols of modern industrialism. There is hardly an underdeveloped country that does not now waste its substance on the symbol of a government-owned or government-subsidized international airline. And there is hardly one that does not want its own steel mill as yet another potent symbol.

Some monuments are inevitable in the course of economic development and may indeed be politically desirable as tangible and dramatic signs of change. If the appetite for monuments were at once so intense as to make them the first claim on a country's resources and yet so limited and satiable that their extent was independent of the resources available, monument-building might be a costly fact of life but would have little relevance to foreign economic aid. Unfortunately, this is hardly the case. The appetite grows by what it feeds on. The availability of resources at little or no cost to the country in question inevitably stimulates monument-building. Thus while foreign aid grants may in the first instance add to the capital available to a country, they also lead to a notable increase in the amount of capital devoted to economically wasteful projects.

Cannot, it will be asked, these problems be solved by our exercising control over the use of the capital we make available to governments? And would they not be avoided even more directly if we adopted the proposal to make funds available directly to private enterprises? Aside from the political problems raised by any attempt at close control of even the funds we give, the answer is no. In the first place, there is a purely technical difficulty. Our grants are only part of the total capital available to a country and of the funds available to the government. It will do no good to control the use of the one part while exercising no control over the other; the effect would simply be to alter the bookkeeping— whatever we regarded as appropriate projects would be treated as financed with our funds, and the monuments would be built with local funds. Effective control would thus require us to control the whole of the capital investment of the country, a result that is hardly feasible on political grounds. But even if it were, the problem would by no means be solved. We would simply be substituting one central planning group for another. This leads to the third proposition: that central planning by government is essential to economic development.

Before turning to this issue, it will be well to consider the assertion that the underdeveloped countries are too poor to save and provide capital for themselves. Here, too, the alleged fact is most dubious. Currently developed countries were once underdeveloped. Whence came their capital? The key problem is not one of possibility but of incentive and of proper use. For generations, India was a "sink" for the precious metals, as the writers on money always put it. There was much saving, but it took the unproductive form of accumulation of specie. In Africa, natives on the very margin of subsistence have, given a market demand for their produce, extended greatly the area under cultivation, an activity involving the formation of capital, though seldom entering into recorded figures on savings. Domestic capital can be supplemented by foreign capital if the conditions are right—which means if property is secure against both private and public seizure. Many low-income countries cannot of course attract foreign capital; in most of these, in fact, locally owned capital is invested abroad, and for the same reason—because there is not an environment favorable to private property and free enterprise. And in this respect, too, government-to-government grants are likely to be adverse to economic development. They strengthen the government sector at the expense of the private sector, and reduce the pressure on the government to maintain an environment favorable to private enterprise. We may and do seek to counteract this effect by using our grants to get "concessions" from the government favorable to private enterprise. But this is seldom anything like a complete offset—the change in the objective power of the government sector is likely ultimately to outweigh by far the imposed restraint on how for the time being it uses that power. The final result of our grants is therefore likely to be a reduction in the amount of capital available from other sources both internally and from the outside.

In short, if any generalization is valid, it is that the availability of capital while an important problem is a subsidiary one—if other conditions for economic development are ripe, capital will be readily available; if they are not, capital made available is very likely to be wasted.

Let us turn now to the proposition that economic development requires centralized governmental control and planning, that it requires a coördinated "development program." This proposition, too, contains an element of truth. Government certainly has an important role to play in the process of development. It must provide a stable legal framework; it must provide law and order, security to person and property. Beyond this, it has an important role in promoting certain basic services, such as elementary education, roads, and a monetary system; it can make an important contribution by extension activities which help to spread knowledge of new and improved techniques. And numerous other activities of the same sort come to mind.

But none of these activities calls for a centralized program for economic development or detailed control of investment. And such a centralized program is likely to be a hindrance, not a help. Economic development is a process of changing old ways of doing things, of venturing into the unknown. It requires a maximum of flexibility, of possibility for experimentation. No one can predict in advance what will turn out to be the most effective use of a nation's productive resources. Yet the essence of a centralized program of economic development is that it introduces rigidity and inflexibility. It involves a central decision about what activities to undertake, and the use of central force and authority to enforce conformity with that decision.

It may well be that in many underdeveloped countries, existing or potential government officials are as competent both to judge what lines of activity will be profitable and to run particular plants as existing or potential private businessmen. There is yet a crucial advantage in letting private business do as much as possible. Private individuals risk their own funds and thus have a much stronger incentive to choose wisely and well. They can be more numerous and they have much detailed information about specific situations that cannot possibly be available to governmental officials. Even more important, however wisely the decisions are made, there are bound to be mistakes. Progress requires that these be recognized, that unsuccessful ventures be abandoned. There is at least some chance that unsuccessful private ventures will be allowed to fail. There is almost none that public ones will be—unless the failure is as flagrant as the British ground nuts venture. The mistake will simply be concealed by subsidy or tariff protection or prohibition of competition. If anything is clear from widespread experience with governmental economic activity, it is that a governmental venture, once established, is seldom abandoned. And surely it is almost as clear that governmental officials are less experimental, less flexible, less adaptive, than private individuals risking their own funds.

What is required in the underdeveloped countries is the release of the energies of millions of able, active, and vigorous people who have been chained by ignorance, custom, and tradition. Such people exist in every underdeveloped country. If it seems otherwise, it is because we tend to seek them in our own image in "big business" on the Western model rather than in the villages and on the farms and in the shops and bazaars that line the streets of the crowded cities of many a poor country. These people require only a favorable environment to transform the face of their countries. Instead there is real danger that the inherited set of cultural and social restraints will simply be replaced by an equally far-reaching imposed set of political and economic controls, that one strait jacket will be substituted for another. What is required is rather an atmosphere of freedom, of maximum opportunity for individuals to experiment, and of incentive for them to do so in an environment in which there are objective tests of success and failure —in short, a vigorous, free capitalistic market.

Thus central control would be a poor way to promote economic development even if the central authorities chose individual projects as wisely as private individuals and with the same end in view. In fact, as we have already seen, the government is almost sure to promote other ends—the national and personal prestige that can be attained through monument-building—so that the case against centralized control is even stronger.

The issues we have been discussing are strikingly illustrated in a report submitted in December, 1956 by the M.I.T. Center for International Studies to the Special Senate Committee to study the Foreign Aid Program. The report studies the problem of how to judge whether a country should be given additional aid. The answer is that the criterion should be whether the country is making an "additional national effort" toward economic development. Two, and only two, "rules of thumb" are given for deciding whether this is the case: "one index that national effort is being mobilized for development is the launching of measures to capture a good fraction of increases in income for the purpose of further investment"; another "measure of national effort . . . is the degree to which a country's leaders have worked out an overall development program."

Here are two of the basic propositions we started with. And the striking thing is that by these tests, the United States would never have qualified as a country making an "additional national effort" toward economic development! We have never had explicit "measures to capture a good fraction of increases in income for the purpose of further investment." Nor have our "leaders" ever "worked out an overall development program." And what is true of the United States is true of every other free nation that has achieved economic development. The only possible exceptions are the economic programs worked out after the Second World War by Britain and some other European countries, and these were largely abandoned because they were failures.

The only countries that satisfy the tests suggested by the M.I.T. report are the Communist countries—these all have measures "to capture a good fraction of increases in income for the purpose of further investment" and all have an "overall development program." And none of these has in fact achieved economic development in the sense of a self-sustaining rise in the standard of living of the ordinary man. In the satellite countries, the standard of living of the ordinary man has quite clearly fallen. Even in Russia, the ordinary man is by no means clearly better off now than before the Communists took over, and, indeed, may be worse off even in terms solely of material comforts. While education and health services have clearly improved, food, shelter, and clothing have all apparently deteriorated for the masses. The achievements of which Russia justifiably boasts are to be found elsewhere: in its heavy industries, its military output, and its space satellites— achievements that from the point of view of the consumer classify strictly as monument building.

It thus seems clear that a free market without central planning has, at least to date, been not only the most effective route to economic development but the *only* effective route to a rising standard of life for the masses of the people. And it is eminently clear that it has been the only route consistent with political freedom and democracy. Yet the M.I.T. report and most other writings on the subject simply take the opposite for granted, without even noting that in doing so they are going against the whole of the evidence to date, and without offering a shred of evidence of their own. This is modern mythology with a vengeance.

What is involved here is no less than another phase of the ideological war in which we are engaged. A central premise of the Communist ideology is that the state must exercise comprehensive control and direction over the economic activities of its citizens; a central premise of Western liberalism is that free men operating in a free market can promote their own objectives without the necessity for an all-powerful state.

Foreign economic aid implicitly accepts this premise of the Communist ideology; yet it is intended as a weapon against Communism. Many who favor it as applied abroad would be horrified at the idea of applying its principles at home. If they accept it, it is because they do not understand what it implies or because they take the word of the "experts" that it is the "only" way to win friends abroad. They, and the experts, are in the state of the man who discovered that he had been speaking prose all his life. Loyal Americans that they are, they have unthinkingly accepted a basic premise of the Communist ideology without recognizing it for what it is and in the face of the available evidence. This is a measure of the success of Marxist thought, which is most dangerous precisely when its products lose their labels.

Despite the intentions of foreign economic aid, its major effect, insofar as it has any effect at all, will be too speed the Communization of the underdeveloped world. It may, for a time, keep some of these countries nominally on our side. But neutral or even hostile democracies are less of a threat to the preservation of a free world than ostensibly friendly totalitarian countries.

An effective program to promote a free and prosperous world must be based on our own ideology, not on the ideology we are fighting. What policy would be consistent with our ideology?

The aim should be to promote free markets throughout the world and maximum reliance by all countries on free enterprise in an environment favorable to competition and to individual initiative. We cannot do this by telling other governments what to do or by bribing them to go against their own natures any more than we can force men to be free. What we can do is to set an example and to help establish an international climate favorable to economic and political freedom; we can make it easier for other countries to take the path of freedom if they wish to.

The most important area in which we can do this is foreign trade. Here, in particular, our policies belie our professions. We profess to believe in free competition and free markets, yet we have erected barriers to "protect" domestic producers from competition; we profess to believe in minimal government interference with economic activity, yet our government imposes quotas on imports and dumps exports abroad because of a policy of government support of farm prices. True, we have also reduced tariffs and barriers to trade in many areas, and these actions, ably supplemented by the unintended effects of inflation, have reduced our trade restrictions to their lowest level in many decades. Yet those that remain, as well as the fresh restrictions that have been imposed, particularly on agricultural products, have, I believe, done far more harm to our foreign relations than any good we have done even temporarily by our economic aid. The rest of the world regards us as hypocrites, and they are at least partly right.

Entirely aside from the problem of foreign relations, these policies do us direct economic harm. They prevent us from using our resources as effectively as we might both at home and abroad; they hurt us as well as the rest of the world. A free trader like myself would like to see them abolished for this reason alone—in order to enable us to have a higher standard of living. But this is only part of the case for free trade, and, in the present context, the lesser part.

A major factor pushing underdeveloped countries in the direction of central planning and of autarchy is their lack of confidence in a market for their products. Suppose, they argue, we do follow the route of free enterprise and free trade, concentrate on producing those things we can produce most cheaply, and count on getting the goods we want to consume through international trade. Is not success likely simply to produce increases in import barriers by the United States and other countries so that we find ourselves all dressed up with a fine export industry and nowhere to go? And, under present circumstances, can one say with any confidence that they are wrong? Ask the Swiss watchmakers and English bicycle producers.

It is not often recognized how widespread are the implications of the restrictions on trade and, in particular, the uncertainty about them. We do not, it will be said, offer a market for the potential products of most underdeveloped countries so that our trade barriers do not affect them. But this is clearly wrong. It is a major virtue of free international trade that it is multilateral not bilateral. Were we to import more from, say, Western Europe, Western Europe would be able to import more from still other countries, and so on in endless chain, so that our own greater exports might go to very different countries than those from whom we purchased products.

Or to take yet another facet of the problem—the effect on foreign investment. In part, such investment is stimulated by trade barriers: if India will not permit the import of complete cars, an automobile company may set up an assembly plant. But this investment is wasted from the point of view of world productivity: it is used simply to do in one country what could be done more efficiently elsewhere. Productive foreign investment is hindered by trade barriers, both directly and indirectly. It is hindered directly, because trade barriers distort the incentives to investment and also make it more difficult for the investor to receive the return on his investment in the currency he wants—a country can earn foreign currency to pay him only by exports. It is hindered indirectly because business and trade relations among nations are a major channel for the spread of information about investment opportunities and the establishment of contacts that make them possible. Commissions of V.I.P.'s assigned the task of finding "investment opportunities" are a poor substitute for the day-to-day contact of numerous individuals engaged in earning their daily living by selling goods and rendering services in a foreign country.

Or again, look for the sources of American influence on foreign attitudes and cultures and where will one find them? Not in the literature disseminated by USIS, useful though that may be, but in the activities of International Harvester, Caterpillar Tractor, Singer Sewing Machine, Coca-Cola, Hollywood, and so on. Channels of trade are by all odds the most effective means of disseminating understanding and knowledge of the United States.

British maintenance of free trade—whatever its motives—was surely a major factor knitting the nineteenth-century world together and promoting the rapid and effective development of many then underdeveloped countries. And trade barriers, currency controls, and other economic restrictions are surely a major factor dividing the twentieth-century world and impeding the effective development of the currently underdeveloped countries.

Suppose we were to announce to the world that we committed ourselves to abolish all tariffs, quotas, and other restrictions on trade by a specified date—say, in five or ten years—and that thereafter we would maintain complete free trade. Can there be any doubt that the effects on our international position—both immediately through the announcement effects and ultimately through the long-run economic effects—would be vastly more favorable than those achievable by any conceivable program of foreign economic aid even if one assigns to that aid all the virtues claimed by its proponents? We would be playing from our strength. We would be offering an opportunity to free men to make effective use of their freedom rather than contributing chains to enslave men.

It would, of course, be better if such action were taken by many nations. But it would be a serious mistake for us to link our actions to that of others; the result would be to slow the movement toward free trade to the pace desired by the most recalcitrant member. Far better to move unilaterally. We would benefit economically and politically from a unilateral move, and we might have far more effect on other countries through example than over the conference table.

A movement toward free trade would affect adversely many particular individuals and concerns—those who have invested talent and capital in "protected" industries. But our mobility and adaptability are such that a gradual movement—over the course of, say, ten years—would give the affected individuals ample opportunity to adjust to the new circumstances with little if any loss. The new opportunities afforded by the expansion of world trade, and the more efficient use of our resources involved therein, would benefit many more than were harmed. After all, the transition to free trade over ten years would have far less of an impact than the technological changes that occur decade after decade and that we take in our stride.

As of the moment, we have a bear by the tail in our foreign economic policy—and unfortunately, it is not the Russian Bear. We get little if any political kudos for continuing economic aid—the recipient countries have come to take it for granted and even to regard it as their right. Yet for this very reason, the sudden cessation of aid would be regarded as an unfriendly and hostile act and would arouse great hostility toward the United States. Thus even if one accepts the arguments of the preceding sections, there remains the problem how to achieve the transition from our present policy to the alternative.

The simplest and least undesirable way seems to me to be to make a final terminal grant to each recipient country. The grant should be fairly generous, say something like two to three times the annual grants we have been making to the country. It should be completely unrestricted and preferably made in the form of a dollar—or even better a Swiss franc—balance on which the recipient country can draw as it wishes. In this way, our own involvement in central planning by other countries could be terminated at once, and the government of the recipient country would attach the greatest value to the grant.

The cost of such a termination program would be sizeable in

the year of termination. But it would be a once-for-all cost rather than the steady and growing drain to which we appear to be on the verge of committing ourselves.

Foreign economic aid needs to be sharply distinguished from direct military aid and defense support even though it may be hard to classify any particular expenditure. Foreign economic aid consists of grants or loans from our government to other governments or to enterprises in other countries for specified projects regarded as contributing to economic development. It includes both technical assistance and grants or loans of money.

The objectives of foreign economic aid are commendable. The means are, however, inappropriate to the objectives. Foreign economic aid, far from contributing to rapid economic development along democratic lines, is likely to retard improvement in the well-being of the masses, to strengthen the government sector at the expense of the private sector, and to undermine democracy and freedom. The proponents of foreign aid have unwittingly accepted a basic premise of the Communist ideology that foreign aid is intended to combat. They have accepted the view that centralized and comprehensive economic planning and control by government is an essential requisite for economic development. This view is contradicted by our own experience and the experience of every other free country.

An effective program must be based on our own ideology, not on the ideology we are fighting. Such a program would call for eliminating the inconsistency between the free trade and free enterprise policies we preach and the protectionist and interventionist policies we at least partly practice. An effective and dramatic program would be to commit ourselves unilaterally to achieving complete free trade by a specified and not too distant date. This would do much to promote an environment and international climate favorable to the rapid development of the uncommitted world along free and democratic lines. It would be an act of truly enlightened self-interest.

Economic Aid Reconsidered

CHARLES WOLF, JR.

Charles Wolf, Jr., is an economist with the RAND Corporation. An expert on development problems in South Asia, he has written extensively in the area and served as government consultant on aid-related matters on several occasions. This article originally appeared in the Summer, 1961, issue of the Yale Review.

THREE YEARS ago, Professor Milton Friedman, of the University of Chicago, wrote a sharply critical article on the subject of foreign aid.[1] The article argued that "despite the intentions of foreign economic aid, its major effect, insofar as it has an effect at all, will be to speed the Communization of the underdeveloped world." Coming from an economist as deservedly distinguished as Professor Friedman, these are inflammatory words. They are accompanied by many others of a similar intensity. But there is a wide gap in the article between the vigor of its criticism and the rigor of its analysis. My main purpose in writing this paper is to suggest just how wide the gap is. Moreover, the subject is perhaps even more timely now than it was when the Friedman article was published. The United States balance-of-payments deficit and the adverse turn of political events in Laos—a heavy aid recipient in recent years—have given arguments concerning the unwisdom of economic aid a new, and I would say ill-advised, palatability and respectability in some quarters.

In the course of these comments, I will be less concerned with making a case *for* foreign economic aid than with dispelling some of the general arguments *against* it which the Friedman article advances. Beyond this, I hope to suggest what I think are reasonable objectives of economic aid—"reasonable" in the sense that there is a significant probability that aid programs can really contribute to them—and to suggest, as well, the distinct limitations of aid as a means of accomplishing other objectives.

Economic aid is, after all, just one instrument of foreign policy.

1. [Reprinted above, pp. 437-451. *Editor*]

Diplomacy, the positioning and composition of the armed forces, military aid, public information and cultural relations, commercial and trade policy are other foreign policy instruments. But this does not mean that *all* foreign policy instruments are applicable to *each* foreign policy objective. Some instruments are, in fact, quite inapplicable to particular objectives simply because there is no predictable relationship between the instruments and the particular objective. The point is obvious, but it is especially relevant to economic aid. Disenchantment with aid often arises from judging it by quite unrealistic objectives in the first place. People who start out from the premise that aid should do more than it realistically can be expected to do, frequently end up convinced that it can do very little, if anything, of value.

Basically, Friedman's criticisms are not ostensibly concerned with the question of objectives at all. He acknowledges at the outset that it is an appropriate objective of United States foreign policy that the less-developed countries "satisfy their aspirations for economic development as fully as possible in a democratic framework." If economic aid can make a contribution toward this end that is sufficient relative to its costs, it presumably would be justified for Friedman, as it would for me. In fact, if the marginal contribution were sufficiently great, the inference would follow that United States resources devoted to economic aid should be expanded—a proposal which has been made by two "task force" reports on the subject to President Kennedy. The burden of Friedman's argument is not that the objective is unsuitable, but rather that economic aid is an ill-suited means for attaining the objective. And his verdict that aid is ill-suited rests on the emphatically negative answers he gives to two questions: (a) is government aid "likely to promote the economic development of the countries to whom it is granted?" and (b) will its "political effects in those countries promote democracy and freedom?"

The second question, he asserts, is "easy to answer and admits of little dispute." Friedman's own answer is based on the following propositions: (1) Aid is extended on a government-to-government basis, and hence tends "to strengthen the role of the government sector relative to the private sector"; (2) "Democracy and freedom have never been either attained or maintained except in communities in which the bulk of economic activity is organized through private enterprise"; and, therefore, (3) Aid reduces prospects of political evolution along democratic lines in underdeveloped countries.

I believe that Friedman's argument is incorrect on two counts. Its factual assertions are inaccurate; and the conclusion drawn wouldn't logically follow even if the factual assertions were assumed to be accurate.

First, on the facts. It is true that aid is extended on a government-to-government basis, but it is not true that economic aid tends to "strengthen the government sector relative to the private sector." Leaving aside for the moment the conceptual ambiguity of the quoted phrase, the facts are more complex, and less conclusive, than Friedman's assertion implies. Often the effect of aid has been to *reduce* the encroachment on the private sector. The point isn't whether government projects *receive* aid, but whether, in the *absence* of aid, the pinch would fall on public or private projects. Probably it would fall on both, but there are two reasons why pressure on the private sector would very likely be greater than on the public sector. The first reason is that the zeal of governments and peoples in many of the less-developed countries for the development of sectors in which private investment has traditionally been negligible would result in a strenuous effort to sustain public investment at the expense of the private sector, in the absence of aid. The *étatisme* which understandably worries Friedman would very likely be greatly increased in a country like India, if foreign economic aid were eliminated or sharply reduced, by drastic efforts to capture private savings for public investment projects. This isn't to say that some efforts to increase private savings may not be warranted and desirable anyhow. There seems to be fairly widespread agreement, for example, among both Indian and American economists who have studied the problem, that additional taxation, even of a mildly regressive sort, would be both feasible and desirable as a way of increasing the resources available for economic development. But, in the absence of aid, measures to capture additional resources for public projects would very likely become so intense and authoritarian that pressure on the private sector would rapidly erode it.

The second reason is that, in the *absence* of aid from the United States, the underdeveloped countries would be very likely to receive increased aid from the Communist bloc. The fact that the Communist bloc would become the only major source of intergovernmental aid would be as important as the increased amount of Soviet aid. One could argue that, *given* substantial and efficient United States aid programs, additional Soviet bloc aid programs need not be feared and might even be welcomed by the United States, as well as by the recipient countries. But, in the absence of United States aid, the Soviet bloc could exploit the additional influence which its monopolistic position would provide. This influence would surely not be directed toward the growth of a vigorous private sector.

There are other ways in which United States aid to government projects helps the private sector. One way is by widening the market for private sector output as a result of the increased public-sector demand. Another is by increasing the supply of inputs which are complementary to private enterprise. Consider, for example, United States aid for projects like community development, or irrigation, or fertilizer distribution, or river valley development. These are, typically, government-to-government projects, but they generally have the effect of providing inputs which raise the productivity of privately-owned agricultural and industrial enterprise. Would their diminution more seriously weaken the private sector or the public sector? On balance, I would say the private sector. At the least, Friedman's general assertion to the contrary is quite untenable.

Next, consider his assertion that democracy depends on the bulk of economic activity being "organized through private enterprise." I can think of no historical example that obviously negates it, although the assertion does leave open how much comprises "the bulk" of economic activity. But granting this assertion, and even if it were true that aid tends to increase the relative size of the government sector, it does not logically follow that the effect of aid will be adverse to democracy and freedom.

It is a tricky business to estimate how much economic activity is "organized through private enterprise," to use Friedman's term. It can, for instance, be measured in terms of how much of the national product is *produced* by private enterprise and how much by government; or by how much of the final produce is *purchased* by private individuals or institutions, and how much by government; or by how much is *expended* by private income earners and how much by government. The second measure will yield a higher figure for the government sector than the first since, in all non-Communist countries, some of what is purchased by government is produced by the private sector. And the expenditure measure will show the highest share for the government sector, because part of government expenditures represents income transfers (like veterans' bonuses, unemployment benefits, interest on the public debt, etc.) which are not included in government purchases of goods and services.

If one is concerned loosely with the question of the extent of government "influence" or "intervention" in the economy, as Friedman is, the third measure is probably the best of the three simply because it is the largest. Considering the underdeveloped country with the best statistics, India, which is also one with a relatively active government sector, the proportion of central government expenditures in gross national product in 1958 and 1959 was 12.6 percent and 12.9 percent, respectively. In the United States by comparison, the corresponding share of federal government expenditures in the national product was 18.8 percent and 19.7 percent, respectively. If we add to federal government outlays those by state governments, the resulting share for the United States was 25.1 percent and 25.7 percent for 1958 and 1959. In India, the share of gross national product represented by central and state government expenditures was 18.1 percent and 18.5 percent for the two years. If the extent of government activity were instead to be measured by product or by purchases rather than expenditures, the figures would be smaller still. However one looks at it, the overwhelming "bulk" of economic activity in India, and to an even greater extent in most other underdeveloped countries, is "organized through private enterprise." The figures above could be doubled and the statement would still be valid.

The point is simply this: even if the effect of economic aid were to increase the relative size of the government sector in underdeveloped countries substantially (a premise which, as we have seen, is highly doubtful), it would still be true, over a wide range of such an increase, that the "bulk of economic activity" would remain "organized through private enterprise." For Friedman's reasoning to hold, we would have to accept the hypothesis that any *increase* in the relative share of the government sector somehow reduces the degree of freedom, or raises the probability that the government sector will eventually encompass the "bulk of economic activity," *even if the increase still leaves the government sector small relative to the economy as a whole.* This is a much stronger hypothesis than the one he explicitly advances. It is one thing to say that democracy requires the *bulk* of economic activity to be in private hands, and quite something else to say that democracy also requires that there be no *decrease* in the share of economic activity in private hands, or that any such decrease reduces the degree of, or prospects for, democracy. As far as I know, there is absolutely no empirical justification for the stronger hypothesis, and Friedman offers none. Some examples seem quite inconsistent with it. In West Germany and Italy, for instance, the private sector was relatively *smaller* in 1959 than it was in the early 1950's, and yet I doubt that Friedman would argue that democracy and freedom have been correspondingly weakened. International comparisons make the stronger hypothesis look still more absurd. The United Kingdom, with a relatively large government sector, would emerge as "less democratic" than West Germany or Italy or India; and the United States as less democratic than West Germany!

The common sense of the matter would appear to be that, in most underdeveloped countries, there is plenty of room for growth in the absolute and relative size of the government sector without compromising prospects for democracy and freedom. Moreover, if expansion in the government sector is itself a response to widespread popular aspirations for accelerated economic growth, the consequence is very likely to be a strengthening, rather than a weakening, of prospects for democratic political evolution in the underdeveloped countries.

To summarize what has been said: A good case can be made for the contention that, as a result of economic aid, the private sector in most underdeveloped countries is very likely to be absolutely and relatively larger than it otherwise would be. Moreover, even if the government sector were to grow relative to the private sector as a *consequence* of aid, rather than independently of aid, within fairly wide limits such growth would be quite consistent with a maintenance of the bulk of economic activity in private hands, simply because the government sector in underdeveloped countries is so small to start with. Finally, whether some growth in the government sector relative to the private sector strengthens or weakens prospects for democracy, is apt to depend on what political, economic, and social changes are accomplished by that growth, and on how responsive the government is to the will of the people—neither of which can be inferred simply from the growth of the government sector alone. Proponents of foreign economic aid shouldn't claim more than this.

Whether or not economic aid results in an expansion in the relative size of the government sector, it remains legitimate to ask, as Friedman does, if such aid is "likely to promote the economic development of the countries to whom it is granted." Friedman again answers, "Emphatically, no," for three reasons: first, the developmental effect of adding to a recipient country's resources is more than offset by the stimulus provided by aid to wasteful use of both the aid and the country's own non-aid resources; second, if a developing country wanted to develop badly enough, it could extract sufficient savings from its own economy to meet its capital requirements without aid; and third, aid tends to sustain or strengthen government planning of economic development, and government planning is the surest way to stifle development. To save space, I have paraphrased his arguments, without, I hope, distorting them. But no matter how they are put, they should be recognized as statements of ideology and doctrine, not of factual or logical analysis.

Consider the first point. Friedman contends that economic aid conduces to wasteful "monument-building" because it makes resources available to underdeveloped countries "at little or no cost." But clearly there are appreciable "costs" attached to aid. I am not thinking here simply of the "hardness" or "softness" of interest and repayment terms, which in most cases I would argue are quite properly lenient, and perhaps should be more so. As long as one accepts the obviously valid assumption that the quantity of aid available isn't unlimited, *there are always appreciable costs attached to aid.* Freshman economics tells us that the "real" cost of using any limited resource for a particular purpose is the returns that are foregone by not employing that resource in its best alternative use. From the standpoint of any recipient country, these "alternative" or "opportunity" costs are positive and large, even if the aid is an outright gift.

Moreover, recognition of the reality of "opportunity costs" doesn't require that the populations or governments of underdeveloped countries attain a high degree of economic literacy. All it requires is that one government ministry be able to recognize that the use of scarce aid resources to build a "monument" desired by another ministry means that much less available for investing in the productive projects desired by the first ministry. And it requires, further, that people outside the government be able to recognize that wasteful use of government resources—whether derived from foreign or domestic sources—means that much less available for meeting the compelling needs of the public itself. Neither of these minimal requirements is unrealistic. Typically, both are actively operative, and their joint effect is generally to conduce toward economic use of the aid that is provided to under-developed countries.

There is still another incentive toward efficient use. The relationship between aid-source and aid-recipient is a continuing one. To the extent that the recipient's anticipation of future aid depends on his efficient use of current resources, he will have a strong incentive to limit monuments and waste. As in the case of opportunity costs, the "future-flow" incentive can operate regardless of whether or what repayment terms are incorporated in government-to-government agreements.

In practice, of course, there are many slips and inefficiencies. Anyone familiar with United States or other international aid programs can't ignore them, and shouldn't defend them. But to say, as Friedman does, that aid is typically wasted because it is costless, is not only bad economics, from a theoretical point of view; it is also a wrong-headed characterization of the actual record of government aid programs.

His second point is based on the contention that external aid is really superfluous. The underdeveloped countries are not too poor to provide capital for their own development. After all, "currently developed countries were once underdeveloped," and they managed to eke out a surplus above subsistence requirements in order to provide capital for their development. The currently under-developed countries could do likewise, simply by offering sufficient incentives to domestic saving and to foreign investment. Their failure to do so results from a lack of will, rather than an absolute lack of resources. If they had the will, foreign aid would be superfluous. Moreover, Friedman contends, aid is even worse than superfluous, because it tends to "reduce the pressure on government to maintain an environment favorable to private enterprise." Consequently, he concludes, "the final result of our grants is therefore likely to be a reduction in the amount of capital available from other sources both internally and from the outside."

There is an eighteenth-century nostalgia to these arguments, but they deserve reply, both because of their source and because of the extent to which they diverge from currently accepted views. Consider, first, the analogy between currently underdeveloped countries, and the currently developed countries before they developed. From an economic viewpoint, probably the main imperfection in the analogy is that the relationship of income and natural resources on the one hand, to population on the other, is tighter in the currently underdeveloped countries. The physical hardship accompanying self-financing of development in the currently less-developed countries would thus be more acute than it was in the seventeenth and eighteenth centuries in Western Europe, or the nineteenth century in the United States. To some extent, this may be offset by the fact that the currently underdeveloped countries are "late-comers" and hence can draw on technological possibilities that were not available to the early arrivals. But the offset is probably only partial. The economic problems of the currently underdeveloped countries are just harder.

None of this touches the core of what is wrong with Friedman's analogy. The big differences aren't economic, but psychological and political. The currently underdeveloped countries live in a world populated by countries which have already developed, and which display the fruits of their development in higher living standards and greater power. The effect of this demonstration is to heighten the aspirations of the currently underdeveloped countries, and to intensify their impatience for development. The acceptable time period for development is consequently much shorter than in the classical examples of development. Diffusion of suffrage in the underdeveloped countries means that governments which tolerate the pace or the inequalities of seventeenth- and eighteenth-century European development will probably not survive. The crucial political difference characterizing the present development context is the obvious one that the currently underdeveloped countries live in a world in which Communism is a tangibly real alternative route to economic development. Hence, the risk of delayed development is just much greater in the currently underdeveloped countries. In effect, Friedman's analogy is misleading because the urgency of development is greater and the available resources smaller in the currently underdeveloped countries than in the classical examples he has in mind.

But what of the argument that the net effect of foreign aid is to reduce the capital that is available by reducing "the pressure on [recipient] governments to maintain an environment favorable to private enterprise"? Implicit in this assertion is the view that in the *absence* of aid, the "environment" would be more favorable to private enterprise. This prognosis seems to me quite unsupported, and, for reasons I've already mentioned above, unsupportable. In general, the effect of foreign aid, as I have seen it operate in South and Southeast Asia, has been to make foreign exchange more readily available to private enterprise, to lower the cost and increase the supply of publicly-provided inputs to private enterprise, and probably to lower the taxes that otherwise would be levied on individual and corporate incomes. In this connection, it is notable that during the past ten years of India's foreign-aided development plans, private enterprise has been more buoyant and expansionist than ever before. I am not denying that private domestic and foreign enterprises have their troubles in underdeveloped countries, or that governmental bureaucracy accounts for much of these troubles through capricious allocations of foreign exchange and through discriminatory collection of taxes from honest firms. What I am suggesting is that, in the absence of aid, these troubles would probably be more acute. Pressures on private enterprise would intensify, not abate. It is, of course, almost as hard to substantiate this prognosis as Friedman's. But besides the Indian example, I would also note that in every underdeveloped country I am familiar with, private business organizations strongly support the need for and desirability of foreign aid. If their interests were adversely affected by aid, it is quite unlikely that they would do so.

Friedman's third reason for asserting that aid does not in fact promote development is that aid sustains and propitiates centralized government planning, and planning is inherently counterdevelopmental. Planning is counterdevelopmental because it tends to be rigid and inflexible while effective development requires experimentation and flexibility. These characteristics are more likely to be obtained under a system of private enterprise than under government planning, because private enterprise provides strong incentives toward careful choice and toward rapid correction of mistakes.

There is an element of truth in Friedman's argument. But the argument is overstated and incomplete. There are powerful reasons why the case for planning is much stronger than Friedman allows. Some of these reasons concern what economic jargon refers to as "external economies" and "decreasing costs." "External economies" relate to the social benefits produced by a particular activity which are not recoverable or appropriable by the proj-

ect's owners or investors. The usual examples include education
and training, public utilities like roads and river valley development, and public health. Since these benefits are "non-appropri-
able," they will obviously not enter into private investors' calculations of the profitability of alternative investment opportunities.
The consequence will be underinvestment in external-economy-
generating activities, and a need for compensating government
investment to offset the deficiency. "Decreasing costs" relate to
activities which result in lower costs as the scale of the activity
increases. Often the scale required for realizing "decreasing costs"
entails investment outlays far beyond what is accessible to private
enterprise in the underdeveloped countries. And even if the investment requirements were met, "decreasing costs" would preclude
the continued existence of many firms and competitive markets.
Without going into the technical ramifications of either "external
economies" or "decreasing costs," the relevant point is that both
considerations will result in underinvestment in potentially high-
priority activities under a regime of private enterprise. Government initiative to compensate for these deficiencies will be necessary if available resources, domestic as well as foreign, are to have
maximum effect on economic growth.

These reasons for active government planning in the underdeveloped countries are supplemented by other strongly practical considerations. Imperfections and rigidities in the market
mechanism are many and notorious in underdeveloped countries.
Although improvements in the flow of information and the mobility of capital and labor are possible and desirable in the underdeveloped countries, these rigidities are deep-seated and durable. The real alternative to some government intervention in these
countries is not a smoothly functioning free market, but a market
pervaded by barriers and rigidities. The distortion in Friedman's
argument arises from comparing an ideal model of a free market
regimen with casual observation of the worst features of government planning. In the real world of the underdeveloped economies, private enterprise and the free market are neither as
flexible or adaptive as Friedman suggests, nor is government
planning as rigid and inefficient. Both the market and planning
have their justifications and shortcomings. As Edward Mason has
put it: "The really good arguments for planning lie in the obvious
inadequacies of the market, and the really good arguments for
the market rest on the deficiencies of planning."

My conclusions from these remarks are in direct contradiction to Friedman's answer to the question of whether aid is likely to promote economic development. There have been examples of "monument building," but, in general, aid has been productively used, and the institutional mechanisms for extending aid have tended to increase the productive use of non-aid resources as well. It is, moreover, definitely not true that aid leads to wasteful use because it is "costless." The existence of alternative uses for aid means that there are always appreciable costs attached to its use in any wasteful activity. Although the bulk of capital requirements for development must be internally generated, the effect of complete self-financing would very likely be to induce the internal authoritarianism which Friedman wishes to avoid, and encourage the erosion of private enterprise which he wishes to protect. Finally, there are both strong theoretical and practical reasons for expecting and encouraging some degree of government planning in underdeveloped countries. True, planning by government can be rigid and inflexible, as can planning by private enterprise. But, more important, government planning that is rigid and inflexible can be improved. Economic aid is probably a much more appropriate tool for improving the quality of planning than it is for affecting the quantity.

In his zeal to discredit foreign aid, Friedman criticizes two criteria that have often been mentioned by advocates of aid as tests of the eligibility of a recipient country for additional aid. The eligibility criteria he criticizes are, first, whether a recipient is taking "measures to capture a good fraction of increases in income for the purpose of further investment," and, second, the extent to which the recipient has "worked out an overall development program." His criticism takes the form of noting that the United States itself would not have been able to qualify for aid under these criteria during the period of its own initial development, that "the only countries that satisfy [these] tests . . . are the Communist countries," and that none of the Communist countries has in fact achieved a continuing "rise in the standard of living of the ordinary man."

Actually, I agree that the particular aid criteria he refers to are vulnerable to criticism. In fact, I have criticized them elsewhere at length for, among other reasons, giving absolutely no attention to the relative productivity or efficiency of resource use in recipient countries in determining aid allocations among them. But the par-

ticular criticisms advanced by Friedman seem to me either misleading or just factually wrong.

The assertion that the United States would not have qualified
for assistance under these criteria is true, but pointless. The
United States didn't receive intergovernmental aid, and the objectives which motivate aid to the currently underdeveloped countries were quite irrelevant to our development in the nineteenth
century. True, Communist countries would qualify under these
criteria (though of course they would be disqualified under the
implicit additional criterion that the objective of aid is to increase
the chances of survival and success of non-Communist political
systems). But it is palpably *untrue* that "the *only* countries that
would satisfy the tests are the Communist countries." Currently,
India, Pakistan, Burma, among others, eminently satisfy the
criteria; historically, Japan would have done so.

Moreover, we should be wary about falling into the trap of assuming that anything the Communist countries do or have done
is necessarily something we should avoid, or encourage others to
avoid. Even if the assumption is often warranted, it sometimes is
not. If, for example, the Communists retain a consequential
capability to wage war with conventional weapons, it doesn't follow that we should avoid doing likewise or encouraging non-
Communist countries to do likewise. If the Communists have
tried to plan their economic development and have adopted
various measures to capture increases in income for further investment, it doesn't follow that we should discourage the underdeveloped countries from doing so.

Friedman's last point, that none of the Communist countries
has achieved increased living standards, is just wrong. Discussions
of foreign aid, or of the uses and misuses of development planning in underdeveloped countries, are not advanced by erroneously asserting, as he does, that planned development in Communist Russia has not raised living standards for the mass of the
people.

So much by way of rebuttal. As I mentioned at the outset, I
have been less concerned here with making a case for economic
aid than with dispelling some of the erroneous arguments against
it which Friedman's article presents. But in conclusion, let me add
a brief comment on the objectives that seem to me reasonable to
attribute to aid, and hence appropriate to apply in assessing its
performance. Frequently, advocates of economic aid, and of in-

creased appropriations, do themselves and their aim a disservice by claiming too much. The unrealistic hopes generated by such advocacy usually return to plague the advocate and weaken his case.

Before suggesting some "reasonable" objectives, it is important to be clear about the "unreasonable" ones. It is as important to recognize the effects that can't (or shouldn't) be sought by extending aid, as it is to recognize the effects that can. By "effects that can't or shouldn't be sought," I mean either that effects aren't predictably related to aid, or, if they are, that they are in general likely to be accompanied by disadvantageous side-effects at least as great as the advantageous effects themselves. From this standpoint, I would include as generally "unreasonable" objectives of economic aid most short-term political returns, such as winning votes in the U.N., weakening or eliminating "neutralism," buying the loyalties and support of particular groups of individuals in the underdeveloped countries, creating and cementing meaningful international alliances, or preventing acceptance by underdeveloped countries of aid from the Soviet bloc. In some cases these objectives may be reasonable, but such cases require especially discerning judgment to be identified and should be treated as exceptions.

There are many other things aid can't do. It can't reliably affect decisions by recipients concerning the "mix" of public and private enterprise they prefer, except perhaps in the negative sense of reducing the resource pressures that would otherwise probably induce recipients to crack down more severely on the private sector. (Incidentally, though Friedman disclaims any divergence of views on objectives, and asserts that his criticisms are confined to means, I wonder whether he doesn't mislead himself. What he seems to be most concerned with isn't whether aid can be used to stimulate development, but whether aid can be used to stimulate free enterprise in the short run.) Nor can aid be expected to bring economic benefits to the United States in the form of greater supplies of raw materials at given prices, larger export markets (other than those financed by aid itself), or "national treatment" of United States investors in their access to local investment opportunities. Finally, economic aid can't be expected to protect recipients against external military threats, and may sometimes even result in increased efforts by hostile forces to disrupt by military means the economic progress that aid itself is furthering.

What remains for the "reasonable" objectives? Aid can provide resources *additional* to those a country raises from domestic or other foreign sources for its own development, and it can provide incentives toward efficient use of the entire package by tying aid increments to productivity. In so doing, it can help provide new opportunities and options to enlist the enthusiasm, energies, and loyalties of peoples and governments in the underdeveloped countries. In addition, aid provides a channel, a working relationship, through which the United States and other developed countries can "illuminate choices" that are open to the recipient countries—to borrow Eugene Black's term. The particular decisions reached by an underdeveloped country—whether they concern industrialization or agriculture, public welfare services or consumption, taxation or price policy—will often be second- or third-best decisions from the standpoint of economic growth alone. But the process of "illuminating choices," of weighing the costs and benefits of alternative actions, can exercise over time a pervasive influence on political as well as economic development. Through its effects on more rapid development, and on rational habits of thought, aid can provide a significant contribution toward enhancing prospects for the survival and vitality of free political systems in the underdeveloped countries. Even if these "reasonable" objectives don't by any means touch some of the main objectives of United States foreign policy, they nevertheless provide strong justification for the economic aid we are extending, and, I would suggest, for making a larger and more disciplined effort in the future.